N. WIEDER

THE JUDEAN SCROLLS AND KARAISM

THE JUDEAN SCROLLS AND KARAISM

BY

NAPHTALI WIEDER

LONDON

EAST AND WEST LIBRARY

PRINTED IN GREAT BRITAIN
AT THE CURWEN PRESS · LONDON · E13
BOUND BY A. W. BAIN & CO LTD · LONDON · E2

PREFACE

In the veritable flood of conflicting theories and diverse hypotheses concerning almost everything relating to the Judean Scrolls and the *Damascus Document* there seems to be one point of substance on which there is a complete consensus of scholarly opinion, *viz.* that a close kinship exists between the people of Qumran-Damascus and the Karaites.

Having regard to this unassailable fact, it appears legitimate to use the rich and variegated literature of Karaism for the purpose of illuminating the literary remains of the Qumran sect; of clarifying obscurities and ambiguities; and of throwing into bolder relief the theological categories of the Sect. The interpreting of Qumranism in the light of Karaism is consequently one of the aims of the present book.

On the other hand our understanding of Karaism, too, stands to gain in no little measure from a comparative study of the two sectarian communities. This is especially true of the theological aspects of Karaism (other than its cardinal thesis—the repudiation of the Oral Law) which have received but scant attention on the part of students of Karaism. Viewed from the vantage-point of Qumran-Damascus, these aspects appear in a new light and furthermore themes, beliefs and concepts hitherto wholly unnoticed make their appearance and thus add fresh and salient features to the Karaite physiognomy.

A considerable part of the source-material adduced in these studies is derived from Karaite Bible exegesis, which mirrors the mind, spirit and theology of the Karaite thinkers who buttressed their sectarian views by an appeal to the prophetic writings. In the past we have been only too ready to dismiss these interpretations as belonging to the realm of the fanciful, as an example of unrestricted homiletical exercise, and hence as devoid of any theological import. In the light of the Qumran literature, however, this type of exegesis must now be given its rightful place: it is *pesher* exegesis. It is difficult to exaggerate the extent to which the Karaite mind and heart were preoccupied with the predictions and allusions they discovered in, or read into, the biblical prophecies and also the *Psalms*; their polemical treatises abound in references and quotations from Scripture cited as proof-texts and based on the *pesher* method. Anachronistic and unwarrantable though this method may appear to us, for them it was not only intellectually enlightening and spiritually uplifting, but also justifiable exegetically: it is not homiletical edification but genuine exegesis. Just as their spiritual kinsmen at Qumran-Damascus have found the history of their own time and sect mirrored in Scripture, so the Karaites firmly believed that contemporary events, the division of the nation into two opposing camps, the apostasy of the rabbis and the rise of their own movement, its mission and destinies, its suffering and ultimate triumph in the messianic era were forecast by the prophets and portrayed in the biblical records. Their conviction of the legitimacy and cogency of this method may be gauged from the fact that many *pesher* interpretations became part and parcel of the intellectual equipment of the Karaite propagandists who used them for polemical and missionary ends, purporting to provide scriptural documentation for their own theses against the opponents whom they obviously hoped to impress, if not indeed to convert, by this kind of documentation. As regards its influence on the Karaites themselves, the *pesher* exegesis was not merely a vehicle of expression, an instrument for rendering preconceived ideas in a biblical idiom, but an important factor in the thinking out and developing of the ideology, and determined contents and phraseology of Karaite literature. The same applies to the Qumran *pesher*.

In order to signalize the standard scriptural quotations invoked by Karaite spokesmen to argue and convince, to remonstrate and censure, I have introduced the term 'Karaite *testimonia*'. More than once we shall have opportunity of demonstrating that the standardized self-designations of the sect, the terms describing the antagonists, or any other scriptural phrase current in Karaite parlance were not mere borrowings of convenient terms and phrases lifted out of their biblical context, but that it is the *pesher* of the whole passage that provides the key to the understanding of the single phrase; in other words, the detached phrase has to be understood as a pointer to the whole passage which, in its entirety, was in the mind of the writer and formed the basis of his argument. The occurrence of identical designations and phrases in the Qumran writings strongly suggests that in Qumran, too, the respective scriptural passages were given a *pesher* exposition and that it was that exposition which formed the basis and justification of applying the phrases in question to the contemporary scene.

As will be noted, the longest chapter in these studies is the first one, dealing with the much-discussed issue as to the meaning of the expression 'land of Damascus'. The search for a solution of the problem involved the writer in an excursion into the field of New Testament studies, and he craves the indulgence of New Testament scholars for having encroached upon an area of research that is not his own.

The main thesis of the chapter is that the 'land of Damascus', i.e., the region of Lebanon and Anti-Lebanon, was believed to be the *locale* where the prelude to the messianic drama would be enacted and the messianic kingdom inaugurated. Corroborative evidence has been culled from rabbinic, Karaite, Jewish-apocalyptic, Christian and Muhammadan literature. The scope of our investigation was then considerably widened by the suggestion that the above idea was identical with the belief that Upper Galilee was destined to be the scene for the ingathering of the exiles and the appearance of the Messiah. The chapter had to be yet further extended by the inclusion of an interpretation of *Mark* 14, 28 (*I will go before you into Galilee*) which was shown to be connected with the rôle of Galilee in the messianic programme.

The last chapter, entitled 'The Book of *Hegeh*' is an entirely independent study, having no relation to Karaism. It bears witness to the phenomenon observed in the last few years that the Judean Scrolls have fertilized research in the most diverse branches of Hebraic studies. In this case, several knotty problems that have engaged the attention of generations of scholars are reopened and, I trust, satisfactorily solved.

In treating the *Damascus Document* as belonging to the literary heritage of the Qumran people I am following the generally accepted opinion which has now received weighty support from the discovery of several manuscripts of this work in the caves of Qumran.[1] I am, however, quite aware that this document includes views reflecting a divergent trend within the Sect, or a different phase in its theological evolution.[2]

The publication of this book was held up by a variety of circumstances It now appears in print due to the efforts of the Chief Rabbi, Dr. Israel Brodie, to whom I wish to express my deep gratitude. I should also like to thank Mr. Raphael Loewe for reading the manuscript.

[1] See J. T. Milik, *Ten Years Discovery in the Wilderness of Judaea*, London 1959 [Studies in Biblical Theology, No. 26], pp. 38, 125.

[2] Cf. *infra*, p. 125 and also 55n.

CONTENTS

ABBREVIATIONS

CDC	Damascus Document (Fragments of a Zadokite Work)
DSD	The Rule of the Community (Manual of Discipline)
DSD A (1QSa)	The Rule of the Congregation
DSH	Habakkuk Commentary
DST	The Thanksgiving Scroll (*Hōdāyōth*)
DSW	The War of the Sons of Light and the Sons of Darkness
1QSb	Collection of Benedictions
BA	*The Biblical Archeologist*
BASOR	*Bulletin of the American Schools of Oriental Research*
B.T.	Babylonian Talmud
Enc. Jud.	Encyclopaedia Judaica
HUCA	*Hebrew Union College Annual*
IEJ	*Israel Exploration Journal*
JBL	*Journal of Biblical Literature*
J.E.	The Jewish Encyclopedia
JJS	*The Journal of Jewish Studies*
JQR	*The Jewish Quarterly Review*
JTS	*The Journal of Theological Studies*
MGWJ	*Monatsschrift für Geschichte und Wissenschaft des Judentums*
N.S.	New Series
O.S.	Old Series
PAAJR	*Proceedings of the American Academy of Jewish Research*
PEQ	*Palestine Exploration Quarterly*
P.T.	Palestinian Talmud
RB	*Revue Biblique*
REJ	*Revue des Études Juives*
The Sect (with capital S)	The Qumran Sect
VT	*Vetus Testamentum*
ZDMG	*Zeitschrift der Deutschen Morgenländischen Gesellschaft*
ZfHB	*Zeitschrift für hebräische Bibliographie*
ZNW	*Zeitschrift für die Neutest. Wissenschaft*
Hadassi	Yehudah b. Elijah Hadassi, *Eshkol ha-Kopher*, Gozlow, 1836

Liq. Qad.	S. Pinsker, *Liqqūtē Qadmōniyyōth* [*Lickute Kadmoniot:* Zur Geschichte des Karaismus und der karäischen Literatur], Wien, 1860
Pithron	*Pithrōn Shenēm 'Āsār* [Commentarius in Librum Duodecim Prophetarum] by Daniel b. Moses al-Qumisi, ed. I. D. Markon (with notes by D. Z. Baneth and E. E. Urbach), Jerusalem, 1958
'The Dead Sea Scrolls'	N. Wieder, 'The Dead Sea Scrolls Type of Biblical Exegesis Among the Karaites' in *Between East and West* [Essays dedicated to the Memory of Bela Horovitz], ed. A. Altmann, London, 1958, pp. 75–105
'The Qumran Sectaries'	*Idem*, 'The Qumran Sectaries and the Karaites', *JQR* 47 [1956–57], pp. 97–113; 269–92

CHAPTER I

THE LAND OF DAMASCUS

THE SECT'S EXODUS TO THE LAND OF DAMASCUS

The object of this chapter is to suggest a reason for the exodus of the Qumran sectaries to the land of Damascus. The historicity of the exodus—universally acknowledged since the discovery of the *Damascus Document*—must still be regarded as unshaken notwithstanding recent attempts[1] to divest the phrase 'land of Damascus' of its plain and simple meaning and regard it as a figurative designation, a 'prophetic name', either for the Assyrian-Babylonian exile,[2] or the area of Qumran,[3] or to see in it a mere symbolic expression for the Sect's 'withdrawal from the normative forms of Jewish life'.

These views, divergent though they may be in matters of geography, have one basic thing in common: they are grounded upon the fact that *Amos* 5, 26–7 was given by the author of the *Damascus Document* a symbolic interpretation (vii, 14–19). It is this interpretation which is the origin of the figurative meaning of the 'land of Damascus'.

However, the fact is that the infusion of the phrase at issue with a figurative sense is not the work of the sectarian expositor. It should be remembered that the interpretation of the

[1] Cf. Isaac Rabinowitz, *JBL*, 73 [1954], pp. 11–35; John M. Allegro, *The Dead Sea Scrolls*, London 1956, p. 101; Theodor H. Gaster, *The Scriptures of the Dead Sea Sect*, London 1957, pp. 14, 34, 110; Frank M. Cross, *The Ancient Library of Qumran and Modern Biblical Studies*, London 1958, pp. 59f.; A. Jaubert, *RB*, 1958, pp. 231, 235.

[2] Rabinowitz, *loc. cit.*

[3] Gaster, Allegro, Cross and others. R. North likewise identifies the land of Damascus with the Qumran area, but he suggests that the designation 'land of Damascus' could be geographically justified; see 'The Damascus of Qumran Geography', *PEQ*, 1955, pp. 34–38. Cf. D. Flusser, *IEJ*, 1959, p. 106, note 24; Cecil Roth, *The Historical Background of the Dead Sea Scrolls*, Oxford 1958, p. 27, note 1. See also the following note.

Amos verses is distinguished by its explicitness: the reader is not left, as is the case in the *Habakkuk Scroll*, to infer or guess by himself the new sense attached to the single words of the scriptural text. The sectarian expositor took pains to point out all the words in the *Amos* passage which he interpreted symbolically:

> *Sikkuth*=the books of the Law[1]
> *The king*=the congregation
> *Kiyyun your images*=the books of the prophets
> *Star*=the Searcher in the Law.

He has, however, nothing to say about 'Damascus', too, having any symbolic significance. Furthermore, the theory equating 'the land of Damascus' with Qumran is vitiated by the fact that the Sect emigrated 'from the land of Judah' (iv, 3; vi, 5) 'to the land of the North' (vii, 13f.); Qumran, however, lies in the Judean desert. This argument could, of course, be eliminated by divesting the latter geographical term, too, of its simple meaning and declaring it a mere symbol—but for this there is no warrant whatsoever. The phrase 'land of Damascus' must, therefore, be understood in its literal, geographical-historical sense.[2]

This being the case, the vexed question must still be asked: What was the reason for the Sect's exodus to the land of Damascus? Various hypotheses have been put forward to account for it—all of them having in common the supposition that the exodus was a forced one, the Sect having been compelled to abandon its settlement at Qumran and seek refuge in the land of

[1] On this equation, see N. Wieder, '"Sanctuary" as a Metaphor for Scripture', *JJS*, viii [1957], pp. 165–75.

[2] See Dupont-Sommer, *VT*, v [1955], p. 127, note 3; H. H. Rowley, *Expository Times*, 68 [1956–57], p. 136; Charles T. Fritsch, *The Qumran Community*, New York 1956, pp. 21–22; Hugh J. Schonfield, *Secrets of the Dead Sea Scrolls*, London 1956, p. 21, note; Cecil Roth, *loc. cit.*; Flusser, *loc. cit.*; J. T. Milik, *Ten Years of Discovery in the Wilderness of Judaea* (Studies in Biblical Theology, No. 26), London 1959, p. 91, note 2: 'It is methodologically unsound to take the phrase "land of Damascus" and, on the strength of a quotation in CD. VII, 14ff. of Amos 5, 26f., to see in it a symbolic name for Qumran. We therefore take it literally.'

Damascus. The Sect is said to have fled in order to escape the persecutions by Antiochus Epiphanes, Simon the Maccabee, King Herod the Great, the Romans, etc.; or else because an earthquake in 31 B.C.E. forced them to leave their habitation and emigrate.

INAUGURATION OF MESSIANIC REDEMPTION IN THE LAND OF DAMASCUS

No attempt will be made here to subject these hypotheses to a detailed criticism; being intricately bound up with the view one takes concerning the date of the Dead Sea Scrolls as a whole, they are all vigorously debated issues. We proceed to present our own thesis which is independent of the question of dating and deviates from other explanations in claiming that the movement to the land of Damascus was a voluntary act, and that it was motivated by messianic conceptions and expectations.

It is almost unnecessary to recall the intense hold which messianism had on the men of Qumran; their life and world-outlook was shaped and dominated by the awareness of the imminent irruption of the 'end'. Messianism, it may be said, is one of the pillars upon which the Sect was founded.[1] The suggestion is here made that the movement to the land of Damascus stemmed from this dominating force in their life: *they betook themselves to the land of Damascus in order to anticipate there the appearance of the Messiah, or, in general, the inauguration of the messianic drama.*

THE 'WILDERNESS OF THE PEOPLES'= 'LAND OF DAMASCUS'

Based on various prophetic utterances, the wilderness assumed a central position in the messianic programme as the scene where the final salvation would be ushered in, and an exodus into the wilderness at a moment thought to be the crucial one became an all-important feature in that programme, particularly in messianically active circles. This is also reflected in the *Rule of the*

[1] See *infra*, pp. 95f.

Community, which makes provision for the time when the members of the Sect will have to proceed to the wilderness in order to prepare the way of the Lord (viii, 12–15), and speaks of 'a time to clear the way in the wilderness' (ix, 19–20). Again, the *War Scroll* (i, 3) begins its description of the eschatological war with the return of the Sons of Light from the 'wilderness of the peoples'. Now, it is this passage in the *War Scroll* which furnishes the first clue to the solution of the question at issue. The land of Damascus is identical with the 'wilderness of the peoples'. The identification is strongly suggested by the fact that, according to the *Damascus Document*, the Sect entered the new covenant in the land of Damascus. It is precisely the 'wilderness of the peoples' which, according to *Ez.* 20, 35–37, will be the scene of the eschatological covenant: '*And I will bring you into the wilderness of the peoples . . . and I will cause you to pass under the rod, and I will bring you into the bond of the covenant.*'[1] That the book of *Ezekiel* exerted a formative influence on the Sect's theology will be pointed out later on.[2]

The 'wilderness of the peoples' is an undefined geographical entity, and the Qumran sectaries located it in the desert of the 'land of Damascus'. It may be stated at once that this view represents a fusion of two doctrines, one which associated the messianic deliverance with the wilderness, and the other which believed the region of Damascus to be the scene of messianic occurrences, as will be shown.

Such coalescence of doctrines is not an infrequent phenomenon, especially in the realm of theological ideas. In view of the great influence of the *pesher*-exegesis on the shaping of the Sect's messiology, it may plausibly be assumed that the command given by God to the prophet Elijah, '*Go, return on the way to the wilderness of Damascus*' (*I Kings* 19, 15)[3] may have been given

[1] See A. Jaubert, *art. cit.*, pp. 234f.

[2] Cf. *infra*, p. 127.

[3] That this verse may possibly have had some influence on the Sect's ideology has also been suggested by A. S. van der Woude, *Die messianischen Vorstellungen der Gemeinde von Qumran* [Studia Semitica Neerlandica], Assen, 1957, p. 55 and Jaubert, *art. cit.*, p. 232, footnote.

in Qumran a messianic reference, according to which it foreshadowed that the return of Elijah at the end of days would likewise occur in the wilderness of Damascus. What considerably increases the plausibility of this suggestion is the fact that, in a tannaitic *'aggadah*, the name 'Damascus' has virtually become synonymous with 'Elijah', on the basis of the same verse from *Kings*—so much so that, thanks to this aggadic 'synonymity', the phrase in *Cant.* 7, 5: צופה פני דמשק could be made to signify *Look out for Elijah.*[1] The association of the precursor of the Messiah with the wilderness[2] as well as with Damascus may well have touched off the identification of the two messianic areas, the 'wilderness of the peoples' and the 'land of Damascus'.

THE 'LAND OF DAMASCUS' IN KARAITE LITERATURE

This, however, is of no more than peripheral interest; our main concern is with the fact of the identification as such and, most important of all, with the idea that the region of Damascus was expected to become the scene of messianic events. It will now be demonstrated that both ideas are also to be found outside Qumran—a fact of no mean importance for our thesis. They were current in Karaite circles, as we learn from Yefeth b. 'Ali's Arabic commentary on *Canticles* (4, 8).[3] The following are the relevant passages, translated into English:

'*Come with Me from Lebanon, O bride; come with Me from Lebanon and glance at My wedding chamber, from the top of the river Barada, from the top of Senir and Hermon.* This chapter reflects the custom of introducing the bride to the bridegroom. It is the custom for the bride to be conducted to the house of the bridegroom and, on her arrival, for the bridegroom to come out and open the gate for her and lead her into his wedding

[1] Cf. *infra*, p. 11.

[2] See *infra*, p. 8, footnote.

[3] Cf. *Rabbi Yaphet Abou Aly . . . In Canticum Canticorum Commentarium Arabicum*, ed. J. J. L. Bargès, Paris 1884.

chamber. Similarly, God will not send to Israel in the lands of the nations a prophet or a messenger, but will deliver them in a manner contrary to what happened in the past when He sent Moses to Pharaoh, to deliver them from his hand and lead them into the desert. Now, in reference to the people of the Dispersion the prophet said (*Jer.* 31, 21): *How long wilt thou turn away coyly, O thou backsliding daughter? For the Lord hath created a new thing in the earth: A woman shall court a man.* The meaning of this verse is: The people of the Dispersion are moving to the extremities of the Fourth Kingdom, saying: "the exile is long and the End is in His hand; we must therefore wait until He sends and delivers us, as He delivered our forefathers from Egypt." The prophet rebuts this argument saying: *For the Lord hath created a new thing in the earth: A woman shall court a man.* The meaning of this is: it is not the custom for a woman to go round in search of a man, but the man goes round searching for a woman. God has now created a new thing; in the first exile, that of Egypt, He sent Moses, and in the time of the Second Temple Cyrus and the prophets summoned them; but now He has commanded them to proceed to the wilderness of the peoples (alone), not under the guidance of a divine messenger. But when they arrive at the boundary of the land, He will send the master Elijah, peace be with him, who will go to meet them, and they will enter (the land) with him. Therefore He said, *with Me from Lebanon*, that is to say, you shall go together with My messenger (Elijah) from Lebanon which is the extreme boundary of Palestine, and it was from there that they went into exile, as the prophet foretold them (*Amos* 5, 27): *I will cause you to go into captivity beyond Damascus*[1] . . . *Thou shalt look from the top of Amanah*, that is the boundary of Damascus, Amanah being a river flowing in Damascus, cf. *II Kings* 5, 12 . . . The sense of the verse is: the exiles will come

[1] In his commentary on *Amos* 5, 27 (MS. British Museum, Or. 2400, fol. 97a), Yefeth explains the implication of the words 'beyond Damascus': previously, in the times of the Kings of 'Aram, the remotest place of exile was Damascus, but now they will be exiled beyond that city, so as to be removed far away from their land, as Ezekiel said (*Ez.* 11, 16): *I have removed them far off among the nations . . . I have scattered them among the countries.*

from East, North and South to the region of Lebanon, Senir and Hermon, and from there they will enter the land together with the master Elijah, peace be with him.'

DEFINITION OF THE 'LAND OF DAMASCUS'

On the basis of the above quotations we have to define the geographical notion 'land of Damascus' as also including the territory of Lebanon, Senir and Hermon, i.e. the region of Lebanon and Anti-Lebanon, perennially dominated by the oasis of Damascus, which is situated on the eastern foothills of the Anti-Lebanon range, in the narrow strip which lies between the mountains and the desert.

The following points arising out of the above quotations may be underscored:

1. The exodus into the 'wilderness of the peoples' is to be undertaken on the initiative of the exiles themselves. In the true *pesher* tradition, Yefeth makes the prophet Jeremiah expostulate with the people of the Dispersion for scattering themselves in the distant regions of the Fourth Kingdom, far away from Damascus, Lebanon, Senir and Hermon, or in other words far away from the land of Damascus, the scene of imminent messianic occurrences. The voluntary march into the wilderness is touched upon by Yefeth also in his comment on *Cant.* 1, 8. In the words:

O thou fairest among women
Go thy way forth by the footsteps of the flock,
And feed thy kids beside the shepherds' tents

he sees a prophetic call to the spiritual leaders of his sect[1] to go and stay with the people in the wilderness and there anticipate the hour of salvation.

2. The region of Damascus, Lebanon, Senir and Hermon is identical with the 'wilderness of the peoples'.

3. The region of Damascus is messianic territory: it is destined to become the assembly area of the exiles, the starting-point of the

[1] 'The fairest of women' is a metaphor for the *élite* of the Karaite sect, see N. Wieder, 'The Dead Sea Scrolls', *etc.*, p. 87.

return march to the homeland, and it will be there that Elijah will make his long-expected appearance, assume the leadership of the exiles and guide them to the Holy Land. That Elijah will appear in the 'wilderness of the peoples' and that he will himself perform the central and most vital act in the messianic drama—the restoration of the exiles to the Holy Land—is mentioned by Yefeth also in other places of his Bible commentaries.[1]

4. It is also not without significance that Yefeth cites the same verse from *Amos* as did the author of the *Damascus Document*. The words *I will exile you beyond Damascus* are adduced to show that the banishment of the nation took place in the region of Damascus, from where the Jews were scattered to the remotest parts of the globe. This region will therefore witness the inaugural

[1] On *Mal.* 3, 23 (MS. British Museum, Or. 2401, fol. 260a) he writes as follows: 'The sages say that the Master of the Worlds took him [Elijah] away from among Israel and hid him in a place concealed from the people. And when the time of the 'End' comes, He will send him to teach the people and to remove disagreement. Israel will enter with him the Land of Israel from the wilderness of the peoples, he will conquer for them the country, take Jerusalem and rebuild the altar. It will be he who will anoint the high priest and the King Messiah and make known the genealogies.' And on *Hos.* 2, 2: 'It may be that the words *and they shall appoint themselves one head* refer to Elijah, peace be with him, who will appear to them in the wilderness of the peoples, according to the opinion of some scholars, and they will enter the land with him, just as they entered it with Joshua.' See the Arabic original in N. Wieder, 'The Doctrine of the Two Messiahs', pp. 16, 18.

According to medieval Jewish apocalypses, both Elijah and the Messiah are expected to appear in the wilderness, see *Midreshē Ge'ullah*, pp. 285, 322, 336; A. Jellinek, *Beth Ha-Midrash*, vi, p. 115; J. D. Eisenstein, *'Oṣar Midrashim*, New York 1915, p. 203. On the other hand, in the messianic schemes of Sa'adya and Hai Ga'on it is only Elijah's appearance that is awaited in the desert, see *Midreshē Ge'ullah*, pp. 121, 122, 136. So also Tobhiah b. 'Eli'ezer (see his commentary on *Canticles*, ed. A. W. Greenup, London 1909, p. 98).

Moses, too, was expected to reappear in the wilderness, according to those rabbinic sources that assigned to him the messianic function of leader of the exiles, cf. the Fragmentary Targum to be quoted *infra*, p. 46 and *Yelammedenu*, quoted by *Yalquṭ*, i, 764; *Exod. R.* 2, 4. Attention should be paid to the words 'all Israel', as well as to the reference to *Hos.* 2, 16 and 17 which clearly show that the two statements refer to the returning exiles and not (or: not merely) to the generation of the wilderness.

phase in the messianic redemption. In different terms, the territory upon which the darkness of the national calamity first descended will be the first to experience the light of the national restoration. Further on, we shall encounter the same argument in such heterogeneous sources as the *Gospel of Matthew* and the *Zohar*.

THE 'LAND OF DAMASCUS' IN QUMRAN MESSIOLOGY

At this juncture it will be convenient to revert to the *Damascus Document*. Apart from the passage (vi, 5) recording the fact of the Sect's departure from the land of Judah to the land of Damascus, there are four other passages in which that geographical term appears—in all of them in a messianic-eschatological context. Three times[1] it figures as the *locale* of the new covenant, and in the fourth passage the advent of the 'Star-Searcher in the Law' is located in that area.[2] The identity of the latter is a moot point; opinions are divided mainly between the priestly Messiah and Elijah.[3] In the present context it makes little difference which of these two messianic personalities is intended. What is important for us is the fact that either the priestly Messiah or the prophet Elijah were expected to appear in the land of Damascus. There is, moreover, good reason to believe that the Messiah son of David, too, was expected to appear there. A new messianic text[4] from Cave IV at Qumran speaks of 'the Scion of David who will arise

[1] vi, 19; viii, 21; xx, 12.

[2] vii, 18–19.

[3] Cf. Y. Yadin, 'The Dead Sea Scrolls and the Epistle to the Hebrews', *Scripta Hierosolymitana* [Publications of the Hebrew University, Jerusalem], vol. iv [1958], p. 54; J. Carmignac, *Revue de Qumran*, i [1958], p. 247; A. Jaubert, *art. cit.* p. 231; Cross, *op. cit.*, pp. 171f., notes 71, 74; D. Flusser, *IEJ*, 1959, pp. 104ff.

[4] See J. M. Allegro, 'Fragments of a Qumran Scroll of Eschatological Midrashim', *JBL*, 77 [1958], p. 353, and also vol. 75 [1956], p. 176. Taking this new text into consideration, I now think (contrary to *JJS*, iv, p. 165) that the phrase הבא דמשק (*CDC* vii, 18f.) has to be rendered 'who *will* come to Damascus', and that a distinction must be made between the *doresh ha-Torah* in *CDC* vi, 7 and vii, 18, the latter being a figure of the future, cf. van der Woude, *op. cit.*, p. 54.

with the Searcher in the Law',[1] and since the appearance of the latter was located in the land of Damascus, it may be concluded that also the Scion of David will make his appearance there, precisely where the above-cited Karaite text expected the appearance of Elijah and a tannaitic text, now to be cited, looked for the advent of the Messiah.

IN RABBINIC LITERATURE

I refer to the interesting discussion[2] between R. Judah b. 'Il'ai and R. Yose b. Durmasqit (or: the son of a Damascene woman) about the meaning of the word חדרך in *Zech.* 9, 1: *In the land of Hadrakh and in Damascus shall be his resting-place*. R. Judah maintained that the word is an appellation for the Messiah who is severe (חד) to the nations and mild (רך) to Israel. Consequently, the phrase 'and Damascus shall be *his* resting-place' referred to the Messiah.[3] R. Yose strongly protested against this interpretation, exclaiming: 'Why dost thou pervert for us the biblical verses?! I call heaven and earth as witnesses that I am from Damascus and there is a place called Hadrakh.' According to R. Yose, the word *His-resting-place* (מנוחתו) is a designation of Jerusalem,[4] and the sense of the verse is that in the messianic era Jerusalem will extend as far as Damascus,[5] where the exiles will assemble and put up their camps. This he finds indicated also in *Cant.* 7, 5:

[1] הואה צמח דויד העומד עם דורש התורה אשר [ימשול] בצי[ון בא]חרית הימים. The reconstruction ימשול is based on several biblical passages where the reign of the Messiah is described by that verb, cf. *Jer.* 30, 21 (see Targum); *Mic.* 5, 1 (see Targum); *Zech.* 6, 12–13 ... איש צמח) ומשל על כסאו); *II Chr.* 7, 18. Cf. also *Jer.* 22, 30.

[2] See *Siphrē* on *Deuteronomy*, ed. M. Friedmann, p. 65a; ed. Louis Finkelstein, p. 7f.; *Pesiqta de-Rabbi Kahana* (ed. S. Buber, Lyck 1868), p. 143a. See also Rashi and Qimḥi on *Zech.* 9, 1.

[3] See the commentary on *Siphrē* to *Deuteronomy* by R. Hillel ben 'Eliakim (11th cent.), ed. by Shachne Koleditzky, Jerusalem 1948, p. 3; W. Bacher, *Die Agada der Tannaiten* (Strassburg 1884), i, p. 395.

[4] On the basis of *Ps.* 132, 14: '*This* [Zion] *is My resting-place for ever.*'

[5] According to R. Yose, 'Damascus shall be *His-resting-place*' means: Damascus shall be Jerusalem.

Thy nose is like the tower of Lebanon which looks towards Damascus.[1]

It is evident that even R. Yose, in spite of his rejecting the interpretation of *Hadrakh* as being an epithet of the Messiah, expounded the verse messianically, and that his exposition, too, presupposes the belief that the region of Damascus will be the *locale* of messianic events, the difference being that this region will now be part of Jerusalem and bear her name.

R. Yose's interpretation appears rather strange and puzzling, and in our view perhaps merits to a greater degree than does the interpretation given by R. Judah b. 'Il'ai the stricture of perverting biblical verses. However, the divergence of opinion between the two Tanna'im must be viewed from an angle other than the purely exegetical. It can be properly understood only against the background of two conflicting messianic conceptions. In contrast to R. Judah's obviously older view, placing the inauguration of the messianic regime in the region of Damascus, R. Yose champions the cause of Jerusalem and accords that privilege and distinction to the Holy City.[2] It is highly significant that he does so by way of compromise, making concessions to the older view: the messianic events are to be enacted in 'Damascus–Jersualem'.

The messianic significance of the land of Damascus is implied in yet another tannaitic interpretation, already briefly referred to, of *Cant.* 7, 5—the verse quoted by R. Yose for a similar purpose. This is how the verse is commented upon in *Siphrē* to *Deuteronomy*:[3] 'If you practise the Law, then look out for Elijah, to whom I said (*I Kings* 19, 15): *Go, return on thy way to the wilderness of Damascus*'. The phrase צופה פני דמשק is taken to mean: 'Look out for Elijah'. The primary idea underlying this remarkable interpretation is the conception which regarded the region of Damascus as the scene of Elijah's appearance.

[1] Cf. *supra*, pp. 5, 8.

[2] According to a tradition reflected in Psuedo-Jonathan on *Gen.* 35, 21 the Messiah will be revealed at Migdal 'Eder (see *Mic.* 4, 8), a place somewhere near Jerusalem, cf. Mishnah *Sheqalim* vii, 4.

[3] § 41 (ed. Friedmann, p. 79b); *Num. R.* 14, 4.

The same conception likewise stimulated the interpretation of *Cant.* 4, 8 by R. Justa'i b. Shunem, found in various talmudic-midrashic sources.[1] '*Come with me from Lebanon . . . look from the top of Amanah, from the top of Senir and Hermon.* Said R. Justa'i b. Shunem, this is a mountain called Amanah, and when the exiles will reach that mountain they will break out into song, as it is said: *Thou shalt sing* (*tāshūrī*) *from the top of Amanah*'. It is here, then, in the region of Amanah, Lebanon, Senir and Hermon that the messianic deliverance will begin, and it is in this area that—according to another *'aggadah*[2]—the nations will bring the exiles as presents to the Messiah,[3] in fulfilment of *Isa.* 66, 20: *And they shall bring all your brethren out of all the nations for an offering unto the Lord.*

The idea may further be detected in the view which anticipated that the Messiah would come from the North,[4] finding support for it in *Isa.* 41, 25: *I have roused up one from the North, and he is come.* Even pentateuchal authority was claimed for it.[5] The divine command: *Turn you to the North* (*Deut.* 2, 3), given to the Israelites when wandering in the wilderness, was interpreted messianically as being addressed to the generation of the last days. We recall that the author of the *Damascus Document* identified the land of Damascus with the 'land of the North' (vii, 13ff.).

[1] *Tanḥuma* (Buber), ii, 11 (p. 59); cf. also the longer version found in the Cairo Genizah and published by J. Mann, *The Bible as Read and Preached in the Old Synagogue*, Cincinnati 1940, Hebrew part, p. 118; P.T. *Shebhi'ith* vi, 5 (36d); *Ḥallah* iv, 8 (60a); *Cant. R.* to 4, 8; *Midrash Shir Ha-Shirim*, ed. L. Gruenhut, Jerusalem 1897, p. 35a. In *Exod. R.* 23, 5 the saying is ascribed to R. 'Eli'ezer b. Yose, see W. Bacher, *Die Agada der Palästinensischen Amoräer*, iii, p. 733, note 9.

[2] *Cant. R.* to 4, 8; *Midrash Tehillim*, ed. S. Buber, pp. 378–9.

[3] See *IV Ezra*, 13, 13; *Ps. Sol.*, 17, 34; T.B. *Pes.* 118b; *Gen. R.* 78, 12 (ed. Theodor-Albeck, p. 932) and also p. 1219; *Midrash Tehillim*, p. 320.

[4] *Lev. R.* 9, 6; *Cant. R.* to 4, 16; *Num. R.* 13, 2. See also the following note.

[5] *Midrash Debharim Rabbah*, ed. S. Lieberman, Jerusalem 1940, p. 22; *Midrash Shir Ha-Shirim Zuṭa*, p. 24; *Midrash 'Aggadah 'al Ha-Torah*, ed. S. Buber, *Deuteronomy*, p. 177; Eisenstein, *'Oṣar Midrashim*, p. 162.

IN MEDIAEVAL JEWISH APOCALYPSES

Turning to the mediaeval apocalyptic writings, we find a striking passage in the apocalypse entitled *The Prayer of Rabbi Simeon b. Yoḥai.*[1] It is embodied in the general portions of the work,[2] as distinct from the bulk of the apocalypse which reflects contemporary conditions. In quoting this late source[3] we assume that many a messianic-eschatological idea of a much earlier date lies embedded in the late Jewish apocalyptic works, derived either from older apocalypses, no longer extant, or even oral traditions which have an astonishing tenacity in persistence. Describing the atrocities of 'the king of fierce countenance' (*Dan.* 8, 23) the named apocalypse says: 'He will go on massacring until he reaches Damascus, but as soon as he reaches Damascus divine rescue and salvation will be granted to Israel.'[4] Here again the national deliverance is bound up with the region of Damascus.

IN QALLIR'S RELIGIOUS POETRY

Our search for traces of the belief under discussion must also extend to Qallir's religious poetry—a veritable repository of national hopes and aspirations. The belief associating messianic occurrences with the district of Lebanon and Anti-Lebanon has found poetic expression in a *piyyūṭ* for the *Musaph* '*Amidah* for the New Year:[5]

[1] A. Jellinek, *op. cit.* iv, p. 122; *Midreshē Ge'ullah*, pp. 277f.

[2] Cf. Yehudah ibn Shemu'el's note, *loc. cit.*

[3] Cf. *Midreshē Ge'ullah*, pp. 174ff.; 254–67; Bernard Lewis, *Bulletin of the School of Oriental and African Studies*, xiii [1949–50], pp. 308–38; S. W. Baron, *A Social and Religious History of the Jews* [2nd ed., New York, 1957], iii, p. 274, note 27; v, p. 353, note 2.

[4] Cf. Yehudah ibn Shemu'el, *loc. cit.*, who refers to *Zech.* 9, 1.

[5] At the end of the *shōphārōth* section, see Israel Davidson, *Thesaurus of Mediaeval Hebrew Poetry*, New York 1924, i, p. 251, no. 7745; iv, p. 278.

Go straight from Hermon	תְּיַשֵּׁר מֵחֶרְמוֹן
To shatter the Red One	לְרוֹעֵעַ אַדְמוֹן,
Cause to snow in Salmon	תַּשְׁלֵג בְּצַלְמוֹן
With the sound of the shofar.	בְּקוֹל הֲמוֹן שׁוֹפָר.

The final conflict with Rome is here associated with Mount Hermon,[1] which is to form the starting-point for the eschatological battle of extermination. We may notice the expression תישר which may also be rendered 'level the way' and which recalls the much-cited messianic verse:[2] *Clear ye in the wilderness the way of the Lord, level in the desert a highway for our God* (*Isa.* 40, 3).

IN THE NEW TESTAMENT

The thesis proposed in the preceding pages is capable of throwing fresh light on three narratives of outstanding importance in the New Testament: Peter's confession in Caesarea Philippi, the transfiguration scene on Mt. Hermon, and Paul's conversion on the road to Damascus. The geographical locations of these central acts in the great messianic drama fit in with the theory about the messianic character of the 'land of Damascus'.

Peter's Confession. According to *Mark* (8, 27), followed by *Matthew* (16, 13), Peter's confession occurred in the district of Caesarea Philippi. Why did Jesus go there? The view[3] that he went there 'for the general purpose of his later Galilean ministry', or in order to seek privacy which he could find 'only at a considerable distance from the scene of his public activities',[4] but

[1] Cf. *infra*, p. 16.

[2] Cited also in the *Rule of the Community*, viii, 14 and in the N.T. (*Mark* 1, 3 and parallels).

[3] E. P. Gould, *The Gospel According to Saint Mark* [International Critical Commentary], p. 151.

[4] Gustaf Dalman, *Sacred Sites and Ways, Studies in the Topography of the Gospels*, London 1935, p. 202. The same reason, among various other explanations, is given by L. E. Elliott-Binns to account for the much larger question why Jesus chose Galilee as the scene of his activities, a fact which 'seems at first sight rather anomalous'. 'There were', he

discloses the embarrassment of finding an explanation of a more satisfactory and convincing nature. Vincent Taylor's observation,[1] in a somewhat different connection, may fittingly be quoted here: 'The reference to "the villages of Caesarea Philippi" by a writer [*Mark*] who so rarely gives place-names commands respect.' A deeper reason must have determined the choice of this district for this crucial messianic event.[2] The place must have some definite connection with the content of the narrative.

In the light of our thesis it appears that the reason is a messianic one, and resides in the fact that Caesarea Philippi, being situated on the slopes of Mount Hermon, belonged to the territory where the prologue of the messianic drama was to be enacted. It is, then, by virtue of its messianic significance that the region of Mount Hermon, a region hitherto unvisited by Jesus, was chosen for the scene where the momentous words were uttered by Peter: *You are the Messiah*. The mention of the district has thus particular pertinency to the narrative which follows.[3] The first acknowledgment of Jesus as Messiah is deliberately, and dramatically, staged in this district. With this acknowledgment the Messiah has been revealed, be it only to the narrow circle of his disciples, and revealed in the very area where his revelation was expected.

The Transfiguration. The closely related vision of the transfiguration[4] in which Jesus is reported to be seen speaking with Moses

says, 'tracts of country where quiet could be found which Jesus would use not only to find rest for His tired spirit, but also as a background for the training of the apostles', see *Galilean Christianity* [Studies in Biblical Literature No. 16], London 1956, p. 24. For our explanation of the choice of Galilee for the beginning of Jesus' activity, see *infra*, p. 23.

[1] Cf. *The Gospel According to St. Mark*, London 1952, p. 374.

[2] 'Simon's confession stands in the middle point of Mark's Gospel. It is variously referred to as the pivot on which his story turns, as its center of gravity, or as the keystone in his Gospel arch' (W. E. Bundy, *Jesus and the First Three Gospels*, Cambridge, Mass., 1955 [Harvard University Press], p. 291.

[3] Against the view of B. H. Branscomb, *The Gospel of Mark* [The Moffat New Testament Commentary], London 1946, p. 144.

[4] *Mark* 9, 2–9; *Matth.* 17, 1–5.

and Elijah and which culminates in the heavenly disclosure: *This is my beloved son*,[1] thus granting divine recognition of Jesus' messiahship, is likewise located in the same neighbourhood, the stage being set on 'a high mountain'. Most modern commentators identify the 'high mountain' with Mt. Hermon.[2] This identification, which is dictated by the context, appears now in its proper theological light: Hermon is messianic-eschatological ground. We are reminded of Qallir's prayer:[3] 'Come straight from Hermon to shatter the Red One.' The question as to why Hermon is not named, but instead a descriptive phrase 'high mountain' is used, may easily and convincingly be answered if we remind ourselves that the phrase in question appears in the well-known messianic prophecy of *Isa.* 40, 9: *Get thee up on a high mountain, thou that bringeth good tidings to Zion . . . lift up thy voice . . . say unto the cities of Judah: Behold the kingdom of your God.* The expression 'high mountain'[4] is a pointer to that prophecy, and *Mark* in employing it intended to imply that the event described represented a fulfilment of that prophecy. We have here a piece of *pesher*-exegesis eminently suitable to the occasion. *Isa.* 40, 9—apart from furnishing one of the key-words of the new faith: 'to preach good tidings'[5]—is the verse that actually contains the

[1] An allusion to *Ps.* 2, 7 used 'as a *testimonium* to the Messiahship of Jesus', see C. H. Dodd, *According to the Scriptures, The Sub-Structure of New Testament Theology*, London 1952, p. 32.

[2] See V. Taylor, *op. cit.*, p. 388.

[3] Cf. *supra*, p. 14.

[4] The description 'high mountain' is in itself a most fitting one, as according to *Deut.* 4, 48 Hermon bore the name הר שיאון which signifies 'high mountain', cf. Köhler-Baumgartner, *s.v.* שיאון; Isaiah Press, *A Topographical-Historical Encyc. of Palestine*, [in Hebrew] Jerusalem 1948, p. 364. Hermon is the highest massif of the Anti-Lebanon mountain range.

It is possible that the prophecy of *Ez.* 17, 22–23 which was given a messianic interpretation by Targum, may also have influenced the association of the Messiah with a high mountain. In the prophetic imagery of Ezekiel a tender branch [=the Messiah] of the cedar [=house of David] will be planted upon *a high mountain and eminent.*

[5] Cf. Alan Richardson, *An Introduction to the Theology of the N.T.*, London 1958, p. 26.

'good tidings' (*evangelion*) of Jesus, which consisted in the proclamation of the arrival of the Kingdom of God.[1] The bringer of good tidings is commanded by the prophet to proclaim on a high mountain: "הנה אלהיכם", which is rendered by Targum:[2] 'Behold the *kingdom* of your God!'[3]

Whatever the precise meaning of the mystical transfiguration vision may be, and whatever special implications its single elements may have, for the purpose of our theme it is sufficient to state the general fact that an occurrence of immense messianic importance was located on Mt. Hermon.

Paul's Conversion. Again, we find that the most crucial experience in Paul's career, which resulted in his conversion and provided him with the credentials for apostleship[4]; the vision in which Jesus of Nazareth, as the risen Messiah, manifested himself to him—this episode of cataclysmic consequences is most significantly placed on the road to Damascus. It was in the land of Damascus, where the appearance of the Messiah was anticipated, that Jesus the Messiah appeared to Paul. And if the recognition of Jesus' messianic character on the part of the other great apostle, Peter, took place in the district of Caesarea Philippi, on the slopes

[1] *Mark* 1, 14; *Matth.* 4, 17.

[2] איתגליאת מלכותא דאלהיכון, 'the kingdom of your God has been revealed'. The rendering of the Targum is suggested and strongly supported by the parallel of *Isa.* 52, 7 where the proclamation of the messenger of good tidings is formulated in the words: *Thy God reigneth*, which the Targum rendered in exactly the same terms: איתגליאת מלכותא דאלהך. The Targum thus equated the two proclamations: הנה אלהיכם = מלך אלהיך.

[3] It should further be borne in mind that verse 3 of the same chapter was interpreted by the evangelists as referring to John the Baptist (*Mark* 1, 2, and parallels). In fact, the entire pericope, *Isa.* 40, 1–11, belongs, as Professor C. H. Dodd has pointed out, to the biblical passages employed as *testimonia* by the writers of the N.T. and which form 'the substructure of all Christian theology', see *op. cit.* pp. 84, 107. 'Here we have, in 40, 1–11, a *locus classicus* of the hope of redemption. The vocabulary of the passage is such as was peculiarly congenial to early Christianity' (p. 84).

[4] *I Cor.* 9, 1: *Am I not an apostle? . . . Have I not seen Jesus the Lord?* See also *I Cor.* 15, 5–9.

of Mount Hermon, Paul's acknowledgment of Jesus' messiahship occurred in the same geographical zone—the region of the Lebanon and Anti-Lebanon.

IN JUDEO-CHRISTIANITY

Another event in the history of Primitive Christianity should be viewed from the vantage-point of our thesis. It is the establishment of the Christian community in Damascus. As Lohmeyer[1] has pointed out—and his view is cited with approval by H. J. Schoeps[2]—its establishment dates back to a period anterior to the persecution of Stephen, i.e. a very short time after the crucifixion of Jesus. The founders, he suggests, may have been none other than the *desposunoi*, the brothers and relatives of Jesus. The most plausible explanation for the choice of Damascus must be sought in the sphere of eschatology. Believing as they did in the immediately impending fulfilment of the *parousia*, they expected the return of Jesus to take place in the messianic territory of the land of Damascus.

Closely related to the preceding point is the fact that one of the two main centres of the Judeo-Christians was in Cochaba[3]—again in the land of Damascus. A dominant factor in Judeo-Christianity was its eschatology: for generations they continued to look for the second coming of Jesus, living in a constant state of preparedness for the irruption of the final era. In view of the messianic significance of the land of Damascus it appears almost natural to expect that at least a section of them should have resorted to the region where the advent of the Messiah was anticipated, just as so many other chiliasts went into the desert to meet the redeemer on the spot of his arrival, which, according to their belief, was to be the desert.[4]

[1] Cf. Ernst Lohmeyer, *Galiläa und Jerusalem*, Göttingen 1936, pp. 55f.

[2] See *Theologie und Geschichte des Judenchristentums*, Tübingen 1949, p. 270.

[3] Cf. Schoeps, *op. cit.* pp. 273ff.

[4] Regarding the emigration of the Jerusalem Christians to Pella in Peraea, which Pliny (*Hist. Nat.* v, 18, 74) included among the cities of the

IN MUHAMMADAN TRADITION

From the Qumran documents, rabbinic, Karaite, apocalyptic, paytanic and Christian literatures, we now turn to Muhammadan sources. Here, too, we find corroborative evidence for the thesis advocated in the foregoing pages.

That evidence resides in the fact that the Muhammadan expectation of the final redeemer which—according to the orthodox belief—centres in the return of Jesus as *Mahdī*,[1] has been associated with Damascus, and that for this a tradition going back to Muhammad himself has been cited. This tradition locates the descent of Jesus on the eastern minaret (*Bāb Djīrūn*) of the great Mosque of Damascus, and it further claims that the last act in the eschatological drama—the killing by Jesus of the Antichrist, the *dadjdjāl*—will be unfolded in the outskirts of that city.[2]

The assumption strongly recommends itself that this tradition has its roots in Christian circles. The great Mosque of Damascus

Decapolis, before the destruction of the metropolis (as reported by Eusebius; see the discussion by S. G. F. Brandon, *The Fall of Jerusalem and the Christian Church*, London 1951, pp. 168ff.), H. J. Schoeps has suggested that the emigration might have been motivated by chiliastic reasons; they might have expected the *parousia* to occur in that district (*op. cit.*, pp. 268, 271). As to the messianic significance of Galilee, see the following pages.

[1] See A. J. Wensinck, *A Handbook of Early Muhammadan Tradition*, Leiden 1927, p. 113.

[2] Cf. M. Steinschneider, 'Apocalypsen mit polemischer Tendenz', *ZDMG*, 28 [1874], pp. 643–44. The tradition is recorded in Muslim's *Ṣaḥīḥ*. See also Hughes, *Dictionary of Islam* (quoting Suyūṭī's *History of the Temple of Jerusalem*), p. 67: 'This is the tower upon which Jesus son of Maria will alight, for Muhammad is reported to have said, "I saw Jesus the son of Maria come forth from near the white minaret, east of the mosque . . . Jesus (it is also said) shall come forth from the White Tower by the eastern gate, and shall enter the mosque. Then shall the word come forth for Jesus to fight with the Antichrist at the corner of the city".' This tradition of Jesus' entrance through the eastern gate may be correlated with another Muhammadan-Christian tradition to the effect that Jesus will enter Jerusalem through the eastern gate [=golden gate], cf. J. Morgenstern, 'The Gates of Righteousness', *HUCA*, vi [1929], p. 10 and *passim*.

was originally the Christian Church of St. John, and when the Muslims took Damascus in 634 the Church was divided between them and the Christian community, to be taken over entirely by the conquerors seventy years later. The expectation of Jesus' descent there must originally have been connected with the Church of St. John, Christian believers expecting the *parousia* to take place in that vicinity.[1]

It is therefore small wonder that the Jews, in their turn, pinned their own messianic hopes on *Bāb Djīrūn*, regarding its collapse[2] as a sign announcing the imminent overthrow of the 'fourth kingdom' and the advent of the Messiah.[3]

'LEBANON' AS AN APPELLATION OF THE SECT

This part of our study may be concluded with a brief observation on one of the 'disconcerting' pieces of exegesis in the *Habakkuk Scroll*. The word *Lebanon* in *Hab*. 2, 17 was taken by the sectarian

[1] The Damascus mosque is the subject of yet another eschatological tradition (Steinschneider, *op. cit.* p. 644), according to which divine worship will still be held there forty years after the world cataclysm. No doubt, the number of forty years is connected with the view that the messianic age will last forty years, cf. N. Wieder, *JJS*, vi [1953], p. 172, note 6.

[2] See A. Jellinek, *Beth Ha-Midrash*, iii, p. 79; iv, p. 120; *Midreshē Ge'ullah*, pp. 194, 273. In these sources *Bāb Djīrūn* is erroneously located in the west of the mosque, cf. Steinschneider, *op. cit.* pp. 639, 641. See also Moses Maimonides, *Epistle to Yemen*, ed. Abraham S. Halkin (English translation by Boaz Cohen), New York 1952, p. 84.

With the collapse of the gate as an eschatological sign, cf. the legend of 'the collapse of the lintel of the Temple' reported by Jerome to have been included among the miraculous events attendant upon the death of Jesus (*Matth.* 28, 51–53) according to the Gospel of the Hebrews. For the eschatological interpretation of these events see Martin Werner, *Die Entstehung des christlichen Dogmas*, pp. 89ff.; English (abridged) edition, *The Formation of the Christian Dogma*, London 1957, p. 33.

[3] Cf. B.T. *Sanh.* 98a, to which attention has been called by N. Brüll, *Jahrbücher für jüdische Geschichte u. Lit.*, ii [1876], p. 198, note, and independently by A. S. Halkin, *op. cit.* p. 84, note 116. W. Bacher (*Ag. d. Tan.*, i, p. 402) quite correctly observed that the reference is to the gate in Caesarea Philippi (not Rome, as Rashi thought), where R. Yose b. Qisma lived. This may be strengthened by the fact that the other sign given by R. Yose is likewise connected with that area—namely the turning into blood of the waters in the Paneas Grotto.

expositor as an appellation of his community (xii, 3–4).[1] What was it that suggested this equation to him? Numerous attempts at explanation have been made, but we must resist the temptation to list them here.[2] In the light of the preceding it would appear that the basis of this interpretation lies in the fact that the Sect, or part of it, sojourned in the region of the Lebanon, awaiting there the advent of the Messiah. The explanation is thus a very simple one: the community is here referred to by the geographical name of the region in which they sojourned—a not uncommon phenomenon.[3]

GALILEE AND THE 'LAND OF DAMASCUS'

In the foregoing pages the 'land of Damascus' figured as the *locale* of the initial phase of the messianic drama. The suggestion is now submitted that this idea is identical with the belief that Upper Galilee is destined to be the *locale* of the ingathering of the exiles and the appearance of the Messiah.[4] Highly suggestive of

[1] The expression '*aṣath ha-yaḥadh* occurs several times as a description of the community as a whole, cf. *DSD*, iii, 2; v, 7; vi, 3, 10, 16; vii, 2, 22, 24; viii, 22. See F. Nötscher, *Zur theologischen Terminologie der Qumran-Texte*, Bonn 1956, p. 59.

[2] Most recently dealt with this question H. J. Schoeps, *Zeitschrift für Rel. u. Geistesgeschichte*, 1959, pp. 70f.

[3] Cf. also the terms 'Heaven' (שמים) as designation of God.

[4] The earliest explicit mention of Upper Galilee as assembly-place of the returning exiles and the appearance of the Messiah (see end of this note) occurs in an apocalypse which has been preserved in the work *Leqaḥ Ṭobh* by Tobhiah b. 'Eli'ezer of Castoria in Bulgaria, composed in the year 1079. By far the greater part of his work is a compilation of material from earlier sources. The passage concerned is introduced by the words 'Said R. Huna in the name of R. Levi' (cf. ed. Wilna, 1880, ii, p. 258; A. Jellinek, *Beth Ha-Midrash*, iii, p. 141; *Midreshē Ge'ullah*, p. 103). As W. Bacher rightly pointed out (*Die Ag. d. Pal. Am.*, ii, p. 432, note 4; see also Strack-Billerbeck, i, p. 161), there is no valid reason for questioning the authenticity of the ascription of the passage to R. Levi, the prominent Palestinian 'Amora of the third century. Other elements in that apocalypse can be traced back to statements by the said 'Amora.

On the other hand, there is no basis for the view frequently met with that the inauguration of the messianic redemption will take place in Tiberias. This is based on a misunderstanding of R. Yoḥanan's saying (B.T. *Rosh ha-Shanah* 31b): ומשם עתידין להגאל. It does not refer to the messianic redemption in general, but merely to the deliverance of

the identity of the two is the fact that the reason given by *Zohar*[1] for the privileged position of Galilee is virtually the same as that given by Yefeth ben 'Ali in reference to the region of Damascus: since Galilee was the territory where the national catastrophe started, the place from where the Jews were exiled and dispersed among the nations, it will therefore be the place where the national liberation will be inaugurated.

From the geographical point of view there is no difficulty in reconciling the two doctrines, as Galilee in its wider sense extends not only as far as Lebanon and Hermon-Anti-Lebanon,[2] but even

the Sanhedrin. What R. Yoḥanan said is that Tiberias, which in his time was the tenth residence ('exile') of the Sanhedrin, will also be its last; from there they will not be exiled any more, but stay in that place until the advent of the Messiah. This interpretation accords with the different formulation of R. Yoḥanan's saying in *Gen. Rabbah* (*shiṭṭah ḥadhashah*) as correctly interpreted by the anonymous commentary on *Gen. Rabbah* (see Albeck's note on p. 1221) and by W. Bacher, *Ag. d. Pal. Amor.*, i, p. 336, note 1. That the saying in question concerned the Sanhedrin only is also manifest from Maimonides' words in *Hilekhoth Sanhedrin* 14, 12: 'There is a tradition', he writes, 'that they [the Sanhedrin] will first return to Tiberias and from there will be transferred to the Temple' (וקבלה היא שבטבריא עתידין לחזור תחילה ומשם נעתקין למקדש). This is a re-interpretation of R. Yoḥanan's words, dictated by the hard facts of history: not only were the Sanhedrin not redeemed, but the institution as such ceased to exist altogether. Maimonides' re-interpretation saves the saying from being relegated to the realm of disproved forecasts and disappointed hopes.

To return to R. Levi, we note that according to him it is the Messiah ben Josef who will appear in Upper Galilee. As is well known, the activity of this precursor-Messiah will mark the inaugural stage in the messianic redemption.

1 On *Exodus*, p. 7b; 8b; 220a: 'There the first calamity happened to them and from there they began to be exiled from all their places and to be dispersed among the nations' (. . . ותמן אתברו בקדמיתא ומתמן שארו לאתגלאה מכל אתרייהו ולאתבדרא ביני עממיא).

2 The natural relationship between these two mountain ranges and Galilee should also be noted. 'The controlling feature of Galilee is her relation to these great mountains.' 'Galilee is literally the "casting forth of the roots of Lebanon" (*Hos.* 14, 5).' 'The opposite range of Hermon dominates the view.' 'How closely Hermon was identified with Galilee, is seen from his association with the most characteristic of the Galilean hills, see *Ps.* 89, 12' (G. A. Smith, *The Historical Geography of the Holy Land*, 1897, p. 417).

up to Damascus.[1] It is significant to note the conclusion arrived at by Ernst Lohmeyer[2] that the New Testament writers used the name 'Galilee' in an extended sense, according to which it included Mount Hermon, Tyre, Sidon and the Decapolis, possibly reaching as far as Damascus.

With this identification in mind, we now return to the New Testament. It is a unanimous Christian tradition that Jesus began his public activity in Galilee. On receiving the news of John the Baptist's imprisonment, which meant the end of the forerunner's work, Jesus proceeded to Galilee and issued his proclamation: 'The time is fulfilled and the kingdom of God is at hand.'[3] Not only do the three synoptic gospels agree on this point but also the fourth evangelist[4] 'similarly calls attention to the fact that the *beginning* of the manifestation of the glory of the Lord was in Galilee'.[5] Likewise in the *Acts of the Apostles* (10, 37) stress is again laid on the fact that the *beginning* was in Galilee. According to Professor Dodd, 'this emphasis on the beginning in Galilee seems to have been integral to the pattern of the *kerygma* from the first'.

This fact is of no mean significance for our thesis. It is in the land of Galilee that the opening phase in the story of Jesus is located.[6] This is perfectly in conformity with the doctrine which regarded Galilee—the land of Damascus—as the area of the initial messianic occurrences.

[1] Cf. *Ezek.* 47, 16–18; Josephus, *Ant.* v, 1, 22 (86); Pseudo-Jonathan on *Num.* 34, 9, 15; see S. Klein, 'Das Tannaitische Grenzverzeichnis Palästinas', *HUCA*, v [1928], pp. 248, 252–3.

[2] *Galiläa und Jerusalem*, pp. 25, 27, 80; H. J. Schoeps, *Theologie u. Geschichte d. Judenchristentums*, p. 271, note 1.

[3] *Mark* 1, 14f.; *Matth.* 4, 12, 17.

[4] *John*, 2, 11.

[5] C. H. Dodd, *According to the Scriptures*, p. 80.

[6] Every bit of information concerning Galilee—including physico-geographical, climatic, demographic and sociological data—has been utilized for discovering a reason which could have led Jesus to choose Galilee as the scene of his activities, see L. E. Elliot-Binns, *Galilean Christianity*, pp. 23–27, cf. also *supra*, p. 14, n. 4.

On the other hand, it is this assumption which enables us to perceive the implication and purpose of the emphasis on the *beginning* in Galilee, to which Professor Dodd called attention.[1] The accentuation of this fact served to demonstrate that this important event in Jesus' life, the prelude to his messianic career, conformed to popular anticipations and satisfied current notions about the Messiah's first appearance, based, as we shall instantly see, on Scripture:[2] Jesus' first action, the proclamation about the arrival of the kingdom of God, was performed in the messianic territory of Galilee, and the people of that territory were the first to hear the 'good news' about the great turning-point in history.[3]

[1] Professor Dodd regarded it as of some importance 'that this element of the *kerygma* persisted so strongly in face of the tendency to canonize Jerusalem as the place of origin of the Christian mission' (*op. cit.*, p. 80, note 1). This seems to imply that the emphasis on the *beginning* in Galilee stems from the opposite tendency—to localize the origin of the Christian mission in Galilee. We are faced with two rival trends, one gravitating towards Jerusalem and the other towards Galilee. If such rival trends ever existed, the unanimity of the evangelists on our point, and especially the fact that even Luke who is regarded as favouring Jerusalem emphasizes that the *beginning* was in Galilee, shows that this fact, at any rate, has no relation to the alleged rivalry, and that its explanation must lie in a different sphere. It is due to the tendency, common to all New Testament writers, to vindicate the truth of Jesus' messiahship by proving that all elements in his career answer to the traditional ideas about the Messiah and his functions. The strong persistence referred to by Professor Dodd is indeed significant, but for the following reason: it shows that the idea of Galilee being messianic territory must have been an important element in the messianic programme of the time, if all the evangelists were at pains to underline that this element had been fulfilled.

[2] How anxious Matthew, for instance, was to impress his readers with the fact that Jesus' actions exactly corresponded with the prophetic forecast, may be seen from his version of the triumphal entry of Jesus into Jerusalem. Contrary to Mark who has one donkey only, Matthew introduced a second one 'in order to exhibit an exact correspondence with the actual wording of *Zech.* 9, 9: "riding upon an ass *and* upon a colt the foal of an ass"' (see Dodd, *op. cit.* p. 127; K. Stendahl, *The School of St. Matthew and its Use of the Old Testament*, Uppsala 1954, pp. 119, 200).

[3] The culminating scene in the messianic drama was, however, reserved for the Holy City. All evangelists represent the triumphant entry into Jerusalem as the climax in the story they are narrating. Nothing can

It is on the supposition here propounded alone that this emphasis on the *beginning* in Galilee really becomes meaningful.

Of even greater significance, however, is the fact that the reason given by *Matthew* for the commencement of Jesus' activity in Galilee appears to be exactly identical with the reason given by Yefeth b. 'Ali for the region of Damascus, and by the *Zohar* for the land of Galilee, as the areas of the advent of Elijah or the Messiah respectively. Following the proof-from-Scripture theology, *Matthew* represents the appearance of Jesus in Galilee as the fulfilment of the prophecy of *Isa.* 8, 23–9, 1, which he quotes as follows:[1]

> *The Land of Zebulun and the land of Naphtali,*
> *The way by the sea, beyond Jordan,*
> *Galilee of the nations.*
> *The people who sat in darkness*
> *Have seen a great light,*
> *And to them that sat in the region of shadow of death,*
> *To them a light has arisen.*

The regions referred to in this quotation are easily harmonized with the extended geographical notion of 'Galilee'. It may be mentioned that according to Josephus the land of Naphtali actually extended as far north as Damascus.[2] Again, one of the geographical entities mentioned in the verse from *Isaiah* is the 'way of the sea' which most probably refers to the *Via Maris*, the great and important highway connecting Damascus with the Mediterranean coast.[3]

convey this more vividly than the highly dramatic frame of the entry. It is here that Jesus himself arranged for the ass-colt to be fetched, and by entering the city riding on an ass deliberately and consciously dramatized the prophecy of *Zech.* 9, 9.

[1] *Matth.* 4, 15–16.

[2] Cf. *supra*, p. 23, n. 1. It may be noted that, in an eleventh-century document, Hadrakh (near Damascus) is styled 'the inheritance of Asher and Naphtali', see Jacob Mann, *The Jews in Egypt and in Palestine under the Fatimid Caliphs*, Oxford 1920, i, p. 196.

[3] Cf. G. Dalman, *Sacred Sites and Ways*, pp. 11, 127, 185.

As to the substance of the quotation, it goes without saying that the evangelist gave the passage from *Isaiah* a messianic interpretation; the terms 'light' and 'darkness' must therefore be understood accordingly.[1] 'Light' is a well-established metaphor for deliverance and freedom,[2] just as 'darkness' is a metaphor

[1] It is usually held that *Matthew* gave the *Isaiah* passage a purely spiritual interpretation, taking 'darkness' to refer to the spiritual darkness in which Galilee was sunk, and 'light' as alluding to the light of Jesus' teaching, which has now appeared over that 'benighted' district. Cf., for example, A. Plummer, *An Exegetical Commentary on the Gospel According to St. Matthew*, p. 47; Alan H. M'Neile, *The Gospel According to St. Mark*, London 1952, p. 44. However, the whole hypothesis about Galilee's spiritual darkness is open to serious question; see Gedalyah Allon, *A History of the Jews in Palestine in the Mishnaic and Talmudic Periods* (in Hebrew), Jerusalem 1953, I, pp. 318–21. See further S. Klein, *'Ereṣ Ha-Galil*, Jerusalem 1945, pp. 18–21 and the literature mentioned there in note 52.

[2] How closely in the Jewish mind the idea of the final redemption has become associated with the imagery of light may perhaps be best illustrated by the fact that in Jewish prayer that imagery was chosen to give expression to the nation's hope and yearning for the advent of the Messiah. This is the case in the formula incorporated in the *Yoṣer*-benediction: 'O cause a new light to shine upon Zion, etc.' (Singer's *Prayer-Book*, p. 39). *Isa.* 60, 1: *Arise, shine, for thy light is come* was used for the same purpose, see J. Mann, *HUCA*, ii [1925], pp. 292, 293, note 63, 295; *Tarbiz* xxii [1951], p. 36 (used by the Palestinian *payṭan* Hedwatha); Ibn Ezra on *Eccl.* 8, 10; L. Zunz, *Die synagogale Poesie des Mittelalters* (2nd ed., 1920), p. 63; I. Elbogen, *Studien zur Geschichte d. jüd. Gottesdienstes*, Berlin 1907, p. 24.

It must be emphasized (against S. Lieberman, *PAAJR*, xx [1951], pp. 399f. and J. M. Grintz, *Sinai*, 1952, p. 15, note 16) that the insertion of *Isa.* 60, 1 into the *Yoṣer*-benediction, the benediction over the light and luminaries, has no relation whatever to the Essene custom (mentioned by Josephus, *Bell. Jud.* ii, 8, 5 [128]) of offering prayers to the sun 'as though entreating it to rise'. The *Isaiah* verse in this benediction has a purely messianic reference.

The messianic symbolism of light also underlies the usage of 'lamp' as a metaphor for the messianic salvation or the Messiah himself, see *Ps.* 18, 29 and the Targum thereto, and especially *Ps.* 132, 17. This symbolism, too, entered Jewish liturgy; a Genizah text (Elbogen, *loc. cit.*) inserted into the *Yoṣer*-benediction the formula 'Light for us the lamp of Thy Messiah', and the '*Amidah* for the New Year—one of the oldest compositions of Jewish liturgy—includes a prayer for 'a rekindling of a lamp unto the son of Jesse, Thine anointed, speedily in our days'. The entire verse (*Ps.* 132, 17) was included in the third benediction—the

particularly for captivity and exile, and the phrase 'those who sat[1] in darkness' stands for 'captives', 'prisoners'. Consequently, what Matthew wants to say is clearly this: the region which was the first to experience the national darkness of captivity, the area which witnessed the deportation and dispersion of the nation, will be the first to experience the great light of the messianic redemption.[2] Matthew's thought is thoroughly Jewish:[3] he thinks

prayer for Jerusalem and the restoration of the Davidic kingdom—of the Grace after Meals, according to a Genizah text, see J. Mann, *ibid.* p. 336 and S. Assaf, *Mi-Siphruth Ha-Ge'onim*, Jerusalem 1933, p. 82. See further *Tanḥuma* (Buber), *Exodus*, pp. 46a, 50a, and Mann's *New Midrash on the Pentateuch*, published in *The Bible as Read*, etc., Hebrew part, p. 251: שמן למאור (שמות כ"ה,ו') זה מלך המשיח שהוא עתיד לפדות את ישראל מן המלכיות ולהאיר להם, שנ' קומי אודי כי בא אורך וגו' (ישעי' ס', א') וכתיב אצמיח קרן לדוד ערכתי נר למשיחי (תה' קל"ב,י"ז).

1 Attention should be paid to Matthew's reading 'those who *sat* in the darkness' (instead of 'walked') which is opposed to both the M.T. and the LXX (As for the reading of A, cf. K. Stendahl, *The School of Matthew*, p. 172). This deviation (if he did not have a different text) is indicative of what Matthew had in mind. As has been said, the expression 'those who *sit* in the darkness' (or 'in the darkness and shadow of death') is a metaphor for captivity, see *Isa.* 42, 7; 49, 9; *Ps.* 107, 10, 14. Cf. also *Mic.* 7, 8 (*when I sit in the darkness, the Lord is a light unto me*) and the messianic interpretation put on it in P.T. *Ber.* i (2c), *Cant. R.* vi, 10, and especially Mann's *New Midrash on the Pentateuch* (*op. cit.*, Hebrew part, p. 220): *When I sit in the darkness*: in [the captivity of] the empires; *the Lord is a light unto me*: through the Messiah, as it says (*Isa.* 60, 1): *Arise, shine, for thy light has come*, this refers to the Messiah (כי אשב בחשך, במלכיות, יי אור לי במשיח שנאמר קומי אורי כי בא אורך, זה משיח). See also *Midrash Ha-Gadol* on *Exodus*, ed. M. Margulies, p. 174.

2 The Targum took the terms concerned in the same sense, with the difference that it interpreted the *Isaiah* verse in relation to the deliverance from Egypt, the first Exodus, whereas according to *Matthew* it alluded the second 'Exodus' in the messianic era.—The targumic interpretation is reflected in the Passover *Haggadah*: 'He brought us forth from bondage to freedom . . . from darkness to a great light' (Mishnah *Pes.* x, 5). The last phrase is moulded on the *Isaiah* verse, the only place in the whole Bible where the phrase 'a great light' occurs.

3 Cf. Ernst von Dobschütz, *Matthäus als Rabbiner und Katechet*, *ZNW*, 1928, pp. 338–48; G. D. Kilpatrick, *The Origins of the Gospel of St. Matthew*, Oxford 1946, pp. 106f.

on the same lines which we encountered in such heterogeneous theological climates as those represented by the *Zohar* on one side, and the 'mourners for Zion'—to whom Yefeth b. 'Ali belonged[1]—on the other.

It is of considerable interest to find that the same interpretation was current in Judeo-Christian circles in the time of Jerome, as we learn from his commentary on *Isaiah*:[2]

> The Hebrews who believe in Christ interpret these passages as follows: 'Of old these two tribes of Zebulun and Naphtali were taken captive by Assyrians and were led away into a strange country, and Galilee was deserted;[3] but as the prophet said, they should be relieved by him [Christ], who should bear the sins of the people.' Afterwards not only the two tribes, but the remnant who dwelt beyond Jordan and in Samaria, were likewise led away into captivity.[4] And this they [the Judeo-Christians] affirm the Scripture to say: 'In the selfsame region whose population had been led captive and had started to serve the Babylonians, and which was first tormented by the darkness of error, that same land should be the first to see the light of the preaching of Christ.'

Here then we have the same line of reasoning: the region which was the first to suffer desolation, the inhabitants who were the first to be affected by captivity and dispersion, will be the first to see the redemptive light of the Messiah. A scrutiny of this quotation suggests that Jerome in recording the Judeo-Christian interpretation superimposed on it a spiritual element of his own. From the whole tenor of the quotation it is evident that the term 'darkness' was taken as symbolic of desolation, captivity and dispersion, and 'light' as a metaphor for deliverance. Jerome, however, so we suggest, made two interpolations which invested the two terms with a spiritual sense,[5] as well: 'darkness'=error and 'light'=

[1] See 'The Qumran Sectaries,' p. 100.

[2] J. P. Migne, *P.L.*, 24, 127. The English translation is by Schonfield, *op. cit.* p. 52.

[3] *II Kings* 15, 29.

[4] *Ibid.* 17, 6; 18, 11.

[5] Cf. *supra*, p. 26, note 1.

preaching of Christ. A reproduction of the passage concerned, with Jerome's interpolations in square brackets, will make this clear:

> The selfsame region whose population had been led captive and had started to serve the Babylonians [and which was first tormented by the darkness of error], that same land should be the first to see the light [of the preaching] of Christ.[1]

Be that as it may, the main idea stands out clearly enough, and its identity with the ideology of Yefeth b. 'Ali and the *Zohar*, on the one hand, and *Matthew* on the other, is beyond doubt. Apart from the slight Christian colouring, the whole quotation might as well have emanated from the two Jewish sources mentioned. But there is yet another point of contact to be noted. It concerns the interpretation of the *Isaiah* verse. According to the messiology of the *Zohar*, the Messiah will be hidden during a period of twelve months in the light of the 'Bird's Nest' as the abode of the Messiah is called. 'After[2] the twelve months, that light will appear between heaven and earth in the land of Galilee, where the exile began, and there will he manifest himself from the light of the "Bird's Nest".'

The suggestion is here ventured that the idea of a light appearing over the land of Galilee has its roots in the messianic interpretation of *Isa.* 8, 23–9, 1, foretelling that the people of that area will see *a great light* and that *a light will shine over them*. The *Zohar* gives an objective reality to the figuratively conceived light of the biblical original, rendering its metaphor concrete, and a real light actually makes its appearance over that territory. The *Isaiah* prophecy will thus be accomplished in its bare literality, as well. The messianic light is no mere figure of speech but a physical phenomenon: a light enveloping the Messiah and actually shining over Galilean territory.

[1] The expression 'light of the Messiah' (אורו של משיח) occurs in rabbinic literature, cf., for example, *Pesiqta Rabbathi* (ed. M. Friedmann), pp. 162a–b. See also *supra*, pp. 26, n. 2; 27, n. 1, and the sources given by V. Aptowitzer, *Parteipolitik der Hasmonäerzeit im Rabbinischen u. Pseudoepigraphischen Schriftum*, Vienna 1927, p. 237, note 13.

[2] *Zohar* on *Exodus*, p. 8b.

If this is correct, then the *Isaiah* verse, though not explicitly cited as proof-text, ultimately lies behind the Galilean ideology of the *Zohar* also.

'I WILL GO BEFORE YOU INTO GALILEE'

The aim of this section is to suggest that the doctrine of the messianic character of Galilee is capable of furnishing a satisfactory explanation of what is commonly called the 'Galilean tradition'. By far the major part of it is concerned with a new interpretation of *Mark* 14, 28: *I will go before you into Galilee*—an interpretation which in itself is important enough to have deserved a separate treatment; it has, however, been included here because of its close connection with the rôle of Galilee in the messianic programme.

In *Mark* 14, 27f., Jesus, after the Last Supper, is represented as saying: *When I am raised up, I will go before you into Galilee*. Likewise, again according to *Mark* (16, 7), the 'young man' at the tomb is reported to have said to the women to go and tell the disciples *that he goes before you into Galilee*. Students of the NT are familiar with the problems which these passages present and the difficulties of how to account for the deviation from the Markan account by *Matthew* and particularly by *Luke*.[1] In the present context the briefest treatment only is possible. Contrary to the commonly held view[2] that the reference in *Mark* to Galilee concerned a resurrection appearance of the risen Jesus in Galilee, in recent years the view has been championed that the oldest tradition did not refer to a post-resurrection scene, but to the *parousia*,[3]

[1] Cf. Vincent Taylor, *op. cit.* pp. 549, 608.

[2] For references see W. G. Kümmel, *Promise and Fulfilment* [Studies in Biblical Theology, No. 23], London 1957, p. 77, note 196.

[3] See, in particular, E. Lohmeyer, *Galiläa und Jerusalem*, pp. 10ff., and *Das Evangelium des Markus*, Göttingen 1937, pp. 312, 356; R. H. Lightfoot, *Locality and Doctrine of the Gospels*, London 1938, pp. 61ff., 73ff.; Willi Marxsen, *Der Evangelist Markus*, Göttingen 1956 [Forschungen zur Religion u. Lit. des Alten u. Neuen Testamentes, Neue Folge, 49], p. 54, and *passim*. For further literature see James M. Robinson, *The Problem of History in Mark*, London 1957, p. 11, note 4.

and reflected the belief and expectation of the earliest Christians that the death of Jesus will soon be followed by his return.

What seems to offer substantial support for this view is the wording of Jesus' pronouncement: *I will go before you.* These words have long been a *crux interpretum* and subject to divergent interpretations on the part of commentators and theologians.[1] The suggestion is here made that the background to these words is to be found in a messianic belief, current in the time of Jesus and founded on a number of biblical passages, such as *Ex.* 13, 21, *Isa.* 52, 12 and *Mic.* 2, 13. It is this belief that will be demonstrated in what here follows, and it is these passages which hold the key to the understanding and significance of Jesus' pronouncement; and it will be shown that the crucial verb προάγειν is but the Greek for הלך לפני, 'to go before', in the two first-mentioned passages, and is equivalent to the expressions 'to go up before', 'to pass on before' and 'to be at the head of' in the third passage.

Let us begin with the third passage which will first be treated in isolation and later linked with the other two verses. I submit that the words: 'I will go before you', were intended as a pointer to, and were meant to re-echo the prediction of *Mic.* 2, 13, according to which the messianic king will *go before* the reassembled flock. It is hardly necessary to point out that such an allusion to a prophetic prediction is in conformity with the 'according-to-Scripture' theology which related the career of Jesus to the traditional messianic conceptions, and which was bent on proving that all events in that career conform to the

[1] Nothing could convey more vividly the perplexity caused by this saying than the theory advanced by two German critics that 'Galilee' does not refer to the northern district of Palestine, but to a place near Jerusalem; see Rudolf Hoffmann, *Galiläa auf dem Olberg* (1896) and A. Resch, *Das Galiläa bei Jerusalem* (1910). More recently, C. F. Evans (*JTS*, 1954, p. 12) has proposed to divest the word 'Galilee' of its geographical meaning entirely and to regard it as a symbolic designation for 'the gentile world'; consequently, the saying would mean: 'I will lead you into the gentile world' (p. 15). Erich Grässer in his comprehensive analysis of *Das Problem der Parusieverzögerung in den Synoptischen Evangelien u. in der Apostelgeschichte* [Beihefte zur ZNW, 1957], p. 30, note 7, chracterizes Evans' view as 'fantastic'.

messianic pattern based on Scripture.[1] The suggestion just made has the merit of supplying an excellent link between the verse under discussion and the one immediately preceding it.[2] The latter, quoting *Zech.* 13, 7, speaks of the scattering of the flock in consequence of the death of the shepherd; verse 28 continues the imagery of the shepherd, by recalling another messianic prophecy which will now, after the resurrection of the shepherd, be fulfilled: the risen shepherd will *go before* the re-assembled flock as messianic king:[3]

> *I will surely assemble, O Jacob, all of thee;*
> *I will surely gather the remnant of Israel;*
> *I will render them as a sheep in a fold;*
> *As a flock in the midst of their pasture . . .*
> *The breaker will go up before them . . .*
> *And their king will pass on before them,*
> *And the Lord at the head of them.*

The words 'I will go before you' assume meaning and significance if they were intended to refer not to a temporary manifestation of Jesus, but to his return as messianic king,[4] in fulfilment of the above messianic prophecy.

Before proceeding to uncover the deeper implication of that prophecy and at the same time to widen considerably the Jewish background of Jesus' pronouncement, we shall demonstrate that

[1] On this problem see C. H. Dodd, *According to the Scriptures*, London 1952. 'The O.T. has exercised a *formative*, even a *creative* influence upon the tradition' (Frederick C. Grant, *The Gospels, Their Origin and their Growth*, London 1957, pp. 147f.).

[2] Some critics held that verse 28 might be an insertion intended to prepare the way for 16, 7, see Taylor, *op. cit.* p. 549.

[3] On the messianic Shepherd-King, see Alan Richardson, *An Introduction to the Theology of the New Testament*, p. 292.

[4] E. Lohmeyer's thesis that *Mark* expects the return of Jesus as 'Son of Man' in contradistinction to 'Messiah' is controverted by R. Bultmann (*Theology of the N.T.*, vol. i, pp. 52f.): 'It is evidently impossible to conceive the titles "Messiah" and "Son of Man" as expressions of two differing theological views about Jesus and hence as distinguishing marks of two different Churches or parties.' Cf. also Marxsen, *op. cit.* p. 66, note 2.

the *Micah* passage was interpreted messianically in Judaism—a fact which has hitherto failed to attract scholarly attention. It may be stated that *Mic.* 2, 13 ranked among the foremost messianic texts, so much so that it entered the liturgy of the synagogue, the worshipper actually praying for its fulfilment. 'The breaker' (הפורץ) was taken as a designation for the Messiah,[1] and Pereṣ, the son of the patriarch Judah, from whom the Messiah would descend, was—according to a midrashic etymology—so called because the 'breaker' will arise from him. 'Their king', was similarly taken as referring to the Messiah, but also to God. The verse is cited in its messianic sense in various midrashic contexts,[2] and it is indicative of the significance it assumed that it figured prominently among the biblical verses of a messianic character recited at the solemn installation of the Exilarch in Babylonia,[3] who was of the royal line of David, and from whose family the Messiah was expected to come.[4] It is there juxtaposed with such outstandingly messianic prophecies as *Isa.* 11, 1–2; 16, 5; *Jer.* 23, 5.

[1] *Gen. R.* 85, 14 (ed. Theodor-Albeck, p. 1049); '*Aggadath* Bereshith (ed. S. Buber, Cracow 1902), p. 129. Another interpretation takes 'breaker' as alluding to Elijah and 'their king' to the Messiah, see David Qimḥi, *ad loc*. This interpretation was also current in Karaite circles, according to Yefeth b. 'Ali's commentary on *Micah* (MS. British Museum, Or. 2401, fol. 30b): וקאל מפסר אכ̇ר אנה קאל עלה הפורץ לפניהם והו אליהו ע"ה ויעבר מלכם לפניהם והו צמח בן דוד ת̇ם קאל ויוי בראשם.

[2] *Gen. R.* 48, 10 (ed. Theodor-Albeck, p. 488); *Lev. R.* 32, end; *Pesiqta Rab.* (ed. M. Friedmann), pp. 29b, 157b, 161a. In the latter place the verse is employed as a messianic peroration: 'In that hour, the Holy One, blessed be He, will reveal His glory and kingdom to all mankind, will redeem Israel and manifest Himself at the head of them, as it is written (*Mic.* 2, 13): *The breaker will go up, etc.*'; *Midrash Bereshith Rabbathi* by Moses ha-Darshan (ed. Ch. Albeck, Jerusalem 1940), p. 185. See further the passages collected in *Yalquṭ ha-Makhiri* on *Micah* (ed. A. W. Greenup, London 1910), pp. 12–16.

[3] Cf. the fragment from the Second Firkowitch Collection in Leningrad, published by S. Assaf in *Ginzē Qedem* (ed. B. M. Lewin), iv, pp. 63f. See also Jacob Mann, *Texts and Studies*, i, p. 208, note 13.

[4] It is significant to note that in a Genizah letter sent to the exilarch, the latter is addressed as זרע הפורץ, 'the seed of the breaker', cf. J. Mann, *The Jews in Egypt and Palestine under the Fatimid Caliphs*, Oxford 1922, ii, p. 347.

The following fact must be considered of even greater significance. In gaonic times it was customary to mention the Exilarch and the two heads of the academies, at Sura and Pumbeditha, in the *Qaddish*, one of the principal prayers of the synagogue. Now, an amplified *Qaddish* of the ninth century, preserved in the Cairo Genizah, adds to the petition for the personal welfare of the Exilarch, the messianic prayer that he may advance at the head of all Israel, in fulfilment of the *Micah* prophecy: *The breaker will go up before them.*[1]

The position this verse had acquired in Jewish messianic thought is perhaps best illustrated by the fact that it was incorporated in a *Qedushah*-composition to be recited on Sabbaths and festivals. Such a special *Qedushah*, long out of vogue among the Jews, is found in a liturgical Genizah fragment in the British Museum.[2] The fourth part of it runs as follows:

אלהיכם אני ואתם עמי,
מלככם אני ואני אמלך עליכם,
ואגלה מלכותי עליכם,
ואקבץ גליותיכם,[3]
ואעבר כמלך בראשכם
[ככתוב[4] על יד נביאך ויעבר
מלכם לפניהם ויי בראשם].

Your God am I, and you are My people,
I am your king, I will reign over you,
I will manifest My kingdom upon you,

[1] This interesting *Qaddish* was first published by A. Marmorstein in *MGWJ*, 1924, pp. 159ff., and re-edited in an amended form by B. M. Lewin, *Ginzē Qedem*, iii, p. 54. Its date is 882–887 C.E. (Marmorstein, *ibid.* p. 151).

[2] MS. Or. 5557. O, fol. 17b. A similar text is found in *Maḥzor Vitry*, p. 175. Cf. also Zunz, *Literaturgeschichte der synagogalen Poesie*, Berlin 1865, p. 85.

[3] These two words are absent in *Maḥzor Vitry*.

[4] The text in square brackets is taken from *Maḥzor Vitry*; the British Museum MS. is damaged.

I will gather together your exiles,
And I will pass on as King at the head of you,
As it is written by the hand of Thy prophet:
And their king will pass on before them,
And the Lord at the head of them.

In this *Qedushah* the *Micah* verse serves as vehicle to articulate the most fervent hope of the Jew, the hope for the advent of the Messiah and the manifestation of the divine kingdom.[1] Such a liturgical phenomenon can shed an illuminating ray on the words: *I will go before you.* In promising his return and the final establishment of the kingdom of God in these words, Jesus had, in effect, promised the realization of the messianic hope in essentially the same terms as expressed in the above *Qedushah*, i.e. had predicted the fulfilment of the prophecy of *Micah* 2, 13.

But Jesus' saying has a yet deeper messianic implication: it is linked with a messiology which had been decisively influenced by the parallelism between the Mosaic and messianic periods.[2] This parallelism is rooted in the Prophets who envisaged the messianic salvation in terms of the exodus from Egypt and the sojourn of the Israelites in the wilderness. The rabbis followed this line, and derived the categories with which to describe the messianic era from the drama of the first redemption, the archetype of the last. The correlation of the two epochs, in general, and the analogy between the 'first redeemer' and the 'last redeemer', in particular, is basic to the messiology of the rabbis[3] as well as to that of

[1] It may further be pointed out that in a Genizah text *Mic.* 2, 13 figures as one the 'kingship' verses (מלכיות), see I. Elbogen, 'Die Tefilla für die Festtage' in *MGWJ*, 1911, p. 596.

[2] Cf. N. Wieder, 'The Idea of a Second Coming of Moses', *JQR*, 46 [1956], p. 359, where it is suggested that the very notion of a messianic forerunner (*Mal.* 3, 23) owes its origin to the correspondence between the two periods.

[3] Cf. V. Aptowitzer, *Parteipolitik der Hasmonäerzeit im rabbinischen und pseudoepigraphischen Schriftum* [Veröffentlichungen der Alexander Kohut Memorial Foundation, Vienna 1927], p. 107 and p. 256, notes 88, 89; see also the following two notes.

the New Testament writers,[1] including Paul.[2] This has now become increasingly recognized.[3]

Now, the phenomenon of the divine cloud advancing before the people of Israel in its wandering through the desert was likewise utilized for the parallelism in question. The rabbis related *Ex.* 13, 21: *And the Lord was* going before them *by day in a pillar of cloud, to lead them the way, and by night in a pillar of fire* to the *Micah* prophecy:

> *The breaker will* go up before them . . .
> *And their king will* pass on before them,
> *And the Lord* at the head of them.

and further with *Isa.* 52, 12: '*The Lord will* go before them.'[4] Just

[1] See the bibliography given by H. H. Rowley, *The Unity of the Bible*, London 1953, p. 19, footnote; H. Sahlin, *Zur Typologie des Johannes-evangeliums*, Uppsala und Leipzig [Acta Universitatis Upsaliensis, 4, 1950]; Jacob J. Enz, 'The Book of Exodus as a Literary Type for the Gospel of John', *JBL* 76 [1957], pp. 208–15; Otto A. Piper, 'Unchanging Promises: Exodus in the New Testament', in *Interpretation*, 11 [1957], pp. 3–22 [mentioned by Enz].

[2] Cf. H. Sahlin's essay 'The New Exodus of Salvation According to St. Paul', published in *The Root of the Vine*, ed. A. Fridrichsen [Essays in Biblical Theology, Dacre Press, Westminster 1953]; E. Earle Ellis, *Paul's Use of the Old Testament*, Edinburgh and London, 1957, pp. 66ff.; 88ff.; 130f.; W. D. Davies, *Paul and Rabbinic Judaism*, London 1948, pp. 102ff.

[3] 'The typological correspondence between the Exodus and the Messianic deliverance was not only generally accepted among the Jews in the time of Jesus, but was also taken for granted in serious theological thinking' (Sahlin, *ibid.* p. 83). 'The New Exodus of Salvation determines the thought of St. Paul as well as the entire Primitive Church. The New Testament can, as a whole, be regarded as a detailed fulfilment of the types of the Old Testament Exodus, God's great act of salvation for the people of His election' (*ibid.* p. 94). Cf. also Jean Daniélou, *The Lord in History* [Engl. translation of *Essai sur le Mystère de l'Histoire*], London and Chicago 1958, pp. 207f.: 'The life of Christ in the Gospels is related step by step to the symbols of the Exodus.'

[4] See *Gen. R.* 48, 10 (Theodor-Albeck, p. 488): וה׳ הולך לפניהם הרי במדבר . . . לעתיד מנין? עלה הפורץ לפניהם; *Tanḥuma*, *Deut.* 1 (both

as the cloud of the *Shekhinah* went before the people in the first deliverance, leading them to the Promised Land, so in the ultimate deliverance the *Shekhinah*, shrouded in a cloud—as all appearances of the *Shekhinah* are[1]—will, together with the 'breaker', lead the dispersed nation back to its homeland.

But the parallelism is extended even further: according to the tannaitic *'Aggadah*,[2] one of the functions of the pillar of cloud was to prepare the way, to level the mountains and raise the valleys—precisely as *Isaiah* (40, 3) depicted the messianic deliverance: *Clear ye in the wilderness a way . . . every valley shall be lifted up and every mountain and hill shall be made low.*

The belief that the Jews returning from the Dispersion will be accompanied by a cloud must have been widespread and deep-seated. According to the Targum of Jonathan on the Prophets, this belief is reflected in yet another prophetic passage, *Isa.* 35, 10 (=51, 11): *And the ransomed of the Lord shall return, and come with singing to Zion, and an everlasting joy shall be upon their heads.* The Hebrew for the last line ושמחת עולם על ראשם is paraphrased by the Targum as follows: 'And a cloud of glory shall form a protective covering [lit. "overshadow"] over their heads.'

versions). In the latter source, as well as in a Genizah text (published by J. Mann, *HUCA*, xiv [1939], p. 349) *Isa.* 52, 12 is cited, instead of the *Micah* verse. On the other hand, in the *New Midrash on the Pentateuch* (Mann, *The Bible as Read and Preached in the Old Synagogue*, Cincinnati 1940, Hebrew part, p. 219) both verses are adduced: גואל הראשון: ויי הולך לפניהם, גואל אחרון: ויעבר מלכם לפניהם וג׳ (מיכה ב׳, 13) וכתיב כי הולך לפניכם יי וג׳ (ישעי׳ נ״ב, 12). וכשם שעשה נסים ונפלאות כמצרים, כך עתיד לעשות להם באחרית הימים, שנ׳ כימי צאתך מארץ מצרים אראנו נפלאות (מי׳ ז׳, 15).

[1] See, e.g., *Ex.* 19, 9; 24, 15; 40, 35.

[2] Based on *Deut.* 1, 33. See *Tosephta Soṭah*, iv, 2 [Zuckermandel, p. 298]; xi, 1 [314]; *Mekhilta*, ed. Horovitz-Rabin, p. 81; *Mekhilta* de-Rabbi Shime'on b. Yoḥai, ed. J. N. Epstein-E. Z. Melamed, Jerusalem 1955, p. 47: ואחד שמקדים לפניהם מתקן להם את הדרכים מגביה להם את השפל ומשפיל להם את הגבוה . . . כענין שנא׳ כל גיא ינשא וכל הר וגבעה ישפלו (ישעי׳ מ׳, 4), ואמר והיתה מסלה . . . (שם י״א, 16) . . . מה לעתיד לבוא כל גיא ינשא . . . כך היה להן בעלייתן מארץ מצרים. See also Pseudo-Jonathan on *Ex.* 12, 37.

This remarkable interpretation[1] must be old; it is taken for granted in an aggadic statement by Rabbi 'Akiba, who cites the verse as proof-text for the repetition of the miracle of the cloud in the messianic age.[2] Nor are these the only biblical passages where this miraculous event is forecast.[3] According to R. 'Akiba it is also presaged in *Isa.* 4, 6: *And there shall be a covert for a shadow in the day-time from the heat, and for a refuge and for a covert from storm and from rain.*[4] 'Covert' (סוכה) stands for the cloud mentioned in the foregoing verse.[5] It may be recalled that the *'Aggadah*

[1] The basis of this interpretation is evidently the phrase 'upon their *heads*'; joy is elsewhere in the Bible associated with the *heart*, cf., e.g., *Jer.* 15, 16; *Ezek.* 36, 5; *Pss.* 4, 8; 104, 15; *Cant.* 3, 11; *Eccl.* 2, 10. It is for this reason that Sa'adya deviated from the Hebrew text and actually translated 'and everlasting joy in their hearts' (*Œuvres Complètes de R. Saadia ben Iosef al-Fayyoûmî*, ed. J. Derenbourg, Paris 1896, iii, pp. 52 and 79). The Targum (and Rabbi Akiba) took *simḥath 'ōlām* as denoting 'a joy of old', i.e. joy experienced in the remote past. The expression is so explained (in an otherwise different interpretation) by R. Simeon b. Laqish in B.T. Shabb. 88a, and it is this talmudic passage which is the source of Rashi's comment on *Isa.* 35, 10.

[2] See *infra*, note 5.

[3] Cf. also the allegorical exposition of *Cant.* 2, 6 (*Cant. R. ad loc.*): '*And His right hand will embrace me*, this refers to the cloud of the *Shekhinah* in the messianic age' (וימינו תחבקני זו ענן שכינה לעתיד לבא).

[4] *Cant. R.* on 1, 8: '*Go thy way by the footsteps* (בעקבי) *of the flock*. R. Akiba said: From the way in which I surrounded them with clouds of glory, as it is said: *And the Lord went before them in a pillar of cloud . . . the pillar of cloud departed not by day* (*Ex.* 13, 21, 22), you may know what I will do to them in the end (בעקב); and so it is written (*Isa.* 4, 6): *And there shall be a covert for a shadow in the day-time*' (צאי לך בעקבי הצאן. ר׳ עקיבא אומר ממה שהקפתי אותם בענני הכבוד המד״א וי׳ הולך לפניהם יומם... לא ימיש עמוד הענן את יודע מה אני עושה להם בסוף, בעקב, הה״ד וסכה תהיה לצל יומם).
See also the following note.

[5] Mekhilta *Bo'* 14 (ed. J. Z. Lauterbach, Philadelphia 1933, i, p. 108): '*To Sukkoth*. R. Akiba says: *Sukkoth* here means only clouds of glory as it is said: *And the Lord will create over the whole habitation of Mount Zion, and over her assemblies, a cloud and a smoke by day, and the shining of a flaming fire by night; for over all the glory shall be a canopy* (Isa. 4, 5) So far I know only about the past. How about the future? Scripture says: *And there shall be a covert for a shadow in the day-time* (*ibid.* v. 6)

assigned to the cloud in the desert yet another function: it surrounded the Israelites on all sides, forming an impenetrable covering to keep off rain, hail and the rays of the sun, as well as protecting them against thorns and snakes.[1] In the view of R. ʻAkiba (or his teacher ʼEliʻezer b. Hyrcanus, as another version has it)[2] the festival of Tabernacles is commemorative of the clouds which enveloped Israel in the desert—a view subscribed to by ʻOnqelos and the Targum of Jonathan.[3] The same miraculous envelopment will occur in the messianic era.

Thus the divine cloud of the first liberation in all its rôles—guidance, preparing the way, and protective envelopment—will reappear in the ultimate liberation. This belief was also given expression in the mediaeval Jewish Apocalypses. One interesting passage may be reproduced here:[4]

and further: *And the ransomed of the Lord shall return, and come with singing unto Zion, and an everlasting joy shall be upon their heads*' (*Isa.* 35, 10). Cf. also *Mekhilta de-Rabbi Shimeʻon b. Yoḥai* (ed. J. N. Epstein-E. Z. Melamed), p. 47; *Gen. R.* 48, 10 (ed. Theodor-Albeck, p. 487); *Lev. R.* 34, 8; *Numb. R.* 14, 2; *Eccl. R.* 11, 1; *Tanḥuma Bo*', 9; *A New Midrash on the Pentateuch* (Mann, *The Bible as Read*, *etc.*, p. 228).

1 See L. Ginzberg, *The Legends of the Jews*, v, p. 438, note 241. Tannaitic sources speak of seven clouds: four on the four sides of the people, one above them, one beneath them and one that preceded them, raising the depressions and lowering the elevations.

2 *Siphra*, *'Emor* 17 (ed. Weiss, p. 103a) and B.T. *Sukk.* 11b. Cf. also *Midrash ha-Gadhol* on *Leviticus* (ed. E. N. Rabinowitz, New York 1932), p. 592.

3 ʻOnqelos rendered the word '*booths*' (*Lev.* 23, 34) by 'booths of clouds', and Pseudo-Jonathan by 'booths of clouds of glory'. This view is shared by such leading medieval Jewish authorities as Saʻadya (in the Arabic translation of the Pentateuch), Rashi and Naḥmanides. The latter insists that this is the plain meaning of the biblical text.

4 *'Othoth ha-Mashiaḥ*, Jellinek, *Beth ha-Midrash*, ii, p. 62; *Midreshē Ge'ullah*, p. 323. Cf. further the apocalypse *Sepher Zerubbabhel* [629–36] first published by Israel Lévi, *REJ*, 68 [1914], p. 140. 'God will cause the heavenly Temple to descend to the earth, and a pillar of fire and a cloud (of incense) will rise up towards heaven and the Messiah and all Israel will follow it on foot to the gates of Jerusalem.' We note that here the pillar of cloud and fire does not accompany the returning exiles, but directs them to Jerusalem from its stationary position above the Temple.

'Michael (the archangel) will blow a long-drawn blast of the *shofar*, and the Holy One, Blessed be He, will bring forth the tribes from the river of Gozan, from Ḥalakh Ḥabor and the cities of Medes[1] . . . And when the tribes will come forth, the clouds of glory will surround them, and the Holy One, Blessed be He, will *go before them*, as it is written (*Micah* 2, 13): *the breaker will go up before them*.'

This belief was given poetic expression in a liturgical composition for Pentecost[2]—a composition which exhibits (as Zulay observed) stylistic features peculiar to Yannai. The *payṭan* saw in the circumstances attendant upon the Sinaitic revelation foreshadowings of the events of the messianic redemption.[3] The

This obviously represents a fusion of two different ideas. The idea of a pillar of cloud and fire rising above the Temple is based on *Isa.* 4, 5. Hai Ga'on in his *Responsum Concerning the Redemption* (*Midreshē Ge'ullah*, p. 140) explicitly refers to that verse. In the apocalypse mentioned this pillar coalesced with the pillar of the Exodus, with the result that although the pillar does not advance before the exiles, it none the less performs the function of a guide: through it they are enabled to find the way to the Holy Land. This view is adopted by Sa'adya (*'Emunoth we-De'oth*, ed. Slutzki, p. 125) who sees in this a literal fulfilment of *Isa.* 60, 3: *And the nations shall walk at thy light, and kings at the brightness of thy rising*. So, too, Hai Ga'on (*loc. cit.*): וכל מי שמבקש לבוא לירושלים רואה ממדינתו את עמוד האש ההוא והולך לאורו עד שהוא מגיע לירושלים, שנאמר (ישעי׳ ס׳, 3) והלכו גוים לאורך. On the other hand, according to the apocalypse *Ma'asē Daniyy'el* (*Midreshē Ge'ullah*, p. 225) the pillar of fire above the Temple merely serves to signalize the rebuilding of the Temple.

One further passage from a mediaeval Jewish apocalypse may be quoted: ובאותו זמן יעיר ה׳ שבטי ישראל ויבואו לירושלים עיר הקדש וימצאו בתורה כתוב (שמות י״ג, 21) ויי הולך לפניהם יומם בעמוד ענן ועוד כתוב (ישעי׳ נ״ב, 12) כי הולך לפניכם יי ומאספכם אלהי ישראל והם מהלכים בעב ובערפל (*Tefillath Rabbi Shime'on b. Yoḥa'i*, Jellinek, *Beth ha-Midrash*, iv, p. 124; *Midreshē Ge'ullah*, p. 282).

1 Cf. *II Kings*, 17, 6.

2 Published from a Genizah manuscript in Oxford by Menaḥem Zulay in *Melilah* v [1955], p. 75. Cf. also the fragmentary text of the same *piyyūṭ*, *ibid.* p. 78.

3 Cf. the liturgical composition for Pentecost by Yannai(?), juxtaposing the occurrences of Sinai with the messianic expectations centring on Mount Zion (M. Zulay, *Piyyūṭē Yannai*, 373).

'exceedingly loud voice of the *shofar*' (*Ex.* 19, 16) signalized the blowing of the great messianic *shofar* prophesied by *Isa.* 27, 13, and the 'thick cloud' (*Ex.* 19, 9) in which the divine glory manifested itself betokened the pillar of cloud by means of which the dispersed will be gathered together:

רָם יָרַד בְּכוֹבֶד בְּעַב עָנָן
לָכֵן יוֹסִיף לְקַבֵּץ פְּזוּרִים כְּשֶׁה בְּעַמּוּד עָנָן.

Significantly, on this point the Karaites are in unison with their Rabbanite brethren.[1] As the sixth miracle to occur in the messianic age Yehudah Hadassi counts the renewal of the pillar of cloud and of fire to guide and shield the exiles.[2] 'As God did in the past with those who left Egypt, of whom the psalmist says (105, 39): *He spread out a cloud for a screen, and fire to give light in the night*, so will He do in the future with those leaving the exile, as it is written (*Isa.* 4, 6): *And there shall be a covert for a shadow in the day-time*.

But this belief is much older than the sources so far quoted would suggest. Already the author of *II Maccabees* (2, 8) anticipated the coming back of 'the cloud as in the days of Moses'. He does not, it is true, explicitly ascribe to it any specific redemptive function, but the fact itself is of significance: the reappearance of the Mosaic cloud had its fixed place in his messianic programme.

The phenomenon of the Mosaic cloud also occupied the mind of Paul, but in keeping with his mystical bent of thought he saw in the envelopment of the cloud the prototypal counterpart to baptism[3]—a rather strange idea which caused some embarrassment to modern Christian critics who characterized it as 'an obscurity which has to be excused as a product of Rabbinical ingenuity'.[4] We are here concerned with Paul's parallel only in so

[1] Already Daniel al-Qumisi saw in the *Micah* prophecy a parallelism to the divine cloud guiding the Israelites in the desert, see *Pithron*, p. 44.

[2] *'Eshkol ha-Kopher*, Alph. 378, letter *'aleph*.

[3] *I Cor.* 10, 2.

[4] Quoted by Albert Schweitzer, *The Mysticism of Paul the Apostle* (2nd ed., London 1953), p. 260.

far as it shows that the incident of the cloud engaged the attention of one of the contemporaries of Jesus in the context of the parallelism between the Mosaic and the messianic epochs.

However, of paramount significance is the fact that the idea of a pillar of cloud and fire fulfilling an actual messianic-redemptive rôle can be traced back to another distinguished contemporary of Jesus: Philo. In contrast to Paul's typological fantasy, Philo conceived of this parallel in realistic terms, assigning to the cloud the rôle of guiding the re-assembled nation to the Holy Land—a rôle it had performed at the time of the first exodus. I refer to the much-debated passage in *De Praemiis et Poenis* 28–29, 164–165 which is here reproduced in Colson's translation:[1]

> For even though they dwell in the uttermost parts of the earth, in slavery to those who led them away captive, one signal, as it were, one day will bring liberty to all . . . When they have gained this unexpected liberty, those who but now were scattered in Greece and the outside world over islands and continents will arise and post from every side with one impulse to one appointed place, *guided in their pilgrimage by a vision divine and superhuman* unseen by others but manifest to them as they pass from exile to their home.

The discussion as to the meaning of the words here italicized is summed up by Wolfson[2] in these words: 'With regard to this passage, there is a difference of opinion among students of Philo as to whether it refers to the Messiah or not. According to one interpretation, it refers to the Messiah as well as to the Logos, thus identifying the two. According to another interpretation, it refers to the Logos but not to the Messiah. According to a third interpretation, it refers to *something like the cloud by which the people were guided in their first deliverance from Egypt*.'

This brief summary is apt to convey the impression, not of course intended by Wolfson, that only the third interpretation

[1] Loeb Classical Library, *Philo*, vol. viii, pp. 417f.

[2] Cf. Harry A. Wolfson, *Philo, Foundations of Religious Philosophy in Judaism, Christianity and Islam*, Harvard University Press, 1948, ii, p. 415.

saw in the divine vision an equivalent to the pillar of cloud and fire. As a matter of fact, all three interpretations share this recognition, which stems from the fact that the pillar of cloud and fire guiding the people through the desert is described by Philo[1] in similar terms.[2] Indeed, the very association of the 'divine vision' with the Logos, shared by the first two interpretations, rests on the fact that the Mosaic cloud had been connected by Philo with Logos[3]-Wisdom,[4] as it had earlier been identified with Wisdom by *Ecclesiasticus*[5] and the *Book of Wisdom*.[6] The question as to whether the Logos enclosed in the cloud was, as Wolfson

[1] Cf. August Gfrörer, *Philo und die alexandrinische Theosophie, oder vom Einfluss der jüdisch-ägyptischen Schule auf der Lehre des Neuen Testamentes*, Stuttgart 1831, i, pp. 528–30; August Ferdinand Dähne, *Geschichtliche Darstellung der jüdisch-alexandrinischen Religions-Philosophie*, Halle, 1834, i, pp. 437f.; James Drummond, *The Jewish Messiah, A Critical History of the Messianic Idea from the Rise of the Maccabees to the Closing of the Talmud*, London 1877, p. 271.

[2] It may be pointed out that Philo's statement that the divine vision guiding the exiles will be invisible except to the exiles themselves is, in fact, predicated in tannaitic literature of the pillar of fire, *Siphrē Zuṭa*, § 33 (ed. H. S. Horovitz, Leipzig 1917 [=Corpus Tannaiticum, III], p. 266): יכול שהיה מאיר על אחרים, תלמוד לומר לעיני כל בית ישראל, לעיני ישראל היה מאיר, לא היה מאיר על אחרים. See also *Siphrē*, § 83 (pp. 79f.).

[3] Cf. the sources mentioned in note 1, and J. Drummond, *Philo Judaeus, or the Jewish-Alexandrian Philosophy in Its Development and Completion*, London 1888, i, p. 185, footnote; ii, 276; M. Friedländer, *Zur Entstehungsgeschichte des Christentums, Ein Excurs von der Septuaginta zum Evangelium*, Vienna 1894, pp. 21f.

[4] *Quis rerum div. her.* 42, 204: 'For on minds of rich soil that cloud sends in gentle showers the drops of wisdom' (Loeb Classical Library, iv, p. 385).

[5] 24, 4. Cf. R. H. Charles, *The Apocrypha and Pseudepigrapha of the Old Testament*, i, p. 397, note 4; M. Z. Segal, *Sepher Ben-Sira ha-Shalem*, Jerusalem 1953, p. 148; Carl Siegfried, *Philo von Alexandrien als Ausleger des Alten Testamentes*, Jena 1875, p. 400.

[6] 10, 17. Cf. William J. Deane, *The Book of Wisdom*, p. 167; Carl Ludwig Grimm, *Commentar über das Buch der Weisheit*, Leipzig 1837, pp. 253f.; Drummond, *Philo Judaeus*, i, p. 185. See also Robert H. Pfeiffer, *History of New Testament Times*, New York 1949, p. 316, footnote.

maintains,[1] none other than the archangel Michael, the guardian angel of Israel, need not detain us here; this question is of no decisive import to our subject. What is important for us is the mere fact that according to Philo a vision similar to that of the pillar of cloud in the desert will go before the people and will be instrumental in accomplishing the central and culminating act in the messianic redemption—the restoration of the scattered nation to its homeland; and Colson[2] is no doubt right in stating that Philo's 'remarkable words' need not 'indicate more than a belief that in the second deliverance the nation would be guided as they were in the first by the Cloud in which was a Θεία ὄψις flashing rays of fire'. Colson followed Emil Schürer who expressed the same opinion, but with absolute definitiveness:[3] 'That this divine appearance is *not* the Messiah,[4] but one analogous to the pillar of fire in the march through the desert, scarcely needs mention.'

[1] *Op. cit.* i, pp. 377f. A different view has been expressed by E. R. Goodenough, *By Light, Light*, Yale University Press, 1935, p. 206, footnote 55: 'the cloud is only another illustration of the λόγος τομεύς'.

It ought to be mentioned that the view that the archangel Michael was enclosed in the cloud, though apparently not to be found in early rabbinic sources, occurs in *Pirqē Rabbi 'Eli'ezer*, chapter 42, where it is said in reference to the same verse alluded to by Philo (*Ex.* 14, 19): 'What did the Holy One, blessed be He, do? He sent Michael, the great prince, and he became a wall of fire between Israel and the Egyptians.' It is noteworthy that Ibn Ezra shared this view, cf. his commentary on *Ex.* 14, 19: ויסע מלאך... הוא השר הגדול ההולך בענן. See further his 'Shorter Commentary' (ed. Leopold Fleischer, under the title *Abraham Ibn Ezra's Commentary to Exodus*, Vienna 1926) on 13, 21 (p. 85).

[2] Vol. viii, p. 418, note a.

[3] See *A History of the Jewish People in the Time of Jesus Christ*, Edinburgh 1898, Second Division, vol. ii, p. 147, note 14.

[4] On the other hand, it cannot be doubted that Philo did believe in a personal Messiah, as it clearly emerges from *De Praemiis et Poenis* 16, 95–97. Cf. Gfrörer, *op. cit.* vol. i, p. 530; Paul Volz, *Die Eschatologie der jüdischen Gemeinde in neutestamentlichen Zeitalter*, Tübingen 1934, §34; C. Guignebert, *The Jewish World in the Time of Jesus* (translated from the French by S. H. Hooke), London 1939, p. 226; Joseph Klausner, *The Messianic Idea in Israel from Its Beginning to the Completion of the Mishnah*, London 1956, pp. 493, 523; *idem*, *From Paul to Jesus*, London 1942, pp. 197f.; Wolfson, *op. cit.* ii, p. 414. F. Gregoire's study, *Le Messie chez Philo d'Alexandrie* (Ephemerides Theologiae Lovanienses, 1935, pp. 28–50) was inaccessible to me.

Here, then, we have a messianic belief that is rooted in the Prophets; held by the author of *II Maccabees*, by Philo, and by Rabbi 'Akiba;[1] articulated in the Palestinian Targum on the Pentateuch and the Targum of Jonathan on the Prophets; embodied in the *Qaddish* and *Qedushah*; reflected in the ceremonial of the installation of the Exilarch in Babylonia; and shared by the schismatic Karaites—a belief which is epitomized in the key expression *to go before*. The pronouncement *I will go before you* ascribed to Jesus has now to be inserted in this distinguished chain of tradition. In using this formula Jesus was not only alluding to the prediction: *The breaker* (=Messiah) *will go up*

[1] This instance may serve as an illustration of the thesis that ideas preserved in late rabbinic compilations, or recorded in the name of an individual rabbi of a late date, may be centuries anterior to both. In the present instance the rabbinic material cannot be dated earlier than the second century, but the idea as such was, in fact, known to Philo. That does not mean that the rabbis are indebted for this idea to Philo, nor that Philo drew upon earlier rabbinic literature, but rather that both Philo and the rabbis are dependent upon a common Jewish tradition. There is good reason to believe that the idea is considerably older than Philo. First, because the parallelism between the first redemption from Egypt and the last redemption in the messianic era goes back to the Prophets, and the belief in the reappearance of the pillar of cloud and fire is but a corollary to that parallelism. This sign of divine protection had obviously made a strong impact on the people's imagination, as may be inferred from the fact that it is repeatedly emphasized in the Pentateuch (e.g. *Ex.* 13, 21; 40, 38; *Num.* 10, 34); is recalled by Moses in his prayer (*Num.* 14, 14) and once more in his farewell discourse to the people (*Deut.* 1, 33); is referred to twice by the psalmist (78, 14; 105, 39) and also twice recounted by the author of *Nehemiah* (9, 12, 19). Secondly, the reappearance of the pillar of cloud and fire, in its protective rôle, is actually forecast by *Isaiah* (4, 5). Thirdly, the author of *II Maccabees* (2, 8) anticipated the restoration of 'the cloud, as in the days of Moses'. I have dealt briefly with the problem of dating rabbinic material in *JQR*, vol. 46, pp. 356–60. For a fuller treatment cf. B. J. Bamberger's article in *JBL*, vol. 68, pp. 115–23. His conclusions may be repeated here: 'A very considerable part of the material preserved in the Talmudic-Midrashic sources is much older than it appears at first sight to be' (p. 123). Again, 'The rabbi whose name appears in our text may have cast the story in its present form, or modified some detail, or provided an old tradition with a new scriptural basis . . . But it does not follow, because a certain idea appears in his name, that he originated or introduced this idea (pp. 116f.). Cf. also S. Sandmel, 'Philo's Place in Judaism', *HUCA*, xxv [1954], pp. 231–3.

before them, and their king will pass on before them, but was, in effect, announcing the re-enactment by himself—as the new Moses and leader of the messianic Exodus—of the incident of the *Shekhinah*[1] going before the people.[2]

The above interpretation of Jesus' pronouncement receives some support from the fact that the Fragmentary Targum describes the advent of the Messiah in very similar terms to those with which Jesus is reported to have predicted his forthcoming advent: 'to lead at the head' (of the flock). Describing the last of the four great nights which are inscribed in the Book of Memorial—the night of Passover on which the messianic redemption will be accomplished—the Targum says:[3]

> Moses[4] will come forth from the desert,[5] and the King-Messiah from Rome, each going at the head of (his) flock,[6] and the Word of God will mediate between them, causing them to walk in harmony; and the children of Israel will proclaim: the Kingdom is the Lord's, in this world and in the world to come.

Significantly, the same Aramaic phrase (דבר בריש) is used by the Fragmentary Targum with reference to the Messiah as the

[1] 'The evangelists attribute to him [Jesus] the fulfilment at once of the prophecies that foretold the coming of God and those concerning the Messiah' (J. Daniélou, *op. cit.* p. 188).

[2] It is interesting to note that according to the Catholic scholar mentioned in preceding note (*ibid.* p. 131), *John* 8, 12 presupposes the identification of Jesus with the pillar of fire. 'The new fire kindled in the Paschal vigil symbolizes the column of fire by which the Jews were guided in their wanderings in the desert, as it is said [*John* 8, 12]: *He who follows me can never walk in the darkness.*' See further *ibid.* pp. 207f. and also R. V. G. Tasker, *The O.T. in the N.T.*, London 1946, p. 52: 'Christ is shown to transfer to Himself the figures of the Exodus (the brazen serpent, the manna, the water, and the fiery pillar).'

[3] On *Ex.* 12, 42; ed. M. Ginsburger on 15, 18 (p. 37). Cf. N. Wieder, 'The Idea of a Second Coming of Moses' in *JQR*, 1956, p. 358.

[4] Ginsburger, *ibid.*: משה יהא נפיק ממדברא ומלכא משיחא יהא נפיק מרומה, דין ידבר בריש ענא ודין ידבר בריש ענא ומימרא דה׳ יהוי מדבר בין תרויהון ואינון מהלכין כחדא ויימרון בני ישראל דה׳ הוא מלכותיה בעלמא הדין ובעלמא דאתי דיליה הוא.

[5] Cf. *supra*, p. 8, footnote.

[6] So according to Codex Paris (Ginsburger, p. 37) and Cod. Vat. (*ibid.* p. 82). See, however, further on in the text.

Targum of Jonathan on the Prophets employs (in the allegorical exposition of *Ezek.* 16, 12) in relation to the cloud going before Israel in the desert[1]—a fact which is indicative of the correspondence between the guide to the Promised Land and the guide to the Promised Kingdom.

The printed editions of the Fragmentary Targum read עננא, cloud, instead of ענא, flock. If this reading be accepted—it has been given preference by some scholars, e.g. M. Ginsburger and Joachim Jeremias[2]—then this targumic passage provides further direct evidence of the belief that the returning exiles will be led by a cloud. Both Moses and the Messiah, who are here represented as sharing in the guidance of the exiles coming from different directions, are accompanied by a cloud.[3]

We can now return to our starting-point. If Jesus' pronouncement concerned his forthcoming *parousia*, the fact that Galilee is named as the scene of so stupendous an occurrence, appears—against the background of our thesis—almost natural. That Galilee—the land of Damascus—should be the first district to be illumined by the light of the messianic kingdom was demanded by the belief of the time, supported by Scripture.[4] Thus, just as the first part of Jesus' pronouncement *I will go before you* reflects a

[1] Represented as divine messenger as in *Ex.* 14, 19. It is noteworthy that Rashi who quotes the allegorical interpretation of the Targum adds as proof-text *Micah* 2, 13. See also *Pesiqta Rab.* (ed. Friedmann), p. 155b.

[2] *Theologisches Wörterbuch z. N.T.*, iv, p. 861.

[3] The much-cited talmudic designation of the Messiah בר נפלי (B.T. *Sanhedrin* 96b) most probably originated in this belief. It was recognized long ago that notwithstanding the aggadic pun נפלת-נפלי [*that is fallen*; Am. 9, 11], the word נפלי represents the Greek for 'cloud', νεφέλη, and that the phrase is to be rendered 'Son of the Cloud'. The data adduced here offer a satisfactory explanation of the origin of this designation.

[4] Marxsen also (*op. cit.* p. 60) has suggested that the Primitive Church expected the *parousia* to occur in Galilee, and thinks that the shifting of the centre of gravity of the *Urgemeinde* from Jerusalem to Galilee is connected with the expectation of the *parousia* there. But on the question 'why Galilee?' he answers that the return of Jesus was anticipated in the same place where his first coming happened. According to the view unfolded in this chapter the reason is a much deeper one, and resides in the belief that the messianic kingdom would be inaugurated in that region.

Jewish messiological idea, rooted in Scripture, so the second part, the geographical location, is in keeping with another messiological idea, likewise rooted in Scripture.

* * *

Our thesis also enables us to account for the divergencies from the original account in the Markan Gospel on the part of *Matthew* and *Luke*—one of the chief problems of New Testament research. The reason for these divergencies seems to lie in the new situation which arose when the promised reappearance of Jesus and the coming of the Kingdom did not materialize. In consequence of the non-fulfilment of the anticipated *parousia*, the original saying *I will go before you into Galilee*, became a serious and critical problem which necessitated either its re-interpretation or a complete recasting of the whole story. The former is manifest in *Matthew*, where the promise of the *parousia* has been transformed into a promise of a resurrection appearance,[1] i.e. a single, fleeting act of self-manifestation of the risen Jesus. And this promise is reported as having been fulfilled: Jesus kept his word and actually appeared to the disciples in Galilee (*Matth.* 28, 16–20). In other words, Jesus' saying has been 'demessianized' and the critical problem of the non-occurrence of the *parousia* eliminated by eliminating the promise.

This 'demessianization', however, suffered from a serious deficiency. If the appearance in Galilee was merely meant to be a resurrection appearance, and not the Messiah's second coming, why should this take place in Galilee? And what then is the purpose of *I will go before you*? The saying had now, apparently, lost all its meaning and significance. Searching questions, similar to those asked in modern times, must have been asked in certain early Christian circles:[2] 'For what reason will not Jesus manifest himself to his followers in Jerusalem, but only in Galilee? And why does he "go before" them, in the meantime? Must he, as

[1] Cf. *ibid.* p. 63.

[2] See J. Weiss, *The History of Primitive Christianity*, pp. 17f.

one risen from the dead, necessarily appear in Galilee? Can he not show himself anywhere, whenever he will? . . . Is he not exalted above limitations of distance and place?'

Hence the complete recasting, the bold transformation of the original narrative, which we find in the case of the Lukan Gospel. In the new version no appearance at all is located in Galilee, and of the original saying of Jesus it is only the formerly vital key-word 'Galilee' that has been retained. The angels' message (24, 6b–7) is now addressed solely to the women, reminding them of Jesus' prediction of his own crucifixion and resurrection (9, 22, 24) made while he *was yet in Galilee*. This radical change which preserved a faint echo of the oldest tradition was dictated by the hard and cruel fact that the expectation of the *parousia* had been disappointed. The unfulfilled promise had to be suppressed.

In fine, Matthew's and Luke's versions alike represent two different attempts[1] to deal with the critical situation created as a result of the non-fulfilment of the promised *parousia*.[2]

* * *

In conclusion, a word or two must be said about a question which forces itself upon our mind: How is it to be explained that relatively few traces only of the Galilean doctrine have been preserved in tannaitic-amoraic sources?

[1] These attempts strongly call to mind the two schools of thought dominating the contemporary scene of New Testament theology: the 'realized eschatology' of Dodd, and the demand for demythologization by Bultmann. Both try to get rid of the *futurist* eschatology; the former by eliminating the predictions of the future by means of exegetical reinterpretation, and the latter by dismissing it as part of a mythological world-view which modern man is unable to accept. Bultmann's own words may be quoted: 'The mythological eschatology is untenable for the simple reason that the *parousia* never took place as the New Testament expected, but that the history of the world ran on' (H. W. Bartsch, *Kerygma and Myth*, 1953, p. 5).

[2] Cf. the conclusion arrived at by E. Grässer (*op. cit.* p. 216): 'In der Redaktion der Evangelisten hat das Problem der Parusieverzögerung seinen festen Sitz! Am deutlichsten bei Lukas.'

The answer to this question can only be conjectural. The reticence of the rabbis may well be a reaction against the new faith. Since Galilee played such a pre-eminent part in the early stages of Christian history, since Galilee was in fact the cradle of the new religion, so much so that its adherents were styled 'Galileans', the talmudic Sages thought it wise to pass over the Galilean doctrine in silence. Jesus' messianic activity in Galilee discredited the rôle which that area was to play in the messianic drama. To this we may add the fact that the hopes entertained particularly by the Judeo-Christians for a return of Jesus had centred on that district.

There is, of course, nothing surprising in such a reaction. Parallels of much greater consequence can be adduced. In their tendency to draw a sharp line of demarcation between normative Judaism and heterodox groups, the rabbis went even to the length of abolishing time-honoured religious practices. It is sufficient to mention two well-known cases: the elimination of the Decalogue from the daily Synagogue service[1] and the abandonment of kneeling and prostration during prayers.[2] These examples belong to the sphere of religious *action*, a sphere which was jealously and meticulously guarded by the rabbis against any change and modification. It goes without saying that the rabbis must have had much less qualms in ignoring the Galilean doctrine which belonged to the sphere of *ideas*, and to the sphere of messianism at that, which was in any case of a rather fluctuating nature and in which much freedom of opinion was allowed.

It was only in post-talmudic sources that the Galilean doctrine received a new articulation—at a time when the *rationale* for keeping silence over it had long been forgotten. This, again, is not unusual. The daily recitation of the Decalogue is likewise illustrative of this phenomenon—the reintroduction, at a later period of a once abrogated custom. After several unsuccessful attempts

[1] See P.T. *Berakhoth*, i, 8 (3c); B.T., *Ber.* 12a.

[2] Cf. N. Wieder, *Islamic Influences on the Jewish Worship* [in Hebrew] pp. 47ff.

at various periods to reintroduce it,[1] the Decalogue was finally readmitted into the Synagogue in the fourteenth century,[2] albeit in a less prominent position and without its recitation having obligatory character; and it is today to be found in almost every Jewish prayer-book.[3]

1 See B.T. *Ber.* 12a; B. M. Lewin, *'Oṣar ha-Ge'onim*, *Meghillah*, p. 67; *Responsa* of Solomon b. 'Adret, i, no. 184; iii, no. 289.

2 Cf. *Ṭur* and *Shulḥan 'Arukh*, *'Oraḥ Ḥayyim*, chap. 1; Solomon Luria, Responsa, no. 64 [translated into English by B. Berliner in *Jews' College Jubilee Volume*, London 1906, pp. 132f.].

3 See Singer's *Authorised Daily Prayer-Book*, p. 87.

CHAPTER II

TORAH AND TRADITION

'HIDDEN AND MANIFEST THINGS'

What is the meaning of the expression 'hidden things' (נסתרות) occurring in the *Damascus Document* as well as in the *Rule of the Community*? What is the nature of these 'hidden things' and what is underlying the antithesis, נגלות–נסתרות, 'hidden and manifest things'? That *nistārōth* does not refer to hidden doctrines or commandments of an esoteric character, as it is sometimes maintained,[1] is quite certain. One has only to consider the following passage in the *Damascus Document*, from which it clearly emerges that the 'hidden things' concern the divine precepts 'which man shall *do* and live thereby', mentioning in particular the observance of Sabbaths and festivals (iii, 12–16):

> But with them that held fast to the commandments of God, who were left of them, God established His covenant with Israel for ever, by revealing to them hidden things in which all Israel had erred: His holy Sabbaths and His glorious festivals, His righteous testimonies and His true ways and the desires of His will, 'which man shall do and live thereby'...

The same conclusion is to be drawn from the passage in the *Rule of the Community* (v, 7–12):

> Every one who enters into the council of the community shall enter into the covenant of God in the presence of all volunteers and he shall obligate himself by a binding oath to return to the Law of Moses . . . [and] to separate himself from all men of iniquity that walk in the ways of wickedness. For they are not reckoned in His covenant, for they have not sought nor searched[2] in His Law to know the hidden things in which they have erred, incurring guilt, and the manifest things they have done high-handedly.

[1] See, most recently, J. Licht, *The Thanksgiving Scroll*, p. 49.

[2] דרש(ה)ו, see Habermann, '*Edah we-'Eduth*, p. 71.

The opponents of the Sect are censured in the first instance for neglecting to search in the Law in order to acquire knowledge of the 'hidden things'. It is obvious that the latter cannot refer to esoteric knowledge, to secret lore entrusted to the initiated few, but to something to which everybody has access, if one but searches for it in the Torah. Indeed, the omission to do so is represented as the principal sin of the opponents on account of which they are stigmatized as 'men of iniquity that walk in the ways of wickedness'. Furthermore, *nistārōth* is used as a correlative to *niglōth*, 'manifest things', which unquestionably refers to religious *practices* which the antagonists are charged with having violated 'high-handedly'.

What, then, lies behind these two terms?

No doubt they denote a fundamental distinction relating to the *precepts* of the Torah which are divided into two categories: (a) *niglōth*, referring to the precepts which are stated in clear terms and there is no doubt as to their meaning and manner of implementation, and hence no dissension exists concerning them; (b) *nistārōth*, on the other hand, are those commandments which are worded in general and vague terms, lacking detailed instructions as to the method of carrying them out, so that their meaning and scope is 'hidden'. It is concerning the interpretation and practice of these that Israel is divided.[1]

We now understand why the author of the *Damascus Document* singled out Sabbaths[2] and festivals as examples of the *nistārōth*.

[1] Cf. I. Rabinowitz, *JBL*, 1954, p. 21, note 50; Friedrich Nötscher, *Zur Theologischen Terminologie der Qumran-Texte*, Bonn 1956 [Bonner Biblische Beiträge, 10], p. 71; Ch. Rabin, *The Zadokite Fragments*, p. 12, notes

[2] Sh. Talmon (*Scripta Hierosolymitana*, iv, pp. 187ff.) explains the association of the Sabbath with the festivals in the *Damascus Document* by the assumption that the Qumran sect reckoned the Sabbath from sunrise to sunrise and not from sunset to sunset, as practised by normative Judaism and Karaites alike. This assumption is flatly controverted by the following *halakhah* in *CDC*, x, 14–17: 'Let no man do any work on the sixth day from the time when the orb of the sun is distant from the gate by its own diameter, for that is what He said, *Observe the Sabbath day and keep it holy* (*Deut.* 5, 12).' Talmon proposes to eliminate this clear evidence by declaring the *halakhah* cited to have been altered by 'the copyist of the *Damascus Document*, who lived in the 10th–11th

These are, indeed, the most striking illustrations of the 'hidden' commandments. The Mishnah[1] aptly describes the Sabbath laws as 'mountains suspended on a hair having a slender scriptural basis and multifarious *halakhoth*'. As to the festivals, apart from the fact that almost the same consideration applies to them as to the Sabbath, they have their own distinctive laws that are indefinite and subject to controversy.[2] But first and foremost their

centuries (or one of his predecessors), whether a Karaite or a Rabbanite', who 'adjusted the text to the current laws prevailing in his community'. This method of eliminating a crucial piece of evidence is hardly admissible. It is instructive to remind ourselves of a similar solution of a vexed problem which has recently been disproved. I refer to the explanation given by a number of students (including the present writer, see *JJS*, iv [1953], p. 168, note 2) for the singular expression 'the Messiah of Aaron and Israel' in *CDC*, xiv, 19, instead of the plural 'the Messiahs' as in *DSD*, ix, 11, as being due to a correction on the part of the mediaeval scribe. In fact, the singular of the mediaeval copy has now been confirmed by the oldest exemplar of the *Damascus Document* found in Qumran Cave IV (4QD^b). See Milik, *Ten Years of Discovery in the Wilderness of Judaea*, p. 125. Another solution will now have to be found for this discrepancy.

As for Talmon's argument from *DSD*, x, 10–14, mentioning the morning prayer first, the fact should be noted that Rabbanite prayer-books begin the order of prayers with the morning service, whereas Karaite prayer-books with the evening service. It goes without saying that one cannot take this fact as evidence of a difference of opinion concerning the beginning of the day and conclude that the Rabbanites reckoned the day from the morning and the Karaites from the evening. Talmon contrasts the passage in *DSD* with the Mishnah *Berakhoth* which deals first with the evening *Shema*ʿ and 'only afterwards does the tractate concern itself with the reading of the *Shema*ʿ in the morning'. Rabbanite prayer-books concern themselves, as said, first with the morning prayers, but nobody would think of deducing from this that there existed a disparity as to the beginning of the day between the Jews in mishnaic times and those in subsequent ages [see Addenda].

[1] *Ḥag*. i, 8: כהררים התלוין בשערה שהן מקרא מועט והלכות מרובות.

[2] Cf., e.g., the controversy about the meaning of 'the fruit of a goodly tree' (*Lev*. 23, 40) which normative Judaism held to be an *'ethrog*, while according to ʿAnan it is an olive. Again, according to the latter the 'four species' were not intended to be taken in the hands, but as material for making the *sukkah*. It is superfluous to mention the long drawn out and heated controversy about the interpretation of the phrase 'on the morrow after the Sabbath' (*Lev*. 23, 11), on which the fixing of Pentecost depended.

observation is dependent on a system of calendation which, as Sa'adya pointed out, is hinted at in the Pentateuch by one single word only—אביב.[1]

It is highly instructive to note that Abraham ibn Ezra in the 'French' version of the introduction to his commentary[2] on the Pentateuch illustrated the obscurity and 'hidden' quality of the pentateuchal commandments by the same two examples of Sabbath and festivals; in the current version of the introduction he limited himself to the instance of the festivals, expatiating at great length on the astounding fact that the calendar regulations, which form the very basis of the festivals, are entirely absent from the Torah.

We can thus also understand the rather surprising fact that, in denouncing his opponents, the author of the *Rule of the Community* lays primary stress on errors committed by them in respect of the hidden commandments, whilst the violation of the manifest ones is given a secondary place—notwithstanding the fact that they were violated 'high-handedly'. One cannot avoid the impression that the infringement of the latter is regarded as of minor importance compared with the misconception of the meaning of the hidden commandments. The explanation is that the violation of the manifest precepts is an act of impiety which must stand condemned by all parties, whereas difference in practice of the hidden precepts is a matter of principle, a question of a divergent conception of the Torah. Significantly, the author of the *Damascus Document* represents the uncovering of the hidden commandments as the purpose and essence of the new covenant: 'But with them that held fast to the commandments of God, who were left of them, God established his covenant with Israel for ever, by revealing to them hidden things in which all Israel had erred.'

[1] Cf. *infra*, p. 75.

[2] See M. Friedlaender, *Essays on the Writing of Abraham Ibn Ezra*, London 1877, Hebrew part, p. 2: כי אין בתורה המקודשת. מצוה שלימה מפורשת. כי לא הזכיר כמה אבות מלאכות ותולדותיהן. ומדות חקות הסוכה ומשפטיהן. גם לא הזכיר הפסחים. איך הם תלויים בירחים. Cf. also Yehudah Hallevi, *Kuzari*, iii, 35. Cf. *infra*, p. 76.

The denunciation of the opponents on account of their failure to search in the Law implies, of course, the Sect's own belief in the possibility of ascertaining the true meaning of the hidden portions of the Torah by means of a thorough and intensive searching in Scripture, *midrash ha-Torah*. This belief is also reflected in the law laid down in the *Rule of the Community*: 'And every matter which is hidden from Israel but was found by the man who searches, let him not conceal it from these out of fear of opposition' (viii, 11–12). The searcher is enjoined not to withhold the findings of his researches into the hidden things out of fear that his interpretations will meet with opposition within his own community, but he should submit them to the judgment of the other members. Acceptance or rejection is decided by a majority vote, as we learn from other passages in the *Rule*.[1]

What has been said so far may be instructively illuminated by a comparison with Karaism, in whose system of thought the distinction between *niglōth* and *nistārōth* and the belief in the possibility of unveiling the latter by scholarly effort formed a basic thesis, and played a vital rôle in the controversy about the Oral Law. The Rabbanites' chief argument was that the written Torah by itself, without the interpretation and supplementation provided by the Oral Law, would be a closed book incapable of fulfilment since so many of its precepts are obscure, undefined and without the particulars indispensable for their application. The Rabbanites' thesis was that the veil of obscurity in which these commandments are shrouded cannot be lifted by the ordinary methods of research and exegesis. Hence the necessity of tradition which elucidates and supplements the written word.[2]

The Karaites, on the other hand, denied both the authority of and the necessity for the unwritten Torah, and proclaimed the principle of the perfectness and sufficiency of the Law of Moses. The psalmist's words (19, 8): תורת יי תמימה, *the Torah of the*

[1] *DSD*, v, 2, 9, 22.

[2] Cf. Sa'adya's statement, as recorded by Ibn Ezra on *Ex*. 21, 24: והכלל לא נוכל לפרש (על דרך) מצות התורה פירוש שלם אם לא נסמוך על דברי חז״ל.

Lord is perfect, became the battle-cry of Karaism. The Torah, they claimed, is self-explanatory, and the meaning of all its parts can be discovered by the exegetical approach on the basis of Scripture alone. Hence search in the Torah was declared to be the supreme obligation of every Karaite. This is the significance of ‘Anan’s motto: חפישו באורייתא שפיר, ‘Search ye thoroughly in the Torah’.[1]

This conviction is emphatically underlined in a passage in *Diqduqē Ha-Ṭeʿamim*[2] containing important points relative to our subject. Ben-Asher insists that the Torah contains nothing which is inherently obscure, referring to *Deut.* 30, 12–14:[3] *It is not in heaven . . . neither is it beyond the sea . . . but the word is very nigh unto thee*, *in thy mouth*, *and in thy heart*, *that thou mayest do it*.[4] Were the words of the Torah, he argues, really hidden and

[1] A. Harkavy (in the Hebrew edition of Grätz' *History of the Jews*, iii, p. 189, note 37; 435, note 140) failed to see the significance of this motto and questioned its authenticity, on the ground that it contained no indication of ‘Anan’s Karaism. See also Salo W. Baron, *A Social and Religious History of the Jews* (2nd edition, 1957), vol. v, p. 389, note 4. See further ‘Additional Notes’ to Chapter II, p. 88.

[2] Edited S. Baer and H. L. Strack, Leipzig 1879, p. 53: ואם ישאל הדורש: מה טעם לזה שיהיו דברים סתומים ולא מגולים, ויהיו על דרך אחת? תשובתו: אילו היה המקרא כולו מגולה לא היה שכר ולא כבוד ליגעים בו וללומדים ולמפרשים . . . ואם יתן אדם דעתו במקרא ויכון לבו לשמים ויחפש ויחקור, ימצא ולא יסתרו ממנו דברי תורה, אם יחקור ויחפש בדעה שלמה ולא יטה לשרירות ולא יהיה אחרי רבים לרעות ימצא ויגלו לו סתרי התורה במקרא ופירוש ובענינים. ואילו היו דברי תורה סתומים וחתומים, היו ישראל ערומים, מן המצות המקימים, ולא היו חוטאים ואשמים, אלא הם גלוים, ויודעים אותם החכמים, ויראי יי התמימים, כי כן משה אבי הנביאים אמר: לא בשמים היא ולא מעבר לים היא כי קרוב אליך הדבר מאד בפיך ובלבבך לעשתו (דברים, ל, 12–14).

[3] It is by reason of their importance for the Karaite ideology that these verses were included in the Karaite liturgy; they were recited immediately before the public reading of the Torah, see Karaite Prayer-Book (ed. Vienna), ii, pp. 137, 168; iii, p. 118. On the principles that determined the selection of biblical passages for the Karaite liturgy, cf. N. Wieder, ‘The Qumran Sectaries’, pp. 110, 288, and ‘The Dead Sea Scrolls’, *etc.*, p. 86.

[4] Cf. also Qirqisani's statement quoted by B. Klar in *Tarbiz*, vol. 15, p. 42, note 48 [=*Meḥqarim*, p. 309, note 202]. Dr. M. Zucker (*Tarbiz*, 1958, p. 66) questioned the exactitude of the parallel, pointed out by Klar, between the statements of Ben-Asher and Qirqisani. Zucker refers to *Kitāb al-Anwār*, p. 124. The truth, however, is that Klar's quotation

sealed, it would have been impossible to fulfil the commandments, and Israel ought therefore not to be regarded as sinful and guilty for not fulfilling them. The same argument, it may be noted, is re-echoed by Yehudah Hadassi.[1] There is however one prerequisite for 'finding' the hidden things: piety. The Torah will yield its secrets to him only who seeks and searches with earnestness, with his heart directed towards heaven. In fact, he claims, the hidden things are known to 'the wise God-fearing perfect ones', i.e. the Karaite scholars.[2] The same claim was made by Moses Ben-Asher when, in a colophon[3] added to his Codex of the Prophets, he says about the Karaite scholars that they 'understand all hidden things and uncover the secret of wisdom'.[4] The 'hidden things' are none other than the obscure passages in the Torah, the סתרי תורה of his son, Aaron Ben-Asher.

Earlier, the same ideas were discussed by Daniel al-Qumisi in a fragment of his commentary on *Leviticus*. As the relevant passage, published by L. Ginzberg[5] without comment, contains a number of errors obscuring its contents, I republish it from the Cambridge Genizah MS., T-S. Loan, 199:

is derived from p. 128, where Qirqisani himself explains *Deut.* 30, 11 (and *Prov.* 2, 4); and it is this interpretation that Klar paralleled with Ben-Asher's words.

[1] '*Eshkol ha-Kopher*, Alph. 171, letter *shin*: שלולי היו דברי התורה עלומים ולא מתבוננים לפני תופסי התורה עדת ישראלים לא היו ישראל חייבים אם לא שמרום כצווי אל אלים. Aaron of Nicomedia reasons in the same manner: הדין נותן להיות הדבור מבואר ושלם. מפני הענשים. אשר יתחייבו לאנשים. איך ידבר הכתוב ברמיזות. ואין ראוי להעשות כזאת (*Gan 'Eden*, p. 2a).

[2] See 'The Qumran Sectaries', pp. 97–113.

[3] See 'Additional Notes' to Chapter II, pp. 89f.

[4] Cf. P. Kahle, *op. cit.* p. 95: המבינים כל נסתרות והמשפירים סוד חכמה. The word *mashpīrīm* is difficult; the rendering 'embellish' does not make good sense: a secret is revealed or uncovered, but not embellished. It appears to me that the expression, for which I was unable to find a parallel, has been impregnated with the connotation, 'reveal', 'uncover', under the influence of the equivalent Arabic root which signifies 'to remove the veil', 'to uncover', 'to make manifest'. Kahle, *op. cit.* p. 96 accepted my rendering. Cf. also *infra*, pp. 93f.

[5] See *Ginze Schechter*, New York 1929, vol. ii, pp. 473–4.

אני דניאל אדבר

אליך כׄיׄ[1] דע[2] כי תורת יהוה נמשלה כמים

ומשכילי דעת והם נביאים[3] יודעי דעת[4]

והם ידעו את המקרא על אפניו למה כתוב

כן ולא כן : על כן נתן יהוה להם את התורה

ממנה גלויה ונודעת וממנה סתורה ונעלמה

והו . . . . [י]ודעים : ולולי סתורה היא לא

היה בה . . . . אל חילוף : ולא . . . . ה

היא ואולם עמוקה היא בדיב[רי] הלשון ולא

ימצאוה[5] ע[קשי לב][6] וישרי לב ימצאו חכמה[7]

אם[8] תבקשנה ככסף וכמטׄ תׄ אז תבין יראת

יהוה ודעת אלהים תׄ : על כן הינחנו[9] [זאת]

בתפלת[נו][10] גל עיני וא]ביטה נפׄ מתׄ : נפׄ מתרׄ

היא נפל[אות התו]רה ככׄ כי[11] יפלא ממך דבר

למשפט וכת[וב] פליאה[12] דעת ממני ודויד

היה יודע ואולם בעבורנו דבר גל עיני ואביטה

והדורש ביראה ובדעת ימצא ככׄ לא[13]

[1] The dots on the word are a sign of deletion.

[2] The expression דע is typical of al-Qumisi's style, see the fragment of his commentary on *Leviticus* in S. Schechter's *Saadyana*, Cambridge 1903, pp. 144, line 1; 145, line 5; 146 line 11. [See Appendix B.]

[3] See *infra*, p. 85.

[4] Sahl b. Maṣliaḥ (*Liq. Qad*. App., p. 36) describes the 'sixty mighty men' (cf. *infra*, p. 119) as משכילים יודעי דעת.

[5] MS.: יבצאות.

[6] The expression עקשי לב is a derogatory epithet of the Rabbanites on the basis of *Prov*. 11, 20 where it is opposed to תמימי דרך. Cf. also תורת יי יעקשו (*Pithron*, p. 45) and עקשו מצות (*ibid*. p. 67). Herein lies the reason (in addition to the pun עקב־עקש) why Sahl dubbed his controversialist, Jacob b. Samuel: העקש (*Liq. Qad*., App., p. 19).

[7] MS.: חכם.

[8] *Prov*. 2, 4–5.

[9] Ginzberg's emendation על כן הוא אומר בתהלות is unfounded. *Ps*. 119, 18, became a Karaite stock prayer, as will be shown further on.

[10] *Ps*. 119, 18.

[11] *Deut*. 17, 8.

[12] *Ps*. 139, 6.

[13] *Deut*. 30, 11.

נפלאת היא ממך: על כן עלינו לחקור היטב
למען למצוא אמת

The fragment includes a number of ideas to which reference will be made in the course of this study; in the present context the following may be noted. Al-Qumisi uses the same verbs, סתר, גלה, to denote the two categories of laws[1] as in the Qumran documents, with the difference that the latter employ the participles *niph'al*, while the former the participles *qal*. He, too, is convinced that the hidden things in the Torah can be uncovered through study and research and cites as support *Prov.* 2, 4 and *Deut.* 30, 11. It is for this reason that the Karaites pray with the Psalmist: 'Open Thou mine eyes that I may behold the hidden portions in Thy Law' (*Ps.* 119, 18). The force of the argument is: were it beyond human power to unravel the secrets of the Torah, the Psalmist would not have asked for it. A similar argument is advanced by Yefeth b. 'Ali.[2] That the psalm-verse became a household prayer of Karaism will be discussed later.

Like Ben-Asher, al-Qumisi emphasizes that research must be allied to piety to succeed; that only they who are upright in heart will find wisdom, but not they who are perverse in heart. Finally, he too claims that the Karaite scholars are in possession of the genuine knowledge of the Torah.

The aspiration of the Karaite scholar, his ideal and yearning, was to be able to contribute to the difficult process of removing

[1] Also used by Nissi ben Noaḥ in his classification of the commandments (*Liq. Qad.* App., p. 11): דעת התורה ועשיית מצותיה מתחלקת על ב׳ חלקים. א׳ מהם מצוה שצוה אל שדי בתורה לעשותה ולשמרה והיא ברורה וגלויה... והשנית מצוה צפונה וסתורה. In another place, however, he uses the same terminology as in the Qumran texts: *niglōth* and *nistārōth*. The term *nistārōth* is also used in Moses Ben-Asher's colophon (59, n. 4). Sahl employs the singular in a collective sense (*ibid.* p. 34): ובראשונה בזמן הנביאים... לא היתה המצוה נסתרת מעיניהם. On the other hand, Aaron Ben-Asher uses the terms *sāthūm-megulleh* (*supra*, p. 58, n. 2).

[2] In his commentary on *Isa.* 29, 9–12 (MS. British Museum, Or. 2501, fol. 33a–b): וקאל אלצאלח גר אנכי בארץ אל תסתר ממני מצותיך (תהלים קי״ט, 19) וקאל גל עיני ואביטה נפלאות מתורתך (שם, שם, 18) פלולא אן אלתבצר פי תוראה אללה ואגב לם יגז ללצאלח אן יסל אללה פי מא ינכרה.

the hiddenness of the commandments, and success therein the highly-valued prize of his scholarly endeavours which filled him with rejoicing and sentiments of gratitude towards God. In a comment on *Isa.* 58, 2, '*They ask Me for true laws*', Yefeth b. 'Ali writes:[1]

> The expression 'true laws' refers to the hidden portions of the Torah. Similarly, it is said about the 'Perfect in the Way' (*Ps.* 119, 62): *At midnight I will rise to give thanks unto Thee for Thy true laws.* And when one of these has been revealed to them they praise God, as it is said (verse 164): *Many times a day I praise Thee because of Thy true laws.*

The same rejoicing is voiced by Sahl ben Maṣliaḥ.[2] Speaking of the Karaites of his own generation, he asserts that God has enlightened their eyes to perceive the obscure parts of the Torah, and adds that at the unveiling of one commandment 'they rejoice as one who finds great spoil'.

THE SYMBOLISM OF 'DIGGING THE WELL'

The process of discovering the 'hidden things' is described in Karaite literature by the imagery of searching for treasures hidden in the ground. The imagery is, on the one hand, illustrative of the difficulty in comprehending the obscure portions of the Torah—one has to penetrate below the surface of literalness, to 'dig' deep in order to unearth the mysteries of the Law—and on the other, it is expressive of the belief that it *is* possible to bring to light the 'hidden things' by human methods of research and investigation.

The symbolism is founded on *Prov.* 2, 4–5: *If thou seek her as silver, and search for her as for hidden treasures, then shalt thou understand the fear of the Lord, and find the knowledge of God.*

[1] MS. British Museum, Or. 2502, fol. 168a: וק׳ „משפטי צדק״ ישיר בה אלי גואמץ אלעלם וכדאך קאל פי תמימי דרך: חצות לילה אקום להודות לך על משפטי צדקך וענד מא ינכשף להם שי מנהא כאנו ימדחון אללה כקו׳ שבע ביום הללתיך על משפטי צדקך.

[2] *Liq. Qad.*, App., p. 35: ובחסדי אלהינו ית׳ שמו האיר כעת את עיני האחרונים וגלה את עיניהם להביט נפלאות מתורתו והם ששים ושמחים בהגלות להם מצוה אחת כמוצאי שלל רב.

From a citation by al-Qirqisani,[1] derived from a lost anti-Karaite work by Sa'adya Ga'on, we gather that the first to have utilized the verse for sectarian purposes was 'Anan himself, who saw in it biblical support for the principle of analogy, *qiyās*, as a legitimate hermeneutic device for deducing laws from the biblical text. The application of this principle together with other exegetical devices was designated as 'searching'. 'Anan was followed in this by Benjamin al-Nahāwendī and, as we have seen, also by al-Qumisi. Thus, it has the authority of the three earliest and most prominent exponents of Karaism. Later, it is frequently harped upon by Karaite scholars like Salmon ben Yeruḥim,[2] Yefeth b. 'Ali,[3] Nissi b. Noaḥ[4] and Yehudah Hadassi.[5]

I venture the opinion that the symbolism of digging the well in the much-quoted passage in the *Damascus Document* (vi, 3–11) was intended to convey the same idea as the Karaite symbolism of digging for hidden treasures: the possibility and the duty to discover by one's own efforts the obscure portions of the Torah. Both imageries have in common the idea of searching for something

[1] *Kitāb al-Anwār wal-Marāqib*, ed. L. Nemoy, p. 79.

[2] *The Book of the Wars of the Lord*, ed. I. Davidson, New York 1934, p. 81, line 69.

[3] In the commentary on *Daniel* 12, 4, ed. D. S. Margoliouth, Oxford 1889 [*Anecdota Oxoniensia*, Semitic Series, I, Pt. 3], p. 141 (Arabic part); Engl. trans., p. 77.

[4] *Liq. Qad.*, App., p. 9: ... בחיפוש התורה והתבונן במקרא כחיפוש על הכסף ברגבי ההרים וכהופיע מטמוני מסתרים שנאמר אם תחפשנה ככסף...

[5] Cf., e.g. Alph. 153, letter *kaph*; 154, letter *ṣadē*; 175, *zayin*, 236, *waw*. The metaphor of 'hidden treasures' also figured in the polemics between Rabbanites and Karaites, see Hadassi, 155, *hē*: דברו עוד להם משכילי ומלמדי נ״ע אם באמת ובתמים ... המקראות והראיות שחפשנו [הקראים] ומטמונים שבקשנו נגלי׳ הכל לעיניכם [הרבנים]. This explains the polemical implication of the sentence reported by 'Aḥima'aṣ b. Palṭi'el (*The Chronicle of 'Aḥima'aṣ*, ed. B. Klar, Jerusalem 1944, p. 19) in the name R. Silano: זכו רבנים ונחלו מטמונים. These words, which so delighted the Palestinian scholars that they revoked the excommunication decree against R. Silano, rebuffs the Karaite boast of having discovered the 'hidden treasures' through their 'searching'; it is the Rabbanites who are in possession of them, received by tradition (נחלו).

hidden. In one instance the hidden thing is symbolically represented as 'water', and in the other as 'treasures'. And just as the 'searching' (חפוש) for the 'treasures' is done by the employment of certain hermeneutic rules, so is the 'digging' of the well done with the help of rules laid down by the *meḥoqeq*.[1] This meaning of the symbolism enables us to explain the association of the 'digging of the well' with the 'hidden things' in a passage in the *Damascus Document* (iii, 13–17) previously cited: '... God established His covenant with Israel for ever, by revealing to them hidden things in which all Israel had erred: His holy Sabbaths, His glorious festivals ... He opened up to them, and they digged a well of many waters; and he that despises them [the waters] shall not live.' The last sentence dealing with the well appears utterly unrelated to its context; one fails to see its connection with the uncovering of the hidden things. In the light of the preceding, however, the sentence receives its full meaning: the sectaries came into possession of the hidden things by 'digging the well'.

A further reference to the well is contained in yet another passage of the *Damascus Document* (xix, 33–34): 'All the men that entered the new covenant in the land of Damascus and have acted treacherously again and turned away from the well of living water shall not be reckoned in the gathering of the people and in their book they shall not be written.' We observe that the faithlessness to the new covenant is expressed by the metaphor 'to turn away from the well'. Obviously the principle conveyed by the metaphor is of such fundamental importance that turning away from it is tantamount to a complete rupture with the Sect's

[1] Note should be taken of the etymological and semantic identity of *ḤFS* and *ḤFR*, see *Job* 3, 21; the Palestinian Targum invariably renders the biblical *ḤFR* by *ḤFS*; cf. also *Ben Sira* 12, 22, ed. M. Z. Segal, p. 75, and the editor's note on p. 80.

Regarding the association of the ideas 'to dig for water' and 'to deduce', 'to elicit', compare the Arabic NBṬ which in the formations IV and X denotes (see Lane) 'he produced, or fetched out, by his digging, the water of the well', and has also the transferred meaning 'he elicited a doctrine of law by his intelligence, or study', or 'he searched out knowledge', 'he found out', 'he brought to light'.

ideology. This is quite in accordance with the above-cited passage, where the discovery of the hidden commandments is represented as the purpose of the covenant. It is further in accordance with the *Rule of the Community* (v, 11) which says of the Sect's opponents: 'These are not reckoned in His covenant for they have not sought nor searched in His Law to know the hidden things in which they have erred'.

As has been said, the symbolism of searching for hidden treasures is a recurrent motif of Karaite literature from 'Anan onward. Significantly, the symbolism of the well, too, is not entirely absent there, as may be inferred from the frequent appeal by Hadassi to *Prov.* 5, 15: '*Drink waters out of thine own cistern, and running water out of thine own well.*' The meaning attached to it is clearly apparent from a passage in which Hadassi contrasts the Rabbanite and the Karaite attitudes to the interpretation of the Torah, saying, in effect, that teachings and perceptual details which are not the outcome of searching in the Lord's Torah 'are accounted as naught'. Those teachings only that result from an exposition of the divine law 'gratify the aspiring souls', as it is written: '*Drink water, etc.*', *viz.* drink the water of the Torah obtained by your own 'digging', your own interpretative work, and not the waters provided by tradition.[1]

A polemical reference to the Karaite interpretation of *Prov.* 5, 15 is found in the work called *The Mishnah of Rabbi Eliezer.*[2] J. N. Epstein[3] already drew attention to a few anti-Karaite

[1] *'Eshkol ha-Kopher*, Alph. 259, *rēsh*: ראיות ודקדוקים ותורות שאינם מתוך דרישת תורת ה׳ מנותן דעות, כולם להבל נחשבות... קנצים דרישות וחקירות... שהם מתוך דוק ביאור תורת האלהים... הם מחיים נפשות תאבות ככתוב שתה מים מבורך ונוזלים מתוך בארך; Alph. 130, *mem:* מזה למדנו כי לנו לדרוש ולחקור ולהבין בדעת... ולא להשען בדעת אחרים... ככתוב שתה מים מבורך. Instructive is the combination of the two metaphors (180, *mem*): הקיצו שכורים וראו דרכים ישרים... וחפשו כמטמונים מים חיים ממקורים להשקות נפש עייפה... וכתוב שתה מים מבורך...

[2] See *The Mishnah of Rabbi Eliezer or The Midrash of Thirty-Two Hermeneutic Rules*, ed. H. G. Enelow, New York 1933, p. 251.

[3] See *HUCA*, xxii [1950–51], Pt. 2, p. 15 (Hebrew section). Cf. also M. Zucker in *PAAJR*, xxiii [1954], pp. 33f. Cf. *infra*, 130n, 212n.

allusions contained in this work. As a matter of fact, a thorough investigation of it in the light of the Rabbanite-Karaite controversy will disclose that the extent of the polemical allusions is far greater than has hitherto been thought and will, in addition, supply explanations for certain distinctive features of this work which have hitherto defied explanation. In the present context I confine myself to calling attention to a change introduced by its author into an aggadic statement which he borrowed from the *Siphrē* on *Deuteronomy*.[1] The two texts, with an English translation, are here juxtaposed:

Mishnah of R. Eliezer	*Siphrē*
ר׳ שמעון בן מנסיא אומ׳ הרי הוא אומ׳ שתה מים מבוריך, שתה מים מדברי חכמים,[2] ואל תשתה מים עכורין ותמשך לדברי מינות.	רבי שמעון בן מנסיא אומ׳ שתה מים מבורך שתה מים של בוראך ואל תשתה [מים] עכורים ותמשך עם דברי מינים.
R. Simeon b. Menasya says, Scripture says: *Drink waters out of thine own cistern*, [this means] drink the waters of the words of the Sages, and drink not turbid waters that thou mayest not be attracted to the words of heresy.	R. Simeon b. Menasya says, [it is written]: *Drink waters out of thine own cistern*, [this means] drink the waters of thy Creator, and drink not turbid waters that thou mayest not be attracted by the words of heretics.

The change of '*the waters of thy Creator*' into '*the waters of the words of the Sages*' is significant. As a result of the change the tannaitic interpretation of the verse was converted into a direct disavowal of the Karaite interpretation, which saw in it a proof-text for the thesis that one may *not* rely on 'the words of the

[1] Ed. M. Friedmann, p. 84a.

[2] This is the correct reading as attested by *Midrash ha-Gadol* on *Leviticus* (ed. E. N. Rabinowitz, New York 1932), p. 519, where our passage is quoted (see J. N. Epstein, *Tarbiz*, iv [1932–33], p. 345) and by al-Naqawa's *Menorath ha-Ma'or* (ed. Enelow, iii, p. 219). The reading מדברי חכמה in the printed edition is the result of a wrong solution of the abbreviation מד׳ חכמ׳.

Sages', but must derive the waters of the Torah by one's own researches. According to the altered text the verse contains a warning precisely against that thesis. This violent change—violent because it removed the exegetical basis of R. Simeon b. Menasya's comment (the play on words[1] בורך–בוראך)—was motivated by polemical considerations.

PROGRESSIVE UNCOVERING OF THE DIVINE LAW

If in the *Rule of the Community*, v, 12 the term *niglōth* bears the meaning of manifest precepts, in other passages (as well as in the *Damascus Document*) the term has a wider connotation; it denotes all those originally hidden precepts which the Sect believed that they had succeeded in uncovering. As soon as one of these had been clarified it automatically joined the ranks of the *niglōth*-category, its observance according to the newly found interpretation becoming obligatory upon the members of the Sect. Thus, with regard to the oath to be taken by new members, the *Rule of the Community* (v, 8–9) provides: 'He shall impose upon himself by a binding oath to return to the Law of Moses . . . to all that has been uncovered of it to the Sons of Zadok, the priests who keep the covenant and seek His will and to the majority of their fellow-members.'[2] In the *Damascus Document* the term 'found' is substituted for 'uncovered': 'to return to the Law of Moses . . . to that which has been found to be done'. The two terms are synonymous.

The clause binding the members to observe the Law not in its entirety, but only as much of it as has been 'uncovered' or 'found', implies the Sect's belief that the Torah had not yet been completely understood, and that there still remained hidden sections which, by reason of their being hidden, could not be applied in practice. No obligation, therefore, was imposed as to their observance. Whether they were not observed at all, or left to the

[1] With this play of words cf. R. Levi's interpretation of *Eccl.* 12, 1 (*Lev. R.* 18, 1, and parallels): וזכר את בוראך, בוראך, בורך, בארך.

[2] See further *DSD*, i, 8–9; viii, 1, 15; ix, 13, 19; *CDC*, xv, 13.

discretion of each individual member who could apply them according to his private judgment, cannot be ascertained from the texts at present available. Such individualism with regard to precepts on which no consensus of opinion could be reached was prevalent among the Karaites.[1]

However that may be, it seems certain that the Sect believed in a progressive uncovering of the Law; its obscurity will be removed gradually, 'from time to time'. That this should be so is, of course, inherent in the Sect's basic approach to the Torah as a book whose exposition depends on the interpretative work of the 'searchers in the Torah'.[2] Such stupendous work as elucidating ambiguities, harmonizing contradictions and inconsistencies and, most particularly, eliciting from the text detailed regulations for the performance of the commandments and deriving new laws for contingencies not provided for in the written text, is replete with difficulties and must of necessity be a slow and protracted process. The Karaites, too, had to reconcile themselves to the same state of affairs, and to acknowledge that the unveiling of the Torah will be done 'little by little' and that 'the days will speak', as Sahl b. Maṣliaḥ expressed himself.[3]

[1] Cf., e.g., Sahl b. Maṣliaḥ (*Liq. Qad.* App., p. 33: ... וישקול דברי המתחלפים והנחלקים, ואשר יעמוד בעיניו באמת ובראיה נכונה ישמור ויעשה. See further Raphael Mahler, *Karaimer* (in Yiddish), New York 1947, pp. 280ff.; 308ff.

[2] The characteristic expression 'searcher in the Law' belongs also to the Karaite parlance; al-Qumisi actually designates the Karaites as *dōreshē Torah* in his appeal to his fellow-sectarians in the Diaspora to come and settle in the Holy Land, pointing out to them that they need not fear the Rabbanites, since the Muslim authorities help the Karaites to live according to the Law of Moses: ואין לכם פתחון פה לפני ײ אם לא תשובו היום אל תורת ײ ואל מצותיו ככ׳ בתורתו כי מתחלת גלות היו רבנין שרים ושופטים בימי מלכות יון ובמלכות רומים ומגוסים פרסיים ולא יכלו דורשי תורה לפתוח פיהם במצות ײ מפחד רבנין כי היו [יראים] עד בוא מלכות ישמעאל כי הם עוזרים תמיד לקראין לשמור כתורת משה. (*JQR*, xii, p. 285). See also *Pithron*, pp. 30 and 56. Noteworthy is Hadassi's form of the expression, מחפשי התורה in which the verb חפש has been substituted for דרש, the former being expressive of the Karaite research method of *ḥippūs* (*'Eshkol ha-Kopher*, 175, *shin*; 226, *'ayin*; 311, *waw*; 324, *gimel*).

[3] *Liq. Qad.*, App., p. 37.

With regard to the Qumran schismatics it is interesting to note that they made, as it were, a virtue of necessity, and (in keeping with their general predeterministic world-view) interpreted this necessity in terms of divine providence: what should become known at certain epochs was part of the divine plan; each epoch will see new knowledge and new laws, providentially determined, added to the body of the unveiled portions of the Torah.[1] Compare the following two passages from the *Rule*:

1. '...and to walk before Him perfectly in accordance with all that has been uncovered for their pre-determined seasons' (i, 8–9).
2. '. . . to walk perfectly in all the ways of God as He commanded for His pre-determined seasons' (iii, 9–10).

While the first passage merely speaks of the precepts as having been uncovered for pre-determined seasons, the second goes beyond it in stating explicitly that it was God who commanded them for pre-determined seasons.

The work of uncovering the true sense of the Law will not be completed in this age; it will come to an end in the immediate

[1] This theory provided at the same time an answer to the question of how to explain the fact of the Torah containing so many 'hidden' portions. To the upholders of tradition the question presented no difficulty, as the obscurities of the written Torah were explained in the unwritten one; cf. the early anti-Karaite polemic incorporated in *Tanḥuma*, *Noaḥ* 3 (see Aptowitzer, *HUCA*, vol. 8–9 [1931–32], pp. 415ff.): ונתן לנו את התורה בכתב ברמז צפונות וסתומות ופרשום בתורה שבעל פה וגלה אותן לישראל. ולא עוד אלא שתורה שבכתב כללות ותורה שבעל פה פרטות. The repudiators of tradition had to grapple with this problem. It was dealt with by al-Qumisi in the fragment printed above; his answer, however, is at present undecipherable because of a lacuna in the text. Aaron Ben-Asher, too, discussed it, evolving the theory that the obscurities of the Torah were intended to give scope for scholars and scholarship: were the entire Torah clear and plain, there would have been no room for interpretative work, no opportunity for scholars, who would thus be deprived of the honour and reward to which they are now entitled for solving the difficulties (see *supra*, 58, n. 2). It is interesting to note that a somewhat similar explanation was given by Origen, who 'was convinced that many of the difficult passages of the scriptures had been made intentionally obscure by the Holy Spirit in order to stimulate the mind of the intelligent student to look for deeper meanings' (*The Interpretation of the Bible* [Edward Alleyn Lectures, 1943], ed. C. W. Dugmore, London 1944, pp. 17f.).

pre-messianic period. That period will see the last results of the 'digging', of the independent search in the Law (מדרש התורה האחרון);[1] the final 'finds' will be made, 'and save them they will *find* nothing'. The remaining difficulties will be removed by 'him who will teach the truth in the end of days'.[2]

'TO RETURN TO THE LAW OF MOSES'

The opposition to tradition on the part of the Qumran sectaries is also suggested by the emphasis on the *Law of Moses* occurring several times in their literature.[3] Thus, a new member on entering the Sect is made to swear 'to return to the Law of Moses', and in the definition[4] of the Sect's faith, מדרש התורה אשר צוה ביד משה, the emphasis on the Mosaic Torah is formulated with a force too conspicuous to be overlooked; instead of the brief term *Torath Mosheh*, a whole relative clause is used. This insistence that by 'Torah' the Mosaic Law is meant is evidently intended to exclude

[1] Cf. *RB*, 1956, p. 61.

[2] *CDC*, vi, 10–11: וזולתם לא ישיגו עד עמד יורה הצדק באחרית הימים This sentence has been the subject of divergent interpretations, the mos recent one being that by Rabin (*Zadokite Fragments*, p. 23) who emendec the text to read: [מוסר] לא ישיגו and translated: 'and without whicl they (or: and others than they) will not grasp [instruction]'. There is nc need for emendation. The sentence is easily explained if we bear ir mind what has been previously said about the uncovering of the penta- teuchal laws by the method of 'searching' and the symbolism of th 'digging of the well', in which context the sentence occurs. We hav only to point out that השיג is already in the Bible synonymous with מצא cf. the parallel expressions השיגה ידו and מצאה ידו (*Lev.* 5, 11 an 12, 8), and *Isa.* 35, 10 where the word ישיגו is rendered by Targun 'they will find' (so, too, by Tur-Sinai in Ben-Yehudah's *Thesaurus* vol. viii, p. 3858, note 3). Now, like the term מצא, the word ישיגו i here employed to designate the outcome of the searching in the Torah In precisely the same meaning—'to find commandments'—the word i used by Hadassi in a passage to be quoted *infra* (p. 83): אדרוש ואמצא ואשיג מצות.

[3] *DSD*, v, 8; viii, 15, 22 (cf. also i, 3); *CDC*, xv, 12; xvi, 2, 5, and als v, 21.

[4] Cf. *infra*, p. 77.

the view that 'Torah' comprises also the oral traditions, that there is an unwritten Torah side by side with the written one.

A comparison with Karaism will be instructive. The term 'the Law of Moses' is a favourite and very frequent expression in the Karaite vocabulary and is used in the exclusive sense of the written text,[1] as opposed to the oral traditions of rabbinic Judaism. Daniel al-Qumisi[2] uses it antithetically to 'man-made commandments'—a hackneyed designation of Rabbanism—and Yehudah ibn Qoreish[3] contrasts the 'Law of Moses' with 'the words of Rabhina and Rabh 'Ashi', the compilers of the Babylonian Talmud. 'To observe according to the Law of Moses' was for al-Qumisi tantamount to adherence to the Karaite faith.[4] Again,

[1] Cf. Pirqoy b. Baboy's view, *infra* p. 72, note 1.

[2] Cf., e.g., *JQR*, xii, pp. 283f.; *Pithron*, p. 9: עזבנו תורת משה לתעות במצות אנשים מלמדה.

[3] *Liq. Qad.*, App., p. 68: ולמה נקבל דברי רבינא ורב אשי ויש בקרבנו תורת משה.

[4] See *supra*, 68, n. 2. See further *JQR*, xii, pp. 286 (twice); 290; 495. The frequent use of the term 'the Law of Moses' may be illustrated by a few references to other exponents of Karaism; Salmon b. Yeruḥim, *Book of the Wars*, p. 78; Sahl b. Maṣliaḥ, in Mann's *Texts and Studies*, ii, p. 88; Hadassi, 121, *ṣadē*; 141, *hē*; 194, *'ayin*. Very revealing are the verses used as epilogue of *Diqdūqē ha-Ṭe'amim:*

Deut. 4, 44:	וזאת התורה אשר שם משה . . .
Ps. 19, 8:	תורת יי תמימה . . .
Deut. 33, 4:	תורה צוה לנו משה . . .
Ps. 119, 72:	טוב לי תורת פיך . . .

The epilogue sums up in biblical quotations the chief features of Karaism. *Ps.* 19, 8 is the famous Karaite slogan, reflecting the idea of the perfectness of the written Torah which needs no oral supplementation. The verses from *Deut.* are expressive of the exclusive belief in the Mosaic Torah. *Deut.* 33, 4 belonged to the Karaite '*testimonia*' for the existence of a single Torah; it is adduced as proof-text, among others, by Salmon b. Yeruḥim, Yefeth b. 'Ali and Elijah b. Abraham. Salmon in his commentary on the *Psalms* (see the extracts in Mann, *op. cit.* ii, p. 85) says that the Rabbanites are called 'arrogant' (*Ps.* 119, 122) because 'they maintain that God gave Moses on Mount Sinai two Laws, but there is only one, as it is written: *Moses commanded us* a *Torah*, and it is further said (*Ps.* 19, 8): *The Law of the Lord is perfect*. As for Yefeth, see the quotation *infra*, 72, n. 1; Elijah b. Abraham: *Liq. Qad.*, App., p. 102. Hadassi (173, end) appeals to *Mal.* 3, 22 and to the two verses from *Deuteronomy*. Verse 4, 44 is invoked by him also in Alph. 225, *'aleph*. Finally, *Ps.* 119, 72 carries the same polemical implication: 'the Torah of *Thy* mouth'.

the prophet Malachi's exhortation (3, 22), *Remember the Law of Moses*, became a sort of Karaite battle-cry.[1]

Our chief interest, however, lies in the phrase in its entirety—'to return to the Law of Moses'—which appears five times in the sectarian writings.[2] Attention has been called to the uniqueness of the phrase which has no parallel in the whole Bible, where even the expression 'to return to the Torah' does not occur.[3] In Qumran it was used with the specific implication 'to embrace the *Qumran* brand of Judaism' and, as mentioned, was part of the oath of admission to membership of the Sect. Characteristically, the Qumranites and the Karaites have this unique phrase in common; it belonged to the Karaite parlance too, and carried the implication: 'to embrace the *Karaite* brand of Judaism'.[4]

[1] Yefeth b. 'Ali in the commentary on *Malachi*, *ad loc.* (MS. British Museum, Or. 2401, fol. 258) writes: וקו׳ תורת משה ישיר בה אלי אלכ̇מסה̈ אספאר אלמסאמה̈ תורה כקו׳ תורה צוה לנו משה וליס ת̇ם תורה בפה. Hadassi cites the verse in numerous places, only a few of which can be noted here: Alph. 3, *qoph* (קרא עוד חתימת כל הנביאים קול אומר זכרו תורת משה . . .); 33, *samekh*; 95, *daleth*; 125, *hē*; 173, end; 259, *rēsh*. Cf. also Aaron b. Elijah of Nicomedia (*'Eṣ Ḥayyim*, ed. F. Delitzsch, Leipzig 1841, p. 175): ועל כן לא נאמין בתורה שבעל פה שהיא תורת הקבלה כפי שאומרים . . . וחותם הנביאים אמר „זכרו תורת משה". It is this polemical import that accounts for the prominent place the verse has been accorded in Karaite liturgy where it is recited (together *Deut.* 33, 4 and 4, 44; cf. 71, n. 4) prior to the reading of the Law, see Karaite Prayer-Book (ed. Vienna), i, p. 86; ii, p. 168. The harping on the *Malachi* verse persisted even in 19th-century Karaism, cf. Simḥa Isaac Lutzki, *'Oraḥ Ṣaddiqim*, 17b–18a. The Karaite exploitation of the verse accounts for Pirqoy ben Baboy's (*c.* 800, C.E.) interpretation of the words *torath Mosheh* as referring to the Oral Law—a fact which L. Ginzberg (*Ginzē Schechter*, ii, p. 572) described as 'very strange'. Its polemical tendency is quite manifest. See further p. 213.

In view of the significance the *Malachi* verse assumed in Karaite thinking, the question may be raised: Was perhaps the *zayin majuscula* (ז׳ רבתי) in the word זכרו intended to draw attention to this significance? There is another instance of a *littera majuscula* at the beginning of a biblical verse of fundamental importance in Karaite ideology—namely *Isa.* 56, 10, on which see *infra*, Appendix A.

[2] *CDC*, xv, 9, 12; xvi, 1–2, 4–5; *DSD*, v, 8.

[3] See P. Wernberg-Møller, *The Manual of Discipline*, p. 95, note 35.

[4] See al-Qumisi, *Pithron*, p. 21; Sahl, *Liq. Qad.*, App., p. 25; Hadassi p. 138a, *s.v. qādōsh.*

THE PRINCIPLE OF SELF-SUFFICIENCY OF THE WRITTEN TORAH

Concerning the oath of admission, the *Damascus Document* has the following to say: 'Therefore a man shall obligate himself by oath to return to the Law of Moses, for in it the details of everything are contained' (xvi, 1–2).[1] This argument, as motivating such a decisive step, so crucial a commitment as a return to the Law of Moses by maintaining that all details are contained in the written Torah, must appear puzzling and strange to a considerable degree.[2] One thing only is immediately quite clear: the

[1] I.e. it contains all the דקדוקים—a term which, in tannaitic usage, indicates the details of the commandments, as distinct from their general wording in the Pentateuch, and which is used to express the rabbinic belief in the divine origin of the oral traditions. Cf., e.g., *Siphra* on *Lev.* 25, 1 (ed. Weiss, p. 105a): מה שמיטה נאמרו כללותיה ודקדוקיה מסיני אף כולם נאמרו כללותיהם ודקדוקיהם מסיני. The term figured also in the controversy about the Oral Law which turned on the question of the origin and validity of the detailed instructions necessary for the fulfilment of the precepts; cf. the 'sermon' about the importance of the Oral Law included in *Tanḥuma*, *Noaḥ* 3: תורה שבעל פה שיש בה דקדוקי מצות; and Pirqoy b. Baboy's insistence that the preceptual details that are in the hand of the Sages were not invented by them nor were they scholarly derivations: ומיכן אתה למד שתורה שבעל פה שהיא ביד חכמים בישיבה שבבבל ודקדוקי מצות שביד חכמים לא למדו אותה מליבן ולא מחכמתן (*Tarbiz*, ii, p. 401; 'Oṣar ha-Ge'onim, *Giṭṭin*, p. 137). Hadassi, on the other hand, denying their divine or prophetic origin says: ... לא מפי ה׳ אף לא הזכרו בדברי תורת ה׳ ... וגם לא דקדקום ופירשום נביאי ה׳ (Alph. 242, *qoph*; see further *ibid.*, letter *yodh*). Noteworthy also is the title conferred on a Karaite *Nāsī'*, David b. Ḥisdai, expressing the Karaite exegete's chief task of harmonizing contradictions and supplying perceptual details: הפתר קושיות התורה ודקדוקי מצות, 'the expounder of the difficulties of the Law and the details of the commandments' (J. Mann, *Texts and Studies*, ii, p. 153).

[2] The phrase כי בה הכל מדוקדק is understood by nearly all scholars in essentially the same sense, differing though they may in the expressions used in rendering it: 'exactly explained' (Schechter); 'accurately treated' (Charles); 'genau angegeben' (L. Ginzberg, *MGWJ*, 1912, p. 676); 'genau dargelegt' (W. Bacher, *ZfHB*, xv [1911], p. 21); 'clearly explained' (Büchler, *JQR*, iii [1912], p. 465); 'clearly stated' (K. Kohler, *Studies and Addresses*, p. 588); 'est dit avec précision'

argument must involve a point of fundamental importance which must have been regarded by the sectarian writer as of sufficient weight and convincing force to induce a decision in favour of a return to the 'Law of Moses'. What is this point, and what is its importance?

The force and import of the argument become clear to us if it is viewed against the background of the controversy about the validity of tradition, in which the question whether the details necessary for the fulfilment of the pentateuchal laws can, or cannot be extracted from the written text without the help of tradition, played a decisive rôle. This has become sufficiently clear from the foregoing pages. We have now to follow it up by demonstrating that that question was in fact the very pivot on which the controversy hinged, and indeed to such an extent that *acceptance or rejection of tradition was made contingent upon it*. This has been expressed with exceptional clarity by Sa'adya Ga'on, the foremost champion of tradition. In the polemical treatise *'Essā' Meshālī* he makes this unequivocal pronouncement:[1]

> Let us now consider carefully and investigate: If the unravelling of all the commandment is contained in the written text of Scripture, then we shall acknowledge that there is no *Mishnah*.

Here we see Sa'adya actually *staking the whole cause of the Oral Law on this argument; it stands and falls with it*. He goes on challenging his opponents to show how one could extract from the written text the details for the execution of the laws of סוכה, מעשר, תרומה, פרט, צצית, שחיטה, נדה, לקט, שכחה, פאה, חלה. Only by means of the divine interpretation embodied in the

(I. Lévi, *REJ*, 1911, p. 208); 'clairement défini' (Lagrange, *RB*, 1912, p. 239); 'minutieusement réglé' (Vermès, *Les Manuscrits du Désert de Judah*, p. 183); 'everything is specified' (M. Burrows, *The Dead Sea Scrolls*, p. 363); 'everything can be learned' (Rabin, *Zadokite Fragments*, p. 75); 'explicitly spelled out' (Gaster, *Scriptures of the Dead Sea Sect*, p. 93). None of the above scholars, however, has even tried to explain the meaning and significance of the phrase in question.

[1] *Rav Saadya Gaon*, ed. J. L. Fishman [=Maimon], Jerusalem 1943, p. 525.

Oral Law are we in a position to fulfil these commandments. It is indicative of the centrality of this argument that Sa'adya reverts to it time and again in several of his writings. In the commentary on *Genesis*, for instance, he inserted a dissertation unfolding the seven famous arguments for the necessity of tradition.[1] As S. Poznansky rightly pointed out,[2] these are in reality only seven illustrations of one single argument: the incompleteness of the written Torah. Again, in a tract against Ibn Saqawaiah[3] the Ga'on dwells on the astonishing fact that while such matters as the work of the tabernacle (*Ex.* 25), the inauguration of its service (*Lev.* 8–9), the numbering of the Israelites (*Num.* 1) and the dedication of the altar (*Num.* 7) are described at great length, an important institution like the intercalation of the year is alluded to by but a single word, *'ābhībh* (*Ex.* 23, 15). It is impossible, he maintains, that the duty of prayer should have been conveyed by a mere allusion in the phrase הוא תהלתך (*Deut.* 10, 21)[4] and civil jurisdiction by the words ונתן בפלילים, 'he shall pay as the judges determine' (*Ex.* 21, 22). This irresistibly leads to the conclusion that the written word must have been accompanied by detailed instructions; and as we do not possess them in writing, they must have been given by word of mouth.[5]

[1] See Salmon, *Book of the Wars*, etc., p. 47, line 42: טופס שבע הראיות הכתובות, אשר ב"פתרון בראשית" לך נכתבות. A fragment of this has been discovered by A. S. Halkin and published in *L. Ginzberg Jubilee Volume*, Hebrew part, pp. 143ff.

[2] *ZfHB*, iii, p. 173, note 8.

[3] Cf. A. Harkavy in *Ha-Qedem*, vol. i, p. 65, and also in *JQR*, 13 [1901], p. 656. That the fragment did not emanate from Sa'adya's כתאב אלתמייז, as Harkavy thought, but from his treatise against Ibn Saqawaiah, has been proved by H. Hirschfeld in *JQR*, 16 [1904], p. 100.

[4] Cf. *Siddur Rabh Sa'adya Ga'on* (ed. I. Davidson, S. Assaf, B. I. Joel), Jerusalem 1941, p. 3* and *Kiryath Sepher*, xxviii, p. 108.

[5] Cf. further Sa'adya's introduction to the Arabic translation of the Pentateuch (ed. J. Derenbourg, p. 4): הכמות והאיכות אינן נכתבות בפירוש בספר התורה ולא נדע למשל כמה פעמים יתפלל האדם בכל יום וכמה היא הצדקה ואיזה גדר המלאכה בשבת. It is this frequent reiteration of the argument on the part of Sa'adya to which Salmon (*ibid.* p. 47) refers: בכל עת תזכרם ברבים לפתות לבבות. The challenge

The same line of defence was taken by other[1] protagonists of tradition like, e.g., Yehudah Hallevi.[2] The strength of his conviction as to the cogency of the argument in question is evidenced by the fact that *he too staked the case of the Oral Law on it*: 'I wish the Karaites could give me a satisfactory answer to questions of this kind, I would not hesitate to accept their view.' Finally, we may again refer to Abraham Ibn Ezra. It is remarkable that this eminent, independent scholar, with all his sharpness and ingenuity uses the same old weapon, and harps on the same motif in defending the Oral Law.[3]

The repudiators of tradition, on the other hand, insisted that the details not explicitly stated are implicit in the biblical text and can be derived from it by the method of 'searching', i.e. by a philological analysis, by defining precisely the terms occurring in

thrown out by the Ga'on was taken up by Qirqisani (see Poznanski, *op. cit.* p. 175; ed. L, Nemoy, pp. 124f.), and by Salmon (*ibid.* pp. 47–50). Salmon's refutations were rebutted by one of the Ga'on's disciples, see the fragment published by M. Schreiner, *ZfHB*, 3, pp. 88f. (cf. *ibid.* p. 172). That the author was a disciple of Sa'adya has been proved by Poznanski, *op. cit.*, 10, pp. 43–52.

[1] The anonymous Rabbanite polemicist (*She'ēlōth 'Attīqōth*, *HUCA*, xxi [1948], Hebrew part, p. 44) asks with reference to the *ṣiṣith*: קשר ציצית צוה לעשותם . . . איך נכין הציצית והתכלת?

[2] *Kuzari*, iii, 35. Controverting the Karaite postulate of the perfectness of the written Torah, he says: 'That which appears plain in the Torah is yet obscure, how much more so are the obscure passages.' Re-echoing Sa'adya he says: 'I want to know the details of circumcision, fringes and the feast of Tabernacles.' Again, 'I desire an explanation of the words "*let no man go out of his place on the seventh day*" (*Ex.* 16, 29). Does this refer to the house or precincts, estate . . . territory, district, or country.' 'I wish to see a Karaite give judgment between two parties according to the chapters *Ex.* 21 and *Deut.* 21, 10 sqq.'

[3] Cf. *supra*, p. 56; in the introduction to the commentary on the Pentateuch Ibn Ezra argues: בעבור שלא תמצא בתורה מצוה אחת בכל צרכיה מבוארה . . . כי אין בתורה חקי השנה מפורשים, ואיך נחשוב החדשים . . . ולמה אין בתורה עליהם עד נאמן רק נ ח פ ש כה וכה רמיזות, ולמה בדברי ת ו ר ה ת מ י מ ה כזאת. וזה לנו האות שסמך משה על תורה שבעל פה. The spaced out words are polemical allusions to the Karaite method of *ḥippus* and to the principle of the perfectness of the Law of Moses.

the text[1] and by logical procedures, particularly by means of inference or analogy, *qiyās*.[2] In short, *the details of the pentateuchal laws are inherent in the written word, are embedded in the text*. And this is also the significance of the words כי בה הכל מדוקדק, 'for in it all details are contained'.

A DEFINITION OF THE SECT'S FAITH

At this juncture we have to point out a fact of considerable importance—that the *Rule of the Community* includes a definition, or characterization, of the Sect's conception of 'Torah', of what they considered to be the distinctive features of their faith. This is contained in a comment on *Isa.* 40, 3: *Clear ye the way of the Lord*. In order to appreciate fully the import of this comment, it must be remembered that the Sect used the term 'the way of the Lord', דרך יי, as a designation for its own conception of Judaism. This is borne out by *CDC*, xx, 18. It should also be recalled that they designated themselves as 'those who chose the way' (of the Lord)[3] and their adversaries were called 'those who deviated from the way' (of the Lord).[4]

Now, the *Rule of the Community* defines 'the way of the Lord' in the following words which may be divided into three paragraphs (viii, 15–16):

1. מדרש התורה [אשר] צוה ביד משה
2. לעשות ככול הנגלה עת בעת
3. וכאשר גלו הנביאים ברוח קודשו.

[1] *'Eshkol ha-Kopher*, 154, *taw*: כי יש בתורת אלהים דברים שנלמדם מעניינם . . . נפתרים במליצת עניינם בדקדוקם ומסורתם ופסוק טעמים . . . נלמדים מענין סופם וראשיתם . . .

[2] The prohibition of marrying a niece is derived by analogy in *CDC*, v, 8f., and also by 'Anan (Harkavy, *Anan's Book of Precepts*, p. 93). Sa'adya composed a special work (כתאב תחציל אלשראיע אלסמעיה) to demonstrate that the details of the non-rational precepts cannot be derived by *qiyās*.

[3] *DSD*, ix, 17f.

[4] *CDC*, i, 13; ii, 6.

1. The search in the Torah [which] He commanded through Moses;
2. To do according to all that has been uncovered from time to time;
3. And according to that which the prophets have uncovered by His holy spirit.

We note that the first place is given to the search in the Torah, special stress being laid, as stated, on 'the Torah which He commanded through Moses'. The doctrine of the progressive uncovering of the Law is contained in the second paragraph. These two points need no further elaboration, having been sufficiently discussed previously. As to the third point, the fact that a reference to the Prophets was embodied in the definition of the Sect's ideology is obviously of basic importance; it is an unmistakable indication of the doctrinal significance of the prophetic writings in the sectarian creed.[1] But what is that significance? At first sight one might be inclined to think that the significance lies in the sphere of messianism, having regard to the prominence given to it in the life and thought of the Sect. However, the context which mentions the Prophets in connection with the application of the Law of Moses does not bear out this interpretation. The text says 'to do' (i.e. to apply the Law of Moses) 'according to all that has been uncovered from time to time and according to that which the prophets have uncovered by His holy spirit'. The prophetic writings are thus assigned a rôle in the process of uncovering the hiddenness of the Mosaic Law.

What this means may be explained by an illustration from Karaism. A prominent Karaite spokesman characterizes his fellow-sectarians by saying 'they seek and search in the Law of Moses and also in the books of the prophets'.[2] Again, he describes

[1] Also in *DSD*, i, 2f. and *CDC*, v, 21f. the prophets are mentioned side by side with the Law of Moses. As Wernberg-Møller (*op. cit.* p. 45, note 6) has pointed out, 'in the Old Testament Moses and the prophets are never mentioned together'.

[2] Sahl b. Maṣliaḥ in *Liq. Qad.*, App., p. 34: הם חוקרים ודורשים בתורת משה ע״ה וגם בספרי הנביאים.

them as 'the disciples of the Torah and the doers according to the words of the prophets'.[1] In this case, we know immediately and with absolute certainty what lies behind the emphasis on the 'search' in the prophetic books alongside the 'search' in the Law of Moses, and further what is meant by the words 'they do according to the words of the prophets'. This is closely connected with the Karaite negation of tradition; having rejected the traditional exposition of the Pentateuch, they turned to the Prophets as a source of elucidation and supplementation of the written Law. The prophets are the authentic revealers of the divine will enshrined in the Torah. Already 'Anan[2] had elevated the prophetic books—and the Hagiographa—to the level of the Pentateuch, investing them with the same legal authority, and this was recognized by all subsequent Karaites as an article of faith.[3]

That the same idea was current in Qumran is implied in the third paragraph of the above definition.

THE APPELLATIONS 'HOUSE OF THE TORAH' AND 'DISCIPLES OF THE TORAH'

This leads us to the expression '*House of the Torah*', בית התורה, occurring twice in the *Damascus Document* (xx, 10, 13)—an expression which gave rise to various interpretations. Apart from the wholly unjustified emendation suggested by K. Kohler,[4] who

[1] *Ibid.* p. 35: תלמידי התורה והעושים כדברי הנביאים Cf. also: יגעים בתורה ובמקרא (*ibid.*); גבורי התורה והמקרא (p. 36).

[2] Cf. A. Harkavy, *Studien und Mitteilungen*, viii, p. xi; B. Klar, *Meḥqarim we-'Iyyunim*, pp. 303f.

[3] See Hadassi, 77, *mem*: משלים וסתומים שדברה תורתך כגון ענין זה [ציצית ותפילין] . . . באו נביאים ופירשום וגלום לעדתך. Among the 'hidden' commandments explained and supplemented by the prophets, Hadassi counts the following: Calendation, the laws concerning the Sabbath, circumcision, the meaning of 'a fruit of a goodly tree' (*Lev.* 23, 40), the making of the *sukkah*, civil jurisdiction, and levirate marriage.

[4] *American Journal for Theology*, xv [1911], p. 410 [=*Studies and Addresses and Personal Papers*, New York 1931, p. 44]. Kohler read בית המורה, 'the house of the teacher (of righteousness)'.

was obviously at a loss to make sense of it as it stands, the expression was taken to signify 'the sectarian centre in Damascus',[1] 'the temple of the Sect',[2] 'a school or place for teaching the Torah',[3] and 'the post-Messianic era of resurrection'.[4]

However, the interpretation demanded by the context and first suggested by Charles[5] is unquestionably correct; the Sect designated itself as 'the House of the Torah'. In the light of the preceding, this is indeed a most fitting designation, descriptive of a basic doctrine of the Sect—exclusive allegiance to the written Torah. Significantly, the Karaites too, who travelled the same path as their kinsmen in Qumran, labelled themselves with a similar epithet conveying the same idea; they called themselves 'Disciples of the Torah', תלמידי התורה.[6] The same implication is carried by the title, derived from *Isa.* 54, 13, 'Disciples of the Lord', למודי יי (אל), which the men of Qumran appropriated to themselves.[7] 'Disciples of the Lord'='Disciples of the

[1] L. Ginzberg, *MGWJ*, 1912, p. 688.

[2] Israel Lévi, *REJ*, 1911, p. 191, note 12.

[3] W. Bacher, *ZfHB*, xv [1911], p. 21; Habermann, *'Edah we-'Eduth*, p. 107; L. Rost, *Theologische Literaturzeitung*, 1953, p. 146; regarded as 'possible' also by Charles, *Apocrypha and Pseudepigrapha of the O.T.*, ii, p. 793.

[4] C. Rabin, *Zadokite Documents*, p. 39. The fact that in line 11 also divine punishment is threatened does not exclude communal punishment of excommunication. Extermination by the sword will be the ultimate fate of the recalcitrant members; the immediate punishment is expulsion from the Sect.

[5] *Loc. cit.* and p. 821. See also W. H. Brownlee, *BA*, 1951, p. 58; G. Vermès, *op. cit.*, p. 171.

[6] *Liq. Qad.*, App., pp. 33, 35; also in a Genizah text published by A. Marmorstein in *Memorial Volume for S. Poznanski*, p. 44: תלמידי התורה ובעלי מקרא; M. Steinschneider, *Catalogus Codicum Hebraeorum Bibliothecae Academiae Lugduno-Batavae*, p. 384 (תלמידי תושיה).

[7] *CDC*, xx, 4. Attention should further be called to the designation 'people of the Torah' occurring in a Qumran text (*RB*, 1956, p. 61: אנשי התורה המתנדבים), which should be compared with the Karaite title בעלי התורה (J. Mann, *Texts and Studies*, ii, p. 1150).

Torah'. Again, this designation, too, the Karaites applied to their own sect.[1]

An illustration of the interchangeability of 'Lord' and 'Torah' is provided by the terms 'the way of the Lord' (דרך יי) and 'the way of the Torah' (דרך התורה), both of which are used to designate the Karaite faith.[2] Noteworthy is the following example in which the two terms are used together; a Genizah document dealing with a case of conversion of Rabbanite Jews to Karaism says: 'They have abandoned their former belief to follow *the way of the Torah* and seek, as we do, *the way of the Lord*'.[3]

ILLUMINATIONAL EXEGESIS

We have now to revert to a problem briefly alluded to above—the seeming contradiction between the *Rule of the Community*, v, 11–12 and the *Damascus Document*, iii, 12–14. While the former clearly implies the duty of uncovering the hidden precepts by scholarly effort, by 'seeking and searching in His Law', so much so that the adversaries are denounced for failing to do so, the latter attributes the uncovering of the hidden things to divine revelation. How are these statements to be reconciled?

A moment's reflection shows that the contradiction is apparent only. We have before us an exegetical theory which may be described as 'illuminational exegesis'. This theory, whilst both regarding scholarly endeavour as essential for the discovery of the true meaning of the Law and insisting on the obligation to search in the Law by means of exegetical and logical devices, believes, on the other hand, that divine illumination is equally necessary to enable the searcher to perceive the hidden things in the Torah and, in particular, to guard him against the dangers of error with which human methods are beset. In other words, human exertion

[1] *'Eshkol ha-Kopher*, 132, *lamed* (למודי ה׳ משכילי עם . . . הם משכילי אבלי ציון בעלי מקרא); 85, *'aleph.*

[2] Cf. N. Wieder, 'The Doctrine of the Two Messiahs', *JJS* 1955, p. 24; *ha-Ṣopheh le-Ḥokhmath Yisra'el*, viii [1924], p. 325.

[3] Cf. H. Hirschfeld, 'A Karaite Conversion Story', *Jews' College Jubilee Volume*, London 1906, p. 91.

and divine illumination are interdependent elements of the process of uncovering the hidden portions of the Torah; the process is an interaction between man and God: man seeks to fathom the divine will and God, in turn, aids man's search by coming to meet him half-way.

ILLUMINATIONAL EXEGESIS AMONG THE KARAITES

The interdependence of scholarly endeavour and divine illumination in biblical exegesis is a recurrent theme in Karaite literature—a phenomenon that has not received the attention of students of Karaism. For polemical reasons, in debating the issue of the Oral Law with the Rabbanites, the Karaites naturally focused their arguments on the possibility of discovering the meaning of the commandments by hermeneutic procedure, independent of tradition. At the same time, being well aware of the difficulties involved in this procedure and knowing the pitfalls that lurk beside its path and, most especially, from their own experience of the slowness of the process, they never failed to stress the necessity for divine aid. This, however, would be granted to those only who engage in serious, unbiased investigation of Scripture and who persevere in the endeavour to penetrate independently into the meaning of the biblical text.

This combination of human and divine factors we meet in the fragment of al-Qumisi's commentary on *Leviticus*, printed above,[1] which mentions not only knowledge as a necessary pre-requisite for finding the hidden things of the Torah, but also piety.[2] This is also the opinion of Aaron Ben-Asher.[3] Vivid expression of the profound anxiety felt in Karaite quarters at the slowness and difficulties of the method of 'searching' is given by Hadassi, in the following quotation:[4]

[1] pp. 60f.

[2] והדורש ביראה ובדעת ימצא.

[3] *Supra*, p. 58, n. 2: ואם יתן אדם דעתו במקרא ויכון לבו לשמים ויחפש ויחקור ימצא ולא יסתרו ממנו דברי תורה.

[4] *'Eshkol ha-Kopher*, 175, *zayin*.

'There are in the Torah hidden things that require seeking and searching in order to know the ways of the Lord, and it is concerning these that the *maskil* asked: "*I am a stranger in the earth, hide not Thy commandments from me*" (*Ps.* 119, 19). The meaning is: I am not a permanent resident in the earth; I do not live for ever; my days and my years are limited and I am unable to spend most of my days in searching in order to find and obtain the commandments of my God. I ask Thee, therefore, to grant me knowledge to understand and observe them "*before I go, and I am no more*", i.e. before I depart from the world, still erring in Thy commandments.'

Hence the frequent mention of the fact that Karaite scholars continually pray for divine illumination. The psalm-verse (119, 18): '*Open Thou mine eyes, that I may behold the hidden things of Thy Law*' became a principal prayer, and looms large in Karaite literature.[1] Already al-Qumisi observed that the Karaites had adopted the verse as their prayer, significantly adding that it was intended from the very outset by King David as a prayer for the sectarian *élite*.[2] Indeed, members of the Jerusalem community of

[1] A few illustrations only will be given: Sahl b. Maṣliaḥ (*Liq. Qad.* App., p. 35): תמימי דרך מתחננים: גל עיני Yefeth b. 'Ali on *Mal.* 3, 22 (MS. British Museum, Or. 2401, fol. 258a): אדׄא טׄהרו שבי פשע ביעקב תרכו אלתשאגל פי אלמשנה ואלתלמוד ואלזמו אנפסהם אלהדׄר פי תורת משה כקׄ מה אהבתי תורתך כל היום היא שיחתי ויסאלו אללה אן יכשף אבצארהם פי כתאבה כקׄו גל עיני ואביטה נפׄל מתו וקאל הוריני יוי דרך חקיך וכתׄיר מתׄל דׄלך.

On verse 23 (fol. 259a) he writes in the same vein: אדׄא טׄהרו שארית ישראל תמימי דרך אלדׄי תרכו אלתעצב ללאבא ואלמעלמין וגׄעלו קצדהם מן כתאב אללה פיעתקדו מא צפא להם מן אלבחתׄ... יסלו אללה אן יכשף אבצארהם אלי טריק אלחק ולא יכׄפי ענהם שיא מן עלם אלפראיץׄ כקׄ גר אנכי בארץ אל תסתר ממני מצותיך. Yefeth writes in similar terms also in the commentary on *Numbers*, MS. British Museum, Or. 2473, fol. 21a. See also *infra*, p. 96.

Two illustrations from *'Eshkol ha-Kopher* will suffice. Alph. 14, *daleth*: דורשים צורם תמיד לגלותם דברי הצופים, דרכי תורתו וחזיון נביאיו ככתוב גל עיני...; 175, *kaph*: ועל אלה המדות יתפללו המשכילים ויאמרו: גל עיני.

See also the verses of *Ps.* 119 placed at the head of the Karaite work *Sepher Bereshith Rabbah* (Steinschneider, Leiden Catalogue, facsimile II); Aaron of Nicomedia, *Gan 'Eden*, p. 81b.

[2] *Supra*, p. 60.

ascetics claimed that divine illumination had in fact been granted to scholars of their own generation. Thus Sahl b. Maṣliaḥ asserts:[1] 'Our God in his mercies has now illuminated the last generation and opened their eyes to perceive the hidden things of His Law . . and every day their knowledge and understanding increases in order to fulfil His word (*Dan.* 12, 4): "*Many shall run to and fro, and knowledge shall be increased*".' Yefeth b. 'Ali, too, speaks of divine revelations having been made to the Karaite 'searchers of knowledge'. In connection with *Dan.* 12, 4 which he—like Sahl in the foregoing quotation—interpreted in relation to his own time and its attendant religious conditions, he says as follows:[2]

> ' "*Many shall run to and fro*", this refers to the *maskilim* and seekers of knowledge . . . they will run over the countries in search of knowledge because scholars will be found in every region; the seekers of knowledge will therefore go to and fro to learn from them; this is expressed by *Amos* (8, 12): "*They shall wander from sea to sea, and from north even to the east; they shall run to and fro to seek the word of the Lord, and shall not find it.*" This shall be at the beginning of their career, but after that God will make revelations to them,[3] since they have sought so ardently.'

The opinion of Sahl and Yefeth, ascribing divine revelation to the last generation of scholars only, is in accordance with al-Qumisi's contention, based on *Dan.* 11, 35 ('*and some of the maskilim shall stumble*'), that 'the first teachers of the *Galuth* stumbled in the interpretation of the commandments', adding 'the last ones will find the truth'. 'Anan himself, belonging as he did to the first generation, was inevitably consigned to stumbling.[4]

[1] *Liq. Qad.* App., p. 35.

[2] Cf. *A Commentary on the Book of Daniel, etc.* (ed. D. S. Margoliouth), p. 141.

[3] In the introduction to his commentary on the *Song of Songs* (MS. British Museum, Or. 2520, fol. 35b) Yefeth says: '. . . the Perfect in the Way to whom God revealed the hidden things of the Torah' (תמימי . . . דרך אלדי כשף את להם נפלאות התורה).

[4] Cf. *JQR*, xii [1921–22], p. 519.

The belief in the superiority of the later scholars is shared by yet another member of the Jerusalem community of ascetics. David al-Fasi,[1] in an allegorical interpretation of *Cant.* 7, 9, contrasts the earlier scholars who are metaphorically designated as 'clusters' (אשכולות)[2] with the later ones who are styled 'clusters of the vine' (verses 8, 9), i.e. 'inspired scholars'.[3] While the former's knowledge was the result of 'searching and deduction', the latter's knowledge is vouchsafed them by the divine spirit.

The belief has found bold expression in the fact that al-Qumisi[4] as well as Moses Ben-Asher[5] went so far as to designate the Karaite scholars as 'prophets'. Behind this daring description lies the belief of divine inspiration having been granted to the scholars in their exegetical work. The prophecy ascribed to them is not of a passive character, a mere receiving of divine communications, but one entailing active human participation; it is the result of an interaction between man and God.

It is very probable that Benjamin al-Nahāwendī's emphatic declaration[6] '*I am neither a prophet nor the son of a prophet*' was prompted by, and directed against, such claims of 'prophecy'. These claims may also have provoked the philosophically minded al-Qirqisani to declare with much emphasis that 'Anan was no prophet, but merely 'a *searcher* who was not free from error and mistake'.[7]

[1] Cf. *Kitāb Jāmiʿ al-Alfāẓ* (*Agrōn*), ed. S. L. Skoss, New Haven, 1936 [Yale Oriental Series—Researches, vols. xx–xxi], ii, p. 335.

[2] See B.T. *Ḥullin*, 92a.

[3] 'Wine' is a metaphor for 'prophecy', see *ibid*. p. 52: ולנא יין תמתׄיל ללנבואת. הביאני אל בית היין יעני בה אלקדס וקד יסמיה „גיא חזיון".

[4] See *supra*, p. 60: ומשכילי דעת והם נביאים יודעי דעת.

[5] See P. Kahle, *The Cairo Geniza* [2nd ed., 1959], p. 97.

[6] See A. Harkavy, *Studien und Mitteilungen*, viii, p. 176.

[7] *Kitāb al-Anwār wal-Marāqib*, ed. L. Nemoy, p. 624, lines 1–3.

THE *MŌRĒH ṢEDEQ*: AN INSPIRED EXEGETE

An inspired exegete,[1] and no more, was likewise the priest, or *mōrēh ṣedeq*, of whom the author of the *Habakkuk Commentary* (ii, 8–10) says that 'God has given [understanding] in [his heart] to explain all the words of His servants the prophets through whom He foretold what was to come upon His people and His land'. Again, on *Hab*. 2, 2 (vii, 1–5) he says:

> God told Habakkuk to write down the things that were to come upon the last generation, but the end of the [last] epoch He did not make known to him. And as for the words '*he that readeth it, may do so swiftly*', this refers to the teacher of the truth to whom God made known all the secrets of the words of His servants the prophets.

The *mōrēh ṣedeq* is thus no more than a 'reader' of the literary records of the ancient prophecies; a commentator who, with divine assistance, is able correctly to 'explain' these records, unlock their secrets and thus make them available to the 'last generation' living in the 'last epoch',[2] to whom they were addressed and to whom they were of vital concern.

This view is in sharp contrast with the fairly widespread opinion that would elevate the *mōrēh ṣedeq* to a rank even higher than that of the prophets, crediting him with 'insight surpassing that of the prophets themselves';[3] with 'an understanding of God's promises that exceed that of the inspired writers themselves';[4] 'what God did not reveal to Habakkuk, He revealed to the Teacher of Righteousness';[5] the knowledge of the *gemar*

[1] Cf. J. van der Ploeg, *The Excavations at Qumran* [*A Survey of the Judaean Brotherhood and Its Ideas*], 1958, p. 168; A. Michel, *Le Maître de Justice*, p. 268.

[2] הדור האחרון = הקץ האחרון, see N. Wieder, 'The Term קץ in the Dead Sea Scrolls and in Hebrew Liturgical Poetry', *JJS*, v [1954], p. 27.

[3] Millar Burrows, *The Dead Sea Scrolls*, p. 284.

[4] J. T. Milik, *Ten Years of Discovery in the Wilderness of Judaea*, pp. 113f.

[5] G. Vermès, *Discoveries in the Judean Desert*, p. 128.

ha-qēṣ which was withheld from the former was granted to the latter.[1]

That opinion can hardly be supported by the relevant passages in the *Habakkuk Commentary*. What emerges from them can be summed up as follows. The pronouncements of the *mōrēh ṣedeq* concerned two closely-related things: (a) the present generation is the 'last generation'; the 'last epoch' in the history of mankind before the commencement of the messianic era; (b) the events of this pre-messianic epoch were forecast by the prophets and are now being enacted on the stage of history. When, however, this epoch of wickedness and tribulation would at last come to an end and be consummated by the advent of the redeemer and the establishment of the messianic kingdom—on that point the *mōrēh ṣedeq* was unable to enlighten his contemporaries; he could not do so, because his knowledge was derived from the prophetic records, and the 'end of the epoch' (*gemar ha-qēṣ*) was not revealed even to the prophets themselves. He knows, it is true, 'all the secrets of the words of His servants the prophets', but this vital piece of knowledge was not contained in the words of the prophets. The whole intention of the author of the *Habakkuk Commentary* in observing that God did not reveal to Habakkuk when the 'end of the epoch' would occur—an observation which has no basis in the text he is commenting upon—was to explain why the *mōrēh ṣedeq* was ignorant of that crucial date.

The Qumran expositor's view that even the prophets were denied knowledge of that vital date is quite in line with a rabbinic saying,[2] expressed in even more emphatic terms, that not even the ministering angels knew the date which remained a secret hidden in 'God's heart'. The view is further shared by the *Acts of the Apostles* (1, 7) where Jesus is represented as saying: *It is not for you to know times and seasons, which the Father hath set within His own authority.*

[1] See D. Flusser, *Zion*, xix [1954], p. 95; *Kiryath Sepher*, 1958, p. 456; F. Nötscher, *Zur Theologischen Terminologie der Qumran-Texte*, p. 166; F. F. Bruce, *Second Thoughts on the DSS*, p. 86.

[2] B.T. *Sanhedrin* 99a; *Eccl. R.*, 12, 10.

ADDITIONAL NOTES TO CHAPTER II

No. 1

(See p. 58, note 1)

The authenticity of the second half of 'Anan's famous dictum has likewise been questioned, chiefly on account of its Hebrew wording: ואל תשענו על דעתי ('And do not rely on my opinion'), which is in sharp contrast with the Aramaic of the first half. There is, however, no compelling reason for doubting its authenticity on linguistic grounds. It is certainly true that the *Hebrew* phrasing did not emanate from 'Anan, who employed Aramaic as his medium of writing. What happened is simply this: 'Anan's Aramaic words were translated into Hebrew by some later copyist for the benefit of Karaite readers unfamiliar with the Aramaic idiom. If Qirqisani's account (Harkavy, *Studien u. Mitteilungen*, v, p. 108; L. Nemoy, *Karaite Anthology*, p. 3) that Hai Ga'on (probably Hai b. David of Pumbeditha, 890–98 C.E.), in co-operation with his father, took the trouble of translating 'Anan's *Book of Precepts* from the Aramaic into Hebrew deserves little credence, it reflects, at any rate, the high value which the Karaite originators of that account set on such a translation, regarding it as a desirable undertaking serving a useful purpose. Unlike their Rabbanite brethren who were reared on the Talmud, the Karaite dissenters, whose studies were confined to the biblical books, were ignorant of the Aramaic tongue; and it is significant that Hadassi, when quoting a simple Aramaic passage from the Talmud, hastens to translate it into Hebrew for the benefit of his readers (233, *ṣadē*).

This explanation is greatly reinforced by the fact that attempts were made to hebraize the first half of the dictum as well. I recall that the only source of the dictum is Yefeth b. 'Ali's commentary on *Zechariah*, and the purely Aramaic form (חפישו באורייתא שפיר) is found in MS. Leiden, Warner 12, of that commentary. This form has become known through L. Dukes who, in 1844, was the first to call attention to it (*Beiträge zur Geschichte der*

Ältesten Auslegung und Sprachelklärung des Alten Testamentes, Stuttgart 1844, ii, p. 26, note 1). However, in MS. British Museum, Or. 2401, fol. 175 (cf. S. Poznanski, *REJ*, 1902, p. 184), the first half of the dictum reads as follows: חַפְּשׂוּ בתורה שפיר. Here, of the original Aramaic formulation only the last word has been left intact. And if such simple Aramaic expressions as the two words affected were regarded as requiring a Hebrew rendering, the hebraization of the second half—which almost certainly ran ... ולא תרחצון—must have appeared as an absolute necessity if it were to be at all intelligible to one not conversant with Aramaic, since the verb רחץ in Hebrew signifies 'to wash'. It is needless to add that complete or partial hebraization of Aramaic statements is a not infrequent phenomenon, even in the talmudic-midrashic literature. See also L. Nemoy in *Semitic Studies in Memory of Immanuel Löw* (Budapest 1947), p. 241, note 17.

No. 2

(See p. 59)

Elsewhere (see my remarks printed in P. Kahle's *Cairo Geniza* [2nd ed. 1959], p. 97) I have pointed out some of the phrases and ideas characteristic of Karaite vocabulary and ideology occurring in Moses Ben-Asher's colophon. One other phrase may be added here—the epithet אנשי אמנה. It is synonymous with אנשי אמת, *men of truth*, a standard honorific self-designation of the Karaites (see *infra*, p. 148). M. Zucker's interpretation of the expression (*Tarbiz*, 1958, p. 69) is unacceptable on purely linguistic grounds, quite apart from other considerations. If it signified 'men of the covenant', and if it referred to Nehemiah and his contemporaries (cf. *Neh.* 10, 1), surely the expression should have run 'men of *the* covenant'—the definite, historical covenant recorded in the Bible. Zucker himself supplies support for this argument: in explaining the expression he actually cites it *with the definite article*, thus unconsciously admitting that his interpretation demanded *ha-'amanah*.

On first consideration one might be inclined to regard our rendering as not plausible on the ground that the usage of *'emunah* in the meaning of 'truth' is rather uncommon. This objection is removed as soon as it is recognized that the employment of the term in this meaning belonged to the style of the period and that it was in vogue with Karaite authors. Thus Aaron Ben-Asher (*Diqduqē ha-Ṭe'amim*, p. 2) designates the prophets צירי אמונה which is equivalent to נביאי אמת, and Sahl b. Maṣliaḥ (*Liq. Qad.* App., p. 41) says of Sa'adya: ולו היה מבקש אמונה, היה יודע; as Pinsker (*ibid.* note 3) already observed the word *'emunah* stands here for *'emeth*. Sahl uses the term in this meaning also on pp. 24 and 26. It is likewise employed by the Rabbanite author of the polemical tract against the Karaites, שאלות עתיקות, cf. *HUCA*, xxi [1948], p. 44, line 3 [Hebrew section], and the new fragment published by A. Scheiber, *ibid.* xxvii [1956], p. 299, line 18. [See Addenda.]

No. 3

(See p. 85, note 5)

In this connection a brief observation may be added on another title applied to Karaite scholars—this time by Moses Ben-Asher's son, Aaron. The title in question—זקני עגולה (*Diqduqē ha-Ṭe'amim*, p. 16)—has been adduced as evidence of Ben-Asher's allegiance to Rabbanism, on the grounds that this honorific designation, deriving from the fact that the Sanhedrin of old as well as the seventy members of the gaonic academies (likewise called 'Sanhedrin') were seated in a semi-circle, 'has no room among the words of a Karaite' (see Aaron Dothan, *Sinai*, 1957, p. 309; M. Zucker, *Tarbiz*, xxvii [1958], p. 73).

Similarly, it has been argued (Zucker, *loc. cit.*) that the Massoretes listed in the *Treatise on the Shewa* (cf. J. Mann, *The Jews in Egypt, etc.*, ii, 43–45 and, especially, P. Kahle, *The Cairo Geniza* [2nd ed.], pp. 75–79, where additional bibliographical material can be found) cannot have been Karaites, since two of them bear the titles ראש הישיבה and החבר respectively—'titles which were only in vogue in the Rabbanite institutions of learning'.

The aforementioned authors have overlooked an important historical fact which nullifies their argument. In imitation of the Rabbanite authorities, Karaite leadership arrogated to itself the time-honoured titles of the ancient seats of learning, adopting not only the title *nasi*', but even such genuinely rabbinic designations as ראש הישיבה and אב בית דין (cf. S. Poznanski, *Babylonische Geonim im nachbabylonischen Zeitalter* [Schriften der Lehranstalt für die Wissenschaft des Judentums], Berlin 1914, p. 126, note 3). How far the imitation went can be gauged from the fact that 'Anan's descendants, the brothers Yehoshafaṭ and Ṣemaḥ, three generations after 'Anan (about the first half of the 9th century) used the precise title borne by the presidents of the Rabbanite academies in Palestine and Babylon alike: ראש ישיבת גאון יעקב. This, of course, implies also that their own academy was designated by the same proud name given to its Rabbanite counterparts: ישיבת גאון יעקב (cf. S. Poznanski, *op. cit.*, p. 128; J. Mann, *Texts and Studies*, ii, pp. 45, 131). And, if we were to give credence to the Leningrad MS. of Yeshu'ah b. Yehudah's (Abū'l Faraj Furqān ibn 'Asad) commentary on the Pentateuch, a Karaite spokesman of the rank of Daniel al-Qumisi himself bore the title *Rēsh Kallah* (A. Harkavy, *Studien und Mitteilungen*, viii, p. 187; Poznanski, *Ha-Qedem* [St. Petersburg], ii, Hebrew part, p. 95, and *op. cit.* p. 128, note 3).

We do not know the ups and downs of the Karaite academy in the Holy Land; but from Ibn al-Hiti's Chronicle we gather that under the presidency of Yoseph ibn Noaḥ (Nuḥ) it experienced a period of prosperity and fame, attracting scholars of the calibre of Yoseph al-Baṣir, the philosopher, and Abū'l Faraj Hārūn, the grammarian (see G. Margoliouth, 'Ibn al-Hiti's Arabic Chronicle of Karaite Doctors' in *JQR*, ix [1896–97], p. 433; L. Nemoy, *Karaite Anthology*, p. 232). Now it is significant that the named chronicler specifically records the fact that Ibn Noaḥ's academy consisted of seventy scholars, that is to say, it was in a position to rival the corresponding Rabbanite institution even in numbers (בחכמה ובמנין), having achieved the quorum of the Great Sanhedrin.

No. 4

(See p. 82)

In 'The Qumran Sectaries', p. 107, I drew attention to a reference by the author of שאלות עתיקות (*HUCA*, xxi [1948], p. 53) to the Karaite claim of divine illumination. In an ironical vein he says: 'Their heart imagines: "the perfect in the way behold the hidden things of the Torah".' Dr. M. Zucker's rejection of my interpretation (*Tarbiz*, xxvii, p. 69, note 49) compels me to revert to this reference. Zucker regards my interpretation as forced because of a linguistic difficulty it allegedly entails, but he did not specify what that difficulty was, and I am unable to detect it. On the other hand, I feel utterly unable to accept Zucker's own view, out of linguistic and contextual considerations. Before proceeding, it will be helpful to reproduce the strophe concerned:

שער אדרת ילבשו למען כחש, והאנשים ימהרו ויחלטו דרך נחש,
ותמימי דרך יראו נפלאות לבם ירחש, תפול עליהם אימתה.

According to Zucker the clause at issue does not refer to the Karaites at all, but to the Rabbanites who are here styled 'the perfect in the way', and it is of them that the author says 'they behold the secrets of the Torah [and] their heart conceives [the correct thing]'.

The following are my objections: (1) Zucker's interpretation, which takes the clause לבם ירחש as co-ordinate to יראו נפלאות, requires a *waw* conjunctive before the former clause. (2) The verb *yirḥash* has no object, and Zucker has to supply one: ת׳ ד׳ יראו נפלאות [ו]לבם ירחש [את הנכון]. (3) The strophe concludes with the curse 'may terror fall upon them', manifestly directed against the people spoken of in the preceding clause, who can therefore be none other than the Karaites. (4) His interpretation does not explain the import of the accusation 'they don a hairy mantle to deceive' and its relevance to what follows.

My interpretation fits the text as it stands, without having to translate a non-existent *waw* conjunctive and without being forced to supply an object; the latter is contained in the text itself: 'Their heart imagines: *the perfect in the way behold the hidden things of the Torah.*' This may be illuminated by Sahl b. Maṣliaḥ's statement: 'The perfect in the way pray: *Open thou mine eyes that I may behold the hidden things of Thy law*', and similar statements to the same effect by other Karaite writers.[1]

Moreover, according to my interpretation all parts of the strophe form a connected whole, embodying ideas that were prevalent in the Karaite-Rabbanite controversy. The Rabbanite author begins by accusing his opponents of false prophecy; he does so by utilizing the imagery employed by *Zechariah* (13, 4) to characterize the false prophets: 'They don a hairy mantle to deceive.' The false prophecy consists in the Karaites' claim that their biblical interpretations are the result of divine inspiration, whereas they are but the product of their 'divinatory method' (דרך נחש). The term 'divination' is frequently used to brand the activity of the false prophets *who say: Thus saith the Lord God, when God hath not spoken* (*Ezek.* 22, 28). See further *Jer.* 14, 14; *Ezek.* 13, 6, 7, 9; 21, 34; *Mic.* 3, 6, 7, 11. This accusation is but another instance of the well-known phenomenon, observable in all polemics, of the two parties each hurling at the other identical charges, and pinning the same pejorative labels at each other's back. The Karaites indulged with special delight in dubbing the leaders of rabbinic Judaism 'false prophets' on account of the biblical interpretations included in the Oral Law,[2] and our Rabbanite author reciprocates.

It is highly probable that in the expression דרך נחש lies concealed an interesting designation of the Karaite exegetical method of 'searching', coined by our Rabbanite author. The Hebrew נחש has been infused by him with the connotation of its Arabic equivalent (נחס),[3] 'to explore, investigate, inquire minutely about'—a linguistic phenomenon often met with among

[1] See *supra*, p. 83, n. 1.

[2] *Infra*, pp. 143–8.

[3] Judeo-Arabic scholars like the grammarian Yehudah Ibn Qoreish (*Risālah*, ed. Barges and Goldberg, Paris 1857, p. 85) and the lexicographer David al-Fasi (*Kitāb Jāmi*', ii, p. 266) identified the two roots. According to J. Barth (*Etymologische Studien*, p. 49, note 4) the meaning '*erforschen, ergründen*' is the primary signification of נחש.

Arabic-speaking Jews[1]—with the result that דרך נחש could convey the same idea as דרך חפוש, the standing title of the Karaite method of Bible exegesis. The term דרך נחש is thus a most felicitous coinage which, through its double meaning, stigmatizes in one single expression the Karaite method of 'searching' as 'divination'.[2]

Paraphrased, the above strophe says: Karaite scholars are false prophets, operating under false pretences: they claim to perceive the hidden things of the Torah through divine illumination, whereas the truth is that their biblical interpretations are nothing but the outcome of their own 'searching-divination'. 'May terror fall upon them!'

[1] Cf., e.g., the usage of the terms סבל, העתקה and הגדה in the sense of 'tradition' under the influence of their Arabic equivalents (N. Wieder, 'Three Terms for Tradition', *JQR*, xlix [1958], pp. 108–21). See also *supra*, p. 59, note 4.

[2] For other examples of Arabic influence on the Hebrew style of our author, see N. Allony, *HUCA*, xxx [1959], Hebrew part, pp. 10, note 66, 12, note 92.

CHAPTER III

MESSIANISM:

THE CORNERSTONES OF BOTH SECTS: SEARCH IN SCRIPTURE AND MESSIANISM

Enough has been said in the foregoing pages to establish the pivotal importance of searching in the Law in the Sect's system of thought. The second pivot around which the Sect's thinking revolved was messianism. If the men of Qumran searched the Torah with a view to discovering the true meaning of the divine precepts, they likewise searched, with equal zeal, the prophetic writings in order to elicit from them, in particular, the secrets of history, the mysteries of the 'end'. The attainment of knowledge in these two spheres was the aim and *raison d'être* of the Sect, the goal of their collective spiritual endeavour. In other words, searching in Scripture and messianism (or: knowledge of the divine commandments and knowledge of the 'end') were the two cornerstones upon which the entire structure of the Qumran community was founded.

It is needless to emphasize that these selfsame subjects were the two principal spiritual forces that dominated the Karaite mind, the distinctive motifs running like coloured threads through the fabric of their literature, sometimes parallel to each other and sometimes intersecting. This will already be obvious from what has been stated up to this point; but it is of no mean importance to find Karaite scholars declaring explicitly the aims of all their intellectual and religious exertions to be not merely the knowledge of the precepts but also the knowledge of the 'end'. These objectives were the ultimate destination at which the travellers on the path of Karaism were hoping, with the assistance of God, to arrive. In an exposition of *Daniel*, chapter 12, according to the Karaite sages we read this piece of *pesher*:[1]

[1] See *A Commentary on the Book of Daniel*, Arabic part, p. 141. The above translation deviates in some points from that of Margoliouth. In the epilogue (p. 151) Yefeth tells us: 'We have explained this chapter in accordance with what we have heard from the teachers of the *Galuth*, or read in their books.'

Many will run to and fro (*Dan.* 12, 4), this refers to the *maskilim* and seekers of knowledge . . . they will run to and fro in the Book of God like those who seek treasures,[1] and as a result of this *knowledge will increase* (*ibid.*); knowledge of two things: of the commandments and of the 'end'. God will not reveal the 'end' until they know the commandments. They [the *maskilim*] are the God-fearing men of whom it is said (*Ps.* 25, 14): *Those who fear God are in possession of His secrets.*[2] These secrets cannot be obtained save by search, cogitation and investigation into the word of God; compare the prayers: *Teach me, O Lord, the way of thy statutes*; *Open Thou mine eyes* (*Ps.* 119, 33, 18).

The point of contact between the two sects regarding a fundamental aspect of this nature must be considered a particularly striking illustration of the community of ideas existing between the two schismatic groups.

INCESSANT STUDY AND PRAYER AMONG THE QUMRAN SECTARIES AND THE KARAITES

An outstanding institution in the Qumran community was the practice of keeping night watches devoted to study and prayer. The *Rule of the Community* (vi, 6–7) contains the following provisions: 'In a place, where the ten are there shall not be absent a man expounding the Torah, day and night continually, one relieving the other.[3] And the Many shall watch together a third part of all the nights of the year reading from the Book, expounding the Law[4]

[1] On this imagery see *supra*, pp. 62f.

[2] Cf. *supra*, p. 84.

[3] על יפות = חליפות; cf. Ch. Yalon, *Kiryath Sepher*, xxviii [1952–53], p. 65; P. Wernberg-Møller, *VT*, 1953, p. 105.

[4] The term *mishpāṭ* is here used in a wider sense, denoting the Law in general. Parallels are to be found in Karaite literature. Daniel al-Qumisi (*Pithron*, p. 37) equates *mishpāṭ* in *Am.* 6, 12 with 'the Torah of the Lord' (משפט היא תורת ה'); the same meaning is implied in Yefeth's interpretation of *Isaiah* 58, 2 and *Ps.* 119, 62, cited *supra*, p. 62.

and praying[1] together'. The most plausible interpretation of the last sentence is that the members of the Sect were divided into three groups that took their turn during one of the three 'watches' into which the night was divided.[2] The first place in these night watches was accorded to the study and exposition of the Torah which was of such outstanding importance in the Sect's religious life, as pointed out in the previous chapter.

The practice of night watches devoted to study and prayer was also in vogue among the Karaites and formed a central institution, especially in the life of the ascetics domiciled in Jerusalem. The scriptural foundation of this practice was considered to be *Isa.* 62, 6–7: *I have set up watchmen upon thy walls, O Jerusalem, they shall never hold their peace, day nor night; ye that are the Lord's remembrancers, take ye no rest.* 'Watchmen' and 'remembrancers' were taken to refer to human beings[3] and the verses made to yield the injunction[4] to appoint 'watchmen' for the purpose of incessant study and prayer. Hence the frequent reference to these verses in Karaite writings.

[1] '*To bless*'='*to pray*', see Mishnah, *Rōsh ha-Shānāh*, end: מי שברך [Rashi: מי שהתפלל], and compare the significant phrase 'to pray benedictions' (e.g. in Mishnah *Ber.* iv, 3; *Tosephta*, Yōm ha-Kippūrīm, v, 14). Pharaoh's words *and bless me also* (*Ex.* 12, 32) are rendered by *Mekhilta*, Onqelos and Pseudo-Jonathan 'and *pray* for me also'. The term הברכה in Mishnah *Ta'anīth*, ii, 5(וגמר את הברכה כולה) is equivalent to *ha-Tephillah*, i.e. the '*Amidah*. The reading of MS. Munich (ואמר כל הברכות כולן) is a paraphrase of an archaic expression. Cf. further L. Ginzberg, *Journal of Jewish Lore and Philosophy*, i, p. 209, note and p. 278.

[2] Wernberg-Møller (*The Manual of Discipline*, p. 104) holds that 'the text refers to vigils in the third part of the night, i.e. the members were to get up at two o'clock in the morning'. This interpretation is not borne out by the text which speaks of 'a third', without specifying which third.

[3] Cf. Sa'adya's view, *infra*, p. 103, note 3.

[4] See al-Qumisi's *Epistle* (*JQR*, N.S., xii, p. 283): ואף כי ציוה ייי לאנשי גלות לבוא אל ירושלם ולעמוד בתוכה תמיד באבל ובצום ובכי ומספד ושק ותמרורים יומם ולילה ככ׳ על חומתיך יר׳; al-Qumisi finds the injunction of holding day and night watches also indicated in *Joel* 1, 14 (*Pithron*, pp. 26f.); Hadassi, p. 10b, letter *ḥeth*: חשו לקיים על חומותיך. . . .

The practice can be traced back to ‘Anan himself. First, the fact may be noted that the recitation of *Isa.* 62, 6b was assigned an important place in ‘Anan’s liturgy. The daily reading from the scroll of the pentateuchal section dealing with the daily sacrifice was concluded with the recitation of certain psalms by the Levites, while the priests recited *Isa.* 62, 6b[1]—and evidently also the subsequent verse which is its direct continuation.[2] The fact that the recitation began in the middle of verse 6 must at first sight appear strange, but the omission of 6a may well be due to its inapplicability in Babylonia (where ‘Anan composed his *Book of Precepts*); full effect to the first half of the verse could be given in the Holy City only.

Secondly, the practice in question was indeed prevalent among the Ananites, the close followers of ‘Anan, as we learn from al-Qirqisani’s *Kitāb al-Anwār wal-Marāqib*.[3] Discussing the seventy days’ fast (from the 13th of Nisan to the 23rd of Siwan) instituted by ‘Anan,[4] al-Qirqisani informs us that the Ananites did not insist that each individual should fast all the seventy days—a practice which they deemed humanly impossible—but permitted the fast to be carried out in shifts. Three people, for instance, were allowed to associate for this purpose and arrange for each one to fast once in three days only. As long as the fast was

[1] See Jacob Mann, ‘Anan’s Liturgy’ in *Journal of Jewish Lore and Philosophy*, i, p. 349.

[2] Mann, not having noticed the significance of this verse, felt impelled to assume that ‘probably the verses of Isaiah were continued till the end of the chapter’ (*op. cit.* p. 333). The recitation of these verses alone is amply accounted for, once their specific sectarian significance is recognized.

[3] Ed. L. Nemoy, p. 918 (transcribed into Hebrew characters): . . . אנהם אגׄאזוא צומהא משאמיר ודׄלך באן ישתרך תׄלתׄהׄ אנפס פיצום כל ואחד מנהם יום מן אלתׄלתׄהׄ איאם ויפטר יומין תׄם יעאוד פתכון אלסבעין קד צאמהא אלתׄלתׄהׄ עלי אן כל ואחד מנהם צאם מנהא אלתׄלתׄ וכדׄלך סאיר אלאמׄהׄ.

[4] For the Ananites’ contention that the fast is alluded to in the Pentateuch, cf. N. Wieder, ‘The Dead Sea Scrolls’, etc., p. 82.

observed by the community as a whole—so the Ananites contended—the law was considered fulfilled.[1]

As an analogy for the collective fulfilment of a religious obligation the Ananites adduced the case of the prayers for the messianic redemption enjoined by the prophet to take place unremittingly, by day and by night. Yet, because of the impossibility for the individual to conform literally to this injunction, alternating watches were instituted for the purpose of carrying out the injunction collectively, by the community as a body.[2] In this analogical deduction (*qiyās*) the day and night watches are taken by the Ananites as an established and generally acknowledged institution.

It was, however, among the Karaite ascetics in Jerusalem in the ninth and tenth centuries that the institution attained great prominence and occupied a position of first importance. It is a measure of its importance that the watches were represented by the chief spokesmen of the ascetics as the very *raison d'être* of their residence in Palestine in general and the Holy City in particular. It was only here that full justice could be done to the exhortation implied in *Isa.* 62, 6: *I have set up watchmen upon thy walls*, O *Jerusalem.* This idea recurs several times in the writings of the ascetic scholars. Thus al-Qumisi, in his *Epistle* addressed to his fellow sectaries in Persia and Babylonia urging them to join the partisans in the Holy Land, represented the holding of the watches as the very purpose of the settlement there:[3] 'Before the

[1] S. W. Baron, *A Social and Religious History of the Jews* [2nd ed.], vol. v, p. 216 writes: 'There is no evidence that this [fast] ever became accepted practice in any Karaite community.' Qirqisani's information shows that the Ananite community did practise this fast.

[2] *Ibid.* p. 919: ואקאסוא [אי אלעאנניה] איגאב אלצום פי אלסבעין יומא משאמיר עלי אלצלוה אלתי קיל פיהא על חומותיך ירושלם הפקדתי שמרים . . . אד כאן מן אלמחאל אן יכון גמיע אלנאס או ואחד או אכתר לא יסכת לא לילא ולא נהארא ואנמא דלך נוב אלתי הי משאמיר . . . פקאל פי הולא אלדין יצלון פי הדה אלנואיב אנהם לא יסכתון לילא ולא נהארא ליס אן כל ואחד מנהם גיר סאכת בל אנמא אראד אן גמלתהם גיר סכות.

[3] *JQR*, xii, p. 284.

ingathering of the exiles come to Jerusalem and stand before the Lord in day and night watches . . . It is therefore incumbent upon you, those who fear the Lord, to proceed to Jerusalem and settle there in order to hold watches until the day of the rebuilding of Jerusalem, as it is written (*Isa.* 62, 7): *And give Him no rest, till He establish, and till He make Jerusalem a praise in the earth.*[1] Or let us take this interesting passage, in which al-Qumisi appeals to his partisans to send at least five people from each city:[2]

> And you, our brethren in Israel . . . arise and come to Jerusalem and let us return to the Lord. But if you will not come because you are totally engrossed in your business and occupation, then send (at least) five men from each city together with their sustenance, so that we may form one fellowship to supplicate our God continuously upon the hills of Jerusalem in accordance with the aforementioned verse: *I have set up watchmen upon thy walls, O Jerusalem.*

The same idea is expressed by Sahl ben Maṣliaḥ in his appeal to the Karaites in the Dispersion to strengthen the sectarian colony:[3] 'And now, our brethren, return to the land of your forefathers to assist your brethren in front of the Hall of the Temple.' 'In front of the Hall of the Temple' was the place where the watches were held, as we gather from Sahl's statement elsewhere:[4] 'God . . . will support the hand of the Karaites who, by means of their good admonitions and writings to their brethren abroad, have assembled in Jerusalem righteous and pious men and have set up alternating watches to pray and to supplicate

[1] This is directed against those of al-Qumisi's partisans who maintained that it was not permitted to settle in the Holy Land prior to the coming of the Messiah; al-Qumisi designated them as הנבלים בישראל, cf. *ibid.* pp. 283, 284, 285. Cf. also Sahl's appeal in Harkavy's *Me'asseph Niddaḥim*, No. 13, p. 198: עתה התקוששו בטרם לדת חק, והם הצרות הבאות לעולם.

[2] *Op. cit.*, p. 285.

[3] *Op. cit.*, p. 199.

[4] *Liq. Qad.* App., p. 30; L. Nemoy, *Karaite Anthology*, p. 112.

before the Hall of the Temple[1] and to implore God to save the
lost sheep and restore them to their cities.'

In this citation the setting up of the 'watches' is likewise represented as the primary purpose of the settlement in Jerusalem.
This is also done by another member of the ascetic community,
Yefeth ben 'Ali, who writes:[2] 'The mourners for Zion will go
from the Dispersion to the Land of Israel and dedicate themselves to continuous study, prayer and supplication. They will
not flag in doing so until the salvation has come.'

But not only was the custom of the 'watches' as such common
to the Karaites and Qumranites; the motive and ideology underlying it were also of the same messianic nature, incessant study
and prayer being intended as a means of achieving the final salvation, a passionate all-out effort to accelerate the advent of the
Messiah. This has become apparent already from the passages
previously cited; a few more illustrations will be found further on.
The mainspring of this extraordinary exertion was the eschatological consciousness of the Karaite ascetics which I have
described elsewhere.[3] Suffice it to recall that they regarded
themselves as the *shābhē pesha'* predicted by the prophet Isaiah
(59, 20) and believed that they were to be instrumental in inau-
gurating the messianic era. Commenting on *Isa.* 30, 19 Yefeth ben
'Ali writes (according to MS. British Museum, Or. 2501,
56b–57a):[4]

> The prophet informs us that repentance of the nation will
> begin among the dwellers of Zion and Jerusalem; to them he

---

[1] Cf. Ben-Me'ir's description (Harkavy, *Studien u. Mitteilungen*, v,
p. 215): ותפילתינו עליכם תדורה . . . בהר הזיתים מול היכל ייי.

[2] See 'The Qumran Sectaries', p. 100.

[3] *Ibid.*, p. 271.

[4] וערף אן אלתשובה תבתדי פי אלאמהֹ מן יושבי ציון וירושלם ואליהם
ישיר בקולה ויקרא אריה על מצפה וגו' ואיצֹא על חומותיך ירושלם
הפקדתי שומרים כל היום וכל הלילה לא יחשו וג' והם אלקום יגֹתמעון
מן אלגלות אלי ציון וירושלם אלי מקום עבודת יי, לבקש ממנו תחנה
בעד עמו ישראל בלבוש שק ואפר ובכי ומספד ואבל תמיד יומם ולילה
מתפללים ומתחננים והם גודרי פרץ אילי הצדק ולהם אתת אלבשארהֹ
לשום לאבילי ציון וג'.

alluded when he said: *And the lion cried, Upon the watch-tower, O Lord, I stand continually in the day-time and I am set in my ward all the nights* (*Isa.* 21, 8).[1] See further *Isa.* 62, 6. All this refers to the people who will come together from the Dispersion to Zion and Jerusalem, to the place of the Temple, in order to intercede for His people Israel in sackcloth and ashes, weeping, lamenting and mourning. They will offer prayers and supplications continually, day and night. They are the *repairers of the breach*, *the terebinths of righteousness* (*Isa.* 58, 12; 61, 3), and to them were given the good tidings of *Isa.* 60, 3ff.

The rôle of inaugurators of the redemption which the Karaites assigned to themselves is graphically illustrated by this interpretation of *Mic.* 2, 13:[2] *The breaker is gone up before them*; the *breaker* is none other than the lilies, the *maskilim*, the *shābhē pesha*ʿ, the Remnant of Jacob. It is they who by their piety and unceasing prayers will break down the walls of the prison (captivity) and bring about the salvation. The idea of the watch-tower (מצפה) dominated the mind of the Karaite expositor and impregnated his exegesis; this is exemplified by the interpretation of *Mic.* 7, 7 (ואני ביי אצפה).[3] The word אצפה was taken by some exegetes as denoting 'I stand on the watch-tower', and as referring to the Remnant, the *shābhē pesha*ʿ who keep guard by night and by day and supplicate for the appearance of the salvation. Indeed the watch-tower may be described as the outstanding landmark in the spiritual world of the Karaite ascetics, and it is

[1] The same *pesher* interpretation is given by David al-Fasi, *Kitāb Jāmi*ʿ *al-Alfāẓ*, i, p. 151.

[2] MS. British Museum, Or. 2401, fol. 29b: עלה הפורץ לפניהם ויריד זמאן מתֿגר אלחבס הו ארץֿ אלגלות... פאדֿא גֿא בה אלקץ נבה פי מא בין אלאמהֿ שושנים משכילים שבי פשע שארית ישראל פהם אלדֿי יתֿגרו הדֿא אלחבס חתי יכֿרגֿו מנה ישראל ומענאה אנהם יסבבו אלישועה בדינהם וצלותהם אלי רב אלעא׳ עלי אלדואם.

[3] *Ibid.* fol. 56a: וקיל אן הדֿא אלפסוק אעראב ען שארית ישראל שבי פשע ביעקב אלדֿי הם מקאם אלדידבאן ליל ונהאר אלי רב אלעא׳ יסאלו אן יטֿהר להם אלישועה אלדֿי קאל ענהם על חומותיך ירושלם הפקדתי שומרים וג׳ ואל תתני דמי לו וג׳.

very significant that they actually designated themselves as 'guardsmen' (אלדידבאן) and 'night-watchmen'.[1]

Turning to the question of how the alternating watches were spent in Qumran, we recall that according to the *Rule of the Community* the programme consisted of (a) readings from Scripture, (b) expositions and (c) prayer. Precisely the same three elements in exactly the same order are mentioned by Sahl ben Maṣliaḥ as constituting the Karaite practice:[2] 'In the days of the "Little Horn" the Lord opened to His people the gates of His mercy and brought them to His Holy City, where they settled and built synagogues in order to read from Scripture, to expound and to pray all the time, and to set up [alternating] watches by night.'[3]

[1] See 'The Qumran Sectaries', p. 100.

[2] Cf. Harkavy, *Me'asseph Niddāḥim*, no. 13, p. 199: ובימי קרן זעירה פתח יי לעמו שערי רחמיו ויביאם אל עיר קדשו וישבו בה ויבנו מקומות בתוכה לקרוא ולפתור ולהתפלל בכל עת ולהעמיד משמרות בלילות. Sahl uses the verb פתר instead of דרש in the *Rule of the Community*. The displacement of the latter by the former is interestingly illustrated by the usage of פתרון in the sense of דרשה, 'sermon', in a letter (J. Mann, *op. cit.* i, p. 315) by the Palestinian Ga'on Solomon b. Yehudah (*ca.* 1025–1051): ויהי אחרי הפתרון ואדבר אל העם דברי רכות . . . והם . . . אומרים לי אתה אומר בפתרונותיך.

[3] Attention may be drawn to Sa'adya's interpretation of two biblical passages adduced by the Karaites as support for the practice of unremittent study and prayer. (1) According to Sa'adya the expressions 'watchmen' and 'remembrancers' (*Isa.* 62, 6–7) are not to be taken literally as referring to men, but metaphorically as signifying three abstract ideas (a) the degradation to which Israel is subjected in exile; (b) repentance; and (c) the divine promise of redemption made to Abraham and the prophets. This interpretation eliminates the strongest support for the sectarian custom (cf. *Oeuvres Complètes de R. Saadia Ben Iosef al-Fayyoumi*, ed. Derenbourg, Paris 1896, vol. iii, p. 140).

(2) *Ps.* 119, 148: קדמו עיני אשמרות ('*My eyes forestalled the night watches*') is another Karaite proof-text (see 'The Qumran Sectaries', p. 101). Sa'adya translated: '*My eyes overcame their drowsiness.*' This 'remarkable' translation was prompted by polemical considerations. (J. Z. Lauterbach, *Saadja Al-fajjumi's arabische Psalmübersetzung u. Commentar* [*Pss.* 107–24], Berlin 1903, p. 58, note 57, remarks: 'Diese Übersetzung . . . ist merkwürdig').

THE TERM *MASKILIM*: ITS MEANING AND MESSIANIC SIGNIFICANCE

One of the illuminating points of contact between the Karaites and the Qumranites is the term *maskil*, which occupies an outstanding place in Karaite terminology and which occurs several times in the Qumran writings, such as the *Rule of the Community*,[1] the *Benedictions* from Cave I,[2] certain unpublished fragments from Cave IV[3] and also in the *Damascus Document*.[4]

How is this term to be translated? What is its significance and what is its origin? These questions concern not only the term in the Qumran writings, where so much of the phraseology is obscure and uncertain, but also its meaning in Karaite usage. As will be shown, even in this latter case, its meaning has not been understood and, most especially, its messianic significance not recognized, although the literature of Karaism at our disposal is by far greater than that of the Qumran Sect, and notwithstanding the fact that a galaxy of distinguished scholars have been engaged in the study of Karaite history and literature for almost a century.

Students of Karaism such as A. Harkavy, A. B. Gottlober, S. Poznanski, I. Markon, J. Mann and L. Nemoy as well as the historians S. Dubnow and Salo W. Baron, and others, understood the term *maskilim* in its intransitive meaning, variously translating it as 'wise men',[5] 'men of understanding',[6] 'scholars',

[1] *DSD*, iii, 13; ix, 12, 21.

[2] 1QSb; Barthélemy and Milik, *Discoveries in the Judaean Desert*, i, pp. 120, 124, 127.

[3] See *ibid*. p. 121.

[4] *CDC*, xii, 21; xiii, 22.

[5] S. Poznanski in Hasting's *Encyc. of Rel. and Ethics*, vol. vii, p. 664; A. Harkavy, 'Zur Entstehung des Karäismus' in Graetz' *Geschichte der Juden* (4th ed.), v, p. 480; J. Mann, *JQR*, N.S., xii, p. 524.

[6] L. Nemoy, *Karaite Anthology*, p. 330.

'*Gelehrte*',[1] 'sages',[2] '*Aufgeklärte*', 'enlightened men',[3] '*Dekende*',[4] '*Einsichtige*'.[5] Accordingly, the term is no more than an epithet of self-glorification like so many others which the Karaites conferred upon themselves. The idea which the epithet was intended to convey is perhaps best expressed in the words of J. Mann and Leon Nemoy. The former says:[6] 'They regarded themselves as the *intelligentsia* of the time (*maskilim*) with the founder of their sect being styled *Rosh Hammaskilim*.' And the latter explains the epithet thus:[7] ' "Men of understanding" (Hebrew *maskilim*) is one of the terms used by the Karaites to designate themselves, as against their benighted Rabbanite cousins.'

This conception of the term is erroneous. It may be demonstrated beyond any doubt that Karaite scholars in the early period of Karaism used the term in its causative sense of 'those who make wise', that is, *teachers*, *guides*, *enlighteners*. It was only in the later period of Karaite history, which began with the destruction of their Palestinian centre by the Crusaders, when the Karaite aggressiveness and missionary propaganda came to an end and the eclipse of the movement set in—it was only then that the term

[1] S. Poznanski in *J.E.*, vol. iv, p. 433; N. Zobel in *Enc. Jud.*, v, 779; L. Nemoy in *Universal Jewish Encyclopedia*, iii, p. 467; *HUCA*, vii, pp. 321, 350. S. Skoss in *Enc. Jud.*, viii, 754 gives both renderings.

[2] A. Harkavy in *J.E.*, vol. vii, 439.

[3] A. B. Gottlober, בקורת לתולדות הקראים [*Kritische Untersuchungen über die Geschichte der Karäer*], Vilna 1865, p. 126: ומה שלקחו להם הקראים התאר הזה ביחוד, יתכן שדרך כל כת חדשה לקחת לעצמה תאר זה, כלומר שדרכה להשכיל ולהבין ולא ללכת כסומא בארובה אחר כל ישן ובזמננו נקראו כן הנאורים, ר״ל האנשים ששכלם נר לרגלם ואור לנתיבתם – דיא אויפגעקלערטען; Weiss, *Dor Dor we-Doreshaw*, iv, p. 49; S. Dubnow, *Weltgeschichte des jüd. Volkes*, iii, p. 465; Salo W. Baron, *A Social and Religious History of the Jews*, v, pp. 233, 257, 401, note 34.

[4] I. Markon, *Korrespondenzblatt des Vereins zur Gründung u. Erhaltung einer Akademie f.d. Wiss. des Judentums*, 1927, p. 21.

[5] Harkavy-Strack, *Katalog der Heb. HSS in St. Petersburg*, 1875, pp. 17, 58.

[6] Cf. 'New Studies in Karaism' in *Yearbook of the Central Conference of American Rabbis*, 1934, p. 221; *Texts and Studies*, ii, p. v.

[7] *Karaite Anthology*, p. 330.

began to lose its original connotation of *teacher* and lingered on among the schismatics—as a survival from a glorious past—in the faded, intransitive sense.[1]

It was Daniel al-Qumisi who first described ʻAnan as *rosh ha-maskilim*;[2] let us therefore inquire of him what a *maskil* is. Fortunately, we have an exceptionally clear definition from his own pen of what he meant by that title. In interpreting the heading of *Ps.* 74 he says as follows:[3] '*Maskil* is one who teaches and instructs Israel in the *Galuth* lest they go astray from the way of the Torah.' As the expression 'the way of the Torah' in Karaite parlance is a designation for the Karaite faith,[4] the definition says in effect: *a maskil is one who preaches Karaism.* In line with this concept of *maskil*, al-Qumisi compares the function of the *maskilim* to that of the prophets. In a comment on *Mic.* 3, 8 (*but I am full of power by the spirit of the Lord . . . to declare unto Jacob his transgressions and to Israel his sins*) he says that this verse refers to the prophets in the period of prophecy and to the admonishers and mentors (*maskilim*) of the people in the *Galuth.*[5]

The same meaning clearly emerges from Yefeth b. ʻAli's comment on *Cant.* 6, 3:[6] 'They (the "lilies") are called *maskilim* and

[1] A similar process took place as regards the epithet 'the Good Figs'. Derived from *Jer.* 24, it originally denoted the 'craftsmen and smiths', i.e. the scholars and spiritual leaders (cf. BT *Sanh.* 38a and parallels) who were exiled to Babylon with king Jehoiachim: the last prophets, Haggai, Zechariah and Malachi, as well as Daniel and his companions; all of whom the Karaites regarded as their spiritual ancestors, cf. Elijah b. Abraham in *Liq. Qad.*, App., p. 101: והם הנקובים נאנחים ונאנקים והוגלו גם הם עם שארית העם ותאנים הטובות החרש והמסגר ודניאל חמו״ע . . . ושארית אחיהם דתם דתנו ושבילם שבילנו; Hadassi, 22, end: המשכילים בעלי מקרא . . . תלמידי התאנים הטובות. Later, however, it was used to designate scholars and pious people in general, cf. Mann, *op. cit.* ii, p. 801, note 176.

[2] Cf. al-Qirqisani, *Kitāb al-Anwār wal-Marāqib*, ed. A. Harkavy, p. 280.

[3] Cf. *ha-Ṣōpheh le-Ḥokhmath Yisra'el*, viii [1924], p. 335: משכיל הוא מבין ומשכיל לישראל אשר בגלות פן יתעו מדרך ייי.

[4] See N. Wieder in *JJS*, 1955, pp. 11–12.

[5] *Pithron*, p. 45: הם נביאים בימי נבואה והמוכיחים ומשכילי עם בגלות.

[6] See the text *infra*, p. 116, note 4.

maṣdiqim because they teach Israel and induce it to repentance, as it is said of the *maskil* (*Isa.* 53, 11): *By his knowledge will my servant make many righteous.*' Another Karaite author, David b. Abraham al-Fasi, supplies this unmistakable triple equation מרשד = מורה = משכיל.[1] This Arabic rendering of *maskil* (מרשד) we also meet in Yefeth b. 'Ali's commentary on *Daniel* where משכילי עם (11, 33) is translated by מרשדי אלשעאב.

More evidential illustrations will be found further on. The evidence so far adduced is, however, quite sufficient to establish our contention and allow us to proceed to point out the significance of the title. First, it describes the Karaite spiritual leaders in their self-assumed rôle as teachers, missionaries and enlighteners. The hey-day of the Karaite schism was characterized by a powerful missionary activity carried out by a group of prominent scholars who, by means of literary productions, Bible commentaries, polemical treatises written in Hebrew and Arabic in prose and in poetic form, as well as by verbal exhortation and by disputations, vigorously propagated their sectarian doctrines. The epithet *maskilim* is expressive of this propagandist function. It is often coupled with such synonymous or analogous terms as מורים,[2] מלמדים,[3] מזהירים,[4] מוכיחים,[5] *teachers*, *instructors*, *warners*, *admonishers*.

[1] See *Kitāb Jāmi'al-Alfāz* (ed. S. L. Skoss), i. p. 225, lines 60–62.

[2] Qirqisani (ed. Harkavy, p. 297) tells us that the Rabbanites asserted 'that they—and not the Karaites—were experts in the Hebrew language and that they were the teachers and instructors' (יזעמון . . . אנהם אצחאב אללגה ואנהם הם אלמשכילים ואלמורים).

Invoking Qirqisani's statement as proof, Harkavy contended (in the Hebrew edition of Grätz's *Geschichte der Juden*, trans. by S. P. Rabinowitz, vol. iii, p. 488, note 183) that the use of *maskil* as a Karaite title is of a 'late date'. The force of his proof is: since in Qirqisani's time the term was used by Rabbanites in reference to themselves, the Karaite usage must date from a later period. Harkavy's contention has been restated by E. Eppenstein in his annotations to Grätz's *Geschichte* (4th ed., vol. v, p. 552, note 1). However, Harkavy's argument is based on a misunderstanding of the above statement. On the contrary, just the opposite conclusion is to be drawn from it—that by the time of Qirqisani's writing (937 C.E.; cf. L. Nemoy, *Karaite Anthology*, p. 44), at the very least, the title *maskil* had already been in vogue among the Karaites. What Qirqisani is saying is that the Rabbanites asserted that it was they,

Its deeper significance, however, lies in the domain of messianism, and reflects the messianic consciousness of the religious

and not the Karaites, who were the *maskilim* and teachers, repudiating the Karaites' right to use these epithets and claiming this honour to themselves. This claim is parallel to, and is of the same nature as, the other claim mentioned by Qirqisani in the same context—that the Rabbanites were the masters of the Hebrew language. This is unmistakably a counter-claim, a rival contention bearing a polemical imprint, intended to deny the Karaite assertion that they were the sole authorities in Hebrew and the exposition of Scripture. It escaped Harkavy's notice that already al-Qumisi, at the beginning of his career, styled 'Anan *rosh ha-maskilim* (see *supra*, p. 106). Two other sources, recovered from the Genizah and unknown to Harkavy, can now be added: the fragments from al-Qumisi's commentaries on *Leviticus* (see *supra*, p. 60) and the *Psalms* (*ha-Ṣōpheh le-Ḥokhmath Yisra'el*, viii, pp. 328–9, and 335).

The rival claim of the Rabbanites that it was the spiritual leaders in their own camp who were the *maskilim*, may be illustrated by Ibn Ezra's interpretation of *Dan.* 11, 33, according to which the words *and the maskilim of the people will instruct the many* referred to the sages of the Mishnah. This interpretation on the part of a scholar like Ibn Ezra is properly to be understood only against the background of the Karaite *pesher*, and it was intended as a rebuff of the Karaites' appropriation of the epithet in question.

As to the rival claims concerning the knowledge of Hebrew, mention may be made of the tract *She'eloth 'Attiqoth*, whose chief purpose is to disprove the Karaite claim; cf. especially *HUCA*, xxi [1948], p. 51, where the Karaite scholars are reported as boasting: 'The Bible is our inheritance' (לנו המקרא נחלה). Another Rabbanite writer likewise taunts his Karaite antagonists for monopolizing the knowledge of Hebrew, Bible and Massorah, challenging them to vindicate their assertion by answering his questions pertaining to massoretic items; see introduction to *Diqduqē ha-Ṭe'amim*, p. xxxviiif.

[3] See al-Qumisi's interpretation of *Zech.* 2, 3 (*Pithron*, p. 63) identifying the 'four craftsmen' with four outstanding *maskilim*: ואולי ארבעה חרשים הם ארבעה מלמדים חכמים יראי ה׳ משכילי עם אשר ילמדו בישראל חוק ומשפט וה׳ יושיעם. The full significance of this interpretation becomes manifest when we remember that in rabbinic literature this verse was invested with a special messianic import, the 'four craftsmen' having been identified with the four messianic figures: the Messiah ben David, Messiah ben Joseph, Elijah and Melkizedek (B.T. *Sukkah*, 52 and parallels; cf. N. Wieder, *JJS*, 1953, p. 162). In identifying the 'craftsmen' with *maskilim* al-Qumisi ascribed to the latter the rôle of artificers of the final deliverance. Cf. also Sahl in *Liq. Qad.*, App., p. 42: ישובו אל ה׳ ואל תורתו בדברי המשכילים והמלמדים; and the quotation from Yefeth b. 'Ali's MS. commentary on *Jer.* 31, 15 explaining

leaders of Karaism who regarded themselves as the inaugurators of the final redemption. The term is derived from the book of *Daniel* chapters 11–12 which the Karaite *pesher* interpreted as

that the *maskilim* are called 'the mother of Israel' because 'they teach and enlighten the people' (מלמדים משכילים), see 'The Dead Sea Scrolls', etc., p. 87, and *infra*, p. 115.

[4] Cf. the introductory paragraph to *Diqduqē ha-Ṭeʻamim*: זה ספר מדקדוקי הטעמים שהחביר ר׳ אהרן בן משה ממקום מעזיה הנקרא טבריה ... המשכילים והמזהירים יזהירו כזהר הרקיע; Hadassi, 33, beginning: משכיל ומ[ז]היר ומצדיק עם ה׳ ותוכחת להביע; Alph. 18, *waw*: המשכילים ומצדיקים ומזהירים.

An outstanding example of Karaite admonitory activity is undoubtedly Sahl's *Epistle* to Jacob b. Samuel which is (so far) unparalleled in Karaite literature. This distinguished 'warner' undertook journeys to various countries for missionary purposes, and it is significant that he describes his activity by the verb 'to warn', which occurs several times in his *Epistle* beginning with the programmatic declaration: אני מבית המקדש באתי להזהיר את בני עמי, 'I have come from Jerusalem to warn the sons of my people' (*Liq. Qad.*, App., p. 27; also on p. 30). Speaking of the duty of the *maskilim*—equated by the Karaite *pesher* with the *three-score mighty men* in *Cant.* 3, 7—towards their Rabbanite brethren, Sahl again describes this duty as 'to warn the people of God' (*ibid.* p. 36): ודעו כי עלינו חוב להזהיר לאחינו ... ששים גבורים וג׳ פתרונו הם ששים חכמים מחכמי ישראל יעמדו ויזהירו עם ה׳ ... ששים משכילים מוכיחים ומלמדים לישראל.

The two epithets, *maskil*, *mazhir*, figure as a title of a Karaite scholar in a text published by Mann, *Texts and Studies*, ii, p. 142. They occur, combined with *maṣdiqim*, in Saʻadya's polemical poem *'Essā' Meshālī* (see *Rabh Saʻadya Ga'on*, p. 519): שילא ושמלאי ... מצ[דיקי ומשכילי] ומזהירי. We witness here the arch-opponent of Karaism wresting these epithets from his antagonists and applying them to the talmudic sages—a well-known device in polemics (against M. Zucker, *Tarbiz*, vol. 27, p. 69). Cf. also *supra*, p. 107, n. 2.

[5] Yefeth b. ʻAli on *Isa.* 43, 8 (MS. British Museum, Or. 2501, fol. 235b) says that the words *the blind people that have eyes, and the deaf that have ears* refer to the Rabbanites who have eyes to see and ears to hear but do not listen to admonishers and *maskilim*. הוצא עם עור ועינים יש וחרשים ואזנים למו ... והם אצחאב מדהב אלתקליד אלדי להם אדאן יסמעו בהא ועינין ינטרון בהא לכנהם לם יסמעו מדבר מוכיחים ומשכילים. [As to the description of the Rabbanites as אצחאב אלתקליד see S. Poznanski, 'Anan et ses Écrits', *REJ*, 1902, p. 183.] Mention may further be made that Yefeth on *Am.* 5, 10 (MS. British Museum, Or. 2400, fol. 93b) interprets the words *they hate the admonisher in the gate* as referring to the *maskil* (verse 13). See further *JQR*, xii, p. 286; *Me'asseph Niddāḥim*, no. 13, p. 203; *Liq. Qad.*, App., pp. 30, 33, 36.

relating to the present time, identifying the *maskilim* of whom it is said (11, 33) that *they will instruct the many* with the Karaite teachers, thus assigning to them the task of preparing the way for the coming of the Messiah through their spiritual and intellectual activity among the people. Karaite writers employ not only the title *maskilim*, but frequently also משכילי עם,[1] 'the teachers of the people', unquestionably derived from the same verse; and it is this verse which they constantly invoke when speaking of their self-assumed task of disseminating the doctrines of their faith among the larger community.[2] From *Dan.* 12, 3 they likewise adopted the title 'justifiers of the many' for the very same reason. It may further be noted that the opprobrious term *marshīʿē berīth* (*Dan.* 11, 32) which figures as contrast to 'teachers of the people' (11, 33) was taken by some Karaite scholars as referring to their Rabbanite adversaries.[3] In fact, *Dan.* 11, 33 and 12, 3 belong to the most frequently cited biblical verses in Karaite literature.

Turning to the Qumran documents, we notice that the generally accepted translation of the term is 'the wise man'. From among the students of the Scrolls who have adopted this translation twelve names, chosen at random, may be mentioned: S. Schechter,[4]

[1] See al-Qumisi, *Pithron*, p. 45; David al-Fasi, *op. cit.*, ii, p. 651, notes; A. Neubauer, *Aus der Petersburger Bibliothek*, p. 112; Yefeth on *Cant.* 1, 2 says: קולה ישקני הו קול משכילי עם מצדיקי הרבים אילי הצדק אלדין עלי ידהם תטהר ישועת ישראל ומלכות צמח. In an ironical vein the Karaites are so styled by the author of *She'elōth 'Attiqōth* (*HUCA*, 1948, Hebrew part, p. 42). The expression שכל מבינים (*ibid.* p. 43, top) which caused difficulties to students of this interesting polemical work (see *ibid.*, note 108) is simply a paraphrase of *maskilim* (מבינים=*teachers*, cf. *I Chr.* 25, 8), necessitated by the alphabetical acrostic.

[2] Cf. al-Qumisi, *JQR*, xii, p. 286: ... והשכילו ללמד לכל יש׳ מצות ייי והוכיחו אותם בדברי שלום ולא בריב ומצה ככ׳ ומשכילי עם יבינו לרבים; Sahl in *Me'asseph Niddāḥim*, no. 13, p. 203; Hadassi, 125, *zayin*; 132, *lamed*.

[3] See *infra*, p. 137.

[4] S. Schechter, *Fragments of a Zadokite Work*, p. li, emended the text to read להשכיל; in note 5, however, he says that 'למשכיל (for the wise man) is not absolutely wrong'.

Dupont-Sommer,[1] Barthélemy and Milik,[2] W. H. Brownlee,[3] O. Eissfeldt,[4] K. G. Kuhn,[5] I. Rabinowitz,[6] H. Bardtke,[7] J. Obermann,[8] D. Flusser[9] and J. Licht.[10] On the other hand, there are those who oscillate between the two alternative renderings. Thus M. Burrows[11] and A. Vincent[12] render the term in the *Damascus Document* (xii, 21) as 'instructor', whereas in the *Rule* (ix, 12), where the same sentence occurs, they translated it 'wise man'. C. Rabin,[13] too, wavers between the two possible meanings; while adopting in the first instance the meaning 'wise man', he also suggests the alternative 'teacher'. Few scholars only seem to have decided definitely in favour of the transitive meaning.[14] But it is this that is the correct rendering, as may be clearly seen from the *Rule*, iii, 13 and ix, 17–18 where the function of the *maskil* is defined 'to instruct and teach, to admonish and guide'. This conclusion is now considerably fortified by the Karaite parallel where the transitive meaning of the term has been established beyond doubt. The Qumran sectaries likewise adopted the term as a result of a *pesher* which interpreted *Dan.* 11, 12 in terms of their own time. Y. Yadin has already called attention to the fact that

[1] *The Jewish Sect of Qumran*, pp. 121, 136, 138.

[2] *Discoveries in the Judaean Desert*, i. p. 120; see, however, p. 113.

[3] *The Manual of Discipline* [*BASOR* Supplementary Studies, nos. 10–12], p. 12; see, however, note 21.

[4] *Einleitung in das Alte Testament* (2nd ed.), p. 801.

[5] *Zeitschrift f. Theologie u. Kirche*, 1952, p. 298: 'für den Einsichtigen (Wissenden)'.

[6] *JBL*, 1954, p. 13, note 7.

[7] *Die Handschriften am Toten Meer*, p. 90.

[8] *JBL*, 1956, p. 286.

[9] *Scripta Hierosolymitana*, iv, p. 247.

[10] *Ibid.* p. 89.

[11] *The Dead Sea Scrolls*, New York 1955, pp. 361, 374, 383, 384.

[12] *Les Manuscrits hébreux du Désert de Juda*, 1955, pp. 141, 142, 191.

[13] *The Zadokite Documents*, p. 62; on p. 66, however, only 'the wise man'.

[14] So, e.g., G. Vermès, *Les Manuscrits du Désert de Juda*, pp. 152, 179; F. Nötscher, *op. cit.* p. 46.

the *War Scroll* was greatly influenced by *Daniel*, chapter 11, from which a number of recurrent expressions were derived.[1] This influence is discernible in other Qumran documents, too. With regard to the term under discussion reference should be made to *Dan.* 11, 33: והמשכילים יבינו לרבים which is re-echoed in the phrase quoted above למשכיל להבין and also in the *Damascus Document*, xiii, 7: ישכיל את הרבים. Of significance is also the fact that one of the key-words in Qumran literature, the term *rabbim*, is likewise taken from that book. Again, the expression 'those who act wickedly against the covenant' (*marshī'ē berīth*) used as a description of the Sect's Jewish adversaries is derived from the same source, the only place in Scripture where the expression occurs. As already noted, the expression is used as antithesis to *maskilim* (cf. verses 32–33). The men of Qumran, who believed that the Final Age had already dawned and were convinced that the prophetic promises were being fulfilled among themselves, dramatized the messianic picture drawn by *Daniel* and adopted certain elements of it in the organization of the Sect, just as they adopted features derived from the analogy between the messianic period and the exodus from Egypt. Consequently, the community in its entirety was looked upon as constituting the 'Many'[2] and its religious guides and teachers as representing the *maskilim*, while their Jewish opponents were regarded as the *marshī'ē berīth*.

[1] See *The Scroll of the War of the Sons of Light against the Sons of Darkness*, Jerusalem 1955, p. 255.

[2] It has been argued that the translation 'the great ones' is a more fitting description of the Sect than 'the Many'. This argument would, indeed, have had some force had the term been specifically coined by the men of Qumran to characterize their community. However, the term is not a creation of their own choosing, but a transference dictated by the sectarian *pesher*; it is by virtue of this *pesher* that they looked upon themselves as embodying the 'Many', and the word evoked in their mind first and foremost the messianic association of its origin in the Book of *Daniel*.

This word, too, is part of the Karaite vocabulary, albeit not in isolation (as in Qumran), but in the phrase מצדיקי הרבים; and here too the expression is messianically charged, originating as it does from the application of the *Daniel* prophecy to the contemporary scene.

THE CORPORATE IDENTIFICATION OF THE *MASKILIM* WITH THE SUFFERING SERVANT

In recent years a view of considerable plausibility has been propounded, *viz.* that the author of the Book of *Daniel* identified the Suffering Servant of *Isa.* 52, 13–53, 12 with the pious of his own day, the *maskilim*.[1] It is worth noting that the connection between the Suffering Servant and the *maskilim* had been anticipated by the tenth-century Karaite Bible commentator, Yefeth b. 'Ali, who was obviously drawing upon earlier sources.[2] The two figures, that of the Servant and that of the *maskil*, are for him identical and he particularly points out the verbal similarity between *Isa.* 53, 11: *My righteous servant will turn the many to righteousness* and *Dan.* 12, 3: *And the maskilim shall shine as the brightness of the firmament, and they that turn the many to righteousness as the stars for ever and ever.* In fact, the Karaite spiritual leaders were conceived of as fulfilling a dual rôle, the rôle of the *maskilim* visualized in *Daniel* as well as that of the suffering figure depicted in *Isaiah*. The features of the Servant were thought to correspond to the traits and experiences of the Karaite *maskilim*, to reflect their self-effacing humility, their suffering and degradation and their rôle of teachers and admonishers of, and intercessors for, the entire nation.

This corporate identification of the Servant is of interest also in view of the community of religious thought between the Qumranites and the Karaites. The thesis has been championed that the former considered their own Sect—or its leadership—as the corporate Servant of the Lord with certain soteriological functions.[3] If in respect to Qumran the thesis cannot as yet be

[1] Cf. H. L. Ginsberg, *VT*, iii [1953], pp. 400–4; W. H. Brownlee, *BASOR*, 1953, pp. 12f.

[2] See *infra*, p. 116.

[3] The question has been discussed, most recently, by John V. Chamberlain: 'Towards A Qumran Soteriology' in *Novum Testamentum*, iii [1959], pp. 305–13; Oscar Cullmann, *The Christology of the N.T.*,

regarded as sufficiently substantiated, it is an indubitable fact that in the Karaite camp the corporate identification indeed had its upholders.

As regards the interpretation of the *Isaiah* chapter by Karaite exegetes we receive the following information from Yefeth b. 'Ali:[1]

> 'Some Karaite scholars are inclined to interpret the chapter in relation to the *maskilim*, resting their view upon two arguments. In the first place, their characteristics answer to the description given in this chapter, and secondly, because of the word למו (in verse 8) which is plural. . . . As to myself, I am inclined with Benjamin (al-Nahāwendī) to regard it as alluding to the Messiah.'[2]

Yefeth did not specify any of the scholars by name who adopted the identification of the Servant with the *maskilim.* Today it is possible to state that al-Qumisi belonged to them. In his exposition[3] of *Ps.* 17 he interpreted *Isa.* 53, 6 (הפגיע בו את עון כלנו) as referring to the *maskil*, the intercessor for the nation (המשכיל הצדיק המפגיע) who by his prayers will bring about the messianic redemption. And in his commentary on *Hosea*[4] he applied verse 3, '*He was despised and forsaken of men*' to his fellow-sectarians.

London 1959, p. 57: 'There is much to be said for the thesis of W. H. Brownlee that the function of the Suffering Servant of God was ascribed to the sect as such, and that this function was concretely realized in the Teacher of Righteousness.' Also H. J. Schoeps in his recent book (*Paulus, Die Theologie des Apostels im Lichte der jüdischen Religionsgeschichte*, Tübingen 1959, p. 137) thinks that the Qumranites applied *Isa.* 53 to the 'Teacher of Righteousness'. This is also the opinion of Dupont-Sommer, *Le Livre des Hymnes découvert près de la Mer Morte* pp. 13ff.

[1] Cf. S. R. Driver and A. Neubauer, *The Fifty-Third Chapter of Isaiah According to Jewish Interpreters*, 1876–77, i, p. 20.

[2] This view is shared by Salmon b. Yeruḥim; see *The Arabic Commentary of Salmon ben Yeruham the Karaite on the Book of Psalms* (Chapters 42–72), ed. L. Marwick, Philadelphia 1956, pp. 113ff.

[3] Cf. *Ha-Ṣōpheh le-Ḥokhmath Yisra'el*, viii [1924], pp. 328f.

[4] *Pithron*, p. 3.

From the casual way in which al-Qumisi cites these verses with the sectarian interpretation attached to them, without specifically drawing his readers' attention[1] to the fact that the chapter from which they were derived is to be interpreted in terms of the *maskilim*, we may perhaps infer that in his time the interpretation in question had already been well known. It may well go back to 'Anan himself, who was not only 'the head of the *maskilim*' (ראש המשכילים), but was also the first to suffer from ostracism[2] and (if we are to give credence to Karaite reports)[3] on whose life attempts were even made by the adherents of Rabbanism. This is at present no more than a plausible conjecture which cannot be supported by more tangible evidence.

David al-Fasi and Joseph al-Baṣīr were also among the scholars who followed this interpretation. The former says that the words *He was oppressed, though he humbled himself and opened not his mouth* (verse 7) are a description of some of the Remnant, that is, the intellectual *élite* of the sect.[4] And the latter explains verse 5, *stricken, smitten of God and afflicted* as referring to the *maskilim*, the 'mother' of Israel.[5] Just as a mother, when protecting her disobedient son from the punishment of his father, becomes herself the target of his punishment, so the *maskilim* who intercede for Israel receive themselves the punishment intended for the nation as a whole. Hence, they are *stricken, smitten of God and afflicted*.[6]

[1] See N. Wieder, 'The Dead Sea Scrolls', etc., note 9.

[2] *Ibid*. p. 106, App., no. 2.

[3] According to al-Qirqisani (ed. A. Harkavy, p. 305) the Rabbanites sought to kill 'Anan but did not succeed (כמא קד טלבו איצֿא קתל ענן פלם יתהיא דלך להם). The same assertion is made by Hadassi, 99, *kaph* (omitted in the printed edition but published by W. Bacher in *JQR*, 8 [1896], p. 436): ובקשו להרוג גם לענן נשיא ישראל ראש הגולה נ"ע בגורלו. יען שחלף וחלק בדבריהם ברוב יראתו ושכלו. ולא נתנו אלהים בידי רשעי ישראל רועיך.

[4] Cf. *Kitāb Jāmi' al-Alfāẓ*, i, p. 104.

[5] To this title see above, p. 108, note 3.

[6] See P. F. Frankel, *MGWJ*, 1872, p. 215.

Reference should further be made to Jacob ben Reuben's compilation, based on earlier sources, where the Servant is identified with the '*maskilim who will receive instruction from the mouth of the prophet Elijah*'.[1] The interpretation was preserved until the fourteenth century, when the prominent Karaite physician and philosopher, Aaron ben Joseph (died *c.* 1320), championed its cause once again.[2]

To return to Yefeth b. 'Ali: it is interesting to note that despite his explicit view that the Servant is to be identified with the Messiah, only a few chapters later he reverts to the corporate identification with the *maskilim*.[3] This is also the case in his commentaries on the *Songs of Songs*,[4] and on the *Book of Daniel*.[5] Here he is particularly explicit, saying: 'In the chapter הנה ישכיל עבדי the prophet says: *By his knowledge will My righteous servant turn the many to righteousness.* In that chapter the groaning of the *maskil*, his griefs and his great knowledge and piety are recorded.'

Obviously the sectarian in Yefeth was stronger than the commentator, who was able to assert himself only when directly confronted with the task of expounding the chapter. Otherwise he followed the partisan tradition which recognized the chapter as a Karaite *testimonium*. The significance which this chapter assumed among the Karaites is best illustrated by the fact that it was

[1] Driver-Neubauer, *op. cit.*, p. 59.

[2] Cf. his *Isaiah* commentary, entitled קצור תכלית ישעיה, ed. Abraham Firkowicz, Gozlow 1835. Mention may also be made of Elijah ha-Melammed's comment on *Ps.* 31, 12 (MS. British Museum, Or. 1263, fol. 334b): רואי בחוץ נדדו ממנו: הם אויבי זה המשכיל . . . וי״א נדדו מרוב החולי ש[נאמר] כאשר שממו עליך (ישעי׳ נ״ב, 14).

[3] MS. British Museum, Or. 2502, fol. 149a: קד ד׳כר פי הנה ישכיל עבדי חסן טאעתה אעני אלמשכיל . . .

[4] On 6, 3 (edited Barges): ... בשושנים פדל אנה עאד אלי ישראל מן אג׳ל אלשושנים אלד׳ין כאנוא סבב חרכתהם אלי תורת יי כקולה ומצדיקי הרבים פהם משכילים והם מצדיקים מן חית׳ אנהם יעלמון ישראל ויסתתיבוהם כקולה פי אלמשכיל בדעתו יצדיק צדיק עבדי לרבים (ישעי׳ נ״ג, 11).

[5] Cf. *A Commentary on the Book of Daniel* (ed. D. S. Margoliouth), p. 140 (Arabic part).

incorporated in their liturgy.[1] I have stated elsewhere[2] that 'one of the principles which governed the choice of scriptural texts for inclusion in the Karaite liturgy was a specific sectarian interpretation placed upon the texts concerned'.

Finally, attention may be drawn to the fact that the Karaite *pesher* exegesis has been extended to other Servant passages as well. The 'I' speaking in *Isa.* 50, 4–9 is, according to Yefeth,[3] the collective 'I' of 'the *maskilim* of the Diaspora', 'the justifiers of the many', and the 'smiters' and 'those who plucked off the hair' (verse 6) are their Jewish adversaries about whose persecutions the *maskil* complained in *Ps.* 69.[4] Again, the author of the *Sermons*[5] expounds *Isa.* 49, 7 at great length and in a rather interesting manner as portraying 'the *maskilim* and mourners for Zion', their characteristic of self-humiliation, their total segregation from the Gentiles and gentile customs, and their glory and illustrious status in the messianic era.

THE ATONING COMMUNITY

Much has been written on the expiating rôle of the Qumran community. Notwithstanding their exclusiveness as a monastic society, they were concerned not merely with ensuring their own salvation but were motivated by the lofty idea of 'procuring atonement for the land',[6] that is, for the entire nation. They were envisaging and making institutional provisions for a time when their small community would be replaced by one embracing 'the whole congregation of Israel',[7] 'from children to women'. It was

[1] See *Karaite Prayer-Book*, II (Odessa), p. 42.

[2] 'The Qumran Sectaries', pp. 110, 288.

[3] MS. British Museum (see p. 116, n. 3), fol. 81b: הדא אלפצל הו מקול עלי משכילי גלות ומצדיקי הרבים עלי מא ידל עליה אלפצל.

[4] Ibid. fol. 83b: ואלאקרב אן יכון אלמכים ואלמורטים מן ישראל אלדי מנהם שכא פי מזמור הושיעני אלהים כי באו מים עד נפש.

[5] Cf. *Zion* (O.S.), iii, pp. 38–41.

[6] *DSD*, viii, 6; 1*QSa*, i, 3.

[7] 1*QSa*, i, 1.

their own piety, their steadfastness in 'keeping the covenant in the midst of wickedness', their constant study of the Torah and their night-vigils that would effect atonement for the people and bring about the national salvation.

As to the Karaite ascetics, we have repeatedly had occasion to refer to their ascribing to themselves the rôle of inaugurators of the messianic redemption. It must now be added that they also made the forthright claim of being instrumental in procuring atonement for the sins of the whole nation. This is, of course, implicit in the identification of the Suffering Servant with their intellectual *élite*. In this connection special mention is deserved by a Karaite interpretation of the words תשים נפשו אשם (*Isa.* 53, 10): '*Thou, O Lord, shalt take his* (the *maskil*'s) *soul as a guilt-offering*, i.e. his fasts shall be acceptable before Thee like a guilt-offering. Just as the latter brings atonement, so the works of the *maskil* will effect the expiation of the sins of Israel.'[1]

The same expiatory function is claimed by the author of the commentary on *Exodus* and *Leviticus* (MS.), preserved in Leiden.[2] Identifying the Karaite sect with the 'Remnant', he says that it was on account of their merit that the divine promise was made: *I, even I, am He that blotteth out thy transgressions for Mine own sake; and thy sins I will not remember* (*Isa.* 43, 25). The expression 'thy transgressions' refers to the capital sins explicitly proscribed in Scripture which will be remitted when the 'Remnant of Israel', that is the Scripturalists, will return.

[1] *Sepher ha-'Osher*, MS. Leiden, Catalogue no. 8, fol. 160a: אתה יי תשים נפשו אשם כמו קרבן אשם מע׳ [= מענהו] אלה התעניות שהוא עושה מקובלים לפניך כמו קרבן אשם. כמו האשם כפור, כן מעשה זה המשכיל, הוא יגרום כפור עונות ישראל... ועונתם הוא יסבל: יסיר מהם עונותיהם.

[2] MS. Warner 3, fol. 226b: ואמר „חטאתיך" (ישעי׳ מ״ג, 24) הם הדתות הרעות אשר עבדו אחרי הנביאים כמו עבודה של ירבעם...ולולי שארית ישראל שבזכותם אמר (שם, שם, 25) אנכי אנכי הוא מוחה פשעיך למעני וגו׳ כאשר יתחלצו ישראל מחקותם ב׳ נשים וימחה וימחוק דתם. ואמר פשעיך כי הם עונות גדולות הכתובות ימחה יי מהם כאשר ישובו שארית ישראל אשר הם בעלי המקרא.
This MS. is identical with MS. St. Petersburg, No. 588, from which S. Pinsker has given some extracts in *Liq. Qad.*, App., pp. 71ff.

Picturesque expression of the expiation idea is afforded by the exposition by Karaite exegetes of the *Zechariah* parable of the shepherd (11, 4–14). The 'thirty silver sheqels' (verse 12) stand for the sixty *maskilim*—identical with the 'sixty strong men' in *Cant.* 3, 7, 'the crown of the nation and its pride'. Thirty sheqels equal sixty half-sheqels, a half-sheqel being the 'expiation money' prescribed in *Ex.* 30, 11–16. Each of the *maskilim* is symbolically represented by the prophet as a 'half-sheqel' which is offered *to procure atonement for your souls* (verses 15, 16), thus describing them, in effect, as mediators of atonement.[1] To use Sahl b.

[1] Cf. Yefeth's commentary on *Zechariah*, MS. British Museum, Or. 2401 fol. 214b: ופסר „שלשים כסף" תלתין (צ"ל סתין) משכיל יקומו פי אכר אלגלות מן ישראל והם „ששים גבורים" אלדי וצפהם פי שיר השירים פיגו מן אלגלות אלי אלקדס והם תאג אלאמה ופכרהא וזעם אן „שלשים כסף" הם „ששים גבורים" לאנה ראי אן כפר נפש אלדי הו כסף כפורים הו מחצית השקל.

Liq. Qad., App., p. 36: וכמו זה אמר זכריה...וישקלו את שכרי שלשים כסף, וגם במשקל ששים גבורים, צדיקים ומשכילים, ואולם שם אמר ששים ופה אמר שלשים להודיע כי בקע הגלגלת לקח והוא כפר נפש, ללמדך כי כמו מחצית השקל כפר לכל נפש ונפש שנאמר ונתנו איש כפר נפשו לה', כן שלשים כסף ששים בקע. ופתרונו ששים משכילים מוכיחים ומלמדים לישראל טמאה וטהרה והם מכפרים עונות ישראל ובהם תבוא הגאולה לישראל ובהמצאם יתכפר עון העדה.

This exposition appears to be identical with one indicated, but not unfolded, by al-Qumisi, *Pithron*, p. 74: ואולם (ואולי ?) הם משכילי עם אשר יקומו בגלות.

The impetus to this interpretation, taking 'thirty silver sheqels' as a metaphor for men outstanding in piety and learning, the Karaite exegetes may have owed to the rabbinic interpretation of the same phrase as alluding to 'thirty pious men' who must be present in every generation, otherwise the world could not exist; cf. P.T. '*Abhodah Zarah*, ii (40c): ורבנן אמרי אילו שלשים צדיקים שאין העולם חסר מהן. In *Gen. R.* 98, 9 (ed. Theodor-Albeck, p. 1260) the interpretation is recorded in the name of Rabh, and the words used by him are: 'thirty mighty men' (שלשים גבורים)—a phrase which must have automatically evoked in the Karaite mind the expression ששים גבורים.

The idea of 'sixty mighty men' might at first appear to be a figment of the Karaite imagination, stimulated by *Cant.* 3, 7. This, however, is not so; the idea is encountered outside the Karaite camp, in the Coptic *Apocalypse of Elijah* (cf. S. Mowinckel, *He That Cometh*, p. 300) which speaks of sixty forerunners of the Messiah. The 'sixty mighty men' whose function is to prepare the way for the messianic redemption are, essentially, 'forerunners' of the Messiah. In fact, in a Genizah fragment of a Karaite commentary on the *Psalms* they are bracketed together with

Maṣliaḥ's words, 'they will atone for the sins of Israel and through them the redemption will come and by their existence the iniquity of the community will be expiated'.

PRINCIPAL AGENTS IN THE ESCHATOLOGICAL WAR

The most striking document discovered in the caves of Qumran is the *Scroll of the War of the Sons of Light against the Sons of Darkness*, the so-called *War Scroll*. It contains a detailed blueprint of the final war in history leading to the annihilation of the heathen powers and the establishment of the divine kingdom on earth.

The doctrine underlying this unique document is the view that the climax in history will not be achieved by divine intervention alone, without human participation, but that Israel will play an active rôle in this mighty drama. This doctrine is obviously inspired by *Ez.* 25, 14: *And I will lay My vengeance upon Edom by the hand of My people Israel; and they shall do in Edom according to Mine anger and according to My fury.* We have here another example of the decisive influence of the Book of *Ezekiel* upon the formation of the Sect's theology.[1] That the Qumran men themselves undertook the stupendous task of drawing up this elaborate military plan for the final war is in itself evidence that they regarded themselves as the principal and decisive actors in that war.

But how are we to account for the amazing fact that 'men of the perfection of sanctity', leading a pious life of asceticism, people withdrawn from the din of the world and dedicated to study and prayer day and night, whose writings breathe anything

Elijah, the messianic forerunner *par excellence*. The fragment (T-S Arabic, 22/17, verso) interprets *Thy rod and Thy staff they comfort me* (*Ps.* 23, 4) as referring to Elijah and the *maskilim*, the sixty mighty men (שבטך ומשענתך המה ינחמוני אליהו ואלמשכילים ששים גבורים).

[1] Cf. *infra*, p. 134.

but a spirit of bellicosity,[1] should have come to look upon themselves as the principal agents in a war of vengeance and total extermination?

The answer to this question is to be found in the sectarians' belief that it will be through the instrumentality of 'the saints of His people' that the divine judgment will be executed upon the heathen nations. This belief is implicit in the entire *War Scroll*, but it is also expressed there with an explicitness too conspicuous to be missed. Here are a few passages: 'The God of Israel has summoned a sword against all the nations, and by the saints of His people He will do mightily';[2] 'for in the hand of the poor[3] Thou wilt deliver the enemies of all lands'; '. . . and by the[4] perfect in the way will all the nations of wickedness be exterminated.'[5] Nor is this belief peculiar to the *War Scroll*; the same conception is reflected in the *Habakkuk Commentary* (v, 4): 'Into the hands of His elect will God deliver the judgment of all nations and by their rebuke all the wicked of His people will be condemned.'[6] The belief is further echoed in the *Rule of the Community* (viii, 6) which assigns to the elect, side by side with the task to procure atonement for the land, the rôle of executors of the divine judgment: 'To render to the wicked their retribution'.[7]

Undoubtedly, this belief the sectarians derived from *Ps.* 149 according to which the 'saints' and the 'humble' will wield the *two-edged sword to execute vengeance upon the nations and punishments upon the peoples* (verses 6–7). True to their *pesher* method, the men of Qumran naturally saw in the 'saints' and 'humble' of

[1] M. Burrows, *More Light on the Dead Sea Scrolls*, p. 357, says about the *DSD* and *CDC*: 'There is . . . not the slightest hint of a martial spirit.'

[2] *DSW*, xvi, 1 (ed. Y. Yadin, p. 348). A similar phrase occurs in vi, 6 (p. 294).

[3] See *The Qumran Sectaries*, pp. 283f.

[4] *Ibid*. pp. 97f; *infra* pp. 206ff.

[5] xiv, 7 (p. 340).

[6] Cf. F. Nötscher, *op. cit.* p. 163.

[7] Cf., further, J. Licht, *The Thanksgiving Scroll*, p. 50.

the psalm the members of their own Sect. Y. Yadin has noticed the influence of *Ps.* 149 upon the *War Scroll*[1] and he very aptly placed at the head of his work[2] the following two lines, from the *War Scroll* and the psalm respectively, showing the identity of view in both sources:

אל ישראל קרא חרב על כל הגואים ובקדושי עמו יעשה גבורה.
רוממות אל בגרונם וחרב פיפיות בידם: לעשות נקמה בגוים תוכחות בלאמים.

The spiritual kinship between the ascetics on the shores of the Dead Sea and the Karaite ascetics manifests itself also in respect of the eschatological doctrine under discussion. It is shared by the prominent representative of the ascetic community, Daniel al-Qumisi who, in expounding *Ob.* 1, 23 (*And the saviours shall come up on mount Zion to judge the mount Esau*), says:[3] 'The "saviours" are the saints of Israel[4] by whose hands God will execute vengeance upon Edom and bring about the salvation of Israel, as it is written (*Ez.* 25, 14): "*And I will lay My vengeance upon Edom by the hands of My people Israel*".' By 'saints' (*ḥasidim*) he means his co-partisans, as it is evident from his comment on *Hos.* 14, 8 where he equates 'saints' with 'mourners for Zion'.[5] This equation goes back to 'Anan who based his demand for the territorial segregation[6] of his adherents on *Ps.* 50, 5: *Gather My saints together unto Me*. Elsewhere al-Qumisi employs another, even more distinctive title for his partisans. Explaining the words *who traineth my hands for war* (*Ps.* 18, 35; *II Sam.* 22, 35) he says: 'The "hands" are the hands of the *Remnant* who are destined to

[1] *Op. cit.* p. 281.

[2] *Ibid.* p. 3; see also p. 17.

[3] *Pithron*, p. 40.

[4] Cf. *DSW*, vi, 6 (p. 294): להפיל חללים במשפט אל ... והיתה לאל ישראל המלוכה (עובדי' 23) ובקדושי עמו יעשה חיל.

[5] *Pithron*, p. 25; also p. 7.

[6] Cf. *infra*, pp. 154ff. This identification of the *ḥasidim* in the Psalter is also shared by the author of the 'Sermons' (*Zion*, iii, pp. 34f.) who interpreted *Ps.* 132, 16 as referring to his co-sectarians: הם הצדיקים החסידים המשכילים משאר׳ ישר׳ שמתענים ומקוננים בצום ובכי...

have a two-edged sword in their hands to execute vengeance upon the nations.'[1]

We notice that he, too, is inspired both by *Ezekiel* and by *Psalm* 149 and that he, also, equates the 'saints' in the psalm with the members of his own sect.

If the Karaite ascetics produced nothing like the *War Scroll*, the theological ground upon which this Scroll rests is nevertheless common to both sects. In essence, the *War Scroll* is but a tangible, concrete expression, a dramatic unfolding of an eschatological idea shared by the two sects alike.

THE SONS OF ZADOK

The messianic consciousness of the men of Qumran, their indulgence in *pesher* expositions and their tendency to dramatize the features in the messianic programme are likewise at the bottom of the rôle which the sons of Zadok play in the life of the Sect.[2] This rôle stems from the dramatization of *Ez.* 44, 15–16.[3] Since they interpreted the *Ezekiel* prophecy not historically but messianically, they had to accord a place in the organization of the Sect to the sons of Zadok of whom the prophet had predicted that they would perform the priestly functions at the end of days.

Some light may be thrown on this phenomenon by Karaite literature. Likewise in Karaite circles the *Ezekiel* prophecy was given a messianic interpretation,[4] and it is this interpretation which is responsible for the close association of the sons of Zadok with the messianic hopes and expectations of the Karaites. When,

[1] *Pithron*, p. 56.

[2] See *CDC*, iii, 20–iv, 4; *DSD*, v, 2, 9; *DSD*a (1*QSa*), i, 2, 24; ii, 3; *Benedictions* (1*QSb*), iii, 22 (p. 124).

[3] *CDC*, iii, 21.

[4] Yefeth b. 'Ali in his commentary on *Numb.* 24, 11 (MS. British Museum, Or. 2475, fol. 35b: ופי זמאן עתיד יכונו כהנים גדולים מן זרע פנחס ע״ה כק׳ (יחז׳ מ״ד, 15–16): והכהנים הלוים בני צדוק וג׳.

for instance, Salmon b. Yeruḥim[1] prays for the final deliverance and rebuilding of the Temple, he couples with this the hope to see the reinstatement into office of the sons of Zadok. Or we may take an example from Yefeth b. 'Ali who, in expounding *Cant.* 7 with reference to the messianic period, sees in '*thy nose*' (7, 5) a metaphorical allusion to the sons of Zadok.[2] These formed an essential part in his messianic pattern and could not be left out in a messianic exposition of the passage.

If we examine the passages in the *Rule of the Community* dealing with the sons of Zadok, we cannot fail to notice that although they are mentioned in the first place they do not possess the sole and final authority either in legal decisions or in the administration of the Sect; other members have a say in these matters, and it is the majority vote, and not the pontifical authority of the sons of Zadok, which is decisive in the framing of the Sect's way of life. Their position was more one of prestige than of real power, and out of keeping with the Deuteronomic legislation (17, 8–12; 21, 5) concerning the legal authority invested in the priesthood.[3]

[1] In the epilogue to the *Book of the Wars*, p. 131:

ירחם עמו הנאדר בגבורותיו
ויחיש לנו נעם בשורותיו
ויבנה ביתו וישכלל חומותיו
. . . .
ובני צדוק הכהנים הקדושים
אשר שמרו את משמרת התורה אל ה׳ הנגשים
חגים וזבחים וכל קרבנות
יקריבו בשירים וזמירות ונגינות.

See S. Zeitlin, *The Zadokite Fragments*, p. 10.
Cf. also Salmon's melodramatic outcry (*Zion*, iii, p. 92): !אחינו
התבוננו וראו איה הכהן הגדול בן צדוק הכהן הנמשח ליי לכהן...

[2] MS. British Museum, Or. 2514, fol. 91b: ויקרב פי תאויל לאפך אנה ישיר בה אלי בני צֹּדֹּק צדוק. The mistake made by the copyist in writing צדק instead of צדוק is noteworthy in view of the reverse case occurring in *DSD*, ix, 14 where בני הצדוק is written instead of ב׳ הצדק. Cf., however, P. Wernberg-Møller, *The Manual of Discipline*, p. 90.

[3] The absolute power of the Sons of Zadok is still reflected in *DSD*, ix, 7, a passage which must reflect an older tradition, as Wernberg-Møller rightly suggested (*ibid.* p. 134, note 16).

The reason for this can only be guessed. It is possible that the spiritual and intellectual stature of the priests who could trace their lineage to Zadok was not considered by the Sect sufficiently high to entrust to them solely and completely the conduct of the religious affairs of the community. On the other hand, the *Ezekiel* passage demanded that a place be assigned to them as religious leaders of the messianic generation; hence their ambivalent position.

This hypothesis enables us to account for a rather curious exposition of *Ez.* 44, 15–16 by the author of the *Damascus Document* (iii, 20–iv, 4). The exposition seems to reflect a phase within the Sect's development (or perhaps a divergent trend), during which the Sect (or the adherents of the divergent trend to which the author belonged) could not persuade themselves to assign to the sons of Zadok a preponderant position of influence. They were therefore compelled to interpret away the whole *Ezekiel* passage, making it refer to the Sect as a whole. By 'the priests' Ezekiel meant 'the penitents of Israel', and by the 'Levites' 'those that joined them', and—most surprising of all—by 'the sons of Zadok' the prophet meant 'the elect of Israel', that is, the sectarian community in its entirety.

An interpretation of this kind to a passage so simple and clear as *Ez.* 44, 15–16 can only have been dictated by the desire to eliminate the scriptural basis for the claim of the sons of Zadok to a dominant position in the messianic period, which the obvious sense of the passage implied, once the passage had been interpreted messianically.

As to the exegetical aspect of the interpretation, the question must be asked: What could have suggested the idea of regarding the term 'priests' as an epithet for the 'penitents of Israel'? On what grounds could such an exegesis be vindicated?

The answer is to be found in *Isaiah*, chapter 61, a chapter predicting the glorious future in store for the 'poor',[1] the 'brokenhearted' that mourned for Zion. In the messianic age, these will bear, among other honorific names, the title 'priests of the Lord'

[1] The Qumran *pesher* on *Ps.* 37 equates ענוים (verse 11) with אביונים, see the text in Licht, *The Thanksgiving Scroll*, p. 243.

(verse 6). Since the men of Qumran looked upon themselves as constituting the community among whom the messianic prophecies were to be fulfilled, they felt justified in taking the term 'priests' in the *Ezekiel* verse as referring to themselves, the 'penitents of Israel',[1] the *shābhē pesha'* of whom it was prophesied that they would see the 'coming of the redeemer unto Zion' (*Isa.* 59, 20). Note should be taken of the fact that from the same chapter (verse 3) the Qumranites also borrowed another of their *sobriquets*, 'the Lord's (eternal) plantation',[2] and, further, that the psalmist of Qumran saw in the 'poor' (verse 1) and 'mourners' (verse 3), for whom 'everlasting joy' (verse 7) is forecast, the members of his own sect.[3]

Here again we have a point of contact between the men of Qumran-Damascus and the Karaites who, also, were conscious of being the community of the 'last days'. Al-Qumisi, in a comment on *Hos.* 2, 1, claims the title 'priests of the Lord' for 'the pious remnant of the *Galuth*', i.e. the adherents of his own sect, explicitly excluding the followers of man-made commandments whom he likewise denies the designation 'My people' (*Hos.* 2, 1).[4] Chapter 61 of *Isaiah* occupied an outstanding position in the Karaite ideology, being as it is the sole source for the appellation 'mourners for Zion'. It is from this chapter that they also derived the title 'terebinths of righteousness',[5] standing side by side

[1] See 'The Qumran Sectaries', pp. 269f.

[2] In conjunction with *Isa.* 60, 21. Cf. J. Licht, *op. cit.*, p. 249, *s.v.* מטעת. It seems that also the idea of the messianic community consisting of 'Aaron and Israel' was exegetically connected with *Isa.* 60, 21—namely with the plural 'plantations' (so, definitely, in the *Isaiah Scroll A*; *Qere'* in MT.). As S. Schechter and other commentators observed, the allusion in *CDC*, i, 6–7 is to the *Isaiah* verse mentioned. A very similar interpretation is recorded by Yefeth b. 'Ali (MS. British Museum, Or. 2502, fol. 203a) according to which the plural 'plantations' referred to the 'house of David and the house of Aaron' (ישיר בה אלי בית דוד ובית אהרן).

[3] *DST*, xviii, 14–15.

[4] *Pithron*, p. 2.

[5] Cf. N. Wieder, *ibid.*, p. 292, note 148; P. Kahle, *The Cairo Genizah* (2nd ed.), p. 97; *supra*, p. 110, note 1.

(verse 3) with the title 'plantation of the Lord' borne by their kinsmen in Qumran-Damascus. This latter fact may be regarded, if nothing else, as symbolic of the close affinity of the two schismatic communities.

CHAPTER IV

THE SECT'S OPPONENTS

'DEFLECTORS FROM THE WAY'

The Sect's opponents are dubbed in the *Rule of the Community* (x, 21) as well as in the *Damascus Document* (i, 13; ii, 6) 'deflectors from the way'. The term is antithetical to the Sect's self-designation 'the perfect in the way'. The 'way' is, of course, 'the way of the Lord'—a term descriptive of the Sect's distinctive brand of Judaism.

To have 'deflected from the way' is a recurrent piece of invective hurled against rabbinic Judaism by Karaite writers. It should be recalled that also the Karaites looked upon themselves as 'the perfect in the way', and that they likewise called their faith 'the way of the Lord'. The phrase employed by them to express the idea of deflection is taken from *Mal.* 2, 8 '*And ye deflected from the way*' (ואתם סרתם מן הדרך). This, like many a biblical phrase employed by Karaite authors, is not merely a borrowing of a convenient scriptural phrase; the whole passage was expounded by the Karaite *pesher* as being directed against the priests and religious leaders during the Second Temple and against their successors, the 'shepherds of the *Galuth*'. It is particularly al-Qumisi[1] who is fond of using the *Malachi* phrase, but it is also to

[1] In the commentary on *Hosea* (*Pithron*, p. 1) al-Qumisi says as follows: 'In the days of the Greek kingdom, their heads, the Rabbanites, placed a stumbling-block before Israel in that they perverted the words of God and said to Israel: "What we teach you is from the Torah." The prophet, therefore, said about them (*Mal.* 2, 8): *And ye have deflected from the way; ye have caused many to stumble* (ובימי מלכות יון שמו ראשיהם רבאנין מכשול לפני ישראל במצות אשר הפכו את דברי אלהים ויאמרו לישראל כי מן התורה אנחנו מלמדים אתכם ועל כן דבר עליהם ואתם סרתם מן הדרך הכשלתם רבים).' And on *Mal.* 2, 8 (*ibid.* p. 78): ואתם יא כהני בית שני ורועי גלות סרתם מדרכי יוי הכשלתם רבים בתורה כי שמתם מכשול לפני ישראל בחלוף המצות ותאמרו זאת מן התורה.

Cf. further *ibid.* p. 8; *Ha-Ṣōpheh le-Ḥokhmath Yisra'el*, ix [1925], p. 140; *JQR*, xii, p. 474.

It is worth noting that the accusation of having 'caused Israel to stumble in the Torah' is repeated by other Karaite writers, too, who

be found in the works of Salmon b. Yeruḥim,[1] Sahl b. Maṣliaḥ[2] Elias b. Abraham,[3] Yehudah Hadassi,[4] and others.[5]

Although the phrase as such does not occur in the Sect's writings thus far published, an allusion to it may perhaps be detected in the expression סרי דרך (*CDC*, i, 13) which seems to have been inspired by סרתם מן הדרך. But if this is no more than a mere allusion, there is an explicit parallel in respect of another biblical verse, which was used by both sects alike to stigmatize deflection from the way on the part of their respective opponents. I refer to *Hos.* 4, 16 to which the *Damascus Document* (i, 13–14) has given a *pesher* exposition:

> And He raised up for them a teacher of the truth to guide them in the way of His heart and to make known to the future generations what He did to the last generation, the congregation of the faithless; they are those that deflected from the way, and the period is that whereof it is written (*Hos.* 4, 16): *Like a deflecting heifer, Israel deflected.*

consequently styled the Rabbanites מכשילי תורה (see *Liq. Qad.*, App., 100) and מכשילים (so Tobias b. Moses in MS. Oxford, Cat. No. 290, fol. 56b: ואל תשימיני מן המכשילים והזדים). It is in the light of this accusation that we have to read the passage in the anti-Karaite polemics which found its way into *Tanḥuma*, *Noaḥ* 5 (see B. M. Lewin, *Tarbiz*, ii [1931], p. 395; *The Mishnah of Rabbi Eliezer*, ed. H. G. Enelow, p. 259) asserting that God established the two academies for the purpose of preventing Israel from stumbling in the Torah: ולפיכך קבע הקב"ה שתי ישיבות לישראל... שמעמידין דבר על בוריו והלכה לאמתה ומביאין ראיה מן המקרא ומן המשנה ומן התלמוד כדי שלא יכשלו ישראל בדברי תורה שנא' (תהלים קי"ט, 165) שלום רב לאוהבי תורתך ואין למו מכשול. For another polemical allusion in *The Mishnah of R. Eliezer*, see *supra*, p. 66.

[1] Cf. *The Book of the Wars*, p. 81, line 57; see also p. 105, line 57.

[2] *Liq. Qad.*, App., p. 29.

[3] *Ibid.* p. 100 (twice); p. 105.

[4] *'Eshkol ha-Kopher*, 104, *hē*.

[5] Mosheh ha-Kohani, *Liq. Qad.*, p. 220; Simḥah Isaac Lutzki, *Sepher 'Oraḥ Ṣaddīqīm*, p. 17b.

It is precisely the same *Hosea* verse that Karaite authors apply to their religious foes.[1] The two sects have thus this piece of *pesher* in common.

THE 'THREE SNARES OF BELIAL'

The *Damascus Document* accuses the opponents of three grievous offences, three 'snares of Belial' in which they were caught: whoredom, unjust acquisition of wealth, and pollution of the Sanctuary (iv, 17–18; v, 6). The accusation of whoredom is substantiated by citing the opponents' practices of polygamy and niece-marriage. The first two charges are repeated in viii, 5, 7 (=xix, 17, 19). Similarly, the *Habakkuk Commentary* accuses the wicked priest of avarice and of 'robbing the poor' (viii, 10; xii, 10) as well as of having polluted the Sanctuary (xii, 8–9).

It is a remarkable fact that the same three offences are laid at the door of rabbinic Judaism by Karaite polemics.

1. To begin with the accusation of whoredom. The 'adulterers' in *Mal.* 3, 5 are, according to al-Qumisi, the rabbis who permit niece-marriage and are guilty of other incestuous practices.[2] These, he maintains, belong to the malpractices which the rabbis have adopted from the Gentiles and which the prophet Hosea was thinking of when he castigated them saying (2, 9): *And she runs after her lovers.*[3] Among the various forms of forbidden marriages on account of which the rabbis are decried, niece-marriage figures prominently and Hadassi, for example, is untiring in fulminating against it time and again.[4] As to polygamy,

[1] Daniel al-Qumisi, *Pithron*, p. 7; Yehudah b. Qoreish, *Liq. Qad.*, App., p. 69; Eliah b. Abraham, *ibid.* p. 102; Hadassi, 334, *qoph.*

[2] *Pithron*, p. 80 [=J. Mann, *Texts and Studies*, ii, p. 81]. According to al-Qumisi the term נאוף denotes all kinds of forbidden marriages. This is also the view of Saul b. 'Anan, see *Liq. Qad.*, App., p. 62. See further B. Revel, *The Karaite Halakah*, p. 70, note 101.

[3] *Ibid.* pp. 3–4.

[4] *'Eshkol ha-Kopher*, 332, end: התירו בת האח וילדי תולדותיה וקבעו זאת ההוראה ללמדה את בני ישראל ולשימה בפיהם להרבות זרע זנונים.... In Alph. 325, *rēsh*, Hadassi reproaches the Rabbis for having

although the majority of the Karaites seem to have permitted it, the view that it is prohibited had its upholders in the Karaite camp,[1] and the fact that Tobias b. Eliezer found it necessary to polemize against it is significant enough.[2]

2. Especially persistent is the accusation of unlawful acquisition of wealth levelled against the leading authorities of rabbinic Judaism who are accused of perverting justice for personal gain, of oppressing and exploiting the defenceless poor. The similarities extend even to phraseology. The *Damascus Document* (i, 19) says about the adversaries that 'they have justified the wicked and condemned the righteous'. Exactly the same words are used by al-Qumisi with reference to the rabbis.[3] By means of the *pesher* method he finds no difficulty in discovering that already Hosea had reproached them for these social crimes. The virulent expression *Those that slaughter men* (*Hos.* 13, 2) is directed, according to him, against the rabbis' spoliation and oppression, which is tantamount to shedding blood.[4] Likewise, the prophetic complaint *They fill their master's house with violence and deceit* (*Zeph.* 1, 9) refers to the officials and judges of the 'shepherds' who take bribes with violence.[5] Other Karaite spokesmen write much in the same vein.[6]

declared niece-marriage to be a meritorious deed: ... רגשו וצרחו ריבונין הקלו והתירו בת האח ובת האחות לאח... והעידו עליו כל הנושא בת אחותו ואחיו בקרב משפחתו עליו הכתוב אומר (ישעי' נ"ח, 9) אז תקרא וה' יענה; cf. also *ibid.* letter *pē*; 104, *'aleph* and p. 135.

[1] See S. Poznanski, *REJ*, xlv [1902], pp. 185f.; S. Schechter, *Fragments of A Zadokite Work*, p. xvii, note 16.

[2] *Leqaḥ Ṭōbh* on *Deut.* 21, 15 (ed. Vilna p. 70): כמה טעות טעו הקראים שאמרו ואשה אל אחותה לא תקח אלו שתי נשים ודבר זה בתורה ובנביאים ובכתובים שהיו ישראל נושאים שתי נשים. See also *ibid.* on *Lev.* 18, 18 (p. 102) and A. Büchler, *JQR*, 1912, p. 434, note 8.

[3] *Ha-Ṣōpheh le-Ḥokhmath Yisra'el*, 1925, p. 139.

[4] *Pithron*, p. 23 [=*JQR*, xii, p. 499].

[5] *Ibid.* p. 57.

[6] See Sahl's acrimonious indictments, *Liq. Qad.*, App., p. 31; *'Eshkol ha-Kopher*, p. 10b, top; Alph. 122, *shin*; 268, *hē*; 120, *mem.*

3. Especially significant is the fact that the imputation of having polluted the Sanctuary is likewise to be found in Karaite literature. To understand this imputation, at first sight so astounding, it is necessary to remember that Karaite controversialists were not content with the defamation of their contemporary Rabbanite opponents, and not even with the vilification of the mishnaic and talmudic sages; they went further back into history and denounced the priests and religious authorities during the Second Temple, from the time of the cessation of prophecy after the death of Haggai, Zechariah and Malachi—one of the most crucial and tragic historical events which resulted, according to Karaite historiography, in the emergence of rabbinic Judaism. The specific crimes with which the rabbinic authorities during that period are burdened were borrowed from certain passages in the Prophets, which were interpreted as reflecting the circumstances during the Second Temple.[1] The accusation of having polluted the Temple has been derived from *Ez.* 23, 38. Hadassi has preserved for us a long list of such charges, all based on the Prophets, which may be reproduced here in an abbreviated form:

> 'From the day when my staff Pleasantness was broken, when prophecy ceased on account of the sins committed by the evil shepherds, in the time of Haggai, Zechariah and Malachi; when after them the staff Injurers[2] that destroyed the vineyard arose . . . they permitted God's people the nine abominations and blemishes of the sacrifices mentioned by Malachi (1, 7, 14; 2, 8)[3] . . . they despised the sacred things and desecrated the Sabbaths of the Lord and polluted His Sanctuary and allowed all kinds of impurity (see *Hag.* 2, 14) . . . as it is written (*Ez.* 22, 8): *Thou hast despised My holy things and hast profaned My Sabbaths*, and again (23, 38): *Moreover this they have done*

[1] Cf. *supra*, p. 129, note 1.

[2] Cf. the passage from Yefeth b. 'Ali's commentary on *Zechariah* (MS. British Museum, Or. 2401, fol. 213b) quoted in my article *Three Terms for 'Tradition'* in *JQR*, xlix [1958], p. 120.

[3] Cf. Eliah b. Abraham in *Liq. Qad.*, App., p. 105.

unto Me: they have defiled My Sanctuary in the same day . . . Such crimes and others like them have the shepherds and sages of the Second Temple multiplied, acting treacherously against the Lord.'[1]

In view of this Karaite parallel I venture to suggest that the charge of having defiled the Temple made in the *Damascus Document* against the Sect's adversaries is nothing but a repetition of the charge found in the Book of *Ezekiel*, no more than a mere echo of the prophet's words. This suggestion appears all the more plausible when we notice that the charge 'they lie with a woman who sees the blood of her issue'[2] is likewise found in *Ezekiel*[3] and—in chapter 22 (verse 10) which also includes the indictment of illicit acquisition of wealth and of whoredom (vv. 11–12). It is significant that a Karaite polemic condemning the rabbis on account of the same offences expressly cites *Ez.* 22, 10.[4]

Further support for the suggestion may be derived from the fact that the Book of *Ezekiel* exerted a far-reaching influence on the Qumran sectaries, supplying them with a number of leading theological concepts. In addition to the ideas just mentioned, there is the dramatization of *Ez.* 44, 15–16 and the rôle which the sons of Zadok played in the life and thought of the Sect;[5] there is the expression גלולים which belongs to the characteristic phraseology of the Sect;[6] again, 'the wilderness of the peoples' which assumed a central position in the Sect's eschatological scheme is likewise derived from that Prophet (20, 35–39), as is the term

[1] '*Eshkol ha-Kopher*, 104, *ḥeth* to *gimel.*

[2] *CDC*, v, 7.

[3] The very phraseology תפם בהם לב ישראל (see Rabin) used by the author of *CDC* in connection with the three snares is inspired by *Ez.* 14, 5, as Schechter already noted (p. xxxv, note 18); see also Charles, *Apocrypha*, etc., ii, 809, note 10.

[4] Hadassi, 333, beginning: התרת העריות והתרת נדות וזבות מקורן הערו. ועליהם כתוב (יחז׳ כ״ב, 10) ערות אב גלה טמאת הנדה ענו בך

[5] Cf. *supra*, pp. 123–27.

[6] See *infra*, pp. 151ff.

'builders of the wall' as an opprobrious title of the opponents.[1] Last but not least, the famous figure of 390 years[2] which forms an important date in the Sect's chronological system has its source in that book, as has long been recognized.[3]

INTERPRETERS OF 'SMOOTH THINGS'

What is the meaning of the term דורשי חלקות with which the men of Qumran stigmatized their opponents?[4] What is the accusation lying behind it? The term as such, the combination of its two nouns, does not occur in the Bible; evidently, it was specifically coined as a derogatory *sobriquet*. What, it is worth asking, determined its formation?

I suggest that the term was coined as an antonym to דורשי התורה, and that *ḥalāqōth* is a description of the opponents' brand of Torah. That *ḥalāqōth* is an antithesis to Torah emerges from the words of the sectarian hymnologist who writes:[5] 'But they are false interpreters and deceiving prophets; they have devised wickedness against me, exchanging Thy Torah which Thou hast imbued in my heart for smooth things for Thy people.' Instead of the genuine Torah they offered the people 'smooth things', i.e. a Torah whittled down and made easy to observe by a lenient interpretation,[6] which resulted in a relaxation of considerable portions of the Law.

How was it that the Qumran sectaries came to use precisely the term *ḥalāqōth* with reference to their adversaries? The answer is

[1] *Infra*, p. 146.

[2] *CDC*, i, 5–6.

[3] Concerning the doctrine underlying the *War Scroll*, influenced by *Ez.* 25, 14, see above p. 120.

[4] See *Pesher Nahum* (*4Qp Nahum*) published by J. M. Allegro in *JBL* lxxv [1956], pp. 90, line 2; 91, line 7; *DST*, ii, 15, 32.

[5] *DST*, iv, 10–11.

[6] Cf. W. H. Brownlee, *The Biblical Archeologist*, 1951, p. 59; Cecil Roth in *PEQ*, 1958, p. 107.

provided by the *War Scroll*[1] from which we learn that the Sect designated the adversaries as מרשיעי ברית, obviously interpreting *Dan.* 11, 32:[2] *And those that act wickedly against the covenant shall seduce* (*or flatter*) *by smooth things* as describing the religious enemies who will allure the people with 'smooth things'.

The foregoing will now be illuminated by a parallel from Karaite literature. First, mention should be made that the accusation of leniency in the interpretation of the Law belongs to the frequent charges levelled against rabbinic Judaism by Karaite polemics.[3] It was by reason of this leniency, they asserted, that they attracted the mass of the people and succeeded in holding sway over the vast majority of the nation who preferred the enjoyment of life made possible by the rabbis[4] to the rigid mode

[1] *DSW*, i, 2 (ed. Y. Yadin, p. 254). Cf. Yadin's note on p. 255 and his Introduction, p. 24. Note further the expression מרשיעי יהודה in *CDC*, xx, 26–27.

[2] Yadin has observed that the whole chapter (*Dan.* 11) greatly influenced the *War Scroll* in general and its first chapter in particular.

[3] Cf. *Pithron*, p. 20: ובמרמה ובכזב פתרו תורתי להקל מצותי. On *Zech.* 10, 3 (*ibid.* p. 72) al-Qumisi says that the wealthy Jews in the Diaspora lent their support to the Rabbanite leaders because the latter made the stringency of the commandments light for them in permitting what is prohibited. Particularly interesting is the following passage (*ibid.* p. 67) in which al-Qumisi ascribes to the Rabbanite leaders a statement declaring that lightening of the yoke of the precepts is permissible so that the people may persist in their adherence to the Jewish religion: הניחו את רוחי (זכרי' ו', 8)...זה הוא דברי רבאנין אשר אמרו בכל המצות יכשר רפוי המצות להקל עול מצות מישראל להיות מנוח לנפשם בגלות למען יעמדו שם על שם דין ישראל. (The expression דין is to be understood in its meaning in Arabic: 'religion').

Qirqisani (*Kitāb al-Anwār*, ed. L. Nemoy, pp. 16–19), Salmon b. Yeruḥim (*The Book of the Wars*, pp. 98–107) and Sahl b. Maṣliaḥ (*Liq. Qad.*, App., pp. 28–30) drew up whole lists of charges of leniency against the Rabbis who permitted what, from their point of view, was prohibited. See also the following note.

[4] Hadassi, 134, *ṣadē*: צעד והלך אחרי התועים והמתעים...וכל אלה עשה למען שעשוע ועדון נפשו ובשרו...ומקל במצות ובדקדוקי חמרי תורת האלהים. The Karaite poet, Moses Dar'i (*Liq. Qad.*, p. 74) says: עינהם היו עורות על חמדם דת קלה, ויעזבו המצות החמורות. Cf. also *Zion* (O.S.), iii, p. 36.

of living demanded by Karaism, which would entail, to mention only two items, an extremely strict observance of Sabbath and festivals and keeping the burdensome laws of purity and impurity.

Karaite writers used the same expression, 'smooth things' (*ḥalāqōth* or *ḥalaqlaqqōth*), to characterize the rabbis' allegedly lenient attitude to the Law.[1] And in this case we are in no doubt about the origin of the expression; it is definitely derived from *Dan.* 11, 32 which was interpreted in relation to the Rabbanites who were consequently spoken of as *marshīʿē berīth*, or simply *marshīʿīm*, just as the Karaites identified themselves with the *maskilim* (*ibid.* verse 33). For all this we have express testimony.[2]

The term under discussion also occurs in the *Damascus Document* in the form דרשו בחלקות. The passage in which it occurs (i, 14–21) includes several points relevant to the subject at hand which may be discussed here.

1. First the phrase להשח גבהות עולם. This has caused students of the *Damascus Document* considerable embarrassment, as may be illustrated by the fact that R. H. Charles[3] placed the phrase in brackets considering it to be an interpolation not fitting into the

[1] Hadassi, 237, *mem*: מזבח וכהן אין ... ולא מורה צדק ללמדם תורה מאושה כי רועיהם התעום בחלקלקותיך, כל אסור וחמור הקלו והתירו על נקלותיהם, ושמו דרך מכשול לפניהם; 132, *lamed*: 'It is further written (*Dan.* 11, 34): ונלוו עליהם רבים בחלקלקות i.e. they [the *maskilim*] will now be joined by many of the people of God who have turned away from the words of the shepherds, who fed [them] with smooth things, with the smoothness of their lips . . . those who previously were unwilling to join and embrace the stringent ways and keep the prohibitions of the Torah of the Lord according to the teachings of the *maskilim*.' In 123, *hē* Hadassi explicitly equates 'the smoothness of their lips' with 'man-made commandments'. See also the following note.

[2] *Ibid.* p. 10b: המו מרשיעי ברית לפניהם ... הם הנקראים ומרשיעי ברית יחניף בחלקות . . . ונכשלו מרשיעיך ביד משכיליך; 125, *waw*: ככתוב אביך הראשון חטא ומליציך פשעו בי (ישעי׳ מ״ג, 27) על דור ירבעם ראשוניך ועל אנשי בית שני מליציך ורועי גלותך, זכרונם לרעה נזכרה מפי עליון ככתוב ומרשיעי ברית יחניף בחלקות וג׳ קראם מרשיעים; *Ibid.* p. 125d: ופושעים יכשלו בם בחלקות מרשיעיך.

[3] See *Apocrypha and Pseudepigrapha*, ii, p. 801.

context, while G. Vermès[1] preferred to omit it entirely. It has been translated 'to bow down the loftiness of eternity' (Schechter); 'to bring low the pride of the world' (Charles); 'causing the eternal pride (or: pride of the world) to become low' (Rabin); 'so that he brought low their iniquitous pride' (Burrows).[2] None of these translations, in my view, satisfy the requirements of the context.

It appears that the rendering 'to bring low ancient heights' is the correct one; we have merely to find the idea behind this metaphor. I suggest that it signifies 'to permit what was formerly forbidden'.[3] 'Height' (or 'hill') is a metaphor for prohibition just as 'valley' and 'plain' are used in rabbinic language as metaphors for permission.[4] This explanation not only suits the context excellently, but is in harmony with the charge brought against the Sect's opponents of having offered the people 'smooth things', mentioned in the very same passage.

2. The construction דרשו בחלקות demands an explanation. In the biblical idiom . . . דרש ב denotes 'to inquire of, to consult'—which meaning, if adopted here, would yield the sentence 'they consulted the smooth things', which is patently nonsensical. Our explanation, however, that *dōreshē ḥalāqōth* was intended as contrast to *dōreshē ha-Torah* and inspired by it accounts also for this construction: דרש בחלקות is used antithetically to דרש בתורה.

3. Regarding the expression ויבחרו במהתלות it is of some interest to note that Salmon b. Yeruḥim[5] in his polemics against Sa'adya uses the term מהתלות—a *hapax legomenon* in the Bible—several times to characterize Sa'adya's arguments in connection with the main controversial issues between Rabbanism and

[1] *Les Manuscrits du Désert de Juda*, p. 160.

[2] *The Dead Sea Scrolls*, p. 350.

[3] J. L. Teicher (*JJS*, 1951, p. 117, note 5) who took the phrase to mean 'abolish ancient customs' came very near this explanation; only 'heights' does not stand for 'customs', but for 'prohibitions'.

[4] Cf. B.T. *Ḥullin* 110a and parallels, and also *Yoma* 74b–75a.

[5] *Op. cit.*, pp. 49, 63, 68, 82.

Karaism, the Oral Law and calendation. It is perhaps a sign of the significance he attached to this term that he nicknamed Sa'adya[1] קושר מהתלות.

4. The charge contained in the words 'they looked out for breaches'—that is, for breaches in the law, for possibilities to circumvent it and avoid its rigidity—was frequently raised by Karaite authors against their opponents.[2] To what extremes they were prepared to go may be seen from the fact that the abusive term 'breachers' (*Dan.* 11, 14; פריצים) was interpreted in certain Karaite circles[3] as referring to the spiritual heads of rabbinic Judaism.

5. The denunciation 'they chose the fair neck'—that is, a life of pleasure and enjoyment[4]—is a recurrent vituperation on the part of Karaite writers of the followers of Rabbanism who are accused, as indicated, of having chosen the rabbanite way of life on account of their love of bodily pleasures.[5]

6. Finally, a word about the phrase 'they abhorred all who walked perfectly'. It is evidently based on *Am.* 5, 10: '*And they abhor him that speaketh perfectly* (*uprightly*)', as noted by the commentators,[6] but with a change of 'speak perfectly' into 'walk

[1] *Ibid.* p. 49.

[2] Cf. Salmon b. Yeruḥim, *op. cit.*, 104; '*Eshkol ha-Kopher*, 132, *nūn*; 140, *ḥeth*; 141, '*ayin* and p. 10a, *pē*.

[3] *Ibid.* 132, *nūn*: ובני פריצי עמך ינשאו להעמיד חזון ונכשלו וג׳ בבית שני נתקיימו אלו ונכללו בעניני זמנך. מן ימי גלות זו קמו רועים מחליפי מצות ה׳ הם הם שנקראו „פריצים" שפרצו תורת ה׳ וגדרה. This interpretation is not shared by Benjamin al-Nahāwendī, who interpreted the verse as referring to five pseudo-prophets, including Jesus; see Qirqisani, *Kitāb al-Anwār*, ed. Harkavy, p. 305; L. Nemoy, *HUCA*, vii [1930], p. 364.

[4] Cf. *Ex. R.* 51, 6: חמי קדל דבריה דעמרם, 'see the [fat] neck of Amram's son!'; *Tanḥuma*, *Ki Tissā'*, 27: חמי צואריה חמי שקיה אוכל מדידן שתי מדידן.

[5] Cf. *supra*, note 35; Salmon, *op. cit.*, p. 82; Yefeth on *Isa.* 29, 20 (MS. British Museum, Or. 2501, fol. 39b) says that the prophet called the Rabbanite leaders לצים: מן חית אנהם יחבון אלזודנה ואלאכל ואלשרב אלדאים ואלארהאט כקולה מערבא ענהם אתיו אקחה יין ונסבאה שכר (ישעי׳ נ״ו, 12).

[6] Already W. Bacher, *ZfHB*, 1911, p. 24.

perfectly'. This is of significance. The term 'to walk perfectly' belongs to the characteristic phraseology of the men of Qumran-Damascus who, it may be recalled, designated themselves as *temīmē derekh*—a designation also adopted by the Karaites.

The application of the *Amos* verse to the persecution of the Sect has its parallel in Karaite literature. Eliah b. Abraham applies it to the hostility evinced towards 'Anan by his contemporaries and to Sa'adya's defamation of him.[1] It may be assumed that Eliah is here following an older Karaite *pesher* which interpreted the verse in terms of sectarian history. In fact, Yefeth b. 'Ali in his commentary on *Am.* 5, 13 equated the *maskil* (verse 13) with 'him that reproveth in the gate and speaketh perfectly'.[2]

THE CHANGERS OF THE BOUNDARY

We now turn our attention to other accusations brought by the author of the *Damascus Document* against the Sect's opponents which are contained in the following passage (v, 20–vi, 2):

> 'In the period of the destruction of the land there arose the changers[3] of the boundary who led Israel astray. And the land became waste, because they spoke rebellion against the commandments of God given through Moses and also through His holy anointed ones, and they prophesied falsely to turn away Israel from following God.'

The phrase 'the changers of the boundary' may first be considered. It is derived from *Hos.* 5, 10, but it is not, as might at first appear, a mere borrowing, lifted out of its context; rather is it a pointer to the entire verse which, as we happen to learn from

[1] *Liq. Qad.*, App., pp. 103, 104: אשר חרף לענן משכיל הגולה כנואם הנואם ודובר תמים יתעבו; מפני זה מאסו לענן לעשותו ראש גלות להתקיים במו ודובר תמים יתעבו.

[2] See *supra*, p. 109, note 5.

[3] See Targum on *Hos.* 5, 10, as well as Onqelos and Pseudo-Jonathan on *Deut.* 19, 14 and 27, 17; hence the rendering *changers*.

both versions of the *Damascus Document*,[1] was interpreted in relation to the Sect's opponents. This is worthy of special note. The usage of a biblical phrase so integrally woven into the text turns out, owing to information elsewhere available, to be founded on a *pesher* of the biblical passage from which the phrase was taken.

The Hosea verse as well as the aforementioned damning epithet by itself were applied by Karaite authors to their own opponents. According to al-Qumisi, '*the princes of Judah are like them that change the boundary*' alludes to the shepherds of the *Galuth* who changed the Lord's Torah and His commandments.[2] Yefeth b. 'Ali, too, took the epithet in question as signifying 'changers of the Lord's precepts',[3] and the epithet itself, without citation of *Hosea*, is used by Hadassi to characterize the Rabbanites.[4] It is significant that he likewise uses its rendering 'changers of the Lord's precepts', for the same purpose.[5]

'THEY LED ISRAEL ASTRAY'

The religious leaders in the opposite camp are accused of leading the people astray. Leaving aside for a moment the nature of the

[1] *CDC*, viii, 3; xix, 15f.

[2] *Pithron*, p. 8: ואולם היו רועי גלות ושריהם כמסיגי גבול מחליפי תורת ה׳ ומצותיו על כן באחרית אשפוך כמים עברה.

To his interpretation of 'princes' as referring to the leaders of rabbinic Judaism, cf. his comment on *Lam.* 2, 9 (*JQR*, 12, p. 279): ... והם רבנין אשר בבית שני אחרי הנביאים ... עליהם כתוב מלכה ושריה בגולה והלא בגוים מלכי יש׳ ראשי גלות ושריהם... . See further 'The Qumran Sectaries', p. 286, note 109.

[3] See *The Arabic Commentary of Yefet ben 'Ali the Karaite on the Book of Hosea*, ed. Philip Birnbaum, Philadelphia 1942, p. 85, line 16: יעני גירו מצות יוי. Yefeth, however, does not explain the verse prognostically. Birnbaum (*ibid.* p. xxii) thought that Yefeth drew upon Sa'adya; as we now see, the explanation 'changers of the commandments' goes back to al-Qumisi.

[4] *'Eshkol ha-Kopher*, 139, *rēsh*: ... וללמוד וללמד מנביאי ה׳ ... או נלמד ממשיגי גבול.

[5] *Ibid.* 132, *nūn*: מן ימי גלות זו קמו רועים מחליפי מצות ה׳; *ibid.*, letter *kaph*: כי כל זמן ימי הרועים לא הזכר שם משכילים כי היו כלם הרועים ההם מחליפי מצות אלהיך.

misrepresentation of Judaism by which they are alleged to have misled them, we note that this is a theme which Karaite authors keep on repeating time and again. The designation 'misleading shepherds' (הרועים המתעים)—modelled after the expression 'the misleading prophets' (*Mic.* 3, 5)[1]—is a recurrent invective with al-Qumisi,[2] just as 'the misleaders' is with Hadassi.[3] Salmon b. Yeruḥim varies the first-mentioned expression into 'the wicked misleaders'.[4] The fact that he[5] as well as Yefeth,[6] who both wrote in Arabic, used the term 'the misleaders of Israel' in Hebrew (מתעי ישראל) shows that it belonged to the standing expressions of the Karaite vocabulary, which are retained in their Hebrew form even in an Arabic text, like, for instance, the term 'the way of the Torah'.

[1] Interpreted by al-Qumisi (*Pithron*, p. 44) as relating also to the leaders of Rabbanism. See also Sahl, *Liq. Qad.*, App., p. 31; Hadassi, 120, *mem*.

[2] *Ibid.* pp. 4 (twice); 8 (twice); 9; 45; 67; 72 (twice); *JQR*, xii, p. 474.

[3] See, e.g., 23, *lamed-mem* (twice); 134, *ṣadē*.

[4] *The Arabic Commentary . . . on the Book of Psalms* (ed. L. Marwick), p. 61.

[5] In the commentary on *Lam.* 2, 14 (MS. British Museum, Or. 2515, fols. 102b–103a) Salmon included an allegorical interpretation of *Cant.* 2, 15, according to which 'the little foxes' are 'those who led Israel astray in the period of the *Galuth*' in contrast to the false prophets of old who were the 'big foxes':
...כשועלים בחרבות נביאיך ישראל היו (יחזקאל י״ג, 4) מתֿל מתעי ישראל בשועלים אלדֿי הם מפסדין אלכרום כקוֿ שלמה (שה״ש, ב׳ 15) אחזו לנו שועלים שועלים קטנים מחבלים כרמים ערף אן האהנא שועלים גדולים איצֿא פשועלים גדולים מתֿל ירבעם בן נבט ובעשא ועמרי ואחאב וסאיר נביאי שקר ואמא שועלים קטנים ישיר אלי מתעיי ישראל פי זמאן אלגלות ועלי מא שרחת פי שיר השירים פי ענין רעה צאן ההרגה (זכריה י״א, 4) וקוֿ הוי רועי האליל עוזבי הצאן (שם, שם. 17) פי אלגֿמיע קאל (יחז׳ י״ג, 9) והיתה ידי על הנביאים החזים שוא והקסמים כזב בסוד עמי לא יהיו ובכתב בית ישראל לא יכתבו ואל אדמת ישראל לא יבאו.
Another example is to be found in his commentary on the *Psalms*, p. 62.

[6] On *Cant.* 2, 15: והולאי אלשועלים הם מתעי ישראל מדרך התורה (so according to MSS. British Museum, Or. 2513, fol. 77b and 2514, fol. 7a; Barges' edition reads: הם אלמינים which appears to be a 'correction' by a Rabbanite reader, who retaliated by making the verse refer to the Karaites who were classified as *minim*). The application of *Cant.* 2, 15 to the Rabbis is shared by Sahl, cf. the polemical poem against Jacob b. Samuel (*Liq. Qad.*, App. 23, top).

The attack on the integrity of the rabbis was rebutted by Sa'adya in the polemical poem *'Essā' Meshālī*.[1] The Karaite controversialist asserted that the sages of the Mishnah misled the people from motives of material gain. The Ga'on pointed out that it was absurd to level accusations of deception against people like Rabbi 'Akiba and his fellow martyrs who 'stretched out their necks to sword and slaughter' and suffered martyrdom precisely because they refused to deceive.

THE ACCUSATION OF FALSE PROPHECY

We now come to the charge of false prophecy—a charge alluded to also in other passages in the *Damascus Document*, to be discussed later. Here mention should be made of the fact that the psalmist of Qumran forthrightly called his opponents '*lying prophets*' and '*deceiving seers*'.[2] They are thus accused of false pretences; of claiming divine origin for something which is but the product of their own minds. To be more specific, they are charged with representing their own interpretations of the Law as emanating from God Himself. The same idea is reflected in the words, 'they spoke rebellion against the commandments of God given through Moses and also through His holy anointed ones', immediately preceding the phrase under consideration. The expression *dibber sārāh* is used of false prophets in *Deut.* 13, 6 and *Jer.* 28, 16; 29, 32.[3]

The description of the religious leaders of rabbinic Judaism as 'false prophets' is a polemical *motif* in Karaite writings. The

[1] See *Rabh Sa'adya Ga'on* (ed. J. L. Fishman), p. 517.

[2] *DST*, iv, 10, 16.

[3] Cf. *Siphrē* on *Deut.*, 86 (ed. M. Friedmann, p. 92a): דבר סרה על יי אלהיכם והרי דברים קל וחומר ומה המזייף דברי חברו חייב מיתה המזייף דבריו של מקום עאכ"ו. See also Rashi on *Deut.* 13, 6: דבר המוסר מן העולם שלא היה ולא נברא ולא צויתיו לדבר כן. It is in this sense that Aaron b. Elijah of Nicomedia employed the expression in reference to the alleged rabbinic falsification of the divine laws (*Gan 'Eden*, 10c): ...ודבור סרה במצות השם להחליף המועדים מזמנם והנה הכתוב צווה אלה מועדי יי. [See Addenda.]

Karaite onslaught was directed not so much against the divergent interpretation of the Torah by the rabbis, however false, in the Karaite view, but against the insistence that this interpretation had been given to Moses side by side with the written Torah. It was this claim of divine origin for rabbinic interpretations that formed the bone of contention between the rival camps and was the principal target of the Karaite attack.[1] The champions of Karaism reiterated that rabbinic Judaism was nothing but a fabrication of the rabbis, 'invented out of their own hearts'—as a common Karaite phrase runs[2]—and that by attributing it to God the rabbis are lying against God and are therefore on a par with the false prophets of old.[3] Zephaniah's strictures: *Her prophets are wanton and treacherous persons* (3, 4) refer to 'the [rabbinic] Bible expounders who are not ashamed of the false interpretations that are contrary to the Torah';[4] and Hosea's words: *They have*

[1] Cf. *Pithron*, pp. 1 and 78 (cited above, p. 129, note 1).

[2] Here are a few examples: al-Qumisi in his *Epistle* (*JQR*, xii, p. 279) writes: ולא מן התורה למדו לישראל כי בדו מלבם מצות; *ibid.* p. 499 (cf. *Pithron*, p. 22): ועוד התעו במצות אנשים מל׳ אשר הם בודים מדעת לבבם.

Sahl b. Maṣliaḥ (*Liq. Qad.*, App., p. 24): ויחפאו מלבם דברים שקרים, לא מפי אלהים ולא מדברי נביאים אמורים, כי אם בדאום מלבם. Hadassi, 359, *zayin*: ... שטרפות האלה מלבם בדו חכמיך כתבו וחקקו מה שלא נכתב ונחקק ונחתם בטבעת המלך (אות כ׳).

Aaron b. Elijah of Nicomedia (*Gan 'Eden*, p. 8b): אין זה כי אם בדיאות הלב... ואולם זה הדבר שבדו אותו מלבם שמוהו כמצות התורה. As is usual with polemicists, Sa'adya (*'Essā' Meshālī*, p. 527) pays back in the same coin and thrusts this charge at his Karaite opponents:

לֹא שָׁאוּל אֶשְׁאָלְךָ לְלַמְּדָם
כִּי מִלִּבְּךָ אַתָּה בוֹדָאם
וְלֹא מִפִּי שׁוֹכֵן מְעוֹנָה.

[3] Al-Qumisi, *Pithron*, p. 67: ...כי הם אומרים שקר על אלהי השמים ומתעים את עם הארץ; Sahl (*ibid.* p. 23): לא יראו מדבר על השם שקרים; Tobias b. Moses (in אוצר נחמד, MS. Oxford, Cat. No. 290, fol. 96a), polemizing against Sa'adya, says as follows: ואם תהיה אתה וכלל קהלך תאמ׳ כי המשנה והגלמוד (= תלמוד) הם דבר יי יתש׳ דבר אותו למשה ע״ה מלה במלה כמ׳ התורה הכתובה דע כי זה שקר אתה מתנבא.

[4] *Pithron*, p. 58.

spoken lies against Me (7, 13) are aimed at both the false prophets of old as well as at the leaders in the *Galuth* who turned the divine commandments into lies.[1] The rabbis are, according to another *pesher*, the *teraphim*, the lying oracles of whom it is said: *For the teraphim have spoken vanity, and the diviners have seen a lie* (*Zech.* 10, 2).[2]

Illuminating is al-Qumisi's interpretation of *Dan.* 9, 24, *to seal vision and prophet*, as forecasting the end of the false prophets. He rejects the common view that the phrase signified the cessation of true prophecy, contending that Daniel foretells here the ultimate elimination of the false prophets (i.e. the Rabbanite spiritual leaders) at the end of the *Galuth*, prior to the coming of the Messiah. He invokes *Ez.* 13, 9, 23, predicting the doom of the false prophets.[3] Revealing is also Salmon's *pesher* on *Zech.* 13, 2: *And also I will cause the prophets and the unclean spirits to pass out of the land*. He has 'no doubt' in his mind that that referred to 'the misleaders of Israel'.[4] How ingrained in his mind the equation of the latter with false prophets was may be illustrated by yet another *pesher* of his, this time on *Prov.* 9, 13–18 which he interpreted as characterizing Rabbanism, represented here, as in *Zech.* 5, 7, under the figure of a (foolish) woman. The reference to false prophecy was read into the words 'stolen waters' (verse 17) on the basis of *Jer.* 23, 30, where the false prophets are described as 'those who steal My words'.[5]

To revert to al-Qumisi; his reference to chapter 13 of *Ezekiel* suggests that he expounded that chapter in relation to the 'false prophets' of rabbinic Judaism, *who prophesy out of their own*

[1] *Ibid.* p. 11.

[2] *Ibid.* p. 72. See further pp. 9 (on *Hos.* 6, 5) and 44 (on *Mic.* 3, 5).

[3] Cf. the Genizah fragment from his commentary on *Daniel*, *JQR*, xii, pp. 459f. The description of the rabbis as 'false prophets' also underlies al-Qumisi's interpretation of *Hos.* 9, 7–8, see *Pithron*, p. 15 (*JQR*, xii, p. 485).

[4] In his commentary on *Ps.* 58, 11 (ed. Marwick, p. 61).

[5] *Ibid.* p. 103. Cf. also Hadassi 180, *mem*: מסתירי עצה מגנבי דברים כנביאי כזב ושקרים.

heart (2, 17), who *say: The Lord saith; albeit He has not spoken* (7). This is borne out by his explanation of verses 17–18 where he expressly states that Ezekiel speaks of 'the shepherds of the *Galuth* who led Israel astray'.[1] This exposition of *Ez.* 13 was also shared by other prominent exponents of Karaism, like Salmon b. Yeruḥim,[2] the author of an anti-Rabbanite polemical treatise,[3] Tobias b. Moses[4] and Yehudah Hadassi.[5] It thus represents a widespread and persistent Karaite *pesher*.

'THE BUILDERS OF THE WALL'

This leads us back to the *Damascus Document* which describes the Sect's rivals as 'the builders of the wall'[6]—a phrase taken from *Ez.* 13, 10. The meaning of the phrase has long been the subject of controversy. S. Schechter,[7] followed by others,[8] saw in it an allusion to the Pharisees who 'raised a fence around the law'. But as Louis Ginzberg[9] rightly pointed out, this interpretation overlooks the fact that the opponents are not merely denounced as 'builders of the wall' but also as 'those who daubed it with whitewash'. There can be no doubt, therefore, that here, as in *Ezekiel*, the phrase is used as a metaphorical description of the

[1] *Pithron*, p. 8.

[2] Cf. *supra*, p. 142, note 5 and his commentary on the *Psalms*, p. 104.

[3] See *Tarbiz*, iv [1933], pp. 42, 194.

[4] Cf. the passage from his '*Oṣar Neḥmad* published by S. Poznanski in *REJ*, xliv [1902], p. 186: ...והוציאו והדיחו את יש׳ בשקרותם בכזבם את עמי שומעי כזב (יחזקאל י״ג, 19) וייגעו בדברי פתיות ואומ׳ בבת קול יאמינו להם לכן קראם אלה „כוזבים" וקרא אלה „שומעי כזב".

[5] Cf. '*Eshkol ha-Kopher*, pp. 10a, end; 135, *s.v.* בתוך.

[6] *CDC*, iv, 19; viii, 12, 18; xix, 25.

[7] *Op. cit.*, p. xxxvi, note 22.

[8] Cf. Charles, *Apocrypha and Pseudepigrapha*, pp. 818f.; I. Lévi, *REJ*, 1911, p. 180, note 2; J. M. Grintz, *Sinai*, 1952, p. 37. M. Z. Segal, *JBL*, 1951, 144: 'Builders of the party-wall'.

[9] *MGWJ*, 1912, p. 286; cf. also R. Leszynsky, *REJ*, 1912, p. 192.

false prophets who by 'whitewashing' the 'wall' of their own making seek to deceive the people as to its real nature and origin, claiming for the constructions of their own minds divine origin and authority: *And her prophets have daubed for them with whited plaster, seeing falsehood, and divining lies unto them, saying: Thus saith the Lord God, when the Lord hath not spoken* (*Ez.* 22, 28).

The designation in question is based on the Sect's *pesher* exposition of *Ez.* 13. That the author of the *Damascus Document* had, in fact, not the detached phrase itself in mind but its context, too, may be proved by his invoking upon the backsliding members of the Sect the curse of *Ez.* 13, 9 against the false prophets (xix, 35). It is significant that the very same verse is also quoted by al-Qumisi[1] and Salmon b. Yeruḥim.[2] Moreover, verse 10 where the phrase at issue occurs is actually cited by Hadassi in relation to the Rabbanites.[3] But the coincidences do not stop here. Salmon and Hadassi use the metaphor of 'whitewashing the wall' to characterize the religious leaders in the rival camp.[4]

'LYING AND DECEIVING INTERPRETERS'

The same idea is conveyed by the terms מליצי כזב, מליצי רמיה which the psalmist of Qumran[5] applied to his religious rivals; they are called 'lying and deceiving interpreters' in the same sense and for the same reason as they were branded by him as 'lying and deceiving prophets'—for deceitfully putting forward their own ideas as emanating from God, like the dishonest interpreter who deceives one party as to what the other actually said by passing off his own words as those of the opposite party.

The question may be put: What was it that suggested the application of the term מליצים to the Sect's rivals? We have seen

[1] See above p. 145.

[2] Cf. *supra*, p. 142, note 5.

[3] See p. 146, note 5.

[4] *The Book of Wars*, p. 84; *'Eshkol ha-Kopher*, 152, beginning.

[5] *DST*, ii, 31; iv, 7, 9–10.

that the condemnatory epithets 'changers of the boundary' and 'builders of the wall' are connected with the *pesher* of the respective biblical passages wherein they occur. It may therefore be assumed that this epithet, too, has a biblical passage prognostically interpreted as its basis. But which passage?

Karaite literature enables us to answer this question with a fair degree of probability. The epithet in question was used in Karaite quarters to describe the religious leaders during the Second Temple and in the *Galuth*. In this case we are in a position to state with certainty that lying behind this usage is a *pesher* of *Isa.* 43, 27 (*Thy first father sinned, and thine interpreters acted dishonestly against me*), according to which 'thy father' referred to the generation of Jeroboam who was considered the inaugurator of rabbinic Judaism, and 'thine interpreters' to 'the false Bible expounders who led Israel astray',[1] or 'the rabbis in the period of the Second Temple and the shepherds of the *Galuth*'.[2]

'MEN OF TRUTH'

In contrast to the 'lying and deceiving interpreters', the men of Qumran were profoundly convinced that they were the sole possessors of the true interpretation of the Torah—a conviction to which expression was given in such designations as 'the house of truth' (*DSD*, v, 6), 'the community of truth' (ii, 24, 26), 'men of truth' (*DSH*, vii, 10; *DST*, xiv, 2), 'sons of truth' (*DSD*, iv, 5, 6). In fact, 'truth' is one of the most frequent words in the Qumran vocabulary; it occurs about one hundred times in the writings so far published.[3]

This exceptionally strong emphasis on truth is shared by the men of Qumran with the Karaites, who likewise claim to be 'men

[1] Al-Qumisi, *Pithron*, p. 3: „ומליציך" הם כל פותרי שקר המתעים את ישראל.

[2] *'Eshkol ha-Kopher*, 125, *hē*; 358, *waw*; 85, *'aleph*; Elias b. Abraham, in *Liq. Qad.*, App., p. 101, lines 3f.

[3] Cf. Yadin's compilation of the passages concerned, *op. cit.* pp. 228–30.

of truth'[1] and styled their way of life 'the way of truth'.[2] Believing as they did that the history of their time had been forecast in Scripture, they took note of *II Chron.* 15, 3, *Now for long periods Israel has been without the God of truth, without a teaching priest, and without Torah* and found in it a mirror of the religious situation of Jewry: the abandonment of the true interpretation of the Torah by the vast majority of the nation. The verse belongs to the *testimonia* of Karaite theologico-historical conceptions.[3]

'KNOWERS OF TRUTH'

This brings us to the title '*knowers of truth*'[4]—again shared by both sects. It is with this title that the author of the *Damascus Document* addressed his fellow-sectarians in the opening sentence of his tract: *Hearken unto me, ye knowers of truth.* The words quoted are derived without modification from *Isa.* 51, 7. In view of the Karaite parallels to be cited instantly, it may be assumed that the whole passage was applied in Qumran-Damascus to the sectarian community.[5] In choosing these words for the opening of his tract the author of the named document implicitly recalled to

[1] Sahl (*Liq. Qad.*, App., p. 35); Nissi b. Noaḥ (*ibid.* p. 11); Yefeth b. 'Ali (*infra*, p. 151, n. 1); Hadassi, 22, end.

[2] Cf. *JQR*, xii, pp. 280, lines 20, 21, and line 2 (fol. 15, verso); 281, 7; 493, top; 503, 21; *Liq. Qad.*, App., p. 33.

[3] *Pithron*, pp. 1, 22, 27; *JQR*, xii, pp. 279, 284; Hadassi, 129, *waw*; 294, *waw*; Aaron of Nicomedia, '*Eṣ Ḥayyim*, p. 3.

[4] There is hardly any need to emphasize that *ṣedeq* in the Qumran texts is simply a synonym of *'emeth*; but the following juxtaposition will be instructive:

עבודת צדק – עבודת אמת
בני צדק – בני אמת
מוכיחי צדק – מוכיחי אמת
דרכי צדק – דרכי אמת

(*DST*, vi, 19; *DSH*, vii, 11; *DSD*, iii, 20, 22; iv, 5, 6; *DST*, fragment 2, 6, vi, 4; *DSD*, iv, 2, 17).

[5] An allusion to *Isa.* 51, 7 is found in *DST*, ii, 35.

the mind of his readers that it was the prophet Isaiah who conferred upon them this honorific title.

Turning to Karaite literature, we find that Sahl b. Maṣliaḥ addressing himself to his controversialist, Jacob ben Samuel, says as follows: 'You have not read the verse: *Hearken unto me, ye knowers of truth . . . fear ye not the taunt of men, neither be dismayed at their revilings*' (*Isa.* 51, 7).[1] In this case, too, the assumption suggests itself that underlying the usage of the *Isaiah* verse is the *pesher* exposition of the entire passage concerned, particularly as Hadassi, too, cites this verse when exhorting his fellow-partisans to ignore the revilings of the enemy.

Now, unpublished sources enable us to establish our assumption as an indubitable fact. From Yefeth's commentary on *Isaiah*[2] as well as from Jacob b. Reuben's *Sepher ha-'Osher*[3] we gather that the entire passage, *Isa.* 51, 1–9, was in fact given a *pesher* interpretation. It is this *pesher* which accounts for the fact[4] that *Isa.* 51, 7–8 (*hearken unto me, ye knowers of truth*, etc.) was incorporated into the Karaite liturgy,[5] and it further explains how

[1] *Loc. cit.*, p. 25.

[2] MS. British Museum, Or. 2502, fol. 87b:
כאן אלפצל אלאול (ישעי׳ נ״א, 1–9) יתכלם פי משכילי עם ופי
ראשי גליות ת̇ם אכ̇ד̇ יתכלם פי אלאכ̇יאר אלד̇י תבעו משכילי עם
פועדהם באלמואעיד אלג̇לילה̈ והו הד̇א אלפצל וסמאהם רדפי צדק
לאנהם אבדא מג̇דין פי טלב אלעדל כמא אוג̇בת אלשריעה̈ צדק צדק
תרדף ת̇ם קאל מבקשי יי והו טלבתהם ישועת ישראל וקדוש השם

And on *Isa.* 51, 7 (fol. 94b): קאל פי אלפצל אלמתקדם שמעו אלי
רדפי צדק פאורא אנהם טלבו אלדין פערף אנהם ענד מא טלבוה וג̇דוה
וצארו עלמא ולד̇לך קאל „ידעי צדק" ת̇ם קאל עם תורתי בלבם פערף
אנהם יצירו ג̇מע בעד כאנו אחאד ופי קו׳ תורתי בלבם שיין אחדהא הו
אלעלם אלד̇י חצל להם בעד אלדראים ואלת̇אני אעתקאדהם
איאהא ונט̇ירה ותורתך בתוך מעי פקד באן לך אן אלד̇י כאנו רדפי צדק
צארו ידעי צדק ואלד̇י כאנו אחאד צארו ג̇מע.

[3] MS. Leiden, Warner 8, fol. 159a: יודעי (צ״ל: רודפי) צדק הם העם הרודפים אחרי דברי הקראים. יודעי צדק המלמדים הגדולים. חרפת אנוש הרבנים. ומגדופתם של רבנים.

[4] Cf. also *supra*, p. 117 and *infra*, p. 200.

[5] *Karaite Prayer-Book*, i, p. 26 (ed. Vilna); ed. Vienna, i, p. 75.

'pursuers of truth' became a frequent Karaite self-laudatory title.[1]

THE OPPONENTS' RELIGION: 'IDOLATRY'

We now come to the problem presented by the term *gillulim*, which belongs to the stock phraseology of the men of Qumran-Damascus; it occurs in three of their outstanding literary productions: the *Rule of the Community*,[2] the *Thanksgivings Scroll*[3] and the *Damascus Document*.[4] The rendering 'idols' or 'idolatry' without any qualification or paraphrase[5] is misleading, as it conveys the idea of actual idol-worship which is out of the question.[6] Some students tried to obviate the difficulty by taking the word to mean 'defilement' or 'filthiness'.[7] This meaning, however, is too

[1] Sahl (*loc. cit.*, p. 27) so styles the predecessors of the Karaites who were forced to lead a crypto-existence before they could come out into the open. Yefeth (*Zechariah* commentary, MS. British Museum, Or. 2401, fol. 174b) styles them 'the people of the truth', saying: 'The people of the truth were humiliated and concealed till the time of the appearance of the "Little Horn".' (פצאר אהל אלחק מנכפצין מסתורין אלי זמאן טהור קרן זעירה). The title *rōdephē ṣedeq* is used by Yefeth in one of his poems, printed by L. Barges, *Rabbi Yaphet ben Heli Bassorensis in Librum Psalmorum*, Paris 1864, p. xxiii (J. Mann, unaware that the poem had already been published, printed it from a Leningrad MS. in his *Texts and Studies*, ii, p. 31); Aaron b. Elijah of Nicomedia at the end of the introduction to his *Kether Torah* (Eupatoria 1866); Kaleb Afendopolo at the beginning of a *responsum* (MS. Leiden, Warner, 52/9); Mordecai Comtino (cited by Joseph Bagi, see Mann, *op. cit.* p. 306); Simḥah b. Solomon Cosdimi in the rhymed preface to his commentary on the Pentateuch (A. Danon, *JQR* [N.S.], xvii, p. 303).

[2] *DSD*, ii, 11, 17.

[3] *DST*, iv, 15.

[4] *CDC*, xx, 9.

[5] Charles, *Apocrypha, etc.*, p. 821, adds in a note: 'in a symbolic sense'.

[6] Against Wernberg-Møller's view that the word 'should be taken in its usual sense of idols', see *Studia Theologica*, 1955, p. 46, and note 1, where other renderings are quoted.

[7] Cf. Rabin on xx, 9 and also on iii, 17. Gaster (p. 51) translated 'the taint of idolatry', and on p. 104, note 18 observed that the author of *CDC* evidently understood the word to mean 'filthiness'. G. R. Driver in *JQR*, xliv [1953], p. 16 came to the conclusion that the word seems to mean 'impure, i.e., idolatrous thoughts'.

indistinct and vague, because too general, to convey any clear, specific notion. The word must bear a *definite* implication, other than actual idolatry. What this implication is is suggested by the psalmist of Qumran when he says about his antagonists: וידרשוכה בגלולים, 'they sought Thee with idols'. No doubt, *gillulim* stands here for the opposing party's brand of religion, their doctrines and practices by which they seek, i.e. worship, God. The antagonists' variety of religion is, then, decried by the Qumran sectaries as 'idolatry'. Phrases like 'they have set idols upon their heart', 'idols of their heart' and the immediate continuation of the psalmist's words just mentioned: 'And the stumbling-block of their sins they put before them' (used also twice by the author of the *Rule* in the same context), are all patterned on *Ez.* 14, 3–4, 7; and this unmistakably points to the Book of *Ezekiel* as the source of the Qumran writers' inspiration. Whether in *Ezekiel*, too, the expression is to be taken in an abstract sense or not, need not detain us here. In view of the Sect's *pesher* method it is quite legitimate to assume that they interpreted the *Ezekiel* pericope in terms of the religious situation of their own time, and therefore in stigmatizing the opposing party's religion as idolatry, could invoke the prophetic authority of Ezekiel.

Precisely the same judgment, exceptionally severe though it is, is passed by al-Qumisi on the type of religion practised by his own opponents; in his repeated declaration that rabbinic Judaism is tantamount to idol-worship, the expression used by him is *gillulim*. What is more, each time he makes this allegation he explicitly refers to the Book of *Ezekiel*. In the *Epistle* addressed to his partisans in the Diaspora he writes as follows:[1]

> Anyone who practises man-made commandments, not those in the Torah of the Lord, is like an idolater. Therefore He spoke rebukingly through Ezekiel to all those who perform precepts other than divine commands: *Go ye, serve every one his idols* (20, 39). Here the prophet informs us that one who worships God by man-made commandments apart from the Torah of the Lord . . . is like an idol-worshipper.

[1] *JQR*, xii, p. 277.

In the same *Epistle* further on he reverts to this topic, hammering in his point:[1]

> Know, that all festivals, statues and ordinances which are not in accordance with the divine command are like the worship of other gods; therefore Ezekiel said: *Go ye, serve every one his idols.*

Another passage by the same author enables us to explain the expression 'the idols of his heart' coined by the author of the *Rule*. It denotes: 'idols' that are but the product of one's heart, that is, practices and beliefs which have no basis in the Torah but are inventions of one's own mind.[2] In his commentary on *Hosea* al-Qumisi writes:[3] '. . . they have led them astray through man-made precepts derived from their heart's understanding, according to their reason and intellect. These are accounted as idols, as it is written (*Jer.* 16, 13): *And there shall ye serve other gods*, and in accordance with the prediction: *Now for long periods Israel was without a true God, without a teaching priest and without Torah* (*II Chron.* 15, 3);[4] and it is further written (*Ez.* 20, 39): *Go ye, serve every one his idols.*' Al-Qumisi reiterates: 'Divine worship which is contrary to the Torah is like idols.'[5]

SOCIAL AND TERRITORIAL SEGREGATION

A salient feature in the physiognomy of the Qumran sect is its rigid isolationism. The oath taken on being admitted to its organization imposed upon the prospective member the obligation 'to separate himself from all the men of iniquity that walk in

[1] *Ibid.* p. 278, lines 20–21.

[2] Cf. *supra*, p. 144 and note 2.

[3] *Pithron*, p. 22; see also *JQR*, xii, p. 499 and vol. 15, p. 387 (on this fragment see J. Mann, *op. cit.* ii, p. 8, note 14).

[4] For the importance of this verse in the Karaite ideology see *supra*, p. 149.

[5] This harsh verdict on rabbinic Judaism is re-echoed by Hadassi, 137, *mem*: וכל הנשען בדעת רועי גלות לבלתי היות מחפש תורת אלהיך מדעתו להבין בין טוב לרע בין תורת ה׳ למצות אנשים מלומדה, כל אלה כנושאים שם ה׳ לשוא ופרועים כעובדי העגל.

the path of wickedness'.[1] As the Sect was convinced that all its contemporaries were walking in the path of wickedness, the oath demanded, in effect, segregation from all people outside their own ranks; and as no exceptions are mentioned, the segregation must have been a total one affecting even the nearest relations. The emphasis laid on this commitment, which must have entailed great personal sacrifice, may be seen not merely from the repeated reference to it,[2] but most especially from the fact that this commitment takes the second place in the oath of admission; it follows immediately after the basic and all-embracing obligation to return to the Law of Moses. The Sect equally insisted on the territorial segregation of its members, concrete evidence of which is the retreat in the desert around the Dead Sea and the formation of smaller groups concentrated in camps, for the running of which special regulations were promulgated.

Such a relentless demand for a total severance of all social contacts with co-religionists who do not conform to the same religious practice, not excluding father and mother, brothers and children, was insisted upon by 'Anan, who was not at any loss to find a scriptural basis for this drastic measure. He, too, prescribed territorial segregation of his adherents who were required to concentrate 'in one place', and also for this he invokes scriptural authority. In his *Book of Precepts* we read this interesting passage:[3]

> It is written (*Ezra* 10, 11): *Now therefore make confession unto the Lord* . . . [*and separate yourselves from the peoples of the land and from the foreign women*]. He enjoins upon us two things:

[1] *DSD*, v, 10–11.

[2] *DSD*, v, 1–2, 10–11; *CDC*, vi, 14–15.

[3] Cf. A. Harkavy, *Studien u. Mitteilungen*, viii, pp. 6–7:
וכת׳ ועתה תנו תודה לייי [והבדלו מעמי הארץ ומן הנשים הנכריות]
קא מזהר לן תרתין מילי פרישו מעמי הארץ דלא למתבו ביניהו ואי
אית לך אשה דלא עבדא כעובדך . . . ואף אב ואם ואחי ובני דלא עבדין
עיבידתא דשמיא כותן מחיבינן למיפרש מינהון דכ׳ האמר לאביו ולאמו
וכל אימת דמערבין ישראל ביני גוים גרמא להון מילתא דעבדין
כעובדיהון דכ׳ ויתערבו בגוים וכל דלא עביד אוריתא ישׂ׳ גוי איקרי
כי היכין דפרישנן.

> (1) Separate yourselves from the peoples of the land[1] and do not dwell among them; (2) If you have a wife that does not conform with your practice . . . and even a father, mother, brothers and children who do not serve Heaven in the same manner as we do, we are duty bound to separate ourselves from them, as it is written (*Deut.* 33, 9): *Who said of his father and of his mother*, [*'I have not seen him'; neither did he acknowledge his brethren, nor knew his own children*]. Whenever Israel mixes with Gentiles this causes them to imitate their works, as it is written (*Ps.* 106, 35): *But they mingled themselves with the nations* [*and learned their works*]. Any Jew who does not practise the Torah is called a Gentile, as we have explained.

'Anan goes on to decree the territorial concentration of his co-schismatics, saying:[2]

> It is our duty to segregate ourselves from them; and all of us must gather together in one place, as it is said (*Ps.* 50, 5): *Gather My saints together unto Me*. And if we do so, the Merciful One will set us apart before Him, in accordance with *Lev.* 20, 26.

Karaite writers of subsequent ages have passed over in complete silence these separatist restrictions of 'Anan.[3] Views echoing

[1] The expression *'ammē ha-'areṣ* signifies here 'Gentiles', as in the verse quoted from *Ezra*. Salo W. Baron (*A Social and Religious History of the Jews* [2nd ed. 1957], v, p. 219) translated 'illiterate people', and on the basis of this translation maintained that 'Anan demanded from his followers 'segregation from the illiterate masses' (*ibid.* pp. 220, 394). However, the whole context of the passage vitiates this translation.

[2] *Op. cit.* p. 7: ומחיבינן למיפרש מנהון ומיבעי לן לאיכנופי כולן בחד דוכתא כי דכ׳ אספו לי חסידי וכד עבדינן הכי רחמנא מפריש לן לקמיה דכת׳ והייתם לי קדשים.

[3] Cf. Harkavy, *op. cit.* p. 196. Simḥah Isaac Lutzki does mention 'Anan's separatism, but in general terms, specifying only the prohibitions of partaking of the Rabbanites' food and intermarriage with them; but he is silent on the prohibition of residing among them and the duty 'to gather together in one place', cf. *'Oraḥ Ṣaddiqim*, p. 18: גזר ואסר לתלמידיו ולכל רעיו ומיודעיו עדת הצדוקים להנזר ולהבדל ולהגזר מעדת הפרושים מכל וכל בתכלית ההבדלה וההפרשה וההגזר במוחלט ואסור לנו לאכול את מאכלם וכך אסר לנו להתחתן בהם.

similar sentiments are, however, not lacking in other Karaite writings. First, mention should be made that 'Anan's harsh, intolerant verdict which would place the followers of rabbinic Judaism on a par with Gentiles is shared by al-Qumisi, who otherwise belonged to 'Anan's fiercest opponents in the Karaite camp. Al-Qumisi delivers himself of this unequivocal judgment:[1] 'Anyone who practises man-made commandments other than the Torah of the Lord, does not belong to the congregation of Jacob and has no portion with the people of Israel.' This is of course an irresistible corollary of his assessment of rabbinic Judaism as being tantamount to idolatry.

Secondly, reference should be made to a passage included in Hadassi's *'Eshkol ha-Kopher* but obviously derived from earlier sources, the gist of which is that association with, and residence among, the Rabbanites is a grievous sin deserving severe punishment. From the rather lengthy exhortation citing numerous biblical proof-texts, the following passage may be given here in translation:[2]

> One who associates with the rebels against God, who hears and keeps silence, sees and restrains himself, but does not depart from their midst is, like them, regarded as one who takes the name of the Lord in vain and will be swept away with them, as it is written (*Ex.* 23, 1): *Thou shalt not accept a false report; put not thy hand with the wicked.* So also one who resides among and associates with them, as it is written (*Num.* 16, 26): *Depart from the tents of these wicked men, lest ye be swept away in all their sin.* It is further written (with reference to Sodom and Gomorrah): *Up, get you out of this place* (*Gen.* 19, 14).

Lastly, the fact should be recalled that Yefeth b. 'Ali in portraying the traits of his co-ascetics[3] specifies as one of their merits that 'they have separated themselves from their parents and brothers who continued to rely upon the previous generations', i.e. on rabbinic traditions.

[1] In his *Epistle*, *loc. cit.*, p. 275.

[2] *'Eshkol ha-Kopher*, 144, beginning.

[3] Cf. N. Wieder, 'The Qumran Sectaries', p. 289.

THE AVENGING SWORD: *ZECH.* 13, 7

In recension B of the *Damascus Document* the following passage occurs (xix, 5–13):

> And all that reject the commandments and statutes the retribution of the wicked is to be rendered to them when God visits the land, when the word which is written by the prophet Zechariah will be fulfilled (13, 7): *O sword, awake against My shepherd and against the man that is My fellow, saith God; smite the shepherd, and the sheep shall be scattered; and I will turn My hand against the rulers*(?). And '*they that pay heed unto Him*' (*Zech.* 11, 11) are *the poor of the flock*. These shall escape in the time of the visitation, but the rest shall be delivered to the sword when the Messiah of Aaron and Israel comes, just as it happened in the period of the first visitation of which He spoke through Ezekiel (9, 4): *To set the mark upon the foreheads of those who sigh and moan*; but the rest were delivered to the sword that executes vengeance of the covenant.

Our interest in the above passage, which represents a coherent whole, centres in the biblical quotations adduced in support of two theological doctrines that loom large in the thinking of the people of Qumran-Damascus: the divine visitation upon the wicked, and the salvation of a faithful remnant. It is highly significant that the prophetic prediction of that visitation the author finds in *Zech.* 13, 7—a passage forecasting the punishment of the faithless shepherd. Obviously, the visitation concerns chiefly the leaders of the nation, conceived under the figure of a shepherd. The author passes on to the explanation of the phrase from *Zechariah* chapter 11, *they that pay heed unto Him*, from which it is manifest that also this chapter was correlated by him to the contemporary scene. This chapter deals with the same theme: the overthrow of the shepherds who neglected and abused the sheep, and like 13, 7, explicitly cited in the *Damascus Document*, summons the avenging sword against them (verse 17):

Woe to the worthless shepherd that leaveth the flock! The sword shall be upon his arm, and upon his right eye.

This will now be illuminated by parallels from Karaite literature. One of the most conspicuous features of Karaite phraseology is the recurrent designation of the heads of rabbinic Judaism as 'shepherds'. This has its origin in the Karaite *pesher* which interpreted the prophetic passages castigating the faithless shepherds, particularly those in the book of *Zechariah*, as relating to them. It is from these passages that Karaite polemicists derived the phraseology with which they characterize their opponents' alleged abuse of office,[1] and it is *Zech.* 13, 7[2] (and also 11, 17) that is cited by them to invoke upon the leaders in the rival camp their final doom, precisely as the author of the *Damascus Document* did.

An early *pesher* on *Hos.* 2, 9 runs thus:[3] 'Israel will not find the originators of these evil laws, because God will exterminate all the shepherds that misguided them [and] their disciples that went after them, as it is written (*Ez.* 34, 10): *I will cause them to cease from feeding the sheep*, and it is further written (*Zech.* 11, 17): *Woe to the worthless shepherd that leaveth the flock*, etc., and also (*ibid.* 13, 7): *O sword, awake against My shepherd*,[4] etc.'

Salmon b. Yeruḥim, commenting upon *Ps.* 58, 11: *The righteous shall rejoice when he sees vengeance* writes as follows:[5]

[1] Cf., e.g., Salmon, *The Book of the Wars*, pp. 82, 113; Sahl, *op. cit.* pp. 31, 32, 33; the Introduction to his *Book of Precepts* in *Me'asseph Niddaḥim*, no. 13, p. 202; Elijah b. Abraham, *op. cit.* pp. 102, 104; Hadassi, 122, beginning.

[2] Rabin's assertion (*The Zadokite Documents*, p. 31, note 20a, 3), followed by A. S. van der Woude (*Die messianischen Vorstellungen der Gemeinde von Qumran*, p. 64), that 'for the Karaite Moses Dar'i (12–13th cent.) the passage [*Zech.* 13, 7] refers to the Messiah' is not borne out by the reference to L. Nemoy's *Karaite Anthology*, p. 142 [Hebrew text in *Liq. Qad.*, p. 99]. All one finds there is that the Messiah is referred to as 'their shepherd' (*rō'ām*).

[3] See *Pithron*, p. 4, top.

[4] Cf. further the comment on *Zech.* 11, 17 (*ibid.* p. 74): וזאת היא נקמת מלמדים לא כתורת משה ע״ה.

[5] Cf. his Arabic Commentary, p. 61; see also pp. 60 (58, 8); 103 (69, 24), and J. Mann, *op. cit.* ii, p. 84.

'When God will take vengeance of them and blot out the remembrance of them from the world, Israel will rejoice, as He promised through Zechariah in the time of the Second Temple to destroy them, saying (13, 2): *And also I will cause the prophets and the unclean spirit to pass out of the land*—undoubtedly referring to those that misguided Israel—and the prophet continues (13, 7): *O sword, awake against My shepherd*, etc.'

How prominent in Salmon's mind the imprecatory words of *Zechariah* were, may be seen from the fact that he invoked against Sa'adya, the chief 'shepherd' of the Rabbanites, a curse derived from 11, 17: 'Woe unto the fool! *His right eye shall be utterly darkened*.'[1]

Yefeth b. 'Ali follows this line of exposition. The divine pronouncement '*O sword, awake against My shepherd!*' refers, according to him, to the vengeance that God will execute upon the leadership of Israel during the time of the Second Temple and the subsequent epochs.[2] It is interesting to note that he explains the words 'smite the shepherd' as being addressed to Elijah the prophet whose function will be to manifest the truth and abolish the leadership of the false shepherds.[3]

Finally, Yehudah Hadassi—in whose encyclopaedic work the term 'shepherds', without the accompaniment of any opprobrious adjective, is the regular appellation of the heads of rabbinic Judaism—re-echoes this exegetical tradition. In censuring the Rabbanite leaders for excommunicating their adversaries and the talmudic sages for saying:[4] 'One may stab an '*am ha-'areṣ* even

[1] Cf. *The Book of the Wars*, p. 118.

[2] MS. British Museum, Or. 2401, fols. 222b–223a: קו׳ חרב (זכרי׳ י״ג, 7) ישיר בה אלי נקם אללה עז וג׳ל אלתי יחלהא אללה פי אלרעאי ופי גבר עמיתי והו אלד׳י תקדם ד׳כרה פי אלפצל אלמתקדם והו קו׳ הוי רועי האליל עזבי הצאן (י״א, 17).

On the latter verse, after giving a literal interpretation, he says as follows (fol. 215b): ... פהד׳א ט׳אהר אלקול ובאטנה הו אן תולא ריאסה ישראל פי אלגלות קום גאהל בכתאב אללה וד׳לך מן זמאן בית שני והם רווס אלגאליה ורווס אלמת׳איב ...

[3] *Ibid*. fol. 223a: וקו׳ הך את הרעה יג׳וז אנה קול ללאליהו לאנה הו אלד׳י יט׳הר אלחק ויבטל ריאסה רעי האליל.

[4] B.T. *Pes*. 49b.

on the Day of Atonement which occurs on a Sabbath'—he pronounces against them the imprecation of *Zech.* 11, 17.[1]

Moving on to the second part of the above quotation dealing with the fidelity and salvation of a remnant, we recall that also the Karaites regarded themselves as the faithful remnant spoken of by the prophets and, further, that they actually appropriated to themselves the title 'remnant'.[2] Moreover, the author of the *Damascus Document* designates the remnant as 'the poor of the flock'; this title, too, the Karaites applied to their own community.[3]

Most significant, however, is the reference to 'those that sigh and moan', who are held up as an example of a minority remaining faithful in the midst of general apostasy, and looked upon by the Qumran sectaries as a source of inspiration in their own plight. The same phenomenon we meet in Karaite quarters. Indeed, Karaite historiographers went even further and claimed that the Karaite community were the physical and spiritual descendants of 'those that sigh and moan'. It was the firmness and perseverance of that ancient group which clandestinely kept the flame of true religion burning, that made the emergence of Karaism in the kingdom of the 'little horn' possible: ''Anan's teachings are the teachings of "those that sigh and moan"; their religion is our religion, and their path is our path.'[4]

[1] *'Eshkol ha-Kopher*, p. 138a, *s.v.* תהלות. See further p. 10a, *'ayin*; Alph. 103, *ṣadē*; 122, end.

[2] See 'The Qumran Sectaries', pp. 278–83.

[3] *Ibid.* p. 288; *Pithron*, p. 66; Hadassi, 15, beginning.

[4] N. Wieder, *ibid.*, p. 279, note 77; Hadassi, p. 10b: גנוזים מסותרים נאנחים נאנקים מדאבות. גמר אמר עבור בתוך ירושלם והתוית תיו על מצחות האנשים הנאנחים ונאנקיך. דבקו יחד במלכות קרן זעירה.

CHAPTER V

TWO SIGNIFICANT TERMS

THE VERB 'TO SEPARATE' IN THE *DAMASCUS DOCUMENT*

Our attention will now be focused on one single expression occurring in a passage of the *Damascus Document* describing the capital sins committed by the opponents. The passage runs as follows (v, 6–7):

וגם מטמאים הם את המקדש אשר אין הם מבדיל[ים] כתורה ושוכבים עם הרואה את דם זובה.

As the Hebrew term for 'separate', or 'set aside', requires an object, which is absent in the text, its explanation has caused difficulty and embarrassment to the translators. The usual rendering 'because they do not separate' adopted, among others, by S. Schechter,[1] Charles[2] and Millar Burrows,[3] is not a translation of the Hebrew; it is simply an infusion of the English meaning of the verb 'to separate' into the Hebrew הבדיל. In English, 'to separate' may be used intransitively in the sense 'to quit each other's company', and may even bear the specific connotation 'to withdraw from conjugal cohabitation'. This latter connotation suits well the context of the passage and it is small wonder that it succeeded in masking the fact that the words 'they do not separate' are not the translation of the Hebrew verb which is transitive and requires an object. Theodor Gaster's translation[4] 'and do not put *them* aside' supplies indeed an object, but the word 'them' is not in the text. Rabin,[5] avoiding an emendation, holds that the *hiph'il mabhdīlīm* stands here for the *niph'al*

[1] *Frag. of a Zad. Work*, p. xxxvi: 'as they separate not . . . and lie with . . .'

[2] *Apocrypha and Pseudepigrapha*, p. 810.

[3] *The Dead Sea Scrolls*, p. 353.

[4] *The Scriptures of the Dead Sea Sect*, p. 76.

[5] *Op. cit.*, p. 19.

nibhdālīm and translates, accordingly, 'they do not keep separate'. This explanation is tantamount to an admission that the term cannot be explained as it stands. But perhaps the best illustration of the difficulty which the term presents was provided by Israel Lévi[1] who, too, felt the need to supply an object, but unlike Gaster's 'them', he supplied 'it' thus making the whole sentence refer to the Temple (!): 'ils profanent le Temple en ne le mettant pas à l'abri.'

It seems that 'Anan's *Book of Precepts* furnishes us with the correct interpretation of the term in question. 'Anan uses the verb מפריש, the Aramaic equivalent of מבדיל, in the specific meaning of 'to give a halakhic decision in matters of purity and impurity and holy and profane'.[2] This restricted meaning obviously derives from *Lev.* 10, 10: *And that ye may separate between the holy and the profane, between unclean and clean.* We suggest that it is in this technical sense that the verb מבדיל is employed by the author of the *Damascus Document*—a sense which fits excellently the context. Note that in vi, 17–18 the author actually uses the full phrase 'to separate between the unclean and clean and to make known the difference between the holy and the profane'.

As a parallel phenomenon we may cite the verb הורה, occurring in the same verse, which in biblical language has the general meaning 'to teach', but in rabbinic idiom it bears the specific implication 'to give halakhic decisions' and is even employed in a more restricted technical sense 'to pronounce judgment on ritual questions (*'issūr we-hettēr*)'[3] as contrasted to matters of

[1] Cf. *REJ*, 1911, p. 181.

[2] Cf. A. Harkavy, *Studien und Mitteilungen*, viii, pp. 22–23. 'Anan compares one who 'discriminates' or 'teaches' (מורה = מליף; see in the text) to a priest ministering in the Tabernacle: he must take off his shoes, wash hands and feet, must do so in a standing posture and in the day time only, and finally, he must be ritually clean: מה אהל מועד לא עילין ליה מסאני... אף מאן דמפריש או דמליף צריך מישלף מסאניה... אף מאן דמפריש או דמליף מיחייב מימשא ידיה וכרעיה מה אהל מועד בעמידה משמשין ביה... אף מאן דמפריש או דמליף מיקם קאים...

[3] Cf. B.T. *Ker.* 13b and *Sanh.* 5a.

jurisprudence. The phrase אין הם מבדילים כתורה is similar to saying אין הם מורים כהלכה, 'they do not decide according to the *Halakhah*', and in our particular case: 'they do not decide this question of purity and impurity according to the Law'.

THE TERM *YŌM HA-TA 'ANĪTH*

The Character of the Day of Atonement According to Qumranites and Karaites

I

The name יום התענית used in the *Damascus Document*, vi, 19 for the Day of Atonement is unparalleled and strikes one as strange in the extreme.[1] The strangeness resides in the usage of the word *ta'anīth* instead of צום; but not in the designation *Day of Fasting*. This latter as well as 'The Fast' *par excellence* are old appellations of *Yōm Kippūr*; they occur in Philo,[2] Josephus[3] and the *Acts of the Apostles*.[4] But the Hebrew terms underlying the Greek in the sources referred to were undoubtedly *yōm ṣōm* and *ha-ṣōm*: both terms occur in the Mishnah[5]; the former was also current among the Samaritans;[6] *yōm ṣōm* is further used in

[1] The phrase מועד התענית in the *pesher* on *Ps.* 37 (*PEQ*, lxviii [1954], pp. 69–75), the meaning of which is not quite clear, probably refers to the date of the Day of Atonement, as Talmon suggested (*Scripta Hierosolymitana*, vol. iv, 180f.). If this is correct, we would have another instance, this time directly from the caves of Qumran, of the fast of *Yōm Kippūr* being called *ta'anith.*

[2] *De vita Mosis*, II, 23 [Loeb Classical Library, vi, p. 461]; *de spec. leg.*, I, 186; II, 193 [Loeb, vii, pp. 205, 427]. Cf. also I. Heinemann, *Philons griechische u. jüdische Bildung*, Breslau 1932, pp. 98. See *infra*, pp. 164, n. 2; 171, n. 1.

[3] *Ant.* XVIII, iv, 3, §94.

[4] 27, 9.

[5] *Ned.* 8, 6 (The Fast); *Men.* 11, 9 (Day of Fasting).

[6] Cf. A. E. Cowley, *The Samaritan Liturgy*, Oxford 1909, ii, pp. 706 (בדן יומה דאתקרי יום צומה); 511; 640 (יום הציאם); 666 (twice); 676 and *passim.*

the liturgy for the Day of Atonement, in the eulogy of the middle benediction of the '*Amidah*;[1] *ṣōm* is likewise contained in the Aramaic expression the 'Great Fast'—another appellation of the Day of Atonement.[2] In fact, *yōm ṣōm* appears also in the Habakkuk Scroll.[3] Nowhere is the name *yōm ha-ta'anīth* applied to *Yōm*

[1] יום צום הכפורים, see *Massekheth Sopherīm*, 19, 4 (ed. M. Higger, p. 326). This form is invariably found in Genizah texts, cf. I. Elbogen, 'Die Tefilla für die Festtage' in *MGWJ*, 1911, pp. 443, 597, 598; J. Mann, *HUCA*, ii, pp. 330, 331; S. Assaf, מסדר התפלה בארץ ישראל in *B. Dinaburg Jubilee Volume* (ספר דינבורג), Jerusalem 1949, p. 129. This formula represents a fusion of *yōm ha-kippūrīm* and *yōm ṣōm*. The Babylonian ritual uses the former only; see *Siddur Rabh Sa'adya*, p. 261; *Seder Rabh 'Amram* (ed. Warsaw), pp. 47a, 47b, 49ab; ed. Frumkin, ii, pp. 345, 347, 351; *Halākhōth Qeṣūbhōth* (ed. M. Margulies, Jerusalem 1942), p. 101.

[2] P.T. *Rosh ha-Shanah*, i, 5 (57b); '*A. Zar.*, i, 1 (39b). The explanation of this name given by Y. M. Grintz, *Sepher Yehūdhīth* [The Book of Judith], Jerusalem 1957, p. 106, that it arose from the fact that on *Yōm Kippūr* besides fasting, also bathing, anointing, wearing shoes and conjugal intercourse are forbidden, is untenable for the simple reason that *Yōm Kippūr* is not the only fast-day on which these are forbidden, see Mishnah *Ta'anith*, i, 6; B.T., *ibid.* 30a. The explanation is to be found in its wide-spread observance: *Yōm Kippūr* was kept by all and sundry, even by people who during the year cared little for religion. This phenomenon, observable in present-day Jewry, is more than two thousand years old, as we learn from Philo's interesting testimony: 'On the tenth day is the fast, which is carefully observed not only by the zealous for piety and holiness but also *by those who never act religiously in the rest of their life*. For all stand in awe, overcome by the sanctity of the day, and for the moment the worse vie with the better in self-denial and virtue' (*De spec. leg.* I, 186 [Loeb, vii, p. 205]). See also *de vita Mosis*, II, 23 [Loeb, vi, p. 461]: 'Who does not every year shew awe and reverence for the fast, as it is called, which is kept more strictly and solemnly than the "holy month" of the Greeks?'

Another name of *Yōm Kippūr* is יומא רבה, 'the Great Day'; it occurs once (?) in B.T. *Rosh ha-Shanah* 21a, and was also in vogue among the Samaritans, see Cowley, *op. cit.*, ii, p. 676: יומא רבה דמתקרי שמה יום צומה (according to MSS. O5 and L17).

[3] *DSH*, xi, 8. The great emphasis laid in this passage on the Day of Atonement as 'a season of rest', 'a Sabbath of rest', was intended to bring into relief the gravity of the wicked priest's action: he attacked the *moreh ṣedeq* on a day on which he was unable, because of the holiness of the day, to defend himself, cf. *Jubilees*, 50, 12; *I Macc.* 2, 32–37.

Kippūr,[1] and its usage in the *Damascus Document* is as strange as it is exceptional.

This deviation from the common usage must have its motive, and it is our thesis that it is connected with a different conception as to how the day should be celebrated. The author of the *Damascus Document* obviously regarded the name *yōm ha-ta'anīth*, *Day of Self-Affliction*, as more in consonance with and more expressive of his conception of *Yōm Kippūr* than *yōm ṣōm*, *Day of Fasting*.

This explanation is both strongly suggested by and derives weighty support from the remarkable fact that Daniel al-Qumisi expressly pleads for the adoption of the term *ta'anīth* in preference to *ṣōm*, the former being a more fitting description of the character of a fast-day.

Before we present his view, a brief preliminary observation will be helpful. The biblical precept concerning the Day of Atonement merely enjoins[2] *Ye shall afflict your souls*, but the nature of the affliction is not defined. Rabbinic sources testify to the difficulty of exactly determining the notion of self-affliction. One particularly relevant tannaitic statement will illustrate this:[3]

> *Ye shall afflict your souls* (*Lev.* 16, 29), you might think one must sit in the sun or in the cold in order to afflict oneself, therefore Scripture says: *And ye shall do no manner of work*; just as the prohibition of work means sit and do nothing, so the affliction of the soul means sit and do nothing.

This amounts to an admission that the expression 'to afflict the soul' as such has a wider application which includes *positive* actions of affliction[4] and it is only the juxtaposition of the clause

[1] Cf. the contrast: בתעניות...וביום הכפורים (Mishnah *Ta'anīth* iv, 1) *Meg.* iii, 4f; P.T. *Yoma*, viii, 1 (44d): ...סלק לגביה ר׳ יהושע בן לוי בלילי צומא רבא...סלק לגביה בלילי תעניתא.

[2] *Lev.* 16, 29, 31.

[3] B.T. *Yoma* 74b. Cf. further P.T. *Yoma*, viii, 1 (44d); *Siphra*, *'Aḥarē Mōth*, vii (ed. Weiss, p. 82b).

[4] On the other hand, mediaeval Jewish Bible commentators distinguish between 'affliction' and 'affliction of the *soul*', the latter signifying 'fasting' only. Abraham Ibn Ezra (on *Lev.* 16, 29) sums up: והכלל כל עינוי שימצא במקרא דבק עם „נפש״ הוא הצום. Naḥmanides, who

ye shall do no manner of work which restricts self-affliction to mere abstinence. The traditional view is that the expression refers only to abstinence from food and drink, i.e. fasting.[1] The designation 'Day of *Fasting*' instead of 'Day of *Self-Affliction*', which one would have expected on the basis of the pentateuchal ענה—*ṣūm* is not used in the Pentateuch in reference to the Day of Atonement—is indicative of the view which limited the scope of affliction to fasting. Only fast-days other than *Yōm Kippūr*, on which other modes of self-affliction also were practised, are described in rabbinic terminology by the word *ta'anīth*.[2]

endorses this view, correctly noticed that Ibn Ezra's polemic (ואחר שיש לנו קבלה אין צורך לחפש) was aimed at the Karaites (לסתום פיהם של הקראים מחוקי שם).

It must however be pointed out that Karaite scholars were divided among themselves on this point. Qirqisani is quite definite that the biblical idiom in question signifies 'fasting' (*Kitāb al-Anwār*, ed. L. Nemoy, p. 915), and so is Yefeth b. 'Ali (see Appendix, no. 2). But this should not be taken to mean that Qirqisani follows the view concerning the character of the Day of Atonement. On the contrary, *Yōm Kippūr*, being a fast-day, he holds, must be kept like all other fasts, and he explicitly refers to *Neh.* 1, 4 from which we see that mourning is a concomitant of fasting. As to Yefeth's view, cf. Appendix. Among the European Karaites, only the ascetic Yehudah Hadassi faithfully adheres to al-Qumisi's strict demands; see *'Eshkol ha-Kopher*, 21, *ṭeth*: טרחם ועניינם לעמוד בתפלתם ולצעוק אל ה׳ בכל לב בצום ובשק ובאפר ובבכי ובמספד. See also 19, *ṣadē*; 20, *shin*; 248, *hē*. For the attitude of later Karaites to this issue, see Elijah of Nicomedia, *Gan 'Eden*, 60a and Elijah Bashyachi, *'Addereth 'Eliyyahu*, 74c.

[1] The halakhic authorities differ as to the character (*mide-'orayetha* or *mide-rabbanan*) of the other prohibitions mentioned in Mishnah *Yoma* viii, 1 (see *supra*, 164, n. 2), but there is general agreement that the *kareth* punishment applies to eating and drinking only. The amoraic efforts (B.T. *Yoma* 76a–78b) to discover evidence that also the other abstentions are called 'affliction' have an interesting parallel in the exertions to adduce biblical proof that the rabbinic prohibitions on Sabbath are designated as 'work' (מנין למקח וממכר והלואה ופקדונות ...דינין טענות וערעורין...קידושין גטין...חשבונות שנקראו מלאכה? תלמוד לומר...). See *Mekhilta de-Rabbi Shim'on b. Yoḥai* (ed. J. N. Epstein–E. Z. Melamed, p. 224).

[2] It is this distinction between the two terms that lies behind the expression 'fast-day of affliction' occurring in the prayer *'anēnū* (to be inserted in the week-day *'Amidah* on a fast-day other than the Day of Atonement): ענו אבינו (יי) ענו ביום צום התענית הזה (צום תעניתנו). The

Al-Qumisi profoundly disagrees with this restrictive interpretation.[1] He, too, considers the clause '*ye shall do no manner of work*' as having a bearing on the scope of affliction, but only insofar as it automatically excludes practices that are technically 'work' and are prohibited as such on a day on which abstention from work is prescribed. This rules out, e.g., plucking of one's hair ('making baldness'), one of the biblical modes of affliction.[2] But other kinds of mortification, though of a positive nature, are required in order to fulfil the commandment *ye shall afflict your souls*. Al-Qumisi therefore demands in addition to abstention from food and drink also the following practices:

1. Standing on the feet in prayer.[3]
2. Abstention from sleep.[4]

expression has disconcerted the prayer-book commentator, A. L. Gordon (*'Oṣar Ha-Tephillōth*, vol. i, *'Iyyūn Tephillāh*, *ad loc.*) to such a degree that he felt constrained to take the word *ṣōm* in its supposed primary meaning of 'gathering' (so Kimḥi) and to render the expression 'fast-day gathering'. However, there is no justification whatever for such a drastic departure from the plain meaning of the word. The combination of the two terms serves to emphasize that this was a fast-day on which, in addition to fasting, also positive modes of self-affliction (e.g. wearing of sackcloth and strewing of ashes) were practised; it is not merely *ṣōm* but also *ta'anith*. This way of describing the full character of the day is paralleled by al-Qumisi's combination of the same terms: צום ועינוי (see Appendix, no. 1). As to the wording of the prayer cited, see L. Ginzberg, *A Commentary on the Palestinian Talmud*, iii, pp. 293 and 299 and the Genizah text published by N. Wieder in *JJS* 4 [1953], p. 72. Also Maimonides' version was ביום צום התענית הזה cf. *Studies of the Research Institute for Hebrew Poetry*, vol. vii [1958], p. 198; the printed editions have תעניתנו.

[1] Cf. Appendix, no. 1.

[2] *Isa.* 15, 2; *Mic.* 1, 16. See also Hadassi, 248, *yodh*.

[3] See Appendix no. 4 at the end of the chapter.

[4] Cf. Hadassi, 248, *hē*. This was also the Samaritan custom, see M. Gaster, *The Samaritans, Their History, Doctrine and Literature* (Schweich Lectures 1923), London 1925, p. 173: 'In it we ıfflict ourselves from evening to evening, men as well as women and children, big and small, except the babes that are sucking at the mothers' breasts. And throughout the day and the night we do not stop reading the holy Law, praying and reciting hymns.' See also A. Cowley, *JQR*, vii [1894], p. 128. The Falashas, too, pass the whole night in prayer, cf. Wolf Leslau, *Falasha Anthology*, New Haven 1951, p. xxxiv. It is well known that the

3. Donning of sackcloth and strewing of ashes.
4. Weeping aloud until one faints.[1]

mediaeval German ḥasidim did the same (*Rabia*, ii, 190; *Ṭur*, *'Oraḥ Ḥayyim*, 619). Cf. the interesting observation by Moses ibn Makhir in his *Seder ha-Yom*, Venice 1599, p. 91b: ויש מי שאינו ישן כל הלילה וכל היום ויש שעומד על עומדו אפילו כל הלילה וענין זה כבד מאד לבעלי תורה תשי כח וראוי להם לחוש שלא יחלו והכתוב הזהיר השמרו בנפשותיכם (ירמי׳ י״ז, 21). אבל מי שהוא ב״ת ויש לו כח לסבול ונדבו לבו לעשות הענין הזה לענות נפשו ביום ובלילה כל מעת לעת מה טוב ומה נעים לו ותשובתו תהיה רצויה ומקובלת וירחמו עליו מן השמים ויקרא לו ה׳ שלום.

[1] For weeping as a concomitant of fasting, see *Joel* 2, 12; *Esther* 4, 1, 3; 9, 31; *II Macc.* 13, 12; *II Bar.* 5, 7; 9, 2; *IV Ezra* 5, 20; 6, 35. As a condition of repentance, see Baḥya ibn Paqudah, *Ḥobhoth ha-Lebhabhoth* vii, 5 beginning, and Maimonides, *Hilekhoth Teshubhah*, ii, 4. Weeping was also in Rabbanite circles a characteristic feature of the *Yōm Kippūr* service, as may be inferred from the frequent references to weeping and tears in the religious poetry for the Day of Atonement. See further J. L. Palache in *ZDMG*, lxx [1916], pp. 251–6; Immanuel Löw, 'Tränen' in *Abhandlungen zur Erinnerung an Hirsch Perez Chajes*, Vienna 1933, pp. 116–19.

Weeping on the Day of Atonement might easily create the impression that *Yōm Kippūr* is a day of mourning and grief, and thus lend support to the heterodox view concerning the nature of the day. It is against the background of this consideration that we have to read the following *'aggadah* explaining 'historically' the institution of the Day of Atonement, the obvious tendency of which is to represent the weeping on *Yōm Kippūr* as 'weeping of joy': ארבעים יום שעלה משה למרום להביא תורה לישראל היו ישראל נוהגין כל אותם הימים צום ותענית ויום אחרון שבכולן גזרו תענית ולנו בתענית למחר השכימו ועלו לפני הר סיני והיו בוכים לקראת משה ומשה בוכה לקראתם עד שעלתה בכייתם לפני הקב״ה. באותה שעה נתגלגלו רחמיו של הקב״ה וקבל אותם בתשובה ובשרה אותם רוח הקדש בשורה טובה מלפניו, אמר להם בני נשבעתי בכסא הכבוד שלי שתהא לכם בכייה זו בכית שמחה ויהא לכם יום כפרה וסליחה לכם ולבני בניכם עד סוף כל הדורות (*Yalquṭ* on *Exodus*, 391; *'Eliyyahu Zuṭa*, ed. M. Friedmann, pp. 180f.).

(This 'historical' explanation of the origin of the Day of Atonement should be contrasted with the one given by the heterodox author of the *Book of Jubilees*, to be dealt with further on in the text.)

On the other hand, the Jews in the Caucasian town of Derbent, among whom the custom prevailed of young maidens dancing and singing in the streets to the accompaniment of musical instruments (see further on in the text), thus giving tangible expression to the festive character of *Yōm Kippūr*, refrained from weeping during the recitation of the *Yōm Kippūr* prayers (cf. J. J. Chorny, ספר המסעות בארץ קוקז, Petersburg 1884, p. 303).

This being the case, the term *ṣōm* conveys merely part of the obligations imposed by the Law; only *ta'anīth*, self-affliction, is comprehensive enough to embrace the above-mentioned obligations as well. Proceeding to nomenclature he has this to say:[1]

> The most apt name for 'fast' is *ta'anīth*, because it conveys the notion of 'self-affliction', as Ezra said (9, 6): *And at the evening offering I arose from my fasting* (תעניתי), *even with my garments and my mantle rent*. Therefore, the meaning of *And ye shall afflict your souls* is fasting with all the afflictions I have mentioned.

Al-Qumisi thus puts the Day of Atonement on a par with other fast-days,[2] demanding that the ceremonial associated with them should be observed on it, as well. Excluded are solely those actions which fall under the prohibition of work. The most conspicuous of the fast-day procedures are, naturally, the wearing of sackcloth and covering oneself with ashes. These acts alone are sufficient to nullify the festal character of *Yōm Kippūr* and impart to it a mournful and sombre aspect.

Al-Qumisi, otherwise a vehement opponent of 'Anan, follows in this important question in the footsteps of the heresiarch. The section of 'Anan's *Book of Precepts* treating of the laws of the Day of Atonement is unfortunately lost; we are therefore denied a detailed knowledge of his views on this most solemn day of the year, but a casual observation in another context sheds an illuminating light on 'Anan's general idea of *Yōm Kippūr*. He insists[3] that on that day, as on all other fast-days, ashes should be strewn

[1] Cf. L. Ginzberg, *op. cit.* p. 486, note 22. For al-Qumisi's usage of the term סגולה cf. *Pithron*, p. 69, and his *Epistle*, *JQR*, xii, pp. 278, 288.

[2] It is against this equalization of the Fast of Atonement with other fast-days that Tobias b. Eliezer polemizes in the commentary on *Leviticus* (ed. Wilna 1880, ii, p. 132): ...ולא עינויין שנוהגין בשאר תעניות כמו שאמר דוד (תהל׳ ל״ה, 13) עניתי בצום נפשי ותפלתי אל חיקי תשוב, הא אין לך למנות אלא ששה עינויים שבמשנתנו.

[3] See J. Mann, *Journal of Jewish Lore and Philosophy*, i [1919], p. 353 (=S. Schechter, *Documents of Jewish Sectaries*, ii, p. 29). Cf. Raphael Mahler, *Karayimer* (in Yiddish), New York 1947, p. 195.

and the curtain of the Ark be covered (with sackcloth). He thus places *Yōm Kippūr* on the same level with an ordinary fast-day.

As in so many other practices of his, in this case too 'Anan is not an innovator; he reintroduced long-abandoned observances, or championed the cause of local usages lingering on in splinter groups, either orthodox or heterodox. In this particular instance he is in essential agreement with the author of the *Book of Jubilees*.

This unique book advanced a unique reason for the institution of the Day of Atonement (34, 13–19)—a reason which outright stamps it as a day of mourning. It was instituted, it maintains, to commemorate the grief and mourning of the patriarch Jacob at the news that his son Joseph was torn in pieces by a wild beast, on which occasion it is said (*Gen.* 37, 34): *And Jacob rent his garments, and put sackcloth upon his loins, and mourned for his son many days.*

> For this reason it is ordained for the children of Israel that they should afflict themselves on the tenth of the seventh month—on the day that the news which made him weep for Joseph came to Jacob his father—that they should make atonement for themselves with a young goat on the tenth of the seventh month, once a year, for their sins; for they had grieved the affection of their father regarding Joseph his son. And this day has been ordained that they should grieve thereon for their sins and for all their transgressions and for all their errors, so that they might cleanse themselves on that day once a year.

This motivation of the origin of the fast reveals in a most transparent manner the author's idea of *Yōm Kippūr* as a day of grief and mourning. He does not specify the ways in which grief should be manifested for the simple reason that this could be taken as universally known from popular practice. In any case, as a day commemorating Jacob's mourning it would require, as a matter of course, weeping and the donning of sackcloth, if not the rending of garments, as the patriarch Jacob did.

The intention of this motivation is, no doubt, polemical. It is designed to inculcate, by establishing on 'historical' ground, the idea that *Yōm Kippūr* is a season of grief. It claims, in effect, that its character had been determined from the very outset by its origin, by its historical association. This is in sharp contrast to the pharisaic-rabbinic view, shared by Philo,[1] which regarded *Yōm Kippūr* as a festival. It is diametrically opposed to the joy and merriment manifested in the festivity arranged by the high-priest for his friends after completing the service at the Temple on *Yōm Kippūr*,[2] and most particularly to the celebrations, jollifications, and dances by the daughters of Jerusalem of which Rabban Simeon b. Gamaliel reported:[3] 'There were no more joyous days in Israel than the fifteenth of Ab and the Day of Atonement on which the daughters of Jerusalem, garbed in white borrowed garments (so as not to put to shame the poor), would dance in the vineyards.'

That this was not an isolated custom is shown by the fact that it spread to the Diaspora and survived in several ancient communities, situated at great distances from each other. Of the Jews in Antioch in the fourth century the Church Father John Chrysostom narrates that they danced barefooted in public squares.[4] This 'golden-mouthed' Jew-hater, chagrined by the fact that many of his own fold participated in the Jewish fast, sarcastically observes that the Jews pretended to fast but they looked like drunkards. No more graphic description of the dual character of the Day of Atonement as Fast-Feast could be given than this picture of fasting, barefooted people indulging in public dancing. The custom of dancing still obtains among the Falasha Jews in Abyssinia where the dancing is performed by men and

[1] *De spec. leg.* I, 187 [Loeb, vii, p. 207]: 'The high dignity of this day has two aspects, one as a festival, the other as a time of purification and escape from sin'; II, 193 [p. 427]: 'The next feast after the 'Trumpets' is the Fast. Perhaps some of the perversely minded who are not ashamed to censure things exalted will say, What sort of feast is this in which there are no gatherings to eat and drink? . . . This the clear-seeing eyes of Moses the ever wise discerned and therefore he called the fast a feast, the greatest of the feasts, in his native tongue a Sabbath of Sabbaths . . .' Cf. also I. Elbogen, *Studien zur Geschichte d. jüd. Gottesdienstes*, Berlin 1907, p. 53.

[2] Mishnah *Yoma*, vii, 4; *Middoth*, v, end.

[3] Mishnah *Ta'anith*, iv, 8.

[4] Cf. *Ben-Chananja*, iii, p. 570.

women separately.[1] In the Caucasian town of Derbent it is customary for the maidens to gather in groups and dance in the streets to the accompaniment of musical instruments.[2] A variation of the custom prevails in Tripolitania where boys between the ages of 9–11, dressed in festive clothes, dance round the synagogue, singing wedding-songs.[3]

This old custom, whatever its origin may have been, vividly and dramatically underlines the festive nature of *Yōm Kippūr*. It is easy to picture in one's mind the striking contrast between worshippers cloaked in sackcloth and covered with ashes, worn out through lack of sleep and continuous standing, and fainting from loud and excessive weeping, on the one hand—and on the other, people dressed in white festive garments with the women wearing their precious ornaments and maidens and young men dancing and singing—a telling picture indeed of the wide gulf separating the two conflicting conceptions regarding the nature of the holiest day in the Jewish calendar.

That the *Book of Jubilees* was studied in Qumran is evidenced by the fact that fragments of about ten manuscripts in the original Hebrew were found in Caves I, II and IV.[4] Further, the author of the *Damascus Document* explicitly referred his readers to this work.[5] Particularly significant is the close link between Qumran and *Jubilees* in a matter of such central importance as the question of the calendar. It seems that a good case has been made out for the view that the calendar of the Sect was

[1] See A. Z. Aescoly, ספר הפלשים, Jerusalem 1943, p. 67; *Encyclopaedia Judaica*, vol. vi, col. 908.

[2] Cf. Joseph Judah Chorny, *Sepher ha-Massa'oth*, p. 303 (see *supra*, p. 168, n. 1); Z. Kashdai, ממלכות אררט, Odessa 1912, p. 40. According to the latter, the musical instruments were played by non-Jews who accompanied the maidens through the streets.

[3] Cf. N. Slousz, מסעי בארץ לוב [*Mes Voyages en Lybie*], Tel Aviv 1943, ii, p. 85.

[4] See J. T. Milik, *Ten Years of Discovery in the Wilderness of Judaea*, p. 32.

[5] *CDC*, xvi, 3–4.

identical with the one advocated by *Jubilees*.[1] On the grounds of these facts and of other affinities some scholars have felt justified in going so far as to maintain that *Jubilees* actually emanated from Qumran;[2] and even if one does not concur with this view, there is no denial that the links are close and striking. It ought therefore to occasion no surprise if the Qumranites followed *Jubilees* not only in fixing the date of *Yōm Kippūr* but also in the manner of its observance.

The designation *yōm ha-taʿanīth*, *Day of Self-Affliction*, is indicative of that observance. We have seen al-Qumisi, for whom *Yōm-Kippūr* was likewise a day of grief, expressly pleading for that designation as a more accurate characterization of the day. As a contrast, it is not uninteresting to mention that the founder of Neo-Orthodoxy, S. R. Hirsch, objects to the use of the German verb *kasteien* ('afflict') with reference to *Yōm Kippūr*, since this verb coming as it does from the Latin *castigare* carries the implication of chastizing and tormenting actions, which are out of harmony with the rabbinic conception of *Yōm Kippūr*.[3]

II

The foregoing discussion has inevitably raised the problems of the evolution of the Day of Atonement and its observances. Naturally, it cannot be our task to deal with these complex problems in this volume; it would require a separate monograph. But in the present context a few observations will be made concerning certain customs still in vogue among the Jews today, which can best be explained as survivals of the ancient fast ceremonial or, like section B *infra*, as a calculated opposition to it. Particular attention will be paid to the practice of wearing sackcloth and

[1] Cf. A. Jaubert, *VT*, iii [1953], pp. 250–64; vii [1957], pp. 35–61; Shemaryahu Talmon, *Scripta Hierosolymitana*, iv, pp. 176ff.; H. H. Rowley, *Jewish Apocalyptic and the Dead Sea Scrolls* (The Ethel M. Wood Lecture, 1957), p. 22.

[2] Milik, *loc. cit.*

[3] See *Der Pentateuch, übersetzt u. erklärt von Samson Raphael Hirsch* (Frankfurt am Main 1920), iii, p. 348.

strewing of ashes, these being the principal and most conspicuous elements in that ceremonial.

A. Let us, then, begin with the practice just mentioned. The Jews of Kurdistan are in the habit of wearing on the Day of Atonement a rope made of goat's hair close to the body.[1] This custom practised by the members of an ancient Jewish community still speaking an Aramaic dialect is not only interesting but highly significant. It is like a beacon of light brilliantly illuminating a dark scene. Manifestly the custom is but a remnant of an original practice of donning sackcloth on the Fast of Atonement, the rope serving as a substitute for the sackcloth garment which is made of the same material. It is another illustration of a phenomenon so frequently met with in the realm of Jewish practice that ancient customs seldom, if ever, entirely disappear without leaving traces behind, be it only in some remote and dark corner in Jewry.

There are a number of reasons suggesting that this element of the fast-ritual was not omitted, at least in circles of rigoristic-ascetic tendencies, on the Great Fast. It must be remembered that wearing sackcloth and putting ashes on one's head were always associated with fasting and were deeply ingrained in the people's consciousness as being integral to a fast-day. The custom is presupposed by *Isaiah*,[2] is graphically described in the Book of *Jonah*,[3] where even the beasts were covered with sackcloth, was practised by Mordecai and the Jews of Susa,[4] by Nehemiah[5] and Daniel,[6] and was given particular prominence in the Book of *Judith* the relevant passages of which are worth quoting:[7]

[1] Erich Brauer, *The Jews of Kurdistan*, p. 260.

[2] *Isa.* 58, 5. See further on in the text.

[3] *Jonah* 3, 5, 6, 8.

[4] *Esth.* 4, 1, 3.

[5] *Neh.* 9, 1.

[6] *Dan.* 9, 3.

[7] *Judith* 4, 9–15.

> 'And every man of Israel cried unto God with great earnestness . . . and they humbled their souls. They, their wives and their babes and their cattle and every sojourner and hireling and servant bought with their money put sackcloth upon their loins . . . and cast ashes upon their heads, and spread out the sackcloth before the Lord; and they put sackcloth about the altar . . . and the people continued fasting many days in all Judaea and Jerusalem . . . And Joakim the high priest, and all the priests . . . had their loins girt about with sackcloth . . . and they had ashes on their mitres.'

Fasting and sackcloth go together also among the Elephantine Jews who, in a letter addressed to the Persian Governor Bagohi in the year 408 B.C.E., confess that since the destruction of their temple they wear sackcloth and fast.[1] *I Maccabees* 3, 47, testifies to the same association, and it is well known that sackcloth and ashes were elements in the fast-ritual of tannaitic and amoraic times.[2] What is indicative of the deep-rootedness of this time-honoured custom is the fact that it persisted up to late gaonic times, as we learn from the detailed descriptions by Sar Shalom, Sherira and Hai of the fast-ritual practised by them.[3]

[1] A. Cowley, *Aramaic Papyri of the Fifth Century B.C.*, pp. 112–14, 120.

[2] Mishnah, *Ta'anith*, ii, 1; B.T. *Ta'anith* 16a. See Me'iri (ed. Abraham Sofer-Schreiber), p. 41; Maimonides, *Hilekhoth Ta'aniyyoth*, iv, 1.

Two other characteristic passages illustrative of the close association between sackcloth and ashes on one hand and fasting on the other may be cited. In the description of Moses' endeavours to escape death (*Deut. R.*, 11, 9) we read: משה... גזר עליו תענית... לבש שק ונתעטף שק ונתפלש באפר ועמד בתפלה ובתחנונים לפני הקב"ה. *Derekh 'Ereṣ Rabbah*, ii, end: וגוזרין צום ומתפלשים באפר ומתכסים בשקים ומורידים דמעות. Note the feature of shedding of tears; see above p. 168, n. 1.

[3] *'Oṣar ha-Ge'onim*, *Ta'anith*, pp. 23, 24. From this description it appears that only the precentor and the priests sounding the *shofar* were clad in sackcloth. In addition, the Ark and the Scrolls of the Law were covered with it: והדר נחית שליח צבור... כדלביש שק וכד נחית שק על תיבותא וספרי וכהני דקימין בשיפורי.

Among the Jews of Yemen the custom of wearing sackcloth on the Ninth of Ab has persisted, at least among the older generation, up to the present time. See also *Massekheth Sopherim*, xviii, 5 (ed. Michael Higger, p. 316): וראשו מתפלש באפר; xviii, 9 (p. 321): וכולם מתפלשין באפר.

All this overwhelmingly testifies to the conjunction of fasting and sackcloth and ashes, the latter being a constant concomitant of the former.[1] In view of this, it would indeed be astonishing if the biblical Fast of Atonement were not observed, at least in some circles, in the conventional manner of fasting.

Exegetical considerations may have added support for this strict view: the commandment *Ye shall afflict your souls*, as indicated, includes other forms of self-mortification in addition to fasting. It could, then, be contended that the Torah explicitly enjoined *self-affliction* and not merely fasting.[2] But there is still another approach to our problem which leads to identical conclusions. I refer to the argument recorded by Levi b. Yefeth ha-Levi[3] —an argument based on the penitential aspect of the Day of Atonement.

Yōm Kippūr, so the argument runs, is an occasion of repentance, a day dedicated to procuring forgiveness of sin; it ought therefore to be observed by performing those devotional and penitential actions which are reported in the Bible as having been performed by those striving to obtain atonement. These actions are the biblical pre-conditions of repentance. The need of fasting, prayer and supplication we learn from Moses who fasted and

[1] See also *Reallexikon für Antike und Christentum* (ed. Theodor Klauser, Stuttgart 1957), vol. iii, cols. 127–36; J. Schümmer, *Die altchristliche Fastenpraxis* (Münster 1933), pp. 75, 185, 213.

Tertullian gives an interesting description of the fast-day ceremonials in heathen communities (*De jejuniis*, 16; Ante-Nicene Library, xviii, p. 151): 'But more than that: the heathen recognize every form of self-humiliation. When the heaven is rigid and the year arid, barefooted processions are enjoined by public proclamation; the magistrates lay aside their purple, reverse the *fasces*, utter prayer, offer a victim. There are, moreover, some colonies where, besides, the people, by an annual rite, clad in sackcloth and besprent with ashes, present a suppliant importunity to their idols, while baths and shops are kept shut till the ninth hour . . . There is, I believe, a Ninevitan suspension of business!' Cf. to this Mishnah *Ta'anith*, i, 6: ונועלין את המרחצאות... ונועלין את החנויות.

[2] Cf. Appendix, no. 2.

[3] See Appendix, no. 3.

prayed on behalf of the Israelites;[1] from the conduct of the Israelites themselves we derive the duty of mourning and discarding beautiful clothes and ornaments;[2] weeping and donning of sackcloth are mentioned by the prophet *Joel* 1, 13 and, finally, the penitential attitude of lowering one's head we learn from Ezra (9, 6). Thus the obligation of mourning, weeping and wearing sackcloth on the Day of Atonement is a corollary to its being a day of repentance.

This is indeed an argument of considerable force seeing that sackcloth and ashes were the regular accompaniments of repentance. This holds true, it may now be added, also of the period of the rise of Christianity, as we learn from *Matthew* 11, 21 and *Luke* 10, 13. Further, the first-century *Tanna*, 'Eli'ezer b. Hyrcanus uses the phrase 'sackcloth and fasting' as equivalent to 'penitence'.[3]

[1] *Deut.* 9, 18.

[2] *Ex.* 33, 4. 'Change of garments and removal of ornaments' figures as the third 'condition' in the penitential discipline of Baḥya ibn Paqudah (*Ḥobhoth ha-Lebhabhoth*, *Gate of Repentance*, v). This is likewise prescribed by Eleazar of Worms (*Roqeaḥ*, *Hilekhoth Teshubhah* 24): צריך להסיר ממנו כל מלבושי תפארתו ולא ישית עדיו עליו ויתאבל ויבכה ויצטער ויתענה. Cf. also B.T. *Rosh ha-Shanah* 26a: 'A sinner must not adorn himself' (חוטא בל יתנאה).

Y. Y. Rivlin (*Tarbiz*, vol. xxvi [1956], p. 25) argues that *Sūra*, vii, 29–30 contains a polemic against the fast of *Yōm Kippūr*. If this is correct, then Muhammad's observation about the removal of ornaments would reflect the custom among Arabian Jews of putting off their best clothes and ornaments on that day.

On the other hand, it is reported of the Jews in Khaibar that on the Day of Atonement they made the womenfolk wear their best garments (see Georges Vajda, 'Jeûne Musulman et Jeûne Juif', *HUCA*, vol. xii–xiii [1937–38], p. 374). This need not be a contradiction; it is quite possible that the Jews in Arabia were divided among themselves on this issue.

[3] *Gen. R.* 84, 19 (edition Theodor-Albeck, p. 1023). The aggadic comment is based on the word וישב which is taken in a technical sense 'he manifested תשובה'. Reuben was the first man to do penitence (בכור לתשובה), see *Gen. R.* 82, 11 (p. 990) and parallels. 'Sackcloth and fasting' are often coupled together in rabbinic literature, see *Gen. R.* 85, 1 (p. 1030); B.T. *Meg.*, 16a; *Esther R.* 10, 6.

A fact of some significance emerges from the views of the leaders of the ḥasidic movement in mediaeval Germany, around Yehudah the Pious of Worms (died 1217). In the true spirit of *ḥasiduth* these pietists were not content, as regards *Yōm Kippūr*, with the halakhic demands of the Mishnah, but imposed upon themselves positive acts of self-mortification such as wakefulness on the night of *Yōm Kippūr* and standing on one's feet during the twenty-four hours of the fast. Since penitence assumed a paramount and central importance in their lives,[1] they were palpably disconcerted by the fact that sackcloth, the penitential dress *par excellence*, is not worn on the Day of Atonement, the day of penitence *par excellence*.[2] More astonishing still, there was not even any prohibition of wearing beautiful garments and ornaments on this day of penitence—a prohibition which one would have expected on the basis of *Ex.* 33, 5: '*Put off thy ornaments from thee, that I may know what to do unto thee*', which implies that the penitent should abstain from donning beautiful clothes.[3] We recall that Karaite ascetics invoked the identical *Exodus* passage for the same purpose,[4] but while they, unfettered by halakhic considerations and traditional usage, drew practical conclusions from it, the ḥasidic devotees, restricted as they were by regard for *Halakhah* and custom, had to find explanations for this anomaly.

The *Sepher Ḥasidim* displays considerable ingenuity in proving both points from Scripture.[5] Sackcloth and rending of garments

[1] Cf. Gershom G. Scholem, *Major Trends in Jewish Mysticism* (Jerusalem 1941), p. 103: 'It [penitence] became the central fact of their existence'.

[2] This omission must have been felt by these *Ḥasidim* to be all the more embarrassing since in their Christian environment (to which they were by no means indifferent, see I. Baer, *Zion*, iii [1938], pp. 1–50) the penitential dress was obligatory for the penitent, who had to wear the *silicium*, i.e. a black, coarse, sack-like garment made of goat's hair; see *Reallexikon f. Antike u. Christ.*, vol. ii, cols. 813f.; iii, p. 131.

[3] See *supra*, p. 177, note 2.

[4] See *supra*, p. 177; Hadassi, 248, *waw*.

[5] *Sepher Ḥasidim* [*Das Buch der Frommen*], ed. J. Wistinetzki (2nd edition, Frankfurt a.M. 1924), p. 49, כתיב (שמות ל״ג, 5) הורד עדיך מעליך ואדעה מה אעשה לך הודיענו שבעל תשובה לא ילבש בגדי

are linked together in *II Kings*, 6, 30; consequently, so it is argued, on a day like *Yōm Kippūr* on which rending of garments is forbidden, no sackcloth is worn. That fine clothes may be worn, the author finds indicated in *Isa.* 26, 15: יספת לגוי יי יספת לגוי נכבדת, which, according to the interpretation he placed on these words, should be paraphrased thus: *Thou hast ordered an 'addition' to the nation, O Lord, Thou hast ordered an 'addition', [therefore] thou shalt honour thyself.* The sense which he extracted from this is: On *Yōm Kippūr*, which is distinguished by two 'additions', i.e. an additional sacrifice and the prohibition of labour, one may honour oneself by wearing fine clothes.[1] He further cites *Joel* 2, 12–13: *Turn ye unto Me with all your heart, and with fasting, and with weeping, and with lamentation; and rend your heart and not your garments.* The prophet, he contends, referred here to the Day of Atonement on which penitence is unaccompanied by rending of garments.

The example from *Sepher Ḥasidim* bears eloquent testimony to the strenuous efforts ascetic spirits had to make in order to reconcile the character of *Yōm Kippūr* as a day of fasting and penitence with the absence thereon of the penitential practices that are recorded so frequently in Scripture, and which conformed to their own ideal and concept of penitence.

But there seems also to be direct evidence that the fast on the

חמודות. וביום הכפורים לפי שהוא יום טוב לא צוה שלא להלביש בגדי חמודות מפני שני דברים שניתוספו בו קרבן מוספין ואיסור מלאכה...ועוד ביום שיוכל לקרוע בגדים יש שק...אבל ביום הכפורים שאינו יכול לקרוע אין שק. כתיב (יואל ב׳ 12–13) שובו עדי בכל לבבכם ובצום ובבכי ובמספד וקרעו לבבכם ואל בגדיכם ושובו זה יום הכפורים שאין בו קריעת בגדים...שצריך לקרוע הלב ולא הבגדים.

The interpretation of *Isa.* 26, 15 as relating to the Day of Atonement is not unparalleled; Yiṣḥaq Ibn Gayyath composed a *piyyūṭ* for *Yōm Kippūr* (יספת אלקים לנחלתך; Davidson, *op. cit.* ii, 3107) which is based on the same verse. On the other hand in *Pesiqta de-Rabbi Kahana* (ed. Buber), p. 189b and *Pes. Rab.* (Friedmann), p. 200a, the verse is applied to the Eighth Day of Solemn Assembly (*Shemini 'Aṣereth*).

[1] Cf. B.T. *Shabbath* 113b: R. Yoḥanan called his garments his 'honourers'. The idea as such is ascribed in mediaeval Jewish writings to Ben-Sira, see M. Z. Segal, *Sepher Ben-Sira ha-Shalem*, Introduction, p. 39.

tenth of Tishri was celebrated with the usual accompaniments of every fast-day. It was J. M. Sachs[1] who first suggested that *Isa.* 58, which became the prophetic lesson (*haphṭarah*) for the Day of Atonement was actually delivered by the prophet on the occasion of the Great Fast. This view was later championed by David Hoffman[2] and has recently been adopted, albeit with some modifications particularly as regards dating, by a critical Bible student like Julian Morgenstern,[3] who convincingly argues that the fast-day of which the prophet spoke could only have been *Yōm Kippūr*. This being the *Sitz im Leben* of the prophetic address, it provides evidence that the prophet's contemporaries celebrated the Fast of Atonement in sackcloth and ashes and in self-humiliation. The prophet himself did not deprecate these practices as such, but only their hypocritical performance; his scathing words were aimed at those believing that these formal observances alone, divorced from righteous and ethical living, would assure them of divine favour:

> '*Should such be the fast that I have chosen,*
> *A day of a man's self-affliction?*
> *Is it to bow one's head down as a bulrush,*
> *Or should one spread out sackcloth and ashes?*
> *Wouldest thou call this a fast,*
> *And a day acceptable to the Lord?*'

The view of normative Judaism concerning the character of *Yōm Kippūr* as a fast-feast has long carried the day, but, as noted, a vestige of a divergent conception has remained in the form of the coarse rope of goat's hair worn by the Jews of Kurdistan.

Another vestige, this time of a literary nature, is to be found in an ancient *widduy* formula figuring as an epilogue[4] to the '*Abhōdāh 'Amiṣ Koaḥ* by Meshullam b. Qalonymus, customary in the

[1] *Kerem Ḥemed*, vii, pp. 124f.

[2] *Magazin für die Wissenschaft des Judentums*, iii [1876], pp. 5f.

[3] *HUCA*, vol. 24 [1952–53], pp. 21f.; 37–39; 63, note 131.

[4] It follows, and is sometimes erroneously combined with, the composition תעינו מאחריך (Davidson, iii, 423) which in the Polish ritual concludes the '*Abhodah* mentioned in the text. In the printed editions of the German *Maḥzor* the alphabetical pieces are differently arranged.

Ashkenazic rite. In the printed editions of the *Maḥzor* according to the German-Polish ritual the formula appears in a truncated form, the second part beginning with the word אבל and containing the reference to sackcloth and ashes having been omitted.[1] The text given below is that of MS. British Museum, Add. 17,055 (Catalogue number 673=A), fol. 159b:[2]

[1] The first part of the formula up to המלך is also found in the *Maḥzor* according to the Byzantine rite, MS. British Museum, Or. 9150, fol. 323b, where it figures among the *Seliḥoth* for the Ten Days of Penitence. It is preceded by the rubric: ואומר וידוי It further appears in *Siddur Romania* (Constantinople 1574), i, p. 43b, among the penitential prayers for the fast of the tenth of Tebeth. Here, too, it is included in the *widduy* section (ואומר זה הוידוי). But the continuation is entirely different and bears no relation to our text.

[2] I have collated A with MSS. British Museum, 674=B; 657=C; 667=D; MSS. Oxford, 1024=E; 1025=F; 1034=G; 1048=I; MS. Vatican, Assemani 320=J; MS. Montefiore (Jews' College), 207=K.

In MS. J our formula occurs on fol. 240a where the copyist recorded the prospective version of *Kol Nidrē* (נוסח אחר להתרת נדרים) and follows immediately after it, together with three alphabetical compositions which are recited at the end of the *ʻAbhodah* mentioned: (1) אר״א תתן אחרית לעמך; (2) אר״א אל תעש עמנו כלה; (3) אר״א תאמר למחות אשמינו. It appears that in some places these were recited also on *Yōm Kippūr* eve. In fact, no. (2) is prescribed for that occasion in *Seder Rabh ʻAmram* (ed. Warsaw), ii, p. 40b.

This custom of reciting *widduy* immediately after *Kol Nidrē* (which is said a short time before the actual commencement of *Yōm Kippūr*) is unparalleled in any of the existing rituals. It is, however, in accordance with the tannaitic *halakhah*, most particularly as recorded in *Tosephta Yoma*, iv, 14 (see also B.T. *ibid.*, 87b), prescribing the confession for 'the eve of the Day of Atonement, at nightfall'. And although the Sages recommended to advance the confession to before the meal, lest one might become confused through excessive drinking, one has to repeat it again after the meal, close to the beginning of the festival; cf. Naḥmanides, quoted by Rabbenu Nissim (RaN) in the commentary on Alfasi *ad loc.*: מצות וידוי של ערב יוה״כ שצריך להתוודות... עם חשיכה סמוך ליום עצמו כדי שלא יהא שהות לחטוא בין הוידוי והיום. It is in order to conform to this view, championed by Naḥmanides, that it became customary among Sephardic and Yemenite Jews to recite before *Kol Nidrē* the *piyyūṭ* לך אלי תשוקתי (I. Davidson, *Thesaurus*, iii, 809); the latter includes a lengthy *widduy* formula. Cf. Mosheh Ibn Ḥabib, *Tōsepheth Yōm Ha-Kippūrīm* on *Yoma* 87b (in his work entitled שמות בארץ): פה ירושלים תוב׳ נוהגים שקודם שיתפללו ערבית אומרים כל הקהל בקשת לך אלי תשוקתי שיש בה וידוי לצאת י״ח הרמב״ן; de Silva, *Peri Ḥadhash* on *'Oraḥ Ḥayyim*, 607, 1.

מה נדבר ומה נצטדק,[1]
מה נענה לממנו מענה,[2]
גמלנו טובות ושלמנו רעות,[3]
ומה יש לנו עוד צדקה לזעוק לפני[4] המלך.[5]
אבל[6] שק ואפר[7] צום וצעקה שועה והודיה[8] אנו מתפללים[9] לפניך,
ואתה תשמע השמים[10] ביום צום הכפורים הזה,[11] ביום סליחת העון הזה,[12]

[1] *Gen.* 44, 16.

[2] Cf. *Prov.* 16, 1.

[3] *Gen.* 44, 4; *I Sam.* 24, 17.

[4] MSS. CDEFGK: פני; BIJ: אל.

[5] *II Sam.* 19, 29.

[6] All MSS. (with the exception of J which is not provided with vowels, and MS. K which vocalizes *'ebhel*—see further on in the text) vocalize the *beth* with *pathaḥ*. This is also the case in editions Pesaro or Rimini (?), *c.* 1520, Augsburg 1537 and Sabbionetta 1557.

[7] D omits: שק ואפר; cf. *infra* in the text.

[8] CEFK, Eliezer b. Nathan of Mayence (in his commentary on the *Maḥzor*, MS. Montefiore [Jews' College], 261, fol. 62b), as well as eds. Sabbionetta, Fürth 1792, and Rödelheim 1803, add: בם.

[9] CEFK, Eliezer b. Nathan, eds. Amsterdam (1768), Fürth and Rödelheim read: מתוודים.

[10] *I Kings* 8, 32, 34, 36, 39.

[11] On a Sabbath the mention of *Yōm Kippūr* was preceded by a reference to the Sabbath: ביום השבת הזה (G); ב' ש' קדש ה' (J); ביום המנוח הזה (BK).

[12] K: סליחות עון ופשע; I is corrupt: סליחות אבותינו; CE: עונינו; F: עונותינו.

The designation of *Yōm Kippūr* as 'the day of pardoning iniquity' occurs in the texts of the *'Amidah* for *Yōm Kippūr* recovered from the Genizah, see I. Elbogen, 'Die Tefillah für die Festtage' in *MGWJ*, 1911, pp. 442, 597; J. Mann, 'Genizah Fragments of the Palestinian Order of Service', in *HUCA*, ii [1925], pp. 330, 331. Also in *Massekheth Sopherim*, xix, 4 (ed. M. Higger, p. 326; here: מחילת). In *Seder Rabh 'Amram* (ed. Warsaw) p. 47a the phrase is not original; it is absent in MSS. Oxford (see Frumkin II, p. 344) and Sulzberger (cf. Alexander Marx, 'Untersuchungen zum Siddur des Gaon R. Amram', *Jahrbuch der Jüdisch-Literarischen Gesellschaft*, v, Hebrew part, p. 34).

כי לכפרה נתת אותו לנו,[1] למחילת עון[2] ולסליחת פשע.[3]

What shall we say, and how shall we justify ourselves? What shall we answer Him from whom answer comes? He hath bestowed good upon us, but we returned evil. What right have we any more to cry unto the King? But we are praying unto Thee in sackcloth and ashes, fasting and weeping, crying aloud[4] and confessing; and do Thou hear in heaven on this fast-day of atonement, on this day of pardoning iniquity; for to obtain forgiveness hast Thou given it to us, for remission of sin and pardoning transgression.

The Palestinian and Babylonian Talmuds[5] know of several formulas for confession of sin for the Day of Atonement. These are distinguished by their brevity and simplicity of style. So, too, is our formula, which manifestly bears the impress of antiquity, composed as it is of quotations and adaptations of scriptural phrases and being devoid of the artificial devices of paytanic productions.[6] Its antiquity is conspicuously apparent

[1] DG: לכפרת חטא (חט); CFI omit: אותו; D omits: לנו.

[2] J: למחול; CEFIK: חטא.

[3] EFI: למחילת חטא ולסליחת עון ולכ׳ פ׳; B: ולכפרת פ׳; CK: ולס׳ ולכ׳ פ׳.
With the latter half of our formula cf. the prayer (patterned on the 'short prayer' said by Rabbi Ṣadoq on Friday evening; *Tosephta Ber.*, iii, 7) recited at the conclusion of the repetition of the *Musaph 'Amidah* on *Yōm Kippūr*: ומאהבתך יי אלהינו שאהבת את ישראל עמך ומחמלתך מלכנו שחמלת על בני בריתך נתת לנו יי אלהינו (את יום השבת הזה) ואת יום צום הכפורים הזה למחילת חטא ולסליחת עון ולכפרת פשע. For a Genizah version of this prayer see Elbogen, *op. cit.* p. 598.

[4] For 'crying aloud' as a concomitant of fasting, see *Jonah*, 3, 8; *Neh.* 9, 4; *Esth.* 9, 31; *I Macc.* 3, 47–54; *Judith*, 4, 9, 12, 15.

[5] B.T. *Yoma* 87b; P.T. *ibid.*, end (45c). Cf. also *Lev. Rabbah*, iii, 3.

[6] To satisfy an artistic taste nurtured on paytanic forms, attempts were made to provide the initial part of the formula with rhyme by adding appropriate phrases. MS. Bodleian, Cat. no. 1160, fol. 154b, adds two such phrases (Note that the second rhymes only after a change has been made in the original text): מה נדבר [פני מישרים דובר] ומה נצטדקה

from the usage of הודייה in the meaning of 'confession of sin', instead of the established term וידוי.[1]

In this formula, then, we find sackcloth and ashes among the features of the Divine Service on *Yōm Kippūr*. It thus testifies that these were, at a time and at a place which cannot be determined, elements of the *Yōm Kippūr* ceremonial. Although the practice had fallen into desuetude, the prayer reflecting it retained a place in the liturgy of the Great Fast, thus preserving for us the memory of that practice. We have here the same phenomenon one meets in connection with kneeling and prostration: Jews up to this day persist in reciting prayers in which kneeling and prostration are spoken of as being practised by the worshipper, when, in fact, the custom had long been abandoned.[2] Or again: Jewish prayer-books still continue to include a prayer, composed in Aramaic,[3] for the dignitaries of Babylonian Jewry, the exilarch and the heads of the academies, many a century after these offices have become defunct.

The uneasiness caused by the statement: 'We pray (or confess) unto Thee in sackcloth and ashes' is clearly mirrored in the divers attempts made to get rid of it.

1. The most radical method employed is that reflected in several manuscripts[4] and in the Polish ritual: they simply

[פני לובש צדקה]. This version has established itself in the Polish ritual. A different version is contained in MS. J and MS. British Museum, Or. 9150, fol. 323b:

מה נדבר [פני מישרים דובר]
ומה נצטדק [פני כל חי לפניו לא יצדק]
ומה נענה לממנו מענה [כי אין בפינו מענה].

The last two additions are also to be found in *Siddur Romania*.

[1] About the synonymity of the two terms cf. Mishnah *Soṭah*, ix, 10 (יוחנן כהן גדול העביר הודיית מעשר) with the *Baraitha* in B.T. *ibid.* 48a (אף הוא ביטל את הוידוי). See further S. Lieberman, *Tosefta Ki-Fshuṭah*, p. 850, note 79.

[2] See *infra*, p. 188, note 5.

[3] Singer's *Prayer-Book*, p. 151.

[4] MS. British Museum, Cat. no. 669 (=Harley 7618), fol. 80b ('German hand of the 13th century') and no. 671 (=Add. 18, 968), fol. 162a (14th cent.); MS. Bodleian, Cat. no. 1160 (=Opp. 166), fol. 154b.

discarded the second half of the formula containing the reference to the custom in question.

2. A less radical procedure was adopted by MS. D: it contented itself with eliminating the crucial words 'sackcloth and ashes'.

3. An interpretative device was applied by the twelfth-century Tosaphist, 'Eli'ezer b. Nathan of Mayence, who, in his MS. commentary on the *Maḥzor*, divested the words in question of their literal meaning, taking them as merely expressing the idea of repentance.[1]

4. The author of the Judeo-German translation of the *Maḥzor* (Luneville edition, 1827) thought to overcome the difficulty by arbitrarily misrendering the Hebrew text. He translated thus: 'We *ought* to go into mourning, don sackcloth and roll in ashes.'[2]

5. Interesting is the change in the vocalization of the word אֲבַל to read אֵבֶל (*mourning*), found in several printed editions of the Ashkenazi *Maḥzor*, but only in one of the MSS. (K). This change must at first appear puzzling in the extreme; it not only fails to remove the difficulty, but actually increases it by explicitly introducing the idea of mourning, and in a syntactical connection which is, to say the least, harsh: 'Mournful, clad in sackcloth and covered with ashes . . . we are praying before Thee.' What was the intention behind this change?

It appears that Wolf Heidenheim's German translation provides a clue to the motive behind this vocalization. Heidenheim, followed, among others,[3] by the translators of the *Maḥzor* into Dutch[4] and French,[5] took the words אבל and שק as forming a construct relation, translating it: *Trauerkleider* (mourning-garments). The scribe or editor first responsible for this construction, which is untenable on grammatical and contextual grounds,

[1] Fol. 62b: פי׳ כל זה תשובה.

[2] מיר געהערין צו מכין טרויאריגקייט שק אן קליידן אין אשי וועלגרן.

[3] Cf. ed. Hanover 1837, 'verbessert . . . von Isaac Berlin'.

[4] G. I. Polak, *Gebeden der Nederlandsche Israëliten voor den Verzoendag*, Amsterdam 1842.

[5] E. Durlacher, *Erech Hatephiloth ou rituel de toutes les grandes fêtes a l'usage des Israélites du rite Allemand*, Paris 1866 (2nd ed.).

seems to have aimed at eliminating at least the disturbing word 'sackcloth'. But what did he mean by 'mourning-garments'? No doubt, what he had in mind was the *kittel* or *sargenes*, the white sack-shaped overall, worn on the Day of Atonement, which, being likewise used as a shroud for the dead, was regarded as a reminder of death and mourning and hence, according to some authorities,[1] to be worn on *Yōm Kippūr*.

This construction was not shared by all translators of the *Maḥzor*. Mention has already been made of the interpretation placed upon the sentence in question by the Judeo-German translator in the Luneville edition. Much earlier, the author of the translation printed in Amsterdam 1768 had understood the term *'ebhel* as being in the absolute state, and had made no attempts to obliterate the plain sense of the words.[2]

B. There is also the custom of wearing white garments on *Yōm Kippūr*—a custom that has given rise to a variety of explanations.[3] It is supposed to be an emulation of the angels, who were believed to wear white; this colour, says another midrashic explanation, symbolizes the confidence and trust of the Jew in a favourable outcome of the divine judgment; white is an emblem of forgiveness on the basis of *Isa.* 1, 18; it was intended as a reminder of the ultimate fate of man, recalling the white shrouds worn by the dead. Needless to say, these and similar explanations are of but homiletical value, incapable of accounting for the origin of the custom.

I suggest that it originated in opposition to, and was meant as a demonstration against, the practice of donning black[4] sackcloth as

[1] See Moses Isserlis, *'Oraḥ Ḥayyim*, 610, 4; cf. *infra*, section B.

[2] מחזור עם כוונת הפייטן כמנהג אשכנז ושאר קהלות קדושות. The translation runs: ...טרויאריגקייט אין זק אונ׳ אש.

[3] See *Yalquṭ, wa-'Ethḥannan*, 825; *'Oṣar ha-Ge'onim, Yōm Ṭōbh*, p. 25; Aaron ha-Kohen of Narbonne, *op. cit.* p. 234.

[4] Cf. *Isa.* 50, 3: '*I clothe the heavens with blackness, and I make sackcloth their covering*' (Ibn Ezra: בעבור שהשק הוא שחור); *Revelation* 6, 12: '*The sun became black as a sackcloth of hair*'; A. J. Wensinck, *Some Semitic Rites of Mourning and Religion* (Amsterdam 1917), p. 69. Cf. also the proverb: אם יתלבן השק, יתחכם הכסיל (*'Oṣar ha-Ge'onim, Ta'anith*, p. 32).

an integral part of the fast and penitential ceremonial. To counteract the view that this dark and gloomy penitential dress must be worn in keeping with the character of *Yōm Kippūr* as a fast-day and a day of penitence and in conformity with the biblical commandment of self-affliction, it was insisted that, on the contrary, a white festive garment should be worn in order to underline the festive character of the Day of Atonement.[1]

The opposition to heterodox practice is particularly evident in the custom of covering the Ark with a white curtain and of robing the Scrolls of the Law with white mantles. The strewing of ashes on the Ark[2] and on the Scroll of the Law[3] was part of the fast-day ceremonial, and from gaonic reports we gather that it was customary to cover them with sackcloth as well.[4] This custom, it may be briefly noted, manifestly developed from the ancient practice, recorded in the Book of *Judith* 4, 12, of covering the *altar* with sackcloth on a fast-day. Heterodox opinion, which put the Fast of Atonement on a par with other fast-days, must have demanded the performance of this ceremony on *Yōm Kippūr* as well. In fact, the Karaite heresiarch prescribed the 'covering of

[1] Contrast this with Jerome's view of penitence: 'The dirty clothes shall serve as a sign of a pure heart', see Ph. Oppenheim, 'Das Mönchskleid im Christlichen Altertum', *Römische Quartalschrift*, *Supplementheft* 28, p. 33. Cf. also *supra*, p. 178, note 2.

[2] Mishnah, *Ta'anith*, ii, 1.

[3] Cf. B.T. *Ta'anith* 16a: ולמה נותנין אפר מקלה על ספר תורה... אמר רבי זירא כי חזאי דיהבי אפר מקלה ע״ג ספר תורה מזדעזע כולי גופאי. This is the reading of MS. Munich and of MS. No. 2, as well as of the *Yalquṭ*, Alfasi, 'Asheri, Isaiah di Trani, and manifestly also of Maimonides and *Ṭur*, see Rabbinovicz, *Variae Lectiones*, *ad loc.*, letters *'aleph* and *beth*. Cf. also the following note.

[4] *Supra*, 175, n. 3. The second Targum (*Targum Sheni*) on *Esther* describing the fast of Mordecai says (on 4, 1): 'They brought out the Scroll of the Law wrapped in sackcloth and covered with ashes (ואפיקו עלוי ספרא דאורייתא כד מכרך בסקא ומפלפל בקיטמא). With regard to the Ninth of Ab, the author of *Massekheth Sopherim* records the custom of wrapping the Scroll of the Law in a black mantle (xviii, 9; ed. M. Higger, p. 321). Cf. also Maimonides, *Hilekhoth Ta'aniyyoth*, iv, 1, and *Keseph Mishneh ad loc*. The custom is still in vogue today among Sephardi and Yemenite Jews.

the curtain' on the Day of Atonement, obviously with sackcloth.[1] The white curtain on the Ark was designed as a protest against the heterodox practice.

C. Another feature peculiar to the Day of Atonement is the practice of prostration. It is highly probable that this practice represents another survival of the ancient fast-day ceremonial.[2] The present-day custom demands three prostrations during the '*Abhōdāh* and once during the '*alēnū* prayer. This has given rise to the view that the practice was meant as a 'memorial of the Temple'. It is, however, a fact that in the Middle Ages prostration took place also during other prayers. For instance, as late as the fifteenth century 'the majority of the people' in Germany stretched themselves out on the ground during the *widduy*, 'confession of sin', which is recited eight times during the day.[3] Further, the repeated and emphatic references to kneeling and prostration in the liturgical compositions for *Yōm Kippūr* must be taken as reflecting prostrations as penitential exercises,[4] and not merely those during the '*Abhōdāh* which are more of a commemorative character.[5] This being the case, it is much more

[1] מכסונן פראסי ושדונן קיטמא דצומא (see *supra*, 169, n. 3). The expression מכסונן clearly means 'covering', and not 'removing' as Mann thought (*op. cit.*, p. 345).

[2] See *Neh.* 9, 1–3; P.T. *Ta'anith*, ii, end [66a]; '*A. Zarah*, iv, beginning [43d]; B.T. *Meg.* 22b. Cf. A. Büchler, *Types of Jewish-Palestinian Piety From 70 B.C.E. to 70 C.E.*, London 1922 [Jews' College Publications, No. 8], pp. 229–30.

[3] *Maharil* (ed. Warsaw 1874), p. 46a.

[4] To the external tokens of penitence as described by Tertullian belong—in addition to sackcloth and ashes, fasts and lamentation ('to groan, to weep and to moan')—also kneeling and prostration (see *Tertullian, Treatises on Penance*, translated and annotated by William P. Le Saint, London 1959, pp. 31, 64, 86; Oscar D. Watkins, *A History of Penance*, London 1920, i, pp. 109, 116, 193). 'The penitents kneel during the whole period of fasting' (Bernhard Poschmann, *Die Abendländische Kirchenbusse im Ausgang des Christlichen Altertums*, Munich 1928, p. 89; *Die Abendländische Kirchenbusse im frühen Mittelalter*, Breslau 1930, p. 152; see also Hasting's *Encycl. of Rel. and Ethics*, vol. 11, p. 856).

[5] One example will suffice (taken from the *qerōbhāh* for the morning service of the Day of Atonement by Meshullam b. Qalonymus; see

plausible to associate the prostrations with the ritual of the public fast-days.[1] The custom, although as good as ignored by the halakhic authorities, has survived to this day in popular usage.

D. Another element of the fast-day ceremonial may be detected in the custom of sounding the *shofar* at the conclusion of the Day of Atonement. In the Ashkenazic ritual only one long drawn-out note, *teqīʿāh*, is blown,[2] but other rituals still adhere to the old custom, which was in vogue in Palestine and backed by the authority of the two Babylonian academies, to sound the full unit תשר״ת.[3] Already Hai Ga'on, who was asked about the reason for this custom, was unable to give a definite reply, and hesitantly proposed that it might have been instituted as a memorial of the Jubilee Year the commencement of which was announced on the tenth of Tishri by the blast of the *shofar*.[4] Hai himself felt the difficulty of this explanation: the Jubilee occurred once in fifty

L. Zunz, *Literaturgeschichte der synagogalen Poesie* [Berlin 1865], p. 109): ...ופשעיהם מתודים ומשתחוים ומודים וכורעים ובורכים וסוגדים וארצה לך קודים.

See *Sepher Minhāg Ṭōbh* by an anonymous Italian *Ḥasid* of the thirteenth century, published in *Ha-Ṣōpheh le-Ḥokhmath Yisra'el*, vol. xiii [1929], p. 234: ועוד כי בתפילת ר״ה וצום כפורים תמצא רוב דברים של כריעה וקידה שאי אפשר שהפייטנים גם הן לא היו כורעים תמיד כל עת התפללם. He goes on to cite a number of piyyutic passages containing references to kneeling and prostration, and concludes: והרבה יש כיוצא בהן אבל היד נלאת מלכותבם כי רבו לאין חקר.

[1] See L. Ginzberg, *A Commentary on the Palestinian Talmud* (in Hebrew), New York 1941, vol. iii, p. 120.

[2] *Maḥzor Vitry*, p. 381 (also on p. 395): שמעתי שתוקעין בארץ ישראל מוצאי יום הכיפורים תשר״ק...ובגולה שלנו לא נהגו אלא תקיעה אחת לזכר בעלמא, זכר ליובל, לבד שבעיר קולונייא נהגו גם תשר״ק; *Sepher ha-Pardes* (ed. H. L. Ehrenreich, Budapest 1924), p. 235; *Siddur Rashi* (ed. S. Buber and J. Freimann, Berlin 1911), p. 94; Eleazar of Worms, *Roqeaḥ* 217: פר״ח תוקעין קשר״ק...ומנהג שלנו במלכות לות״ר לתקוע רק תקיעה אחת לומר נצחנו השטן.

[3] See preceding note; *'Oṣar ha-Ge'onim*, *Yoma*, p. 43; *Seder Rabh 'Amram* (Warsaw), p. 49b; ed. Frumkin, ii, p. 359; Isaac ibn Gayyath, *Sepher Shaʿarē Simḥah* (ed. I. D. Bamberger, Fürth 1861), i, p. 65a; *Shibbolē ha-Leqeṭ* (ed. S. Buber), p. 299; *Sepher ha-Manhig* (ed. Berlin), p. 62a; David Abudraham (Warsaw), p. 156; Yemenite Prayer-Book (ed. Jerusalem), ii, p. 123a.

[4] Ibn Gayyath, *loc. cit.*; *'Oṣar ha-Ge'onim*, *Yoma*, p. 42.

years, while the custom commemorating it is practised every year.[1] He suggested an alternative reason: that it is done in order to 'confound Satan'. Mediaeval authorities advanced various other hypotheses, only a few of which will be mentioned, to illustrate the difficulties they encountered in attempting to fathom the origin of this custom. The sounding of the *shofar* is a sign of 'victory over Satan';[2] it is a means of intimidating him;[3] it signalizes the fall of the night so that the children who fasted may be given food;[4] it betokens acquittal in judgment;[5] it marks the departure of the *Shekhinah*;[6] it is the earthly equivalent to the heavenly voice which, according to an *'aggadah*, proclaims at this hour: *Go thy way, eat thy bread with joy* (*Eccles.* 9, 7).[7]

It may safely be asserted that also this custom has preserved an ingredient of the ancient fast-ritual in which the sounding of the *shofar* played an important part. Dating back to biblical times, it persisted for millennia. We meet it first in *Joel* 2, 15: *Blow the horn in Zion, sanctify a fast, call a solemn assembly*. It is again encountered in the Hasmonaean period:[8] *And they fasted that day, and put on sackcloth, and put ashes on their heads . . . and they sounded with the trumpets, and cried with a loud voice*. It had its fixed place in the tannaitic 'order of fasts',[9] was observed in gaonic times when the blowing was still performed, as it had been

[1] Cf. *Tosaphoth*, *Shabbath* 114b, *s.v.* ואמאי: ולא כמחזורים שכתוב בהן שהתקיעה זכר ליובל כי למה תוקעין בכל שנה ושנה וכי היה יובל בכל שנה ושנה.

[2] Eleazar of Worms (see p. 189, note 2).

[3] Isaac Abba Mari, *'Iṭṭur* (Wilna 1874), p. 217.

[4] *Tosaphoth, loc. cit.* Cf. also L. Ginzberg, *A Commentary on the Palestinian Talmud*, iii, p. 22.

[5] *Shibbolē ha-Leqeṭ*, *loc. cit.* The author's brother, Benjamin, gave two other reasons (*ibid.*).

[6] Joel Sirkes, *Bayith Ḥadash*, *'Oraḥ Ḥayyim*, 624.

[7] Abudraham, *loc. cit.*; *Maharil*, p. 50a.

[8] *I Macc.* 3, 47–54. Cf. 4, 39–40.

[9] Mishnah *Ta'anith*, ii, 5; *Tosephta*, *Ta'an.*, i, 14 (ed. Zuckermandel, p. 216).

in mishnaic times, by priests,[1] and it was adhered to by the Jews in mediaeval Spain[2] and Italy.[3]

It is, then, this ancient custom, unrecognized and relegated to an inferior position at the conclusion of the fast, which has tenaciously maintained itself to this day.

E. Finally, the custom still prevalent today of visiting the cemetery on the eve of *Yōm Kippūr* stems likewise from the ancient fast-ritual. On public fast-days it was the practice for the congregation, clad in sackcloth, to repair to the cemetery where services were held and the *shofar* blown.[4] Although not mentioned in the Mishnah, the practice is accepted by Palestinian *'Amora'im* of the third century who advanced different reasons for it.[5] It was taken over by the early Church: on 'station'-days divine services were held either on the cemetery ground itself or in its vicinity.[6] It has been traced back to Rome as early as 258 C.E. At the time of the Church Father John Chrysostom (347–407) the custom was already so old that its origin and reason were not known any longer. Chrysostom tried hard to find a specifically Christian explanation for the practice of his contemporaries to arrange services on the Saturday preceding Easter, 'the Great Sabbath' (also 'the Holy Sabbath'), in cemeteries.[7] The explanation is simply this: 'the Great

[1] *Supra*, p. 175, note 3.

[2] Cf. Naḥmanides' 'Discourse for the New Year' published in *Ha-Ṣōpheh le-Ḥokhmath Yisra'el*, vol. i, p. 154: לפיכך נהגנו אנו בספרד לתקוע בשופרות בתעניות של התרעה שאין עושין כן בצרפת כלל. See also Me'iri on *Ta'an.* 16a (ed. Sofer-Schreiber, pp. 47–49).

[3] Vogelstein-Rieger, *Geschichte der Juden in Rom* (Berlin 1896), i, p. 306. See also D. Goldschmidt in *Scritti in Memoria di Sally Mayer* (Jerusalem 1956), pp. 77ff. (Hebrew part).

[4] Cf. Rashi, *Ta'anith* 16a, quoting the Palestinian Talmud (not in the current text).

[5] P.T. *Ta'anith*, ii, 1 [65a]; B.T. *loc. cit.*

[6] See J. Schümmer, *Die altchristliche Fastenpraxis*, p. 149 and Index, *s.v.* Friedhof; Athanasius, *Apolog. pro Fuga*, 6 (*A Select Library of the Nicene and Post-Nicene Fathers of the Christian Church*, Oxford and New York 1892, iv, p. 257).

[7] Schümmer, *op. cit.*, pp. 148, 143, 144.

Sabbath' was an important fast-day and was therefore celebrated with the attendant ceremony of a public fast.

The ancient ceremony of visiting the cemetery on a fast-day observed on account of drought persisted, particularly among the Yemenite Jews, who while still in their native land were in the habit of carrying the Scrolls of the Law to the '*me'ārāh*', as the graveyard is called by them, and reciting there prayers for rain.[1] It was further practised on the fast of the Ninth of Ab,[2] on the eve of *Rosh ha-Shanah*,[3] which was also a fast-day, and especially on the eve of the Great Fast of Atonement.[4] The latter custom aroused some opposition on the part of certain rabbinical authorities, who argued that the eve of *Yōm Kippūr* was no fast-day. But it is obvious that the visit, which should take place on the Day of Atonement itself, is here transferred to the preceding day because of the festive character of the Fast of Atonement.

[1] Yehudah Ratzhaby in *Reshumoth*, N.S., i, pp. 116, 117; iv, p. 193; *Maharil, Hilekhoth Ta'anith* (ed. Warsaw 1874, p. 37a); *Shulḥan 'Arukh, 'Oraḥ Ḥayyim*, 579, 2; Joseph b. Mosheh, *Leqeṭ Yosher* (ed. J. Freimann, Berlin 1903), i, p. 115.

[2] *Tosaphoth*, *Ta'anith* 16a, *s.v.* יוצאין; *Shulḥan 'Arukh*, *ibid.* 559, 10.

[3] *Maharil*, *Hilekhoth Rosh ha-Shanah* (p. 37b); Isserlis, *'Oraḥ Ḥayyim*, 581, 4. On the custom among the Portuguese Jews in Surinam (Dutch Guiana) see J. D. Oppenheim in '*Edoth* (A Quarterly for Folklore and Ethnology), iii (Jerusalem 1948), pp. 86f.; English translation, pp. lxxiv f.: 'The day before the New Year a special service is held in the Portuguese Synagogue beginning at 4 o'clock in the morning. At day-break (about 6 o'clock), the congregation leaves the Synagogue and goes to the Portuguese cemetery where prayers are said, and the people afterwards visit the graves of their deceased. This service is attended by many Jews who do not frequent the Synagogue on other days of the year; by Jews living in mixed marriages; and by many non-Jews of Jewish origin; apart from the regular attendants of the services. After the official prayers even people without relatives buried in this cemetery remain for some time in the grave-yard, meditating or praying among the graves.'

[4] Isserlis, *'Oraḥ Ḥayyim*, 605. For Alexandria, see 'Eliyyahu Ḥazzan, מנהגי נא אמון (Alexandria 1894), p. 25a; for Salonika, David Joseph, *Beth David*, *'Oraḥ Ḥayyim*, p. 111a; for Germany, *Leqeṭ Yosher*, i, pp. 116, 140; Yoseph Yuspa Hahn of Nördlingen, *Yosiph 'Omeṣ* (Frankfurt a. Main, 1928), nos. 956, 986.

APPENDICES

I

Daniel al-Qumisi's views on the character of the Day of Atonement are contained in two fragments of his lost commentary on the Book of *Leviticus*. The first was published by L. Ginzberg in *Ginzē Schechter*, vol. ii, pp. 485–6, and the second by Jacob Mann in *JQR*, vol. xii [1921–22], p. 473. The latter is a direct continuation of the former. Both fragments are here printed together, copied anew from the manuscripts.

אך בעשור[1] כתׄ בלשון אך לעשותו סגולה מכל הימים לצום ולעינוי ככׄ[2] ועניתם את נפׄ ודע כי לא כתׄ הנה פתרון עינוי זה: ואולם למען כי ביאר אחריו וכל מלאכה לא תעשו[3]: בזאת ידענו כי הוא עינוי נפש שלעולם הבא ולא עינוי מלאכת העולם הזה: ודע כי עינוי נפש ליהוה הם פנים פנים: לחדל מאכילה ושתיה ולעמד על רגלים בתפלה הרבה הרבה עד עינוי הנפש: ולהחליף בגדים בלבוש שק ואפר ולבכות בקול עד עטיפת רוח עד יהיה תום עינוי נפש: וסגולת[4] שם צום נקרא תענית כי הוא עינוי כאשר אמר[5] עזרא[6] ובמנחת הערב קמתי מתעניתי וב [קׄ בׄ ומׄ על כן] ועניתם את נפשותיכם הוא צום בכל אלה עינויים אשר ביארתי: ובימי אבתינו בשבת לבטח בארץ ישראל היו מהם לובשי שק כאשר מצאנו בישעיה[7] לך ופתחת השק מעׄ מתנׄ: כי היה חגור שק: ומהם לבשו שק בעת צרה כאשר ביאר בחזקיה[8] ויתכס בשק ויבא בית יהוה: וכׄ וישלח את חלקיהו[9] אשר על הבית ואת שבנא הסופר ואׄ זקׄ הכהנים מתכסים בשקים אל יש בׄ אׄ הנביא: וביום צום

[1] *Lev.* 23, 27.

[2] *Ibid.*

[3] *Ibid.*, verse 28.

[4] MS.: וסגולה.

[5] Here the second fragment begins.

[6] *Ezra* 9, 5.

[7] *Isa.* 20, 2.

[8] *II Kings* 19, 1–2.

[9] M.T.: אליקים.

אשר צמו כלם לבשו שק ככֹ[1] נאספו בני יש בצום ובכי ואדמה עליהם: ובימי מרדכי כתֹ[2] אבל גדול ליהודים וצום ובכי ומֹ שׂ ואֹ יצע לרֹ: ומרדכי ידע את כל אֹ נעֹ ויֹ מֹ אֹ בגֹ ויֹ שק ואפר: על כן כתֹ בתוכֵחה[3]: הכזה יהיה צום אבחרהו יום ענות אֹ נפֹ הֹ כֹ רֹ ושׂ ואפר יצע: כי כן היה מנה[גם] ל[פנים] כי יום כיפורים יום גדול ונורא הלא לעש[ות אותו ככ]ל צומות.

2

Extract from Yefeth b. 'Ali's commentary on *Leviticus*, MS. British Museum, Oriental 2399, fol. 141a–b:

פנקול אנה אדׄא דׄכר לפטׄ ענוי מן גיר אן יקרן מעה נפש ליס פיה דלאלהׄ עלי אלצום דון גירה מתׄל קולה[4] להתענות לפני יוי אלהינו ומתׄלה להבין[5] ולהתענות לפני אלהיך פימכן אן יכון פיה אלצום וגירה וקד לא ידכׄל פיה אלצום ואדׄא קרן מעה נפש פאלקצד פיה אלצום דון גירה כקו[6] למה צמנו ולא ראית ענינו נפשנו ולא תדע ומתׄלה ונפש[7] נענה תשביע וקד דׄהב קום אלי אנה יגׄב מע אלצום גירה מן אגׄל דׄלך קאל ועניתם ולם יקל צומו פאוגׄב ענד דׄלך אלתשקי פי אשיא אכׄר מע אלצום מתׄל אלתעב פי אלצלאהׄ ואלחפא וגיר דׄלך והדׄא הו מסלך אלרבאנין[8] והדׄא אלתפסיר לא יתׄבת מן אגׄל אן תׄם שיךׄ כביר

[1] *Neh.* 9, 1.

[2] *Esther* 4, 3, 1.

[3] *Isa.* 58, 5.

[4] *Ezra* 8, 21.

[5] *Dan.* 10, 12.

[6] *Isa.* 58, 3. The division of opinion among the Karaites on this point (see *supra*, p. 166) is glaringly exemplified by Yefeth b. 'Ali himself: his argument from *Isa.* 58, 3 is at variance with his own view in the commentary on the *Isaiah* passage (MS. British Museum, Or. 2505, fols. 17b–18a). Whereas he here regarded the phrase '*we afflicted our souls*' as parallel to '*we fasted*', deriving the general conclusion that 'affliction of the soul'='fasting', in the *Isaiah* commentary he took the phrase '*we afflicted our souls*' as implying practices other than fasting, such as putting on sackcloth and spreading of ashes and sleeping on them. (ודׄכר שיין צום וענוי ואלענוי הו לבאס אלמסח ובסט אלרמאד ואלנום עליה כמא קאל שק ואפר יצ׳ע).

[7] *Isa.* 58, 10.

[8] This assertion is very strange; Yefeth entirely ignores the fact that this was al-Qumisi's view and ascribes it instead to the Rabbanites, to whom he imputes the opinion that if one failed to tire oneself out through prayer one had not fulfilled the commandment *ye shall afflict your souls*.

או זמן או צבי לא יקדר עלי אלתשקי פי אלצלאה[1] פליס יגוז אן נקול אנה קצר ען ואגב ועניתם נפשותיכם.

3

Extract from the *Book of Precepts* by Levi ben Yefeth ha-Levi, MS. Leiden, Warner 22, fols. 91b–92a; collated with MS. Oxford (Bodleian Library), Cat. No. 857, fol. 55b:

הדבור בענוי. כבר נתחלף הדבור בו, מקצת האנשים יראה כי אמיתתו הוא הצום בלבד בעת אש׳ יסמיך אותו על הנפש ויזכיר אותה עמו והורה על זה באמרו[2] עניתי בצום נפשי וגם אש׳ יחזק זה באמ׳[3] ונפש נענה תשביע. וזה האומ׳ רחוק כי אילו היה אין שם ענוי נפש אלא בצום לא היה מוצרך[4] לומ׳ עניתי בצום נפשי וזה יגוש כי כבר יהיה ענוי נפש באין צום וזה ידוע באין פוגה בלא כתוב. ומקצ׳ טען כי ענוי נפש יהיה במעשים קשים ובהליכת אורח[5] וברעב ובצמא ובלבוש שק וכיוצא בו כל אש׳ יהיה בו ענוי. וכל אש׳ יהיה ממין המעשים האסורי׳ כבר יצא בכתוב שנ׳[6] וכל מלאכה לא תעשו בעצם היום הזה וגו׳ ונשאר עמו הענוי אש׳ [אין][7] בו מעשה אסור כמ׳ שימנע נפשו מן המאכל והמשקה והתענוגות מן ריח בשמים וכלי שיר לשמוע אותם ולהלוך יחף ועומד להתפלל לילה ויומם ולא ינום ולא יישן... ומקצ׳ האנש׳ יראה כי יתחייב מזה אשר לו תליאה בכפור כמו המניעה לאכול ולשתות והוא ידוע מן הכתובי׳ במקרא וכן להתנפל לפניו ית״ש ולחלות ולהתחנן ולשאול כאש׳ ידענו מן מעשה משה על׳ ה׳ אש׳ התפלל בגלל יש׳ שנ׳[8] ואתנפל לפני יוי וגו׳ לחם לא אכלתי ומים לא שתיתי על כל חטאתכם וגו׳ ויחל[9] משה [192a] את פני יוי וכיוצא בזה. וכי יהיה הוא ע״ה

[1] Cf. Moses Ibn Makhir's remarks, quoted *supra*, p. 167, note 4.

[2] *Ps.* 35, 13.

[3] *Isa.* 58, 10.

[4] MS. Oxford: מן צרך.

[5] Based on *Ps.* 102, 24. Cf. Hadassi, 248, *yodh* and Tobias b. Eliezer, *op. cit.* ii, p. 132: ואע״פ שיש עוד ענויים במקרא כגון (תהל׳ ק״ב, 24) ענה בדרך כחי... אין זה דרך יוה״כ להיות מהלך בדרך.

[6] *Lev.* 23, 28.

[7] Missing in MS. Leiden; correct in MS. Oxford.

[8] *Deut.* 9, 18.

[9] *Ex.* 32, 11.

עשה כל זה בגללם וכל שכן לעשות הם בעבור נפשתם על פי אש׳ יוכלו עליו. וכן להתאבל ולהסיר הבגדים החמודות והחליפות הטובות והעדיים וכיוצא בהם שנ׳[1] וישמע העם את הדבר הרע הזה וי׳ ו׳ ש׳ א׳ ע׳ ע׳ וכן לבכות וללבוש שק שנ׳[2] וגם עתה נאום יוי שבו עדי בכל לבבכם ובצום וב׳ וב׳. והשב מעונותיו כי אש׳ יזכור אש׳ עשה יכאב לבו וידאג שנ׳[3] כי עוני אגיד ואדאג מחטאתי. והיה פניו על הארץ בוש ונכלם שנ׳[4] אלהי בושתי ונכלמ׳ ואמ׳[5] כי אחרי שובי נחמתי וגו׳ וכזה וכיוצא בו כלו מן תנאי התשובה.

4

Al-Qumisi's view that the twenty-four hours of *Yōm Kippūr* must be spent in a standing posture as an exercise of self-affliction is not an innovation on his part, but goes back to an ancient Palestinian custom. Mentioned in *Pirqē R. ʻEliezer* (ch. 46), a work composed not earlier than the beginning of the 8th century, it sprang into prominence in the Middle Ages when the ḥasidic circles in Germany advocated its observance. See *Rabia*, ii, p. 190 (פרושים); *Sepher ha-Manhig*, p. 62 (חסידי צרפת). In the printed edition of this work an entire passage has been omitted by *homoioteleuton*; it should read, according to MS. Oxford, Cat. No. 900, as follows: מכאן יש לי סמך [להדליק את הנירות בליל הכפור. אב״ן הירחי. וזה שנהגו חסידי צרפת לעמוד ביום הכפורים כל היום מצאתי סמך] לדבר בפרקי ר״א; ʼAsher b. Yeḥiel, Yoma 24 (נהגו באשכנז הרבה בני אדם); *Ṭur*, *ʼOraḥ Ḥayyim*, 619 (אנשי מעשה באשכנז); Moses Isserlis, *Darekhē Mosheh*, 619, 10.

The difference between the German *ḥasidim* and al-Qumisi is a legal one; whereas the former practised the custom as a voluntary, supererogatory act of piety, the latter declared it to be obligatory, as being implied in the biblical commandment. The view held by L. Ginzberg (*Ginzē Schechter*, ii, p. 638) that the Rabbanite observance of this custom was the result of Karaite influence, cannot be sustained, even if one were prepared to

1 *Ibid.* 33, 4.

2 *Joel* 2, 12.

3 *Ps.* 38, 19.

4 *Ezra* 9, 6.

5 *Jer.* 31, 19.

concede the possibility of such an influence on *Pirqē R. ʿEliezer*. It has been overlooked that the custom is already referred to by Qallir in a *piyyūṭ* incorporated in the Ashkenazi ritual (in the section of the *Musaph* composition beginning אז מלפני בראשית; I. Davidson, *Thesaurus*, etc., i, no. 2155). Qallir's words are worth quoting, as they eloquently express the penitentiary nature of standing on the feet as an act of self-mortification:

הביטה וראה... דליות שוקים ומצב רגלים דריכת מתנים ומעד קרסולים. גשים יחפים בענוי עיפים.

O look and see . . . the weakness of the legs, the standing of the feet, the bending of the loins and the tottering of the ankles. They approach Thee barefoot, weary with affliction.

With Yannai's Qerōbhōth now at our disposal, we are able to trace the practice to an even earlier period than that of Qallir. The *'aggadah* in *Pirqē Rabbi ʿEliezer* mentioning the custom of standing must emanate from an old Midrash, since it was known to Yannai who recast it in poetical phraseology (see M. Zulay, *Piyyūṭē Yannai*, Jerusalem 1938, p. 341). Comparing the conduct of Israel on the Day of Atonement to that of the angels, he says that just as the angels, having no joints, stand on their feet, so 'our congregation stands today erect on the feet' (קהלינו היום ביושר מצב רגל).

The fact that mediaeval Jewish authors refers to the practice as a Franco-German custom should not be taken to imply that it was unknown in other countries. Under the influence of the ḥasidic movement in Germany, whose religious values and ascetic practices carried weight with the average pious Jew, the ascetic exercise of standing penetrated wider circles. But individuals observed it even in Spain before the rise of the ḥasidic movement in Germany. It has gone unnoticed—so far as I am aware—that the custom is mentioned by Yehudah Hallevi (died 1141) in his *Kuzari*, iii, 5: 'The fast on this day is such as to make one almost equal to the angels, because it is spent in humility and contrition, standing, kneeling and offering songs and hymns of praise.' Of some significance is, further, the fact that the custom is also practised by the Jews in Kurdistan (cf. Erich Brauer, *The Jews of Kurdistan* [in Hebrew], Jerusalem 1947, p. 260).

CHAPTER VI

THE KARAITE *PESHER*

EXEGESIS OF THE BOOK OF PSALMS

Not the least remarkable aspect of the *pesher* phenomenon is the fact that the *Psalms* were also subjected to this mode of interpretation, i.e. they were looked upon by the Qumranites and Karaites alike as prognostications for the 'end of days' and consequently as referring to the events of their own respective periods.

The first prominent Karaite to have done so is none other than 'Anan himself, as may be seen from the fact that he prescribed the recitation of *Ps.* 74 for the liturgy of the New Moon and festivals. This liturgical institution is founded on a *pesher* which expounded the psalm as relating to the strife between the Karaites dissenters and their Rabbanite foes, foretelling—and denouncing—the rabbinic innovation of fixing the festivals by calculation instead of by observation of the new moon.[1]

Subsequent Karaite writers followed suit. The argument in support of this method ran something like this: It is impossible to assume that King David, or any other of the psalmists, actually experienced sufferings and degradations such as are described in several psalms.[2] Nor—to take another example—could King

[1] *Kitāb al-Anwār wal-Marāqib* (ed. L. Nemoy), p. 631, lines 5–11. Cf. N. Wieder, 'The Qumran Sectaries', pp. 111f.

[2] Hadassi (93, *mem*) after enlarging upon the prognostic contents of *Ps.* 90 lists 22 examples derived from *Pss.* 6, 13, 31, 35, 38, 44, 69, 74, 77, 79, 88 and 102, all of which have to be explained prognostically: מכל אלה אירע למשה ע״ה? הלא בעבור גלותיים אמרם. וכן לדוד ע״ה כלום אירע שאמר עניתי בצום נפשי; סבבוני כלבים; יחלקו בגדי להם ועל לבושי יפילו גורל... כלום אירע לדוד המלך ע״ה מכלל הדברים האלה, או לאסף הראש או לאיתן או להימן או לידותון או לשאר משורריך. צעקות ותחנות מאלו על לשון הדורות האחרונים נבאו משורריך.

To denote the idea that a psalm or a prophecy was written with reference to the 'last generation' Karaite authors employ several expressions, foremost among which is the term על לשון 'on behalf of', 'in the

David, being in possession of the knowledge of the hidden portions of the Torah, have asked for himself *Open Thou mine eyes that I may behold the hidden things of Thy Law* (*Ps.* 119, 18).[1] As psalms like these cannot possibly have been written in reference to their authors, they must be considered as pertaining to 'the last generation'.

In the present state of Karaite literature it is hardly possible to give even an approximately full survey of the prognostic exegesis of the Psalter by the champions of Karaism. The following lines are intended merely to indicate what use they made of this method. The examples given were chosen with a view to demonstrating how profoundly the 'karaitized' psalms influenced thought and phraseology of the Karaite schismatics.

To begin with Daniel al-Qumisi. From the few fragments of his lost commentary on the *Psalms* which have been preserved[2] we learn that he interpreted *Ps.* 17 as applying to the *maskil*.[3]

name of', with which I have dealt in 'The Qumran Sectaries', p. 282, note 94, where I pointed out that the Hebrew term was a translation of the Arabic עלי לסאן, likewise used by Karaite writers for the same purpose. To the list of Rabbanite writers using this term add Samuel ha-Nagid in *Ben Mishle*, no. 883 (*Diwan of Shemuel Hannagid*, ed. D. S. Sassoon, Oxford 1934, p. 224); David Qimḥi on *Isa.* 59, 9; Maimonides, *Hilekhōth Qiddūsh ha-Ḥodesh*, iv, 17.

The term בעבור is used by al-Qumisi in the fragment of his commentary on *Leviticus*, printed above, p. 60. Hadassi in the foregoing quotation employs both terms.

The expression אערב ען occurs frequently in Yefeth b. 'Ali's Bible commentaries, so, for instance, on *Cant.* 2, 15 (MS. British Museum, Or. 2520, fol. 60a): ואערב אסף ען אכיאר דלך אלזמאן ואני כמעט נטיו רגלי (תהל' ע"ג, 2); Mic. 7, 7 (Or. 2401, fol. 56a): וקיל אן הדא אלפסוק אערב ען שארית ישראל שבי פשע; Deut. 30, 1 (Or. 2479, fol. 60a): כמא אערב ענהם אלמשורר וקאל שש אנכי על אמרתך (תהלים קי"ט, 162).

[1] *Supra*, p. 60.

[2] Published by A. Marmorstein in *Journal Asiatique*, 1916, pp. 199–209, and also in *Ha-Ṣōpheh le-Ḥokhmath Yisra'el*, vol. viii [1924], pp. 327–37; vol. ix [1925], pp. 129–40.

[3] *Ha-Ṣōpheh*, viii, p. 328: וזה המתפלל משכיל. The heading '*Ps.* 13' on p. 327 is an error; read: '*Ps.* 17'. This fragment (MS. 7) is badly preserved and exhibits a number of *lacunae* which make considerable parts of it impossible to understand. Elijah ha-Melammed drew upon this

Very interesting is his explanation of the title at the head of *Ps.* 77 which was apparently taken by him as *noṭariqon*:[1] ידותון = דת תורה. This ingenious device enabled him to contend that the psalm was said in reference to those who walked in the 'Lord's Torah' in the *Galuth*, *viz.* the adherents to Karaism.[2] The question in *Ps.* 82, 2: *How long will ye judge corruptly?* is addressed to the Exilarch and the heads of the academies who pervert justice, teach that which is contrary to the 'Lord's Torah', justifying the guilty and condemning the innocent.[3] Likewise, the statement (verse 5): *They know not, nor understand, they walk in darkness* refers to the heads of Israel and its rulers in

commentary, and the interpretation of verse 4 which in the printed text is utterly unintelligible reads in his compilation as follows (MS. British Museum, Or. 1263, fol. 331b): לפעלות אדם. אמר למה שמרתי נפשי מכל רע כי ידעתי כי יש לבני אדם שכר ופעלה לכל מצוה. בדבר שפתיך. ובעבור שדברת על ידי משה מצות על כן שמרתי נפשי מארחות פריץ הוא הרשע שפרץ מה שבנה משה.

The interpretation is noteworthy; al-Qumisi takes the words (17, 4) *I have kept me from the ways of the breacher* as referring to the founder of Christianity 'who broke down what Moses had built'; see 139, n. 3.

Elijah also quotes the explanation of verse 5, introduced by 'some say', which may be given here: וי״א תמוך תמכתי במעגלותיך הוא דרך עגול יסובבנו אל דרך אחרת, כן במצות דרכים ישרים ודרכים [עגולים] יחפוץ [= יעני .Ar] החכם יראה אנה הולך כמו שאמר ארבעה אבות נזיקים ויש לכל אב חוקים אין להם שיעור.

Al-Qumisi distinguishes between laws that can be obtained by a straight and direct route, i.e. by a mere reference to the Pentateuch where they are clearly stated, like the 'four chief torts', and the innumerable derivatives that are arrived at by the circuitous route (מעגל) of inference or analogy (*qiyās*, *heqqesh*)—the principal hermeneutic device of the Karaites, which, in their view, makes the Oral Law superfluous. This figurative interpretation of מעגל is also used by Elijah ha-Melammed in his exposition of *Ps.* 23, 3 (fol. 333b): ישובב אל חכמת תורתו ויורני וינחני אל המעגלות הם הקשות והפליאות של תורה.

It may further be noted that the sentence about the 'four chief torts' seems to emanate from an early unknown Karaite work, written in rhyme.

[1] *Op. cit.*, vol. 9, p. 134: על ידותון הלכי בדת ובתורה: שירה זאת נאמרה על הלכי בתורת ײ׳ בגלות ככ׳ על ידותון.

[2] Regarding the term 'the Torah of the Lord' as an appellation for the Karaite concept of Judaism, see my article in *JJS*, 1955, pp. 24f.

[3] *Ibid.*, p. 139; see *supra*, p. 124.

the *Galuth*—an explanation repeated by him elsewhere[1] and adopted by other Karaite exegetes.[2]

Three psalms bearing the heading על שושנים, *Concerning the Lilies*,[3] allude, according to Yefeth b. 'Ali, to the Karaites (45, 69, 80).[4] These three figure also among the psalms mentioned by Elijah ha-Melammed[5] as referring to the 'Remnant': 5, 22, 45, 60, 69, 80. This brings us to *Ps.* 22 which was eminently suited for a sectarian application. The self-description of the speaker *I am a worm, and no-man, the reproach of men, and despised of the people*—a description which recalls the traits of the Suffering Servant (*Isa.* 53, 3)—is not merely a reflection of the actual state of the detested and derided sect, but it is at the same time expressive of the humility which characterized the 'Mourners for Zion'. The heading of *Ps.* 22, *Concerning the Hind of the Dawn* is, according to David al-Fasi, a figurative epithet of the 'Remnant' who rise at dawn to divine worship as the thirsty hind runs to the water in the early morning.[6] A graphic picture of the sect's poverty is contained in verse 18, '*I count my bones*', i.e. I tell them (the shepherds of the *Galuth*) of my poverty but they

[1] *Pithron*, p. 66.

[2] In a fragment of an anonymous commentary on the *Psalms* (MS. British Museum, Or. 2519, fol. 82b) we read: ... וכאנו דאים פי אלחשכה יתהלכו והי אלרתב אלדי להם מתל אלמשנה ואלתלמוד.

[3] See *infra*, p. 205, note 1.

[4] In the commentary on *Cant.* 2, 1 (MS. British Museum, Or. 2513, fol. 63b) Yefeth writes: וממא ידלנא איצׄא עלי אן אלישועה תטׄהר פי זמאן אלשושנים הו מא ראינא ידׄכר אסמאהם פי אלתהלות פי ג׳ מואצׄע אעני ענואן ג׳ מזאמיר והי רחש לבי (45) הושיעני אלהים (69) רעה ישׂ (80).

[5] MS. British Museum (see 200, n. 3), fol. 328b: ... וי״א על הנחילות על אבילי ציון כי הם כצאן נחילות וי״א הוא כלי מכלי השיר, ויש שיפתור על מכאוב הלב, ויחלה הלב מרוב יגונות הגלות. וטוב מכולם על השארית וכן מצאנו ו׳ מזמורים בתחלתם על השארית הא׳ זה והב׳ הושיענו אלהים (69) והג׳ רועה ישר׳ (80) והד׳ על אילת השחר (22) והה׳ על שושן [עדות] מכתם (60) והו׳ רחש לבי (45).

[6] *Op. cit.*, vol. i, p. 77. A different interpretation of the title is given by Yefeth, see *Der XXII Psalm . . . von R. Jephet ben Eli Ha-Bacri*, ed. Theodor Hofmann (Tübingen 1880), p. 7. This interpretation is also found in Elijah ha-Melammed's compilation, see N. Wieder, 'The Qumran Sectaries', p. 283, where the relevant passage is quoted.

have no compassion and exact contributions.[1] That in verses 17, 21, the Rabbanite antagonists are likened to dogs is in accord with the Karaite *pesher* on *Isa.* 56, 10: *They are dumb dogs that cannot bark*, and on verse 11 (*The dogs are greedy*), which was also taken to refer to the leaders of Rabbanism.[2] Noteworthy is further Yefeth b. 'Ali's interpretation of the phrase *they shoot out the lip* (verse 8) as describing the enemy's imitation of the way the Karaites prayed, cried and entreated.[3] No doubt, this refers to the prayers and lamentations during the alternating watches at the Temple site by the 'Mourners for Zion'. Yefeth, who was one of them, must have experienced such scornful mimicry himself. The same complaint was earlier made by Salmon b. Yeruḥim, as we shall instantly see.

A good example of how the 'karaitized' psalms influenced the language of Karaite authors is furnished by the use they made of *Ps.* 102, and particularly of *Pss.* 69 and 109. Salmon, in the diatribe in which he holds up to ridicule the anthropomorphic passages in the Talmud, utters these curses against the Rabbanites:[4] 'Those who say and believe this, may their habitation be desolate and destroyed, and may God remember the iniquity of their fathers.' Why, one wonders, just these curses? Analysing the sentence we find that the first is based on *Ps.* 69, 26 and the second on *Ps.* 109, 14. As a further illustration may serve a passage from *'Eshkol ha-Kopher* delineating the traits of the Karaite ascetics, which is made up of complete verses and truncated quotations from *Pss.* 69 and 102.[5]

[1] Elijah ha-Melammed, fol. 333a: ... אספר להם דלותי ולא ירחמוני כי אם יקחו גם הם הפסיקות.

[2] Sahl in *Liq. Qad.*, App., p. 23, top; Hadassi, 123, beginning. As is customary in polemics, writers in the opposite camp reciprocated and bestowed the same designation upon the Karaites. Abraham ibn Daud in *Sepher ha-Qabbālāh* (A. Neubauer, *Mediaeval Jewish Chronicles*, Oxford 1887–95, vol. i, p. 79) called the Karaites 'dumb dogs that cannot bark', and so does Simon b. Ṣemaḥ Duran in his *Magen 'Abhoth* (Livorno), ii, p. 31a.

[3] *Op. cit.*, p. 8: ומעני יפטירו הו מא יחאכונה כיף יצלי ויצרך ויטלב.

[4] *The Book of the Wars*, p. 124.

[5] *Eshkol ha-Kopher*, p. 10b.

As a matter of fact, the practice of using these psalms to characterize the pious within the sect is met with centuries earlier than Hadassi. Al-Qumisi,[1] speaking of the suggestion made concerning the members of his party that 'those who abandon Rabbanism, its festivals and laws are doomed to die of hunger and in distress', contends that to suffer contempt is 'the criterion of the God-fearing in *Galuth*', which he proves by appealing to *Ps.* 69, 8 as well as to *Isa.* 53, 3. This association of the psalm with *Isaiah* chapter 53 is significant; it shows that just as some Karaites regarded themselves as the Suffering Servant,[2] so they saw themselves in the innocent sufferer of the psalm. The practice is followed by Yefeth b. 'Ali, who drew upon *Pss.* 69 and 102 in his portrayal of the 'Perfect in the Way'.[3]

The utilization of the psalms mentioned is founded on and justified by their *pesher* exposition. As to *Ps.* 102, I have already mentioned elsewhere Salmon's claim that the psalm represented 'the prayers of the Remnant'.[4] The heading, *tephillah le-'ani*, was understood as 'the prayer of the poor'—'poor' being an honorific title of the Karaite *élite*, bearing both a sociological and religious connotation. The corpus of the psalm described the circumstances and feelings of the persecuted sect, that became a victim of enmity and a subject of scorn (verse 9), and suffered from ostracism (7–8). It depicts their sighing for the Temple (verse 6), their night-vigils (verse 8),[5] their yearning for Zion (15), and even that characteristic feature of the ascetics—ashes—is not absent:[6] *I eat ashes like bread and mingle my drink with weeping* (10). Lastly, it gives expression to the sect's conviction that they will be instrumental in bringing about the restoration of Zion (17–18).

[1] *Op. cit.*, p. 3.

[2] *Supra*, pp. 113–17.

[3] *JQR*, xlvii [1957], p. 290.

[4] *MGWJ*, 1901, p. 520; cf. 'The Qumran Sectaries', note 117.

[5] The phrase '*I watch*' was interpreted as referring to the night-watches (Elijah ha-Melammed, fol. 353a): שקדתי ישקוד בתפלתו עד אשמורת הראשונה ועוד יקום בחצות הלילה.

[6] *Ibid.*, fol. 353a: זכר האפר כי הוא עליו תמיד.

As to *Pss.* 69[1] and 109, the two main imprecatory psalms of the Psalter, the features of these were found to bear an extraordinary resemblance to the facts of the sect's life, and hence looked upon as a predictive description of its plight. The sufferer is either the Karaite congregation as a whole or its leaders, whose piety and zeal for the Temple earned them the derision[2] of the 'wicked of Israel', upon whom a series of fierce imprecations are piled up.[3] From the exposition of single verses, mention may be made of Salmon's interpretation of *Ps.* 69, 13: *They that sit in the gate*

[1] *Ps.* 69 bears the title *concerning the lilies*, and is thus already through this alone earmarked as a composition prefiguring the 'lilies'—a well-known Karaite epithet (see N. Wieder, *ibid.*, note 80).

[2] On *Mic.* 6, 16 al-Qumisi says (*ibid.*, p. 47): וגם הטובים בכם חרפת אחיכם ישראל ישאו ככ׳ (תהלים ס״ט, 11) . . . ואבכה בצום נפשי [ותהי לחרפות למו], אחיכם שנאיכם מנדיכם (ישעי׳ ס״ו, 5).

The *Isaiah* verse is the chief Karaite 'testimony' for the excommunication of the sect; see my study 'The Dead Sea Scrolls', pp. 93–99. This study was written before the publication of al-Qumisi's *Pithron*, from which we now learn that he, too, applied the verse to the Karaite-Rabbanite strife (p. 47).

[3] Karaite spokesmen made ample use of these imprecations in their vituperations against the Rabbanites (see *supra*, p. 203). Yefeth reverts to the imprecatory psalms in several places of his Bible commentaries, either just to call attention to the fact that the sufferer in them is the 'pious sect' and the oppressor the Rabbanites [=the wicked of Israel], or to give vent to his feelings by invoking upon the latter the curses of the psalms concerned. In a fragment of his commentary on the Psalter (MS. British Museum, Or. 2519, fol. 75a=Cat. No. 327, fragment xv) we read as follows: וכמא פעל אללה תעאלי בדואג כדאך יפעל בכל מן יסעא בישראל ויודיהם פי אלגלות והם רשעי ישראל אלדי דעא עליהם פי מזמור אלהי תהלתי אל תחרש (109) ופי הושיעני אלהים (69) בקולה שפך עליהם זעמך וקאל פי אכר כלאמה ימחו מספר החיים (ס״ט, 29). תם ערף אן אלצאלח יפרג אללה ענה ויפרחה בקולה ואני עני וכואב (שם, 30) וקאל יראו ענוים וישמחו דרשי אל ויחי לבבכם (שם 33: ראו ענוים ישמחו).

Further, on *Cant.* 2, 2 (*as a lily among the thorns*) he explains that the 'wicked of Israel' are figuratively designated as 'thorns' because they harm Israel, adding that it was upon them that the pious imprecated the curses of *Ps.* 69, 23–29 (MS. British Museum, Or. 2513, fol. 64a): פיחתמל אן יכונו רשעי ישראל אלחוחים לאנהם מודיין לישראל וכמא קאל ענהם טובם כחדק (מיכה ז׳, 4) ותואעדהם אללה באלהלאך כמא שרחנא פי הוי רועי האליל עזבי הצאן (זכרי׳ י״א, 17) ודעא עליהם אלצאלח יהי שלחנם לפניהם לפח וג׳ ימחו מספר החיים.

talk of me; and I am a song of the drunkards. The reference is to the drinking banquets of the Rabbanites at which they imitate how the Karaites wail for Zion, mourn over the destruction of the Temple, and the way they intone the Book of *Lamentations*.[1] This mimicry can be illustrated by a citation from a recently discovered fragment of an anti-Karaite treatise describing how the Karaites, dressed in black, with the womenfolk sitting separately, wail and lament: 'Ah, Ariel!'[2]

PSALM 119 IN KARAITE IDEOLOGY

The most prominent example of the *pesher* interpretation of the Psalter among the Qumranites and Karaites alike is the exposition of *Ps.* 119. The several Scrolls containing this psalm recovered from Cave IV,[3] and most especially the exceptionally frequent occurrence of the term *temīmē derekh* and its cognate forms in the Qumran texts, bear testimony to the importance which the men of Qumran attached to this eight-fold alphabetical composition which their copyists took pains to write out stichometrically and alphabetically.[4] The Sect identified itself with the 'Perfect in the Way' mentioned in the first verse of the psalm, going so far as actually to adopt this term as a laudatory self-designation.

The Karaites also appropriated that title to themselves, claimed that the psalm was composed by King David 'on their

[1] *The Arabic Commentary*, etc., p. 100.

[2] Published by A. Scheiber in *HUCA*, xxviii [1956], p. 300: קודרים ישבו לשכות לשכות/ הם יספדו „הוי אריאל" במבוכות/ ונשיהם לבד יושבות מבכות/ קול נהי וקול צוחה.
That the women played an important part in the lamentations of the 'Mourners for Zion' is graphically described by one of the participants, Sahl b. Maṣliaḥ, in a passage in which he tells us of women wailing and lamenting in Hebrew, Persian and Arabic, adding that they also instruct their daughters in this practice: ובתוכה נשים מקוננות וסופדות בלשון הקדש ובלשון פרס ובלשון ישמעאל ומלמדות לבנותיהן נהי ואשה רעותה קינה... והאנשים והנשים באפר מתפלשים, צמים ומתענים בלבוש שק (*Me'asseph Niddaḥim*, no. 13, p. 203).

[3] J. T. Milik, *Ten Years of Discovery in the Wilderness of Judaea*, pp. 27f.

[4] *Ibid.*

behalf'[1] and that it contained an anticipatory description of the current religious situation. The speaker is identified with either the Karaite community or its intellectual core, the *maskilim*, whose outstanding features the psalm portrays. I have substantiated this elsewhere by ample references to Karaite literature, which led me to the conclusion that the psalm was 'a basic religious document of Karaism' and that it exercised a profound influence on the sect's ideology.[2] I further pointed out that it was included in the Karaite liturgy from the time of 'Anan, who ruled that its recitation should be spread over the whole week, and that it was studied on Sabbath afternoons during the seven weeks between Passover and Pentecost.[3] The initiation of this custom was also ascribed to 'Anan.[4]

I have since had the opportunity of studying the still unpublished commentary on *Ps.* 119, entitled עשרה מאמרות,[5] in the introduction of which the author, Kaleb Afendopolo, deals with the importance of the psalm for the Karaites; this fully confirms the view I had formed about it and which I summed up in the statement that 'it may be styled *the evangelion of the Karaites*'. Afendopolo characterizes the themes contained in the psalm as 'the roots of religion and the fundamentals of faith'. It deals with such cardinal principles as the exclusive belief in the written Torah and the possibility of discovering the hidden things of the Law by means of 'searching'; it enjoins and encourages the Karaite believer fearlessly to adhere to his faith in face of enmity and scorn; it alludes to the 'mighty rebellion' of the Rabbanites in asserting that they are in possession of a second Torah, and it foretells the persecution of the Karaite sect. In general, 'the subjects of this psalm concern the roots of the controversy between the Rabbanites and ourselves', and it was for this reason that the

[1] *Supra*, p. 199, note 2.

[2] *The Qumran Sectaries*, pp. 97–113.

[3] *Ibid.* pp. 111f.

[4] See the extract (no. 2) from Kaleb Afendopolo's work at the end of the chapter.

[5] MS. Leiden, Warner 30/5 (also Warner 52/10).

psalm was read in Karaite synagogues on each of the seven Sabbaths between Passover and Pentecost, since the fixation of the date of the latter formed one of the principal points of controversy between the two camps.

An interesting illustration of the position of *Ps.* 119 in Karaite thinking is supplied by Judah Maruli II of Constantinople (died 1593) who composed a liturgical poem in imitation of Ibn Gabirol's *Kether Malkhūth* to be recited, like the latter, on the Day of Atonement.[1] In order to 'karaitize' the theological and cosmological ideas which he derived from Gabirol's composition, Maruli enclosed them in an alphabetical frame consisting of verses from *Ps.* 119 in such a way that each strophe begins with a verse from that psalm. This close connection of the poem with the psalm was designed to stamp the doctrines contained in the former as karaitic, i.e. consistent with the Karaite faith. Maruli could hardly have contrived a better device to indicate this than by marking his composition with verses taken from the 'evangelion of Karaism'.

The Karaites' exposition of the psalm in question and their appropriation of the title 'Perfect in the Way' is presupposed in the Rabbanite work *Seder 'Eliyyahu Rabbah*[2]—a work which contains a considerable number of passages of a polemical nature directed against Karaite teachings and beliefs.[3] Such a passage, which can be correctly understood against the background of Karaite ideology only, is found there on page 69. Already its introductory statement is unmistakably polemical: 'It is a bad sign if a man despises a good life in this world.' This disparagement of the ascetic is aimed at the ideal of the Mourners for Zion, who preached and practised renunciation of worldly goods, and regarded asceticism as the hall-mark of the pious man.[4] The passage concludes with the interpretation of *Jer.* 31, 7, saying:

1 *Karaite Prayer-Book* (Vienna), iii, pp. 79ff; Abraham Danon, 'The Karaites in European Turkey', *JQR* (N.S.), xv [1924–25], p. 329.

2 Edition of M. Friedmann, Vienna 1900.

3 See W. Bacher, *MGWJ*, xxiii [1874], pp. 266–294.

4 *The Qumran Sectaries*, pp. 283ff.

This refers to the sages and their disciples who dedicate themselves to the study of the Bible, Mishnah, *Halakhoth* and *'Aggadoth*, and it is of them that the psalmist says: *Happy are the perfect in the way.* Thus, rebutting the Karaite contention, the Rabbanite author insists that the 'Perfect in the Way' are none other than the Rabbanite sages and scholars who repudiate asceticism and are devoted to the written and the oral Law alike.

It is instructive to compare this passage with the portrayal of the 'Perfect in the Way' by Yefeth b. 'Ali.[1] He begins by asking, 'Who are these Perfect in the Way?', and answers, 'We say that these are the sect of the Karaites who hold fast to the Lord's Torah, have abandoned man-made commandments and do not rely on Mishnah, Talmud, *Halakhoth* and *'Aggadoth* which are replete with error and are contrary to the Lord's Torah'. After describing their separation from their nearest relatives and after depicting their strict asceticism he concludes: 'And it is to them that the psalmist referred with the words *Perfect in the Way.*' The contrast is conspicuous and the interdependence of the two sources can hardly be denied. Attention should also be paid to the same emphatic wording employed in both sources to underline their respective views: the *Seder 'Eliyyahu* has ועליהם הוא אומר אשרי תמימי דרך, and Yefeth b. 'Ali ואליהם ישיר בקולה תמימי דרך.

Nor is this the only attempt made by the Rabbanite author of the named work to combat the Karaite conception of the psalm. Whereas in the aforementioned interpretation he followed the method of his opponents insofar as he, too, interpreted the psalm in reference to his contemporary generation, in another place[2] he claimed that the title 'Perfect in the Way' related to the pious of the earliest periods of mankind: Adam, Noah, the three patriarchs, Judah and Joseph. And in this instance, too, he uses the same emphatic formula, designed to exclude an alternative interpretation: 'And it is of them that the psalmist said: *Happy are the perfect in the way.*'

[1] *Ibid.* pp. 289–91.

[2] *Seder 'Eliyyahu Rabbah*, p. 35.

APPENDIX

Extracts from the treatise עשרה מאמרות by Kaleb ben Elijah Afendopolo, MS. Leiden, Warner 30/5, fols. 210b (no. 1) and 221b–222a (no. 2):

1

ומן החלופים ההם חלוף אחד הוא מחרת השבת הבא תוך שבעת ימי מצה שיום החמשים יום ממנו הוא יום חג השבועות יום מתן תורה כפי קצתם עׄהׄ וכבר ידעת איך הוסיפו החכמים עׄהׄ בתפלות השבע שבתות שבין אלו הימים חבורים ופסוקים מורים על החלוף שבינינו ובינם[1] בעניין זה כמו שעשו כן ביום ז׳ עצרת וביום מועד חג השבועות כמו שידוע העניין בסדר התפלה. הנה כמו כן תקנו קדמונינו וסדרו להיותנו קוראים בבית הכנסת לעת נטות השמש בכל שבת ושבת משבע השבתות אלו שבין מחרת שבת בראשית שחל להיות תוך שבעת ימי מצה ובין יום מתן תורה שהוא אחרי חמשים יום לקרוא הפרקים והם מזמור אשרי תמימי דרך ההולכים בתורת יי עם פתיחתו[2] וחתימתו כמו שכתוׄ בסדור תפלות השנה. כי במזמור הזה

[1] Cf. 'The Qumran Sectaries', pp. 110, 288; 'The Dead Sea Scrolls', p. 86; *supra*, p. 117. This principle of selecting scriptural texts for inclusion in the Karaite liturgy was expressed with exceptional candour by Elijah b. Moses Bashyachi ('Addereth 'Eliyyāhū, p. 105b): ואם יש חלוקה בקדוש היום ההוא בינינו ובין אחינו בעלי הקבלה מוסיפים פסוקים ומזמורים כנגדם להורות שהם נוטים בזה מדרך האמת כגון בראש חדש שאומרים [מפר אותות בדים וקסמים יהולל] משיב חכמים אחור ודעתם יסכל (ישעי׳ מ״ד, 25); כי התרפים דברו און והקוסמים חזו שקר (זכרי׳ י׳, 2) וזולתם שמרמיזים בטעות בעלי הקבלה בענין הקדוש ברדפם אחרי החשבון. וכן עשו בממחרת השבת. Cf. Hadassi, 19, beginning, and *Karaite Prayer-Book*, i, p. 13 (Vilna 1868).

The relevance of the *Isaiah* and *Zechariah* verses to the controversy about the calendar resides in the Karaite *pesher*, according to which the rabbinic method of calendation which utilizes astronomical computations was denounced by the prophets as 'sorcery' or 'divination', and the Rabbis as 'sorcerers' or 'diviners'. It is on the grounds of this *pesher* that Karaite writers dubbed the rabbinic method of calendation as חשבון הקוסמים, 'the calculation of the sorcerers'; see the extracts from al-Qumisi's *Book of Precepts*, in A. Harkavy, *Studien u. Mitteilungen*, viii, p. 189; *Pithron*, pp. 44, 46; Sahl b. Maṣliaḥ, *op. cit.* p, 150; 'Eshkol *ha-Kopher*, 104, *beth*; 192, *shin*; 195, *qoph*.

[2] The recitation of the psalm was usually prefaced by *Isa*. 49, 16 and 62, 6–7. These introductory verses were intended to indicate the identity of the 'Perfect in the Way'; they are none other than the 'night-watchmen' on the walls of Jerusalem, see 'The Qumran Sectaries', pp. 110f.

תועלות גדולות ודברים מורים לעניינים רבי התועלת כמו שנבארם מאחרי כן א״יה. וכבר נמשך המנהג מאבותינו ואבות אבותינו מזמן הרב רבינו ענן הנשיא ראש הגולה אשר פתח דרך התורה והאיר עיני בני מקרא ורבים השיב מעון ועברה הוא ז״ל היה תלמידו של (ברוך) גנאי ברוך ע״ה שהיה תלמידו של עזרה הכהן[1] ע״ה. מאז נמשך המנהג עד היום הזה לקרוא במזמור זה ברבים בכל שבת ושבת משבע השבתות כפי שאנו מתנהגים היום כאשר אתה רואה.[2]

2

ונתחיל ונאמר התאנים[3] הטובות ע״ה בחרו מזמור אשרי תמימי דרך לקראו ברבים בכל שבת ושבת משבע השבתות מפני סבות. הסבה הא׳ כונתם הראשונה ז״ל והיא בעבור שמזמור זה מורה על היות התורה אמתית ואחת אין לה שנית. ויורה על מעלת ואשור האיש המודה בה לבדה מבלתי שיודה בזולתה. ופחיתות ורוע מזג האדם שמודה בזולתה עמה או בלתה ויורה גמול המודה בה לבדה ומקיים המצות והאזהרות על פי פשוטם הנכון שאין בו שגג או טעות מבלתי היות הפכי או סותר למה שישפוט השכל האנושי המאמת. וכי המעיין בה והחוקר בדבריה ומחפש מצפוניה יגלו לו נפלאות ועניינים אלהיים מועילים להשארת הנפש אחרי המות אשר הוא סוף כל האדם. ויורה על ענש המודה בזולתה והשוגג או הטועה במצות ואינו מקיימם על פי פשוטם הנכון אלא יגבר תאותם החמרי על השכל וכדי להתגבר על אויביהם ולהשתרר על אנשי זמנם וזולתו הורו דברים שלא כדין התורה ואיימו לבות האנשים והיו חוטאים ומחטיאים כירבעם בן נבט. וכי אין ראוי לאדם לירוא משום נברא מהנבראים בלכתו אחרי דרך התורה וברדפו אחרי עשיית המצות ושמירת האזהרות אלא ראוי להיותו הוגה בתורה שבכתב אע״פ ששרים ומלכים יאשימוהו ויגנוהו על זה. וכי ראויה התחנה והבקשה לו ממנו יתע׳ להדריך האדם בדרך אמת עד שישמור ויעשה גזרתו הנכתבת כפי כונתו יתע׳ ולהסיר ממנו דרך שקר אשר הוא הפך או סותר לאמת שנכתב בתורתו יתעלה. וכי יש בו פסוקים רבים מורים על המרי העצום שעשו בני בירב באמרם שתורה שנית יש להם והיא פירוש לתורה שבכתב והיא תורת הפה שהורו הם: סורו ממני מרעים ואצרה תורת אלהי (114); עת לעשות לה׳ הפרו תורתך (126); צמתתני קנאתי כי שכחו דבריך צרי (139) וזולתם הרבה. וכי יש בו פסוקים מורים על היות לאנשים השומרים תורת ה׳ לבד ואינם שומעים לקול

[1] Cf. *Liq. Qad.*, p. 24; App., p. 186.

[2] See also J. Mann, *Texts and Studies*, ii, p. 1419, note 57.

[3] On this title see *supra*, p. 106, note 1.

מלחשים וילדי נכרים רבים אויבים וצרים והם מתקוטטים עמהם אולי ישיבום מדרכם הרעה וממחשבתם הזרה שחשבו שלא כתורת השם יתֹעֹ כמונו היום עם בני בירב. הנה כל אלה העניינים שהורו בם הפסוקים שבמזמור הזה כלם הם עקר המחלוקת שבין הרבנים ובינינו. לכן בחרו משכילי עם עֹהֹ זה המזמור לקראו ברבים בשבע השבתות[1] עד שיבחן האמת מן השקר ויראה בין עובד אלהים לאשר לא עבדו כאשר יתנו העם לב להבין דבריו.

והסבה השנית היא בעבור היות המזמור הזה כולל כל חלקי התורה שבהם נכללת והם עשתי עשר עניינים.[2] והם דרך תורה עדות פקודים מצוה אמירה דבור משפט צדק אמונה חוקים שהם נמצאים בכל פסוק ופסוק מפסוקי מזמור זה שהם קעֹו פסוקים זולת פסוק אֹ שנמלט מהם והוא ערוב עבדך לטוב (122). שזה רמז על היות התורה אחת לאמה וברה ליולדתה.[3] וזולתה

[1] With the relationship between this custom and the Rabbanite practice of studying Mishnah *'Abhoth* on the Sabbaths between Passover and Pentecost, I propose to deal in a separate paper; for the time being, see L. Finkelstein, הפרושים ואנשי כנסת הגדולה [*The Pharisees and the Men of the Great Synagogue*], New York, 1950, pp. 24ff.

[2] The *Massorah Magna* on verse 122, calling attention to this feature of the psalm, speaks of ten expressions only, which are explained as being corresponding to the Ten Commandments. The text of the massoretic passage (as printed in *Miqra'oth Gedoloth* and in Christian D. Ginsburg's edition of the *Massorah*, London 1883, ii, p. 758) needs emendation: instead of *ṣedeq*, which does not appear *alone* in any of the verses, read *'emunah*, which figures as the sole expression in verse 90. Kaleb Afendopolo must have had such a corrupt text before him, and on discovering that verse 90 contained none of the expressions listed in his text, but only *'emunah*, added this latter expression to the ten of his text, thus arriving at the total of eleven.

[3] *Cant*. 6, 9. Underlying Afendopolo's usage of the verse is the interpretation placed on it by the Karaite allegorical exegesis as referring to the uniqueness and self-sufficiency of the written Torah. Yehudah Hadassi invokes the verse with great frequency, cf. 25, *nūn*; 98, *yodh*; 131, *qoph*; 132, *zayin*; 173, *shin*; 226, *nūn*, and *passim*. It is against this Karaite claim of the written text of Scripture being sufficiently 'clear' without the help of tradition that the author of *The Mishnah of Rabbi Eliezer* polemizes (p. 249; cf. *supra*, pp. 66, 130): אימתי היא ב ר ה, כשאתה מקבלה מאבותיך שהן בקיאין בכתב ובלשון ובפירוש. ואם אינו שומע להן הוא אויל ינאץ מוסר אביו (משלי ט״ו, 5). וכי יש אויל גדול מזה, הוא סומך על אביו בכתב ובלשון ואינו סומך עליו בפירושו. אבל הט אזנך ושמע דברי חכמים. Cf. J. N. Epstein, *HUCA*, xxiii, Part 2 [1950–51], p. 15.

זדות וגאות ובדיאה מלב[1] אנשים זדים.[2] וזהו שאמ׳ אל יעשקוני זדים. רצונו ערוב והטיב והכשיר לעבדך לטוב על היות שומר תורתך שעליה נאמ׳ על ידי חותם הנביא׳ זכרו תורת משה עבדי[3] ולא לזולתה להושיעני ושלא יעשקוני זדים ובודים על שאיני שומר תורתם שזדו והרשיעו ובדו מלבם שלא כתורתך.[4]

[1] On the accusation that the Oral Law was but an invention of the Rabbis, see *supra*, p. 144, note 2.

[2] For *zedim* as an opprobrious title of the Rabbanites cf. 'The Qumran Sectaries', p. 103, and add now *Pithron*, p. 4.

[3] *Mal.* 3, 22. The verse became a battle-cry of Karaism; see *supra*, page 72, note 1. Afendopolo, too, makes ample use of this biblical verse in various places of his tract. One example may be quoted. In eulogizing the Hasmonean rulers and imputing to them the Karaite belief in the sole authority of the written Torah, he writes thus (fol. 217b): ואת אלהי ישראל היו עובדים ואת מצותיו שומרים כאשר כתובים בתורתו יתע׳ שעליה נאמר על פי חותם הנביאים זכרו תורת משה עבדי.

This eulogy, it may be observed *en passant*, is not incompatible with the Karaite rejection of the festival of Ḥanukkah. That rejection was not motivated by a negative attitude towards the Maccabees, but stemmed from the basic tenet of Karaism that insisted on Scripture as being the exclusive source of all religious legislation and opposed any post-biblical innovation, be it in the form of a law or a festival (such as the second day of the holidays in the Diaspora). '*Thou shalt not add thereto*' (*Deut.* 13, 1) is one of the pillars of the ideological structure of Karaism, and its spokesmen do not tire of citing it time and again. As to Moses Ben-Asher's reference to the Hasmonean victory over the Greeks, cf. M. Gertner's observation in P. Kahle's *The Cairo Geniza* (2nd ed.), p. 105.

[4] Cf. Salmon b. Yeruḥim's interpretation of verse 122 in J. Mann, *Texts and Studies*, ii, p. 85.

CHAPTER VII

THE 'BOOK OF *HEGEH*'

A STUDY IN THE SEMANTICS OF THE ROOT הגה

PART ONE

I

Notwithstanding the veritable spate of speculations and conjectures, the character of the work mostly cited as the 'Book of *Hagu*'[1] remains as mysterious as it was nearly fifty years ago when the *Damascus Document* first emerged from the limbo of the Cairo Genizah. It has been variously rendered as:

Book of Explanations,[2]
Book of Study,[3]
Book of Meditation,[4]
Book of Deduction,[5]
Book of Swearing,[6]
Book of Exposition, Study and Interpretation,[7]
Book of Moaning,[8]

[1] *CDC*, x, 6; xiii, 2; xiv, 7–8 (?); *DSD* A (1*QSa*) i, 7.

[2] L. Ginzberg, 'Eine Unbekannte jüdische Sekte', *MGWJ*, 1912, pp. 306f.; 417f.: *Buch der Erklärungen*. For a detailed criticism of his view see *infra*, p. 233, footnote.

[3] Theodor H. Gaster, *The Scriptures of the Dead Sea Sect*, p. 85; H. J. Schoeps, *Zeitschrift für Religion und Geistesgeschichte*, vol. iii [1951], p. 331.

[4] Barthélemy and Milik, *Qumran Cave I*, p. 112; G. Vermès, *op. cit.* p. 157, and others.

[5] H. E. Del Medico, *The Riddle of the Scrolls*, p. 413.

[6] A. M. Habermann, *'Edah we-'Eduth*, pp. 27f.; 121. Habermann surmises that part of the 'Book of *Hagu*' has been preserved in the *Damascus Document*, xv–xvi, which contains regulations relating to swearing.

[7] A. M. Honeyman, *JJS*, iv [1953], p. 132.

[8] M. H. Goshen-Gottstein, *VT*, vol. viii [1958], pp. 286–8.

Book of Decisions,[1]
Book of the Correct Text [of the Bible],[1]
Book of the [prophet] Haggai,[2]
Book of Hegai.[3]

It has been suspected to be 'a secret book of halakhic decisions';[4] 'the Torah with the interpretation of the teachers of the sect';[5] 'a sort of Canonical Scripture from which it [the sect] deduced necessary precepts';[6] 'das Haupthandbuch für das Studium der Lehre der Gemeinde';[7] 'the oral Law, or Mishnah of the sect'.[8] It has been identified with the Torah; with the *Rule of the Community*;[9] with the *Thanksgiving Scroll*.[10] Even the ingenious *'Atbash* cypher[11] was put into the service of unravelling its mystery, with the result: *The Book of Proof*, or *The Book of Test*.[12] Perhaps the crowning piece of these exegetical adventures is derivation from the Greek, with the resultant translation: *The*

[1] Both renderings were proposed by L. Ginzberg, *op. cit.*, p. 418.

[2] Charles, *Apocrypha and Pseudepigrapha*, ii, p. 825, note 2; H. J. Schoeps, *ZNW*, 1952, p. 254, note 1. While Charles considered this interpretation 'possible', Schoeps declared it to be 'zweifellos'.

[3] H. Neil Richardson, *JBL*, lxxvi [1957], p. 120.

[4] Charles, *loc. cit.*; P. Wernberg-Møller, *The Manual of Discipline*, p. 123: 'this book was a halakic handbook in which were recorded the regulations of the society'.

[5] A. Büchler, *JQR*, N.S. iii [1912–13], p. 452, note 68.

[6] S. Poznanski, *Jewish Review* (London 1911), p. 278.

[7] Paul Kahle, *Theologische Literaturzeitung*, 1952, p. 403.

[8] L. Ginzberg, *loc. cit.*; Schoeps, *loc. cit.*; Ch. Rabin, *The Zadokite Documents*, p. 50.

[9] W. H. Brownlee, *The Biblical Archeologist*, xiii [1950], p. 54. See also M. Z. Segal, *Tarbiz*, xxii, p. 137.

[10] G. Molin, *Lob Gottes aus der Wüste*, Freiburg, 1957, p. 10.

[11] את בש. In this device the first letter of the alphabet is equated to the last, the second to the last but one, and so on.

[12] Hugh J. Schonfield, *Secrets of the Dead Sea Scrolls*, p. 3.

Book of the Leader,[1] or, according to a different derivation:[2] *The Book of the Holy One*.[3]

II

If a fresh attempt is here made at solving the riddle, it is done in the hope that even if the proposed solution should fail to find the acceptance anticipated by its author, the way to be traversed in the investigation will prove to have its own value.

The mystery surrounding our book stems from the regrettable fact that the Qumran texts afford no indication of its contents. All we are given is a name, and all conjectures are of necessity focused on that name, trying to extract from it if not the secret of the book's contents, at least a clue to its general complexion. An added difficulty lies in the uncertainty concerning the vocalization, and even the correct spelling of the word.

The present attempt, too, will centre on the title, and endeavour to elicit the character of the book from the meaning of its name. Before proceeding to that task, account should, however, be taken of the few data about the book contained in the sectarian texts. These data, to be sure, are by themselves incapable of deciding the issue; but they possess sufficient weight to reinforce considerably the semantic argument to be set out presently. At any rate, on the ground of these data at least a *prima facie* case can be made out in favour of the solution we suggest below.

The general and most obvious conclusion to be drawn from the data alluded to is that the book in question was of basic importance for the sectarian community; of utmost and all-embracing significance for their religious life: the knowledge of it was regarded as an indispensable prerequisite for the office of judge,[4] and any

[1] A. Dupont-Sommer, *The Jewish Sect of Qumran and the Essenes*, London 1954, p. 60, note 10.

[2] Schonfield, *op. cit.*, p. 2.

[3] Mention may also be made of Israel L'evi's suggestion that the book was a treatise beginning with the word הֱגוּ, 'meditate!' (*REJ*, 1911, p. 196, note 2). Cf. also M. J. Lagrange, *RB*, 1912, p. 231, note 4; W. Bacher, *ZfHB*, xv [1911], pp. 20f.

[4] *CDC*, x, 4–6.

group of ten members had to be headed by a priest conversant with it.[1] In view of the indisputable fact that it was the Bible which occupied the supreme position in Qumran-Damascus, being not merely the code of law regulating the entire life of the Sect, but also the foundation of the eschatology which exercised so powerful an influence on their world outlook; and in view of its being, furthermore, the book which the Sect regarded as mirror and record of its history in the past and its destiny in the future, the *Book of Hagu* will most likely have been the Bible itself, a book which formed the object of their intense study, by day and by night, wherever the minimum number of ten members resided.[2]

Then there is the important provision requiring that the *Book of Hagu* be taught to every member of the Sect from his earliest youth.[3] In a Scripture-centred and Scripture-dominated society such as the Qumran community was, the Book of Books is the most obvious candidate for this central and exalted position: to be the work with which each and every member had to become acquainted at an early age. The ruling of the Mishnah[4] may be recalled which required that at the age of five years a child had to be instructed in the Bible—and this at a period when the Bible no longer was the sole subject of study in the educational scheme of the rabbis.

III

From this general consideration we now turn to the morphological and semantic aspects of the problematic הגו. First, its spelling and vocalization. Two things may now be taken for certain: (a) that הגו=הגי;[5] the scribe of the *Damascus Document*

[1] *Ibid.* xiii, 2; xiv, 7–8 (?).

[2] *DSD*, vi, 6–7.

[3] *DSD* A (1*QSa*), i, 6–7.

[4] *'Abhoth*, v, 21.

[5] The spelling with *yodh* is attested in *DSD* A (1*QSa*); cf. also Barthélemy and Milik, *op. cit.*, p. 113.

misread the *yodh* for *waw*—a not infrequent error on his part; and (b) that the word הגי=הֶגֶה[1]—a spelling which is quite in consonance with the orthographic habit of the writers of the Dead Sea Scrolls.[2] In fact, the biblical הֶגֶה (in the meaning of 'moaning')[3] is actually spelt with *yodh* in one of the *Hodayoth*.[4] We have now to speak, as M. H. Goshen-Gottstein recently observed, of *Sepher ha-Hegeh*.

And as to its meaning, we shall demonstrate—in line with the general argument which led us to postulate that the name *Sepher ha-Hegeh* hides nothing but Scripture itself—that the noun הֶגֶה is synonymous with מִקְרָא, 'reading', the most common appellation for the Bible, and that *Sepher ha-Hegeh* denotes *The Book of Reading*, i.e. the Bible.

Most of the renderings of the word *hegeh* are based on one or other of the possible meanings that the root *HGH* is credited with according to the dictionaries. It appears that one semantic aspect of *HGH* has not been utilized for our purpose—the fact that *HGH* may simply mean 'to read'[5] and that it is exactly

[1] It is not uninteresting to note that the first to have proposed this reading long before the discovery of the Qumran texts, was L. Ginzberg, *MGWJ*, 1912, p. 417. See now Goshen-Gottstein, *op. cit.*, p. 287.

[2] See Ch. Yalon, *Sinai*, 1950, p. 286; Y. Yadin, *The Scroll of the War*, etc., p. 297; Goshen-Gottstein, *loc. cit.* and the other studies mentioned *ibid.*, note 3.

[3] *Ez.* 2, 10.

[4] *DSH*, xi, 21.

[5] The common rendering of *HGH* is 'meditate' and hence the most frequent translation of '*Sepher he-Hagu*' is: '*Book of Meditation*'. It is noteworthy that Rashi regarded 'meditate' as the only meaning of our root in the whole Bible (see on *Josh.* 1, 8; *Ps.* 1, 2). Rashi's general observation was perhaps provoked by Menaḥem b. Saruq's contrary opinion (*Maḥbereth Menaḥem*, ed. Filipowski, London 1854, p. 68) that *HGH* and its derivatives signify 'speech' (ענין מלל הם). Already the thirteenth-century *piyyūṭ* commentator, R. Abraham b. Azriel ('Arūgath ha-Bosem, i, p. 43; ii, p. 36) took issue with Rashi on this score, observing that he overlooked *Job* 27, 4. R. Abraham's own view is that in connection with 'heart' it signifies 'thought', but with 'tongue' it denotes 'speech'. This is also Abraham ibn Ezra's view. On the other hand Josef Qimḥi denies that it ever denotes 'reading or speech'; its

identical in meaning with קרא. It is this meaning which holds the key to the solution we are seeking. Of decisive consequence, however, is not the bare meaning 'to read', but the fact that *HGH* was used to denote, in particular, the public reading of the Law in the Synagogue. Its exact synonymity with *qārā'* is well exemplified by its employment in such standing phrases like 'the reading of the Law' and 'the reading of *Shema*''.

To substantiate these contentions we shall have recourse chiefly to the liturgical poetry of the Synagogue—a much neglected source of linguistic material still awaiting serious and systematic exploitation which, if undertaken, will bring to light meanings and shades of meanings of numerous Hebrew words and phrases not listed in any dictionary and capable of clearing up obscurities in other branches of Hebrew literature.[1] A case in point is the term קץ in the meaning of 'time', 'period', which, when met with in the *Damascus Document* and the Qumran texts, caused surprise among students in all fields of Hebraic studies. That this meaning frequently occurred in Hebrew liturgical poetry, has gone wholly unnoticed.[2]

IV

It will be convenient to cite first examples of the use of the verb *HGH*, to be followed by the nominal derivatives הגיון and הגה. The first three examples are derived from Qallir's poetry.

sole meaning is 'to stammer, mutter'. His son David Qimḥi records (*Sepher ha-Shorāshīm, s.v.* הגה): וכתב אדני אבי ע״ה כי הכל הוא לשון גמגום וצפצוף ואין בו קריאה ודבור כי פירוש ובתורתו יהגה: כל כך יהיה קורא בתורה עד שבכל שעה אפילו שלא בשעת קריאה יצאו הדברים על פיו ויופיעו משפתיו. Qimḥi's view can be endorsed as far as the *primary* meaning is concerned, see H. L. Fleischer in J. Levy's *Neuhebräisches u. Chaldäisches Wörterbuch über die Talmudim u. Midrashim*, i, p. 278; G. R. Driver, *Semitic Writing from Pictograph to Alphabet* [Schweich Lectures, 1944], London, 1948, p. 90, note 3.

[1] See the very instructive study by the late M. Zulay on the language of Yannai: עיוני לשון בפיוטי ינאי in *Studies of the Research Institute for Hebrew Poetry*, vi, pp. 165–248.

[2] See N. Wieder, 'The Term קץ in the Dead Sea Scrolls and in Hebrew Liturgical Poetry', *JJS*, v [1954], pp. 22–31; M. Wallenstein, *VT*, iv, pp. 211–13.

1. In the *qerōbhāh* for the first day of Passover Qallir says with reference to the custom of reading on that day the section beginning with *Lev.* 22, 26, that is, 'the pentateuchal section dealing with *ox*':[1] ...להגות בו בקץ ערך ענין שור

2. In the same composition he expressed the above idea in different terms but retained the root *HGH* for 'reading':[2] ...בכן זכרון שור אהג בזה מועד.

3. In the *qerōbhāh* for the special Sabbath, *Pārāshath Sheqālīm*, on which *Ex.* 30, 11–16 is read in the Synagogue, Qallir says as follows:[3]

This section is to be read at this time, so that her [Israel's] *sheqels* should precede the *sheqels* of the enemy and despiser [Haman].	פרשה זאת להגות בקץ זה פלסיה להקדים לפלס צר ובוזה.

4. Likewise in connection with the scriptural lesson for the above-named special Sabbath, one of the earliest Palestinian *payṭanim*,[4] Pinḥas ha-Kohen, says:[5] סידור שקלים הגות בו להתעלה.

5. In the *'Abhōdāh* composition of the old French ritual,[6] in a passage describing the High Priest's preparations for the Day of Atonement, we read these words: ... ורגיל יהגה בפיו לקח ויהגא בספר חמודות. This is based on Mishnah *Yoma* 1, 6, requiring the High Priest to occupy himself either with the exposition or just with reading of Scripture, in order to keep wakeful during the eve of *Yōm Kippūr*. The Mishnah continues: 'If he was conversant with reading of Scripture, he would read,

[1] For the full quotation and an English translation thereof see my article mentioned in the preceding note, 220.

[2] *Ibid.*, p. 26.

[3] *Ibid.*, pp. 26–27.

[4] Pinḥas is mentioned by Sa'adya Ga'on among the earliest liturgical poets, Yosē ben Yosē, Yannai and Qallir; see Sa'adya's *Agron*, published by A. Harkavy in *Studien u. Mitteilungen aus der Öffentlichen Bibliothek zu St. Petersburg* (St. Petersburg 1891), v, p. 50. See further A. Marmorstein in *Ha-Ṣōpheh* (Budapest), v [1921], pp. 225ff. and M. Zulay, *op. cit.*, i, p. 150 and v, p. 121.

[5] *Ha-Ṣōpheh*, p. 253.

[6] Entitled אתן תהלה; I. Davidson, *Thesaurus of Mediaeval Hebrew Poetry*, i, no. 8958; I. Elbogen, *Studien z. Gesch. d. jüd. Gottesdienstes*, p. 160.

if not they would read before him . . . Zechariah b. Qabutal says: Many times I read before him in the book of *Daniel*.'

6. The poet Isaac Ibn al-Shami,[1] a contemporary of Yehudah Hallevi, in a poem written in honour of the *ḥazzan* in Algeciras, Spain, praising him for making no mistakes when reading the Law, likewise uses the root *HGH* to denote the scriptural reading in the Synagogue: ולא ישגה בעת יהגה בדת אל.

7. Yoḥanan ha-Kohen b. Yehoshu'a,[2] author of the '*Abhōdāh* which was customary in the Italian rite, reformulates in the following words the description of the Mishnah of how the Elders of the Court read before the High Priest *Lev.* 16, the pentateuchal section (*seder*) prescribed for the Day of Atonement:[3] לוית כבודו בין זקני שבת. להגות לפניו בסדר.

8. With regard to the reading of the *Shema*', we find Yannai[4] employing the verb *HGH*[5] in the following sentence: בכן לדורותם נהגה קרית שמע.

9. The employment of *HGH* in connection with the reading of the *Shema*' is also to be found in a poem by Shelomoh b. Yehudah (Ibn Gabirol?) who says:[6] הגות[7] ערבית אל תשבית, 'Do not neglect the reading (of the *Shema*') in the evening'.

[1] See J. Schirmann, 'Poets Contemporary with Moses ibn Ezra and Yehudah Hallevi', *Studies of the Research Institute*, etc., vi, p. 259.

[2] Davidson, *op. cit.*, i, no. 2272; Elbogen, *op. cit.*, p. 84.

[3] Mishnah *Yoma*, i, 3.

[4] M. Zulay, *Piyyuṭē Yannai*, p. 240.

[5] Cf. P.T. *Ber.*, i, 8 (3c): והגית בו יומם ולילה, שתהא הגיית היום והלילה שוין ('*And thou shalt read therein day and night*'—the reading [of the *Shema*'] of the day and the night are to be alike). *Josh.* 1, 8 (and also *Ps.* 1, 2) was interpreted as referring to the reading of the *Shema*', see B.T. *Menaḥoth* 99b and *Midrash Tehillim* on 1, 2 (ed. S. Buber, p. 16).

[6] S. Baer, *Seder 'Abhodath Yisra'el*, p. 776. Ch. N. Bialik and J. Ch. Rawnitzki included this poem in their collection of Ibn Gabirol's poetry (Tel-Aviv 1932), ii, pp. 228f., insisting on Gabirol's authorship against H. Brody and others (*ibid.* p. 144, notes).

[7] S. Baer (*loc. cit.*) reads הֶגֶה which is, however, not in accordance with the metre of the poem. The different readings (another is the imperative of *HGH*) were already noted and discussed by the thirteenth-century *piyyūṭ* commentator, R. Abraham b. Azriel, '*Arūghath ha-Bosem*, ii, pp. 2–3.

V

Turning to the cognate substantive הגיון, we note that it was used by the earliest known liturgical poet, Yosē b. Yosē, with reference to the reading by the High Priest of *Lev.* 16, mentioned above:[1]

תאר[2] שעיר לראש המדבר משכוהו לשנן בחוקי העשור

. . . .

תם הגיונו פשט וטבל ועטה שמונה בגדים . . .

The word *hegyōnō* signifies 'his reading', namely the High Priest's reading of the 'laws of the tenth [day of Tishri]', alluded to before.

The word occurs in this meaning also in Sa'adya's polemical poem *'Essā' Meshālī*,[3] where the Ga'on says of the Massoretes: חסר ויתר בהגיונם, that is, they differentiate in their reading between defectively and *plene* written words.

VI

At this juncture the fact should be noted that *HGH* in *Josh.* 1, 8 and *Ps.* 1, 2 is rendered in LXX by μελετάω—a root which in Judeo-Greek as well as in Judeo-Spanish (in the form *meldar*, or *melder* among Spanish-Portuguese Jews in France) is used in the sense of 'to read Hebrew' and in the specific connotation 'to read the Pentateuch in the Synagogue',[4] corresponding to the

[1] The quotation is derived from Yosē b. Yosē's '*Abhodah* אזכיר אלוה which Sa'adya incorporated in his Prayer Book, see *Siddur Rabh Sa'adya Ga'on*, ed. I. Davidson, S. Assaf, B. I. Joel (Jerusalem 1941), p. 274.

[2] תאר ='to go, depart' (on the basis of *Josh.* 15, 9, 11), cf. *Siddur Rabh Sa'adya Ga'on*, p. 413: תאר היום 'the day departed', and the Genizah text published by R. Edelmann, *Zur Frühgeschichte des Maḥzor* [Bonner Orientalische Studien, Heft 6], Stuttgart 1934, p. 16: תאר ליפנים, 'he went inside'.

[3] *Rabh Sa'adya Ga'on* (ed. J. L. Fishman), p. 509.

[4] Cf. D. S. Blondheim, *Les parlers Judéo-Romans et la Vetus Latina* (Paris 1925), pp. 76–78.

Judeo-German *leinen*. It is surely not insignificant that this usage coincides exactly with the meaning of *HGH* exemplified in the foregoing citations.

VII

In the examples so far given the verb *HGH* figured as precise equivalent of *qārā'*, and the noun *higgāyōn* as synonym of *miqrā'*[1] or *qerī'āh*. It will now be demonstrated that the same semantic development which took place in respect of the former—the transition of meaning from 'reading' to the 'book' that is read[2]—

[1] The word *miqrā'* is often employed simply as *nomen actionis* of *qārā'*, like *qerī'āh*, and interchanges with it; cf. *miqrā' megillāh* (*Tos. Meg.*, *i*, 4; B.T. *Meg.* 6b) and *qerī'ath megillāh* Mishnah *Meg.* ii, 5; *miqrā' pārāshāh* (B.T. *Yoma* 5b).

[2] Also the *nomen actionis qerī'āh* or *qeriyyāh* (so vocalized by S. Baer, *Diqdūqē ha-Ṭe'āmīm*, p. 33 and Ben-Yehudah, *Thesaurus*, xii, 6183; L. Blau, *Einleitung in die Heilige Schrift* [Budapest 1894], p. 12, note 1, prefers the vocalization *qerāyāh*) is employed to denote the entire Bible, see *Diqdūqē ha-Ṭe'āmīm*, pp. 24, 41, 42, 72–77, and *passim*. The term also occurs in Menaḥem b. Saruq's *Maḥbereth* (ed. Filipowski, p. 20: אבל מצאנו בכל קריות ספרד בספרים המוגהים... ובקריות טבריה), and in a Byzantine document, dated 1252 C.E. (see J. Mann, *op. cit.*, i, p. 52). It was widely used in German-Jewish circles in the 12th-13th centuries, as may be seen from the literature emanating from those circles. It occurs in the *Itinerary* of Pethaḥyah of Ratisbon where it is narrated that Samuel b. 'Ali of Baghdad had a learned daughter well versed in Bible and Talmud who used to give instruction in Bible through a window; she herself was within the building while the students were outside below, and could not see her: ...ור' שמואל יש לו בת אחת והיא בקיאה בקרייה ובתלמוד, והיא מלמדת הקרייה לבחורים והיא סגורה בבניין, דרך חלון אחד, והתלמידים בחוץ ואינם רואים אותה. (L. Grünhut, *Die Rundreise des R. Petachjah aus Regensburg*, Jerusalem 1904, p. 10). MS. Leipzig and Wagenseil's edition have twice *qerī'āh* (*loc. cit.*). See also *ibid.*, p. 12: ובארץ בבל לומדים פירוש רבינו סעדיה שעשה מכל הקרייה ומשׁשה סדרים. It occurs several times in *Sepher Ḥasīdīm* (ed. Wistinetzki): §825: כיון שאדם רואה שאין בנו זוכה לתלמוד ילמוד לו הלכות גדולות ומדרשים וקרייה (ed. Bologna, §308: *qerī'āh*); §748: ...יעסוק במדרשים או בקריאה אם עסק אדם בקרייה. See further *ibid.* §1504; Maḥzor Vitry, p. 462; *REJ*, 52 [1906], p. 204.

Aramaic, too, has its equivalent to *miqra'*: קרא or קרייא; for references see L. Blau, *op. cit.*, and particularly W. Bacher, *Die exegetische Terminologie der jüdischen Traditionsliteratur* (Leipzig 1905), ii, pp. 195f.

occurred also in the case of *higgāyōn* which assumed the connotation of Torah or Bible.[1] A single example of this meaning was cited from one of Sa'adya's *piyyūṭim* preserved in the Cairo Genizah.[2] It will be shown that the printed sources provide ample evidence of this meaning and, moreover, enable us to trace it back to a few centuries before Sa'adya, to the second known liturgical poet, Yannai.

1. Affirming his belief in the immutability of the Torah, Yannai says of God: כי הגיונך לא תמיר, 'Thou wilt not change Thy Torah'.[3] This should be compared with the words of the Qumran hymnologist:[4] להמיר תורתכה and with the formulation of the same belief in the well-known dogmatic poem *Yigdal*:[5] ולא ימיר דתו.[6]

2. Likewise Yannai,[7] in a poem contrasting Israel's infidelity

[1] A similar semantic development underwent the word *midrash* which in *II Chr.* 13,22 is used in the meaning of 'book', as rendered by LXX; see W. Bacher, *op. cit.*, i, p. 104; J. N. Epstein, מבואות לספרות התנאים [*Prolegomena ad Litteras Tannaiticas Mishnah, Tosephta et Interpretationes Halachicas*], Jerusalem 1957, p. 501; Otto Eissfeldt, *Einleitung in das Alte Testament* (2nd ed., 1956), pp. 658, note 2 and 659f.

[2] See Habermann, *op. cit.*, p. 156, in the name of M. Zulay: *sepher higgāyōn*. The whole *piyyūṭ* was later published by the latter in *Tarbiz*, xxiii [1952], pp. 117–18.

As will be shown further on, in certain phrases *dāth* and *higgāyōn* interchange. In this instance too we find in Yannai's *qerōbhōth* (*Piyyūṭē Yannai*, p. 138) and in Sa'adya's *'Azhārōth* (*Siddur Rabh Sa'adya Ga'on*, p. 201, top) the expression *sepher dāth*. We have, then, the following fourfold equation:

ספר תורה
ספר דת
ספר הגיון
ספר הגה

[3] *Piyyūṭē Yannai*, p. 333.

[4] *DST*, iv, 10.

[5] Singer's *Prayer Book*, p. 3.

[6] Note the correspondence *tōrāh-dāth-higgāyōn*; cf. n. 2; p. 228, n. 4; p. 235.

[7] *Ibid.* p. 293.

to God with God's loyalty to Israel,[1] says: דברי הגיונך הימרנו, 'we have changed the words of Thy Torah'. דברי הגיון stands for דברי תורה.

The following three examples are derived from Sa'adya's writings.

3. Dealing with the aggadic symbolism of the four species of plants prescribed for the feast of Tabernacles, according to which the willow, possessing neither taste nor fragrance,[2] is representative of people possessing neither good deeds nor learning, Sa'adya says:[3] ירודים ממעש ומהגיון, 'deficient in deeds and in Torah'. This is equivalent to the midrashic 'they have neither Torah nor good deeds'.

4. In a poem the subject matter of which is the revelation at Sinai we read the following words:[4] וישמעו מאמריו ויקבלו הגיונו 'they heard His utterances and accepted His Torah'. One immediately notes that the expression קבל הגיון corresponds to the mishnaic קבל תורה.

5. The following example is taken from *Sa'adya's Polemic Against Ḥiwi Al-Balkhi*, a treatise written in rhymed prose to rebut Ḥiwi's attacks against the Bible and Jewish theology. The relevant passage runs:[5]

אור יי אשר נראה מתחלה בחזיונות. לא הוא האנשים ולא אחד מדמיונות.
כי אחרי לכתם עודנו נצב ככתוב בהגיונות.

The last words of this quotation, not translated by the editor, Israel Davidson, mean: 'as it is written *in the Torah*', and the reference is to *Gen.* 18, 22. The words ככתוב בהגיון correspond

[1] The two alphabetical compositions, on p. 333, no. 6 and on p. 293, no. 7, are counterparts. The former underlines God's inseparable attachment to Israel and the Torah, and the latter contrasts this attachment with Israel's faithlessness to God and its violation of the Torah.

[2] *Pes. de-Rabbi Kahana* (ed. S. Buber), p. 185a; *Lev. R.* 30, 12 and parallels.

[3] *Siddur Rabh Sa'adya*, p. 245, line 10.

[4] *Ibid.* p. 387, line 7.

[5] See *Saadia's Polemic Against Ḥiwi Al-Balkhi*, ed. Israel Davidson, New York 1915 [Texts and Studies of the Jewish Theological Seminary of America, vol. v], p. 68, no. 53.

to the common phrase ככתוב בתורה. The plural, imposed by the requirement of the rhyme, is philologically not unwarranted; it is paralleled by הכתוב, which is applied in tannaitic and amoraic terminology in both singular and plural in the sense of Torah or the entire Bible.[1] In this, Sa'adya is preceded by Qallir who, too, employs the plural of *higgāyōn*, albeit with the masculine ending as dictated by the rhyme of the strophe concerned.[2]

6. A particularly interesting example is found in the paytanic compositions of Samuel the Third, member of the 'Sanhedrin' in Palestine (*c.* 1100 C.E.).[3] Re-phrasing the famous saying of Simon the Just in Mishnah *'Abhoth*, i, 2, he says as follows:[4]

קבעת בנין עולם על שלשה יסודים:
רחש הגיון וכפר שגיון ותגמול חסדים.

Thou hast established an everlasting edifice
upon three foundations: study of Torah,
expiation of sin, and practice of charity.

[1] W. Bacher, *op. cit.*, i, p. 92; ii, p. 95; L. Blau, *op. cit.* p. 18. Cf. further *Gen. R.* 48, 18. Rashi still uses *ha-Kethubhim* as a designation of the entire Bible (B.T. *'Erubhin* 65a) בצר אל יורה. בדקתי אחר המקרא הזה ואינו בכל הכתובים ושמא בספר בן סירא הוא.

[2] See the *qerōbhāh* published by P. F. Frankel in *Jubelschrift zum neunzigsten Geburtstag des Dr. L. Zunz* (Berlin 1884), p. 207: *dath hegyōnīm*. The same phrase is also used by Yehudah Hallevi (*Diwan des Abu-l-Hasan Jehuda ha-Levi*, ed. H. Brody [Berlin 1930], iv, p. 90; ed. S. D. Luzzatto [Lyck 1864], p. 30a). The combination *dath higgāyōn* should be compared with the expression *dath miqrā'* occurring in *Pirqē Rabbi 'Eli'ezer* 46 in the meaning of 'written Law' in contrast to *dath mishnah*, 'oral Law': [משה] יושב לפני הקב"ה כתלמיד שהוא יושב לפני רבו קורא בדת מקרא ביום ושונה בדת משנה בלילה. It is employed, too, by Neḥemiah b. Shelomoh b. Hēman ha-Nasi' (*Studies of the Research Institute for Hebrew Poetry*, iv, p. 230). This is another illustration of the interchangeability of *miqrā'* and *higgāyōn*.

[3] I. Davidson, *Ginzē Schechter*, iii, pp. 50f.; J. Mann, *The Jews in Egypt and in Palestine under the Fāṭimid Caliphs* (Oxford 1920) i, pp. 27ff.; M. Zulay in *Ginzē Kaufmann* [*Genizah Publications in Memory of Prof. Dr. David Kaufmann*, Budapest 1949], i, p. 103; M. Wallenstein, *Some Unpublished Piyyuṭim from the Cairo Genizah* (Manchester 1956), pp. 78f.

[4] *Ha-Ṣōpheh* (Budapest), viii [1924], p. 160.

The phrase *raḥash higgāyōn* is equivalent to *talmūd Torah*.[1]

7. Meshullam b. Qalonymus in the *'Abhōdāh* composition *'Ammiṣ Koaḥ*,[2] customary in the Ashkenazic ritual, recasts the mishnaic description of how the High Priest was kept awake by lecturing on the Oral Law and by reading from Scripture, in the following words: שיח[3] מדרש בפה ובכתב הגיון. The expression כתב הגיון[4] stands here for *miqrā'*, 'Scripture',[5] and not for 'Pentateuch'; the hagiographical books of *Job*, *Ezra*, *Chronicles and Daniel*—and not the Pentateuch—were used for the purpose indicated.[6] It is instructive to compare Meshullam's words with Yosē b. Yosē's formulation of the same idea:[7] נעימות מדרש ומקרא ישוחחו.

8. The aforementioned Meshullam b. Qalonymus employs our term in yet another combination, as in the following sentence:[8] דורשי הגיון דת משיבת נפש. This combination in which *dōreshē higgāyōn* took the place of *dōreshē Tōrāh* is especially illustrative of the interchangeability of the two terms.

9. The *payṭan* Shim'on b. Yiṣḥaq b. 'Abun in a *qerōbhāh* for the second day of Pentecost,[9] in which the Torah is personified and

[1] The usage of the רחש in the specific connotation of 'study' (the Torah) already occurs in Yannai's compositions as well as in Qallir's. The former says (*Piyyūṭē Yannai*, p. 277): רוחשים בדת ארוכה מארץ; and the latter (in a *piyyūṭ* published by A. Scheiber in *Ginzē Kaufmann*, p. 10): ... רוחשת בדת.

[2] Davidson, *Thesaurus*, i, 5703.

[3] See *infra*, p. 229, note 3.

[4] In this instance, too, we are able to adduce a similar combination in which *dāth* takes the place of *higgāyōn* (cf. 225, n. 2; 227, n. 2)—namely כתב דת used by Yehudah Hallevi (*loc. cit.*).

[5] It is, however, equally possible to understand the phrase as though the words were reversed: והגיון בכתב, 'and reading from the written law'. *Higgāyōn* would then be opposite to *midrash* and בכתב to בפה.

[6] Mishnah *Yoma*, i, 6.

[7] *Siddur Rabh Sa'adya Ga'on*, p. 270, line 133.

[8] In the *qerōbhāh* אימך נשאתי; Davidson, *Thesaurus*, i, 3513.

[9] A. M. Habermann, *Liturgical Poems of R. Shim'on Bar Yiṣḥaq* (Jerusalem 1938), p. 93.

represented as claiming that God had pointed out to her the patriarch Jacob as one worthy to study the Torah, writes as follows: ויורני הנה זה נעים ונחמד ונאה לו בהגיונך ללמד.

10. In a *qerōbhāh* for the Great Sabbath by Ḥanan'el b. 'Amnon, enumerating the laws for Passover, this sentence occurs:[1] חמץ לבער כהגיון יקרה. It is interesting to note that *higgāyōn* is here treated as a feminine noun—no doubt by reason of its synonymity with Torah.

VIII

As previously indicated, the segolate noun *hegeh*, also, was employed to signify the act of reading of the Law and of *Shema'*, taking the place of *miqrā'* and *qerī'āh*. Two illustrations will be given.

(a) Yosē b. Yosē[2] describes the scriptural exposition and reading by the High Priest on the eve of *Yōm Kippūr*, previously mentioned, with these words: שעשוע[3] מדרש והגה[4] כתבי הקדש.

[1] The *piyyūṭ* was published from *Seder Ḥibbūr Berākhōth* by I. Davidson in *JQR*, N.S. xxi [1931], pp. 256–66. The passage cited is on p. 258, top. Abraham Schechter, *Studies in Jewish Liturgy* (Philadelphia 1930), p. 73, erroneously ascribed it to *Shabbath ha-ḥodesh*. Ḥanan'el b. 'Amnon is otherwise unknown. A. Schechter's attempt to identify him with a scholar mentioned in al-Ḥarizi's Taḥkemōnī has been proved by S. H. Kook to lack any foundation (*Sinai*, 1952, p. 128).

[2] The citation is taken from the *Abhodah* אתה כוננת עולם ברב חסד (Davidson, *ibid.* i, 8815), once customary in the old French ritual. It was discovered by S. D. Luzzatto, who printed it as an appendix to the second volume of his edition of the Italian *Maḥzor* (Livorno 1856). The citation is on p. 214a. Cf. further I. Elbogen, *Studien etc.*, pp. 79f.

[3] The sentence should be translated: 'Study of *midrash* and reading from the Hagiographa.' Meshullam b. Qalonymus' formula, cited above, which is evidently influenced by Yosē b. Yosē, has שיח מדרש. Here, too, the word שיח should be translated 'study'. Both words are rendered by LXX μελέτη (see Hatch-Redpath, *Concordance of the Septuagint*, ii, p. 908), which in Judeo-Greek bears the meaning of 'study' (cf. D. S. Blondheim, *op. cit.* pp. 76ff. and 167; *supra*, p. 223). S. Lieberman (*Hellenism in Jewish Palestine*, p. 109, note 62) calls attention to Hesychius' definition of μελετάω: *to exercise oneself in*. It may be noted that Rashi on *Ps.* 119, 16 explains the word אשתעשע by אתעסק which signifies precisely 'exercise oneself in'. Rashi derived the word from

(b) In Qallir's liturgical composition for the *Musaph 'Amidah* on *Shabbath Sheqālīm*, when *Ex.* 30, 11–16 is read in the Synagogue, the refrain of each benediction runs as follows: בצדק הגה ערך כי תשא. These words may be rendered into the more common Hebrew phraseology: בזכות מקרא סדר כי תשא 'through the merit of[1] reading the pentateuchal section[2] of *Kī Tissā*''.

IX

In view of the exact correspondence between *miqrā'* and *hegeh*, and bearing in mind that the name the Bible was given in

שעה and referred to *Isa.* 17, 7 and *Ex.* 5, 9; in both places, however, Rashi gave different interpretations from that here implied. Note however 'Onqelos's rendering of ואל ישעו (*Ex.* 5, 9): ולא יתעסקון.

Shim'on b. Yiṣḥaq b. 'Abun, too, uses the term שעשוע in the sense of 'study' in a *piyyūṭ* for the New Year (Davidson, *op. cit.*, iii, p. 140, 1543): נסמכת בשעשוע דת גחלתיך ('She relies on the study of Thy fiery Law'; cf. *Lev. R.* vii, 3; *Pes. de-Rabbi Kahana* [Buber], p. 60b; *Zohar*, *Deut.* 270).

It is further noteworthy that Moses Ben-Asher in his *Song of the Vine* (see now P. Kahle, *The Cairo Genizah*, 1959, p. 84) employed the word שעשועים in relation to the reading of the Bible: שעשועים התקינו טעמי מקרא 'for the reading of Scripture they established the accents'. Cf. *supra*, section vi.

[4] Yosē b. Yosē's two formulations together with Meshullam's formula yield this significant treble equation:

מדרש – מקרא
מדרש – הגיון
מדרש – הגה

[1] The word בצדק in the meaning 'through the merit of' occurs rather frequently in liturgical poetry; cf., e.g. Yannai (*Piyyūṭē Yannai*, pp. 79, 81); Qallir in the prayer for rain uses it several times (see Ashkenazic *Maḥzor* for the eighth day of Tabernacles); Pinḥas ha-Kohen (*Studies of the Research Institute for Hebrew Poetry*, v, p. 138); Hedwatha in a composition for Passover (*Tarbiz*, xxii [1951], p. 38) uses the expression six times, at the end of the first three and last three benedictions of the '*Amidah*, in reference to Abraham, Isaac, Jacob, Aaron, Moses and the Messiah.

Julian Morgenstern (*HUCA*, xxiv [1952–53], p. 28) translated *Isa.* 58, 8: והלך לפניך צדקך 'and thy merit shall go in front of thee', observing (note 71) that 'here *thy merit* . . . seems the most appropriate translation'. This translation gains substantial support from the usage of the *payṭanim* who have preserved this connotation of the word *ṣedeq*.

[2] To ערך = סדר cf. *supra*, p. 221 and N. Wieder, *JJS*, 1954, p. 24, note 11.

rabbinic Judaism, both in Hebrew and Aramaic, was *Reading*,[1] it ought to cause no great surprise to learn that in Qumran, too, they designated the Bible in essentially the same manner: *The Book of Reading*, using the precise equivalent to *miqrā'*. If, then, the position which *Sepher ha-Hegeh* occupied in Qumran led us to envisage the Bible under the cover of these two Hebrew words, our investigation of the root *HGH* and its derivatives *higgāyōn* and *hegeh* has shown that the expression *Sepher ha-Hegeh* is, in fact, a most fitting appellation for Holy Scripture, being quite in keeping with the equivalent appellations in Hebrew and Aramaic.[2]

X

So far as *higgāyōn* was concerned we were in a position to muster ten instances illustrating its synonymity with Torah (and Scripture). Torah in its wider sense signifies the entire Bible. As regards *hegeh*, too, examples of its usage in the sense of Torah can be adduced. It must, however, be emphasized that our explanation of *Sepher ha-Hegeh* does not depend on them. The rendering *The Book of Reading* is sufficiently warranted by the evidence of *hegeh* bearing the connotation of 'reading'. None the less, the examples add considerable weight to our explanation; they show that the same semantic development which took place in the case of *miqrā'* (and *higgāyōn*)—the shift of meaning from 'reading' to the object of reading—occurred likewise in the case of *hegeh*. Here are three examples.

1. In a most interesting *piyyūṭ* for Pentecost ascribed to Qallir and preserved in a Genizah manuscript in the Kaufmann Collection, we read this strophe:[3]

[1] Cf. W. Bacher, *op. cit.*, i, pp. 119f.; ii, p. 117; L. Blau, *op. cit.*, pp. 9f.; M. Wilensky, *REJ*, lxxxiv [1927], pp. 72–80.

[2] *Supra*, p. 224, note 2. Note also the Syriac *qeryānā* (lit. 'reading'), and the Arabic *Qur'an* (Koran) which signifies 'reading' or 'reciting' (Wellhausen, *ZDMG*, lxvii, p. 634; J. Horovitz, *Der Islam*, xiii, p. 67). Reference may also be made to the Latin *lectio* which not only assumed the meaning of 'passage', 'chapter', but was employed in the mediaeval Church to designate the *Epistles*; see Albert Sleumer, *Kirchenlateinisches Wörterbuch*, p. 468.

[3] M. Zulay in *Melilah*, v [1955], p. 70.

וירד יי על הר סיני/ לגלות לעניו צפונות ליפניי/
ששה בכתב בהגא עיניניי/ וששה בהלכות שינוניי.

The burden of these lines is that God revealed to Moses six books of the Bible[1] in written form and the six orders of the Mishnah in oral form. The term *hege*' denotes here 'Bible'. The addition of עיניניי may be illuminated by the similar combination דת עניני, occurring in a poem by 'Ohebh b. Me'ir, a contemporary of Yehudah Hallevi.[2]

2. In an ancient poem[3] in which the anonymous author juxtaposes worldly possessions which man should not covet, and the Torah which should form the sole object of his desire—a poem which gained wide currency and became the target of an attack by Salmon b. Yeruḥim—the following strophe occurs:

אילני פירות/ בגדי תפארות/ גפני פורות/ למה תחמוד;
דת יקרה/ הגה מיוקרה/ ומשנה ומקרא/ חמוד תחמוד.

The words הגה מיוקרה are parallel to דת יקרה[4] and allude to the Torah. Note that the term *hegeh* is treated as a feminine noun; this is not merely because of the requirement of the rhyme but, as in the case of *higgāyōn*, because the feminine gender is in accordance with the meaning of *hegeh* as 'Torah'.

3. The third example is derived from the Hebrew version of Sa'adya's *Sepher ha-Galuy*.[5] Speaking of the decision to commit the Oral Law to writing, Sa'adya says that our forefathers, seeing the global dispersion of the nation and fearing lest the Torah be

[1] The five books of the Pentateuch and the book of *Job*, see B.T. *Bab. Bath.* 14b.

[2] J. Schirmann, *op. cit.* iv, p. 279.

[3] Edited by M. Zulay on the basis of eight Genizah manuscripts in the *Memorial Volume for Rabbi Kook* [=*Sinai*, 1945], p. 287.

[4] An even closer parallel is obtained if הגה מיוקרה is juxtaposed to דת מיוקרת used by Josef ibn Abitur (*Kiryath Sepher*, xxx [1955], p. 246).

[5] See the fragment published by S. Schechter in *Saadyana, Geniza Fragments of Writings of R. Saadya Gaon and Others* (Cambridge 1903), p. 5.

forgotten (ויגורו על ההגא לבלתי השכח), collected every word which had been transmitted by tradition from of old . . . and called the collection Mishnah. The word *hegeh* stands for 'Torah'.[1]

[1] Formerly (*JQR*, xlix [1958], p. 114) I took *hege'* to mean 'word'; the meaning 'Torah' appears to me now to be more appropriate.

L. Ginzberg ('Eine Unbekannte jüdische Sekte', *MGWJ*, 1912, pp. 306–7) contends that the word *hege'* means here 'explanation', and the reference is to the Oral Law which is an explanation of the written one. Similarly, *sepher ha-hegeh* in the *Damascus Document* is rendered by him *Book of Explanations*, i.e. the Oral Law of the sect (see *supra*, p. 215). These renderings are founded on the contention that *HGH* bears the meaning 'explain' (*erklären*), for which Ginzberg cites two proofs: B.T. *Ber.* 63b and *Gen. R.* 49, 2 (also *Tanḥuma*, ed. Buber, i, p. 79). These passages do not bear out his contention. The word יהגה in the dictum לעולם ילמוד אדם ואחר כך יהגה does not signify 'explain'; ילמוד implies explanation, too [Ginzberg: 'mechanisch aneignen']; cf. Rashi's comment on the parallel passage in B.T. '*A. Zarah* 19a: ילמד אדם מרבו עד שתהא גירסת התלמוד ופירושו שגורה לו בפיו. The word יהגה has here the ordinary meaning 'to think' with the implication 'to reason, argue, deduce' (see Jastrow's *Dictionary*, *s.v.* הגי), as rendered by Rashi in *Berakhoth* יעיין, and fully explained in the parallel passage: יעיין בתלמודו לדמות מילתא למילתא להקשות ולתרץ, 'he should scrutinize his learning with a view to making comparisons and thrashing out difficulties'.

The second passage invoked by Ginzberg runs: ומעמיד אני מהם משה שהוא הוגה בתורה בשבעים לשון שנאמר (דברים א׳, 5) הואיל משה באר את התורה [read with *Tanḥuma* and MSS. Paris, Stuttgart and Munich: הוגה (את)התורה]. At first sight this passage appears indeed to afford strong support for Ginzberg's contention, since הוגה is here equated with באר which is usually rendered *he explained*. On closer consideration, however, we note that this is not so. The verb באר like its synonym פרש may simply denote 'to state clearly, express, proclaim' (see in particular M. Zulay's investigation in *Studies in the Research Institute*, etc., vi, pp. 173–7). This is also the meaning of *HGH*: *to pronounce*, *recite* (see Jastrow). Consequently, what the above talmudic passage says is this: Moses *proclaimed* (not explained) the Torah in seventy languages, see Mishnah *Soṭah*, vii, 5. The sentence has been correctly translated by L. Blau, (*op. cit.* p. 98): 'Moses hat die Torah in 70 Sprachen *ausgesprochen*.' Cf. also Jastrow, *s.v.* באר (p. 135).

[It is noteworthy that Maimonides in *Hilekhoth Qeri'ath Shema'*, ii, 9, still uses the verb באר in the sense 'to pronounce': וצריך לבאר ז״יין של תזכרו 'one has to pronounce clearly the letter *zayin* in the word תזכרו' (*Num.* 15, 40)].

One further observation should be made concerning Rabin's view that הגו stands for 'Mishnah'. He writes (*Zadokite Documents*, p. 50): 'In the early Lam. R., proem I (read: II), *hogim* appears by the side of

The reason given by Sa'adya for reducing the Oral Law to writing—the fear lest the *Torah* be forgotten—is the usual motivation which we meet with, for instance, in Sherira's famous *Epistle*[1] and in Rashi's comment on the respective talmudic passage.[2] The disappearance of the oral Torah through forgetfulness was considered tantamount to the disappearance of written Torah, since the latter, without the interpretation contained in the former, is incapable of fulfilment.

XI

We previously had occasion to draw attention to the fact that the terms *dāth* and *higgāyōn* interchange in certain corresponding phrases.[3] The same phenomenon is observable in the case of *dāth* and *hegeh*.[4] It will be instructive to tabulate such interchanges as well as those instances in which *miqrā'* and *tōrāh* are involved. All instances in this tabulation have been mentioned in the foregoing pages. They vividly illustrate the usage of *higgāyōn* and *hegeh* as equivalents to *tōrāh*, *miqrā'* and *dāth*:

mashnim Mishnah-teachers; thus h. [=hagu] is an etymological substitute for *mishnah*.'

The passage in *Lam. R.* reads as follows: מאן אינון נטורי קרתא? אילו סופרים ומשנים שהוגים ומשנים; 'who are the guardians of the city? These are the Bible-teachers and the Mishnah-teachers, who [the former] teach the Bible and [the latter] give instruction in the Mishnah.' Thus, *hogim* and *mashnim* are not synonyms but opposites. The verbs הגה and שנה are correlative terms like the frequently occurring קרא ושנה. As to the correlatives *sopherim-mashnim*, see P.T. *Ḥag.* i, 6 (76c); *Pes. de-Rabbi Kahana* (Buber), p. 120b; *Lev. R.* 9, 2; Aramaic: ספרין ומתניין.

[1] *'Iggereth Rabh Sherira' Ga'on*, ed. B. M. Lewin (Haifa 1921), p. 20 ('Spanish version'): וחזא [רבי] דקא ממעט לבא וקא מסתם מעין החכמה ומסתלקא תורה.

[2] B.T. *Giṭṭin* 60a: כיון דלא אפשר מליכתב שנתמעט הלב והתורה משתכחת; *ibid.* 60b: מכאן אתה למד שהתלמוד לא ניתן ליכתב אלא מפני שהתורה משתכחת. So also Jacob b. Yehudah of London in the preface to his *'Eṣ Ḥayyim* (see David Kaufmann, *JQR*, v, [1893], p. 367): ורבנו הקדוש חבר ספר המשנה . . . כדי שלא תשתכח התורה.

[3] See notes pp. 225, n. 2; 227, n. 2; 228, n. 4.

[4] *Supra*, p. 232, note 4.

הגה עניניי – דת עניניי
הגה מיוקרה – דת מיוקרת (יקרה)
כתב הגיון – כתב דת
ספר הגיון – ספר דת
מעש והגיון – מעש ודת[1]
דת הגיון – דת מקרא
הגיונך לא תמיר – ולא ימיר דתו
הגה – מדרש
מקרא – מדרש
הגיון – מדרש
קבל הגיון – קבל תורה
ככתוב בהגיון – ככתוב בתורה
דברי הגיון – דברי תורה
דורשי הגיון – דורשי תורה

XII

In conclusion, a word should be said in justification of the view that *Sepher ha-Hegeh* signified the 'Bible', i.e. the whole canon. On the basis of the examples adduced one could as well assert that it signified just the Pentateuch, and not the Bible as a whole. Two considerations, however, advocate the first alternative. First, the fact that the Pentateuch is referred to in the Qumran texts by its regular title *tōrāh*;[2] and secondly, the data about the book. Messianism and eschatology played, as repeatedly noted, a central rôle in the Sect's ideology and vitally affected their life; it stands therefore to reason that the knowledge, for instance, of the Prophets and the Book of *Daniel*, the very foundations of their messianic-eschatological doctrines, should have been regarded a vital element in the spiritual corpus to which the Sect turned for guidance, no less vital—and from the viewpoint of edification and encouragement certainly of greater necessity—than a knowledge of the Pentateuch. Add to this the Sect's attitude to the prophetic writings as a source of elucidation and

[1] *Supra*, p. 226 and *Siddur Rabh Sa'adya Ga'on*, p. 245, line 3.

[2] Cf. S. Schechter, *Fragments of a Zadokite Work*, p. xvi.

interpretation of the written Torah. Hence it is much more likely that the insistence, e.g., that the priest heading a group of ten members should be versed in the *Book of Hegeh*, referred to the Bible as a whole and not merely to the five Books of Moses.

PART TWO

It almost looks as if the root *HGH* and its derivatives were predestined to become the subject of a multiplicity of explanations,[1] covering a wide range of conceivable and inconceivable theories. One is inclined towards such a 'fatalistic' view on finding that, in addition to the *hagu* of Qumran-Damascus with its chequered history, there are other derivatives of the same root that have had a strikingly similar career. It appears now that the meanings of *hegeh* and *higgāyōn* established by the preceding evidence put us in a position to dispel at last the obscurity in which these expressions have long been enveloped, and to furnish a satisfactory explanation of the passages in which they occur.

I

Let us begin with the term *higgāyōn* in the famous apothegm of R. Eliezer b. Hyrcanus[2] מנעו בניכם מן ההגיון, 'Keep your children away from *higgāyōn*,' the sense of which has been disputed for over eleven hundred years, since the days of Ṣemaḥ Ga'on who was the first, according to the sources at present available, to have proffered an explanation of it. The similarity of fate between *hagu* and *higgāyōn* extends to the circumstance that the latter, too, was considered by scholars to represent a corruption of other Hebrew words. Leopold Löw[3] suggested that the correct reading was גליון and the sense of the maxim: 'Keep your children away from the [*Evan*]*gelion*.' And in recent years a scholar of the calibre of G. Allon contended that the word was a scribal error for גאון to which he assigned the meaning

[1] Even its meaning in the Bible was a moot point, see *supra* 219, n. 5.

[2] B.T. *Ber.* 28b.

[3] *Ben Chananja*, iv [1861], p. 31.

'plutocracy'.[1] But the similarity goes even further; in the case of *higgāyōn*, too, a Greek derivation had been advocated: it hides the word *hagio*, and what R. Eliezer said was: 'Keep your children away from reading the Hagiographa.'[2]

We must, however, resist the temptation to list here all the various interpretations placed upon the apothegm mentioned—interpretations ranging from 'childish talk'[3] to 'philosophic speculation' (logic,[4] dialectics, sophistry),[5] from 'reading apocryphal

[1] *Tarbiz*, xxi [1950], p. 107, note 9; מחקרים בתולדות ישראל [*Studies in Jewish History in the Times of the Second Temple, the Mishnah and the Talmud*], Jerusalem 1957, i, p. 314, note 9. It may be noted that already N. Brüll connected R. Eliezer's dictum with the saying in *'Abhoth de-Rabbi Nathan* (ed. S. Schechter, p. 34a). Brüll, however, who was uncertain as to the meaning of *higgāyōn*, hesitantly proposed the translation *Gerede*; see *Jahrbücher für jüdische Geschichte und Literatur*, ix [1889], p. 137.

[2] See the Hebrew translation by A. Z. Rabinowicz of W. Bacher's *Die Agada der Tannaiten* (2nd ed. Berlin 1922), i, p. 74.

[3] This is an alternative interpretation given by Rashi in *Ber. ad loc.*

[4] Cf. *'Oṣar ha-Ge'onim*, *Berakhoth*, ii, p. 39. The interpretation is attributed to Hai Ga'on in a letter by the Maimunists of Castellon (de La Plana) embodied in *Minḥath Qenā'ōth* by 'Abba Mari (Don Astruc) of Lunel (Pressburg 1838), p. 172. It is cited as a gaonic comment, without mentioning Hai Ga'on, in letter no. 91 (*ibid.* p. 169) by Mordecai b. Isaac of Carpentras.

R. Eliezer's apothegm (with the interpretation of *higgāyōn* as signifying 'logic') was employed by the anti-Maimunists as a weapon in their struggle against philosophic studies (cf. also *ibid.* letter no. 13, p. 49). The rationalists, on the other hand, insisted that the apothegm referred to children only. This distinction between self-education and education of children, quoted by S. Lieberman (*Hellenism in Jewish Palestine*, p. 103) in the name of Rabbi Israel of Toledo (died 1326), can be traced back to earlier authors. It is mentioned by Jacob Anatoli in the introduction to his Hebrew translation of Averroes' commentary on Aristotle's *Logic* (see M. Steinschneider, *Catalog der Hebr. Handschriften in der Stadtbibliothek zu Hamburg*, 1878, p. 182; J. Freimann in *'Oṣar Ṭōbh* [Hebrew Supplement to *Magazin f. die Wissenschaft des Judenthums*], xi [1884], p. 33): ואם יאמר אומר הלא רבותינו ז״ל מנעו החכמה הזאת כי הם אמרו מנעו בניכם מן ההגיון, נשיב לו השמע לאזניך מה שאתה מוציא מפיך כי הם אמרו בניכם ולא אמרו עצמיכם. It is also cited (but rejected) by the Qabbalist Abraham Abulafia (see Jellinek, *Philosophie und Kabbala*, Leipzig 1854, p. 14); it is alluded to by Naḥmanides in his letter addressed to the French rabbis in the

books'[1] to 'reading the Gospels'. Our interest lies in the most commonly held interpretation, adopted by Rashi,[2] according to which the apothegm warns against too much reading of Scripture on the part of the children. In the light of the data we have produced concerning the meaning of *higgāyōn*, this interpretation is brought out into full relief: it rests on the equation of *higgāyōn* with *miqrā'*.[3] The interpretation is old; it goes back to the aforementioned Ṣemaḥ Ga'on[4] who actually employed the

controversy between Maimunists and anti-Maimunists (קובץ תשובות הרמב"ם ואגרותיו, Leipzig 1859, p. 10c); Shem Tobh b. Joseph Falaquera, *Moreh ha-Moreh* (Pressburg 1837), p. 170.

[5] S. Lieberman, *op. cit.* pp. 103, 109, note 62.

[1] A. Marmorstein in איים, London 1927, Section III, p. 16.

[2] Rashi, *Ber. ad loc.*: לא תרגילום במקרא יותר מדאי משום דמשכא. Samuel b. Me'ir (Rashbam) on *Gen.* 37, 1 (ed. David Rosin, Breslau 1881, p. 49) quotes R. Eliezer's saying in these words: אל תרבו בניכם בהגיון. This reading is obviously a reformulation of the saying in accordance with Rashi's interpretation. Cf. Profiat Duran's ingenious explanation of Rashi's words 'too much' in the introduction to his *Ma'aseh 'Efod* (ed. J. Friedländer and J. Kohn, Vienna 1865, p. 5).

[3] J. Freimann (*loc. cit.*) was amazed at Rashi's interpretation, asking rhetorically: 'Where do we find the noun *higgāyōn* having this meaning? Is there an example for it either in biblical or in rabbinical language?' (כי מה ענין הרגל במקרא יותר מדאי אצל „הגיון"? ההוראה הזאת לשם „הגיון" מאין תמצא? היש דוגמתה בלשון תורה או בלשון חכמים?) The answer to these questions has now been supplied. The restrictive clause 'too much' is, of course, not implied in the word *higgāyōn*; it is an interpretative addition by Rashi himself.

[4] *'Oṣar ha-Ge'onim*, *Berakhoth*, ii, p. 40: פירש רב צמח גאון מנעו בניכם מן ההגיון מלהגות במקראות שהן נוטין למינות. In the current text of Rashi the reason for restricting the teaching of the Bible to children reads: משום דמשכא. In view of the fact that Rashi's interpretation is evidently derived from Ṣemaḥ Ga'on who motivates the prohibition by saying: 'it leads to heresy', it is very plausible to assume that the original reading in Rashi was: משום דמשכא למינות, 'because it seduces to heresy' (cf. B.T. '*A. Zarah* 27b: שאני מינות דמשכא), and that the word מינות was omitted because of the censor.

As to the fear of heresy, it is interesting to note what Abraham Ibn Ezra reports in connection with *Ps.* 89: והיה בספרד חכם גדול וחסיד וזה המזמור היה עליו קשה ולא היה קורא אותו ולא היה יכול לשמעו בעבור כי זה המשורר ידבר כנגד השם הנכבד קשות.

A. Geiger (in Blumenfeld's *'Oṣar Neḥmad*, iii [1860], p. 116) conjectured that the 'eminent and pious scholar' was no other than the

word *miqrā'* to explain *higgāyōn*. If this interpretation is correct—as it appears to the writer to be[1]—then we have here evidence that *higgāyōn* was used in the connotation of 'Bible' already in the first century C.E.

II

The second illustration of the 'ill-fate' of *HGH* is the word עגה or אגא in a tannaitic statement found in B.T. *Sanhedrin* 101b. One cannot fail to be struck by the diversity of etymologies and interpretations to which this word was subjected. Even the expression *hagu* with all its numerous explanations appears to be eclipsed by the interminable discussion that has centred on this word since gaonic times. Here again the fact of its spelling being different in the various sources added in no mean measure to the confusion.[2] Rashi's two interpretations alone, clearly bearing the imprint of implausibility—one deriving the word from לעז and assigning to the phrase לשון עגה the meaning 'foreign tongue',[3] and the other identifying it with עוגה, circle[4]—are sufficiently

celebrated poet and philosopher, Yehudah Hallevi (?). Cf. also N. Ben-Menaḥem in the volume *Rabbi Yehudah ha-Levi* (ed. Israel Zemorah, Tel-Aviv 1950), p. 340, note 30.

On the other hand, Samuel Shallum, the first editor of ספר יוחסין (Constantinople 1566) 'censored' Ṣemaḥ Ga'on's interpretation and eliminated it from his edition, obviously regarding the assertion 'it leads to heresy' as unwarrantable. The passage has been restored in Filipowski's edition (London and Edinburgh 1857, p. 124).

[1] Cf. Abraham Geiger, *Jüdische Zeitschrift f. Wissenschaft u. Leben*, v [1867], pp. 204–5.

[2] A most puzzling reading: בלשון עבא is cited without explanation by Yehudah b. Barzillai al-Bargeloni in his commentary on *Sepher Yeṣirah* (*Commentar zum Sepher Jezira von R. Jehuda b. Barsilai aus Barcelona*, ed. S. J. Halberstam, Berlin 1885, p. 115).

[3] לשון עגה. לעז שאינו הוגה באותיותיו בלשון הקדש שלנו אלא שאר לועזין, עגה לשון בלעגי שפה (ישעי׳ כ״ח, 11).

[4] עגה לשון עוגה מקום שיש בו חבורת בני אדם שמדברין דברי חול. Jacob Mann, too, connects the word with *'ūgah*, circle, but (deviating from Rashi) grafts on to our phrase an even more far-fetched interpretation: '*language of mysticism* referring to the use of the circle in mystical action' (see *Oriental Studies, Paul Haupt Anniversary Volume*, Baltimore and Leipzig 1926, p. 445).

indicative of the difficulties mediaeval commentators encountered in dealing with the phrase at issue.[1] Modern commentators, too, have spread their net far afield: in addition to Arabic[2] and most especially Samaritan,[3] the Greek language also has been appealed to for help, and furnished, as far as I am aware of, at least two alternative etymologies.[4]

Before advancing our interpretation a brief recapitulation of the problem will be helpful. The Mishnah (*Sanhedrin*, x, 1) records 'Abba Sha'ul's statement: ההוגה את השם באותיותיו אין לו חלק לעולם הבא, 'one who pronounces the Divine Name according to its letters has no share in the future world'. To this a *Baraitha* in B.T. *Sandedrin* 101b adds the qualifying condition: ובגבולין ובלשון עגה, that is, the condemnation refers only to the country, i.e. outside the Temple, and only if uttered בלשון עגה. As regards the orthography of the last word, it should be pointed out that '*Arukh* and Yehudah b. Barzillai Albargeloni[5] spell: אגא. This word is found in the Samaritan Targum as translation of the Hebrew נקב (*Lev.* 24, 16). Already A. Geiger[6] correctly recognized that אגא is the equivalent of the mishnaic הגה, and in our days an eminent student of Samaritan language and literature[7] regarded this as 'self-evident'. There is

[1] See the discussion of the different interpretations in *Yad Ramah* on *Sanhedrin*, *ad loc.*, by Me'ir b. Ṭodros ha-Levi Abulafia (Salonica 1798).

[2] See A. Kohut, *Aruch Completum*, vol. i, p. 20, in the name of David de Lara.

[3] See *infra*, p. 249.

[4] Benjamin Mussafia in his *Supplement* to Nathan b. Yeḥi'el's '*Arukh*, (*Aruch Completum*, *loc. cit.*) and J. Levy, *Neuheb. u. Chald. Wörterbuch*, i, p. 17.

[5] See *supra*, p. 239, note 2.

[6] In *ZDMG*, xv, p. 414; '*Oṣar Neḥmad*, iii, p. 118 [=קבוצת מאמרים, ed. Samuel Poznanski (Warsaw 1910), p. 99]. To Geiger's explanation of the talmudic phrase see L. Ginzberg's observation in the last named source, p. 394.

[7] Z. Ben-Ḥayyim, *The Literary and Oral Tradition of Hebrew and Aramaic Amongst the Samaritans* (in Hebrew), Jerusalem 1957, ii, p. 588, note 291.

hardly any need to emphasize that such interchanges of gutterals as exhibited in הגה – אגא – עגה is a linguistic phenomenon as frequent as it is natural. But it will be instructive to adduce the various forms in which a word consisting of the same consonants, *HGH* (but designating a certain type of thorn), appears in the sources.[1] They are האגא, היגי, אגא, אגה, הגא, הגה, האגה; and in the plural: היגין, אגין, חגין.

Consequently, the expression בלשון אגא is but a phonetic variation of בל' הגה and is thus equivalent to בל' מקרא; it signifies, I submit, *in the pronunciation of the reading of the Law*, or simply 'in the way of scriptural reading', that is, in the accurate, distinct pronunciation used in the reading of the Law in the Synagogue, in contradistinction to the lax everyday speech, neglecting the correct pronunciation of consonants and vowels alike. Nothing can better illustrate the strict accuracy demanded in scriptural reading than the painstaking work of the Massoretes, the guardians of that accuracy. We may further remind ourselves of the talmudic exhortations to pay meticulous heed to the pronunciation of the letters when reading the *Shema*'.[2] The expression הגה באותיות conveys the same idea as דקדק באותיות used with reference to the distinct reading of the *Shema*'.

Accordingly, what the phrase ובלשון אגא says is this: 'Abba Sha'ul's severe condemnation of anyone who pronounced the Tetragrammaton applies to him only who utters it in a clear and accurate manner, pronouncing all its four letters and in their distinctive value; one, however, who used the colloquial idiom in which one of the letters had been elided or changed is not to be condemned, as in fact he has not uttered the Tetragrammaton at all but some other word. The Tetragrammaton, entirely consisting of weak letters, was especially exposed to mispronunciation

[1] *Tosefta*, *Shebhi'ith*, v, 6 (7) and *Kil'ayim*, iii, 5; see S. Lieberman, *Tosefta Ki-Fshuṭah*, New York 1955, pp. 551, 634; ed. Zuckermandel, p. 68.

[2] Mishnah *Ber*. ii, 3; B.T. *Ber*. 15b; P.T. *Ber*. ii, 4 (4c). Cf. *supra*, p. 233, footnote.

and was subject both to elision and interchange,[1] especially in districts reputed for laxity in pronunciation of Hebrew and Aramaic alike. A case in point is the Samaritan pronunciation as recorded by the Church Father, Theodoret: 'Ιαβέ (or: 'Ιαβαί).[2] Such a form might be a symbol of or a substitute for the four-lettered Name but not the Name itself, and one who uttered it had not violated the prohibition of 'pronouncing the divine name *according to its letters*'.[3]

[1] An interesting example of the neglect of the *hē* is furnished by the inscription of the Synagogue in Capernaum (ספר הישוב i, p. 94) where the engraver spelt תי לא ברכתה (*may he be blessed*) instead of תהי לֵה ב׳. Similar examples are to be found in Genizah fragments of the Palestinian Talmud: תפשיטה לך instead of תי [= תהא] פשיטה לך; דיהא = דיי; cf. J. N. Epstein, *Tarbiz*, iii [1932], p. 130 and note 10; E. Y. Kutscher, *Studies in Galilean Aramaic*, *ibid.* xxiii [1952], p. 52.

The elision of the *hē* also occurs in the Qumran texts; see *DSH* viii, 30: שלהבתה > שלבתה and *DSD* v, 10: ולהתהלך > ולהתלך (M. H. Goshen-Gottstein in *Scripta Hierosolymitana*, iv [1958], p. 110). About the change of *yodh* into *'aleph*, see *ibid.* p. 114.

[2] Cf. G. F. Moore, *Judaism in the First Centuries of the Christian Era*, i, pp. 426f.; iii, pp. 128f. See now Z. Ben-Ḥayyim, 'On the Pronunciation of the Tetragrammaton by the Samaritans' in ארץ ישראל, מחקרים בידיעת הארץ ועתיקותיה [English title: *Eretz-Israel*, *Archaeological, Historical and Geographical Studies*], iii, pp. 147–54. The author reaches the conclusion that the only reliably attested pronunciations of the Tetragrammaton by the Samaritans are: *shema'*, and *yūt-ī-bā-ī* (spelled out for י.ה.ו.ה.). He agrees, however, that the pronunciation in one word as reported by Theodoret may be accurate as far as antiquity is concerned (p. 150). Cf. also *idem* in הכינוס העולמי למדעי היהדות [*World Congress of Jewish Studies*, 1947], i, p. 152. For Hebrew and Aramaic examples of the orthographic changes of *waw* into *beth* see J. N. Epstein, *Mābhō' le-Nūsaḥ ha-Mishnah*, pp. 1223ff. and E. Y. Kutscher, *Tarbiz*, xxi [1950], p. 201.

[3] This may be exemplified by the custom still prevalent among pious Jews who, having a reverential reluctance to utter or write down even divine appellations other than the Tetragrammaton, pronounce and write: קל, אלקים instead *'el*, *'elohim*. In Genizah texts the latter appellation is often spelt without *hē* (אל״ים) or even without *lamed* (א״ם); cf., e.g., Mann, *HUCA* ii [1925], p. 336; *The Jews in Egypt, etc.* ii, pp. 110, lines 5, 7; 114, lines 16, 18, 122, line 55, and *passim*.

Of greater relevance is the fact that in the Aquila fragments published by F. C. Burkitt (*Fragments of the Books of Kings According to the Translation of Aquila*, Cambridge 1897) the Tetragrammaton is transliterated in palaeo-Hebrew letters, with the significant alteration of the

The above explanation enables us to understand a gaonic interpretation[1] of the same phrase which has hitherto remained unexplained. It runs: מהו בגבולין לשון עגה? שקורא את השם כצורתו. What the Ga'on says is this: the phrase לשון עגה means 'reading of the Divine Name in accordance with its form', that is, doing full justice to that form by pronouncing all its consonants, articulating the sound values signalized by them. This agrees with, and is illuminated by, what has been said above in elucidation of the phrase.

III

The interpretation of *leshōn hegeh* as being equivalent to '*miqrā*'', the traditional manner of scriptural reading, makes it possible for us to solve yet another riddle involving that phrase.

waw into *yodh*: יהיה. This 'most remarkable circumstance' is not the result of a confusion on the part of the scribe as Burkitt (*ibid.* p. 15) thought, but is a deliberate change. On the other hand, in some hexaplaric MSS., where the name is written in square characters, the *yodh* was changed into *waw* for the very same reason. An example of omission is supplied by a fragment of the LXX found in Cave IV where the Tetragrammaton is represented by a trigrammaton: IAÔ (P. W. Skehan, 'The Qumran Manuscripts and Textual Criticism', VT Supplement iv, p. 157; J. T. Milik, *Ten Years of Discovery in the Wilderness of Judaea*, p. 30). [See Addenda.]

A different kind of change is the substitution of *daleth* for the last *hē* (יהוד) occurring in an Aramaic papyrus and other sources (cf. A. Epstein, מקדמוניות היהודים, Jerusalem 1957, ii, p. 107; V. Aptowitzer, *Das Schriftwort in der rabbinischen Literatur* [*Sitzungsberichte d. Phil.-Hist. Klasse d. Kaiserlichen Akademie d. Wiss.*, Bd. 153, 1906], p. 10, note 2; *idem*, in *Jewish Studies in Honour of Professor J. L. Landau*, Tel-Aviv 1936, p. 58; *Samuel Krauss Jubilee Volume*, Jerusalem 1937, p. 102, note 28). This form appears in the Brescia Bible of 1494 (see J. Z. Lauterbach, *PAAJR*, 1931, p. 40, note 3).

Mention should further be made of the formula used by witnesses in the proceedings against a blasphemer (Mishnah *San.*, vii, 5): יכה יוסה את יוסה (the reading יוסה is well attested, see J. N. Epstein, *op. cit.* p. 1268). According to the '*Arukh* the word יוסה stands for the Tetragrammaton, the *hē* having been replaced by *samekh.*

All these are different devices inspired by the same motive and pursuing an identical objective: to avoid the profanation of the name of God.

[1] M. Z. Weiss, *Seridim min ha-Genizah* (Budapest 1924), p. 80.

Among the hermeneutic principles of the Talmud enumerated by Sherira Ga'on in his *Epistle*,[1] the following words occur: אם של מקרא אם של מסורת לשון עגה. The presence of לשון עגה in this context is wholly enigmatic and none of the interpretations of that phrase hitherto proposed is capable of explaining it.[2] According to our explanation, however, its presence is satisfactorily accounted for as being explanatory of the controversy[3] יש אם למסורת – יש אם למקרא, whether the traditional reading (pronunciation) or the spelling of the biblical text should guide us in biblical exegesis. In other words, whether לשון הֶגֶה should serve as a guide or not. The term *miqrā'* in this exegetical maxim does in fact demand an explanation, since it is not employed in one of its usual applications, but has quite a specific connotation embodying the idea *the official pronunciation used in the synagogal reading of the Pentateuch*—and this is exactly what *leshōn hegeh* means.[4]

IV

We now turn our attention to a passage in which the word אגה figures in a different combination. In a letter by the Ga'on of Pumbeditha, Ṣemaḥ b. Palṭoi, prefacing a halakhic *responsum* sent to an unidentified country, we read the following passage:[5] לא תפשע מן פרושי אגה דשלמאי ואגה דרבנן ובתאי כולהון וקארית שלמא עליהון בשם. The intriguing words of strange appearance אגה דשלמאי rightly disconcerted the editor, the late Prof. S. Assaf, who confessed that he did not know their meaning.[6]

[1] *'Iggereth R. Sherira Gaon* (ed. B. M. Lewin), p. 48 ('French version').

[2] The editor, in a footnote, referred the reader to a Glossary at the end of the book where he explained the expression; but the Glossary never appeared.

[3] B.T. *Sanh.* 4ab.

[4] MS. Oxford II has the words ל' עגה immediately after *miqrā'*; accordingly, the former is directly explanatory of the latter.

[5] S. Assaf, *Teshubhoth ha-Ge'onim mi-Tokh ha-Genizah* [*Gaonic Responsa from Geniza MSS.*], Jerusalem 1928, p. 76.

[6] *Ibid.* note 2.

He hesitantly suggested the emendation of the second word into דשלמאני, 'pious, righteous', and taking the term אגה to denote 'suffering'. The sentence as a whole would then mean: do not omit to mention the suffering of the pious and scholars, etc. However, apart from the linguistic difficulties and the necessity of a textual emendation, the interpretation proposed fails to do justice to the context.[1]

A clue to the correct understanding of these strange words is provided by the phrase וקארית שלמא עליהון which in itself deserves our attention. The phrase 'to call peace on somebody' is not recorded in any Hebrew or Aramaic dictionary.[2] What is its precise meaning? There cannot be the slightest doubt that it denotes 'to greet' or 'to convey greetings to somebody'; it occurs in Arabic as well as in Syriac[3] in this specific meaning and, moreover, it has become part of the Hebrew vocabulary of Arabic-speaking mediaeval Jewish writers. Samuel ha-Nagid in a farewell poem dedicated to a friend setting out on a journey says:[4] ועת תגע לעיר מבצר בחסדך קרא את שלומי על מבורך, 'and when you have reached the fortified city, kindly convey my greetings[5] to Mebhorakh'. A perfect (albeit unobtrusive)

[1] Another interpretation, much nearer the truth, has been given by S. Abramson (*Tarbiz*, xix, p. 104) who rendered the expression by *debhar shelomi*.

[2] See p. 246, note 1.

[3] Payne Smith, col. 3713; all references are from Bar Hebraeus.

[4] *Diwan of Shemuel Hannaghid* (ed. D. S. Sassoon), p. 57, poem 84, line 11.

[5] In Arabic the expression is used for both 'greet' and 'convey greetings'. In the extract from Samuel ha-Nagid (and also *op. cit.* p. 74, line 31) it bears the latter meaning. In this sense it is further employed by the famous controversialist of Maimonides, Me'ir ha-Levi Abulafia, in a letter published by H. Brody (*Studies of the Research Institute for Hebrew Poetry*, ii, p. 88): באתי לחלות פניך . . . לקרוא מיטב שלומותי לאדוני . . . הנשיא. On the other hand, in the citation from al-Ḥarizi (see also the following note) it signifies 'to greet somebody'. Naḥmanides 'hebraized' our expression, adapting it to the biblical שאל לו לשלום, in the letter to his son, Naḥman, written soon after his arrival at Jerusalem in the year 1267 (see Abraham Yaari, *'Iggeroth Ereṣ Yisra'el*, Tel-Aviv 1934, p. 85): ותקרא לי לשלום בני ותלמידי ר' משה. Cf. also the expression *qeri'ath shalom* cited further on in the text.

Arabism. Likewise Yehudah al-Ḥarizi writes:[1] ואסור אליו לקרוא שלומי עליו, 'I went to him in order to greet him'. Now we have seen above that the noun אגא - אגה is the semantic equivalent to קריאה; consequently, the expression אגה דשלמא translated into Hebrew would run קריאת שלום, 'greeting, salutation'. This Hebrew expression does, in fact, exist: it figures in a Genizah letter dated Ṣo'an (=Fusṭaṭ), Marḥeshvan 1453 (=1141 C.E.).[2] The writer complained that his correspondent had not written to him for some time nor sent greetings through others: ואפילו קריאת שלום על פי אחירים.

The excerpt from Ṣemaḥ Ga'on's letter is therefore to be rendered thus: 'Do not omit to convey [to them] my own greetings and those of the scholars and all the lay leaders; and do salute them by name.'[3]

V

Another occurrence of our phrase is to be found in a liturgical composition by Sa'adya Ga'on, characterizing ten Divine Names.[4] With respect to the four-lettered Name, which takes the eighth place in his characterization, he has this to say: והשמיני ארבע אותיות הכתובות בלשון עגא ואינן נאמרות אילא במקדש מפי כהן גדול. M. Zulay[5] was of the opinion that by לשון עגא the Samaritan script is meant and that Sa'adya referred here to the practice known from Aquila and the Dead Sea Scrolls to transliterate

[1] *Taḥkemōnī* 26. Also *ibid.*: ומהרתי אליו לקרוא שלומי עליו. This reference is given by Ben-Yehudah, *Thesaurus*, vol. xiv, p. 7134, without, however, indicating its special connotation.

[2] J. Mann, *The Jews in Egypt, etc.*, ii, p. 279, line 30.

[3] The addressee is asked that, in conveying the greetings to the leaders of the community, he should mention them by name; cf. *Ginzē Qedem*, iii, p. 19. As to the custom of sending greetings to the Diaspora communities by the Ge'onim, see the letter by an unknown Ga'on to the head of the Baghdad community אחזנו מנהגינו לברכך . . . לדרוש שלומך כמו נהגו ראשי ישר' לדרוש בשלום אבירי עמם וגדולי מקום ומקום. (S. Assaf, *Teqūphath ha-Ge'ōnīm we-Siphrūthāh*, Jerusalem 1955, p. 292).

[4] S. Abramson, *Tarbiz*, xxi [1950], p. 63.

[5] In the Hebrew daily newspaper הארץ of 7th April, 1950.

the Tetragrammaton into Palaeo-Hebrew characters.[1] This view, attractive though it may appear at first sight, is difficult to sustain. First, it is extremely improbable that that practice persisted as late as Sa'adya's time without any trace of it having been preserved in any source other than the *piyyūṭ* mentioned. Secondly (and this is the stronger argument) it is hardly conceivable that Sa'adya would have used in relation to the Divine Name the expression ל׳ עגא which—if it designated the Samaritan language—etymologically signified 'corrupt, barbarous tongue'. The choice of this expression must appear all the more infelicitous as there are other names for the old Hebrew script to choose from: כתב עברי, כתב ליבונאה, רעץ (or: דעץ) which, furthermore, are apter designations, referring as they do specifically and exclusively to the *script*.

I think that the explanation proposed by S. Abramson is the correct one. 'It seems', he writes, 'that Sa'adya intended to say that [although] the four-lettered Name is written in explicit language, it is not permitted to pronounce it.' Abramson did not touch upon the etymological aspect of the crucial expression but sensed, as it were, the substance of the passage. This is of interest; it turns out that the sense he attached to the passage is quite in harmony with the meaning of its key-expression as established by the foregoing investigation. But a few words of explanation are still needed.

In endeavouring to decipher Sa'adya's difficult *piyyūṭīm* one has often first to delve below the surface of the single words and try to get at the main idea he most likely intended to express. In the present case, this is not difficult. Sa'adya set out to characterize the Tetragrammaton. Now there is a traditional way of doing this—a way which, according to a talmudic statement,[2] is already indicated in the very pentateuchal verse that introduces

[1] This is based on a passage in Qirqisani's *Kitāb al-Anwār wal-Marāqib* where our expression occurs and it is usually taken—see however further on—to refer to the Samaritan way of reading the Pentateuch. Sa'adya would, then, have used it in an extended sense: Samaritan *script*.

[2] B.T. *Pesaḥim* 50a; *Qiddushin* 71a.

that Name (*Ex.* 3, 15): '*This is My name for ever, and this is My memorial unto all generations*; the Holy One, blessed be He, said: Not as I am written am I read; I am written with *yodh hē*, while I am read as *'aleph daleth*.' In other words, the salient feature of the four-lettered name is the discrepancy between its spelling and its pronunciation—a fact that was regarded as an anomaly peculiar to this *aeon*, to be eliminated in the future world.[1] Any description of the Tetragrammaton would naturally have to mention this outstanding characteristic, as in fact mediaeval writers do.[2]

This is also what Sa'adya did. The Ga'on says, in effect, that although the four-lettered Name is written in 'accurate idiom' (ל׳ הגה), that is, it may be fully spelt out in *writing*, no one is allowed to utter it in that idiom (which otherwise adheres scrupulously to the written text), except the High Priest in the Temple.

VI

It seems to me that the view that ל׳ עגה signified 'the accurate pronunciation used in synagogal reading of the Bible', finds confirmation in a casual remark by Qirqisani. Censuring the Samaritans for their corrupt reading of the Torah, he says as follows: 'Their reading of the Torah is at variance with that of the entire nation from East to West—that is what the Rabbanites call ל׳ עגה.'

Contrary to the usual interpretation, I venture to suggest that the last sentence could be taken to refer to 'the reading of the

[1] *Ibid.*

[2] A few examples will be given. Tobias b. Eliezer commenting on the Divine Name in *Num.* 1, 1 says (*Leqaḥ Ṭobh*, p. 161): השם הנכבד והנורא אשר לא קריאתו ככתבו; Abraham Ibn Ezra superscribed the eighth chapter of his treatise on the Divine Name *Sepher ha-Shem* (ed. G. H. Lippmann, Fürth 1834, p. 17a) with these words: 'Concerning the pronunciation of the name that is written but not uttered'; a more telling example is found in a liturgical composition by Yehudah Ibn Qoreish, a contemporary of Sa'adya (*Ha-Ṣopheh* [Budapest], ii, p. 72): השם המפורש נכתב ולא נקרא/ אותיותיו ארבע לספירה/ ולא כמכתבו קריאתו פתורה.

entire nation from East to West'.[1] While other sections of Jewry suppressed their dialectal differences when it came to the reading of the Bible in the Synagogue and followed the massoretic tradition which united them all, the Samaritans repudiated that tradition—the tradition of ל' הֶגֶה.

[1] *Kitāb al-Anwār wal-Marāqib* (ed. L. Nemoy, p. 185): קראתהם אלתורה̈ עלי כ̇לאף מא יקראהא ג̇מיע אלאמה̈ מן אלשרק אלי אלגרב – ודלך̇ מא יסמיה̈ אלרבאניון לשון עגה – מע מא ד̇כרנאהא ענהם מן אלזיאדה̈ ואלנקצאן אלד̇ין יסתעמלונהמא.

Should this construction be proved untenable, Qirqisani's statement would go to show that the explanation of the expression at issue as 'corrupt tongue' and as referring to the corrupt Samaritan idiom goes back to gaonic times and—in view of the divergent gaonic interpretation (*supra*, p. 243)—that already at that period the meaning of the expression was disputed. The meaning 'corrupt tongue of the Samaritans' derives its main support from R. Mani's statement (P.T. *Sanh.* x, 1, 28b): כגון אילין כותאי דמשתבעין, 'like the Samaritans when they swear', which was held to be identical in substance with בל' עגה in the *Baraitha*. However, the wording of R. Mani's saying ('when they swear') accords much better with the meaning 'accurate pronunciation'. What R. Mani says is that the condemnation of one who utters the Divine Name *according to its letters* applies to one only who pronounces it in an accurate manner, as the Samaritans do *when they swear*. The implication of the italicized words is: although in speech and reading the Samaritans are reputedly lax in their pronunciation, they make a point of uttering the Tetragrammaton accurately ('according to its letters') *when swearing*. Cf. also M. Grünbaum, *ZDMG*, xvi [1862], p. 404, note 1.

ADDITIONAL NOTES TO CHAPTER VII

No. 1

HIGGĀYŌN=QUR'AN

At once interesting and significant is the case in which *higgāyōn*, being semantically equivalent to Qur'an [=*miqrā'*], was used, with the qualifying addition 'false' (הגיון שוא), as a crypto-designation of the Muhammadan Bible. It occurs in the liturgical poem שננו לשונם (I. Davidson, iii, 1986) by an unidentified *payṭan*, Shemu'el (S. L. Rapoport in *Kerem Ḥemed* [Goldenberg], iv, p. 33, note 1, identified him with the celebrated Samuel ha-Nagid). In the current editions of the poem, which is directed against Christians and Muslims, the relevant strophe is either mutilated or drastically altered; the reference to Christianity has been either entirely omitted (*'Oṣar ha-Tephilloth*, ii, p. 54) or substituted by a hardly intelligible phrase: עין רעיון (S. Baer, *Seder 'Abhodath Yisra'el*, p. 628; Julius Fürst, *Das Buch Jozeroth*, Leipzig 1852, p. 14). The correct text reads as follows: אלה בשגיון עון גליון, ואלה בהגיון שוא קנאוני. As to the expression *'āwōn gillāyōn*, this is a well-known cacophemistic adaptation of *evangelion* (cf. B.T. *Shabbath* 116a), and it is for this reason that it has been eliminated or replaced. But the meaning of the parallel expression הגיון שוא has not been recognized. The mediaeval *piyyūṭ* commentator, Abraham b. 'Azri'el (*'Arugath ha-Bosem*, ii, p. 130) explained it by 'words of falsehood', and modern translators rendered it 'false logic' (H. Arnheim, *Jozeroth für alle Sabbathe des Jahres*, Glogau 1840, p. 11; Abraham Geiger, *Salome Gabirol und seine Dichtungen*, Leipzig 1867, p. 28). However, it is obvious that what is required by the context is the Muhammadan counterpart of the Christian *Evangelion*. This is in fact the case: the expression is a disguised reference to the Qur'an which, as has been said, etymologically signifies 'reading' and is thus synonymous with *higgāyōn*. The above strophe says then: 'These [the Christians] incited me [to apostasy] by the error of the Gospel, and these [the Muhammadans] by the falsehood of the Qur'an.'

No. 2

LESHŌN HEGEH = 'STANDARD' HEBREW

The explanation of the term *leshōn hegeh* as 'the pronunciation of Hebrew used in the synagogual reading of the Bible' gains added significance in connection with the view about the existence side by side of two Hebrew dialects, convincingly put forward by E. Y. Kutscher, *The Language and Linguistic Background of the Isaiah Scroll* [in Hebrew], Jerusalem 1959, pp. 34ff. Basing himself on Bergsträsser and utilizing Ze'ev Ben-Ḥayyim's *Studies in the Traditions of the Hebrew Language*, Madrid-Barcelona 1954, Kutscher distinguishes between 'standard' and 'substandard' Hebrew. The former was in use in the Synagogue reading of the Bible, and faithfully guarded and preserved by the Massoretes. The latter—'identical with Vernacular Hebrew' and reflected in the Isaiah Scroll (1QIsA)—was employed in other spheres of life, especially in Jewish liturgy where some of its features (like the much-discussed pronomial suffix *-ākh*, instead of the massoretic *-khā*) have survived, chiefly in Sephardic and Yemenite Prayer Books, until this very day.

In 'leshōn hegeh' we have, then, a tannaitic name for 'standard' Hebrew.

CONCLUDING REMARKS

The large number of resemblances between Qumranism and Karaism set forth in these studies,[1] though marshalled with the aim of mutual illumination, inevitably raises the question: Did the Qumran documents emanate from Karaite circles? These final observations will be devoted to answering this question.

Quite apart from other considerations, such as archeological and paleographical data, on purely theological grounds the answer must be an emphatic 'No'. There is no need to draw up a list of differences between the two sects; it is sufficient to refer to two fundamental doctrines of far-reaching implications, dualism and predestination, doctrines which imparted a distinctive atmosphere to the most outstanding work of the Qumran literature, the *Rule of the Community*. The dualistic world-view, dividing the world into two hostile realms, the realm of 'light' ruled by the 'prince of lights' and the realm of 'darkness' under the domination of the 'angel of darkness'—this piece of gnostic speculation is completely alien to the Karaite world outlook. And so is the closely related doctrine of predestination, which divides mankind into two diametrically opposed sections of Truth and Evil, and holds that thoughts and actions of all men are pre-ordained by an initial divine plan which remains unchangeable forever and determines all human character and behaviour. This religious and ethical predestinarianism is foreign to Karaite thinking. It is pre-eminently these all-pervasive principles, which must have

[1] See also my other studies cited in the foregoing pages, and the article 'The Doctrine of the Two Messiahs Among the Karaites', *JJS*, 6 [1955], pp. 14–23. To the theme of this article it may now be added that the prominence given to the messianic high priest in Karaite messiology is also reflected in Salmon b. Yeruḥim's interpretation of *Jer.* 3, 15: *And I will give them shepherds according to My heart*. 'The shepherds', says Salmon, 'are the Messiah son of David and the high priest, as it is said (*Zech.* 6, 13): . . . *and there shall be a priest upon his throne*' (see his *Arabic Commentary on the Book of Psalms*, ed. L. Marwick, p. 62). Likewise, Jacob b. Re'uben in *Sepher ha-'Osher* on *Isaiah* (MS. Leiden, Warner 8, fol. 159a) explains *Isa.* 51, 5: *My righteousness is near*, as denoting 'the bearers of My righteousness (*ṣedeq*), that is, the priest and the Messiah'.

affected the whole mentality, piety and religious experience of the Qumran people, that immediately convey the clear impression that the spiritual climate on the shores of the Dead Sea was so dissimilar to that of Karaism that an identification of the two sects must be precluded.

We have to take the Scrolls for what they are: first-hand evidence of the existence of a hitherto *unknown Jewish sect* and a record of its way of life and thought. The attempts to identify the people of Qumran-Damascus with one or other of the historical movements or sects are unavoidably driven to practising the Procrustean method of cutting and stretching: 'cutting' facts and 'stretching' theories. The image of the Qumran sect as reflected in the texts before us does not square with the pictures of the historical sects as portrayed in the ancient sources. It is true that the Qumranites share qualities and characteristics with each one, but they are identical with none. It may be said that the glaring contradictions between the various historical identifications and reconstructions propounded and vigorously championed by competent and responsible scholars is in itself a phenomenon so disquieting as to constitute sufficient reason for doubting the validity of any of the proposed identifications. The same applies to the Karaites. Overwhelming though the correspondences between them and the Qumranites may be, they do not postulate an identity.

In short, it cannot possibly be maintained that the Qumran documents originated in Karaite quarters; that they are, however, essentially karaitic in character cannot reasonably be denied.

But how are we then to account for the strikingly close kinship between the two sects? We cannot refrain from stating our own view, however briefly, on this intriguing problem. In the absence of documentary data we are naturally thrown back upon theory and hypothesis but, fortunately, not upon blind conjecture. It may reasonably be assumed that the remnants of the Qumranites formed one of the dissident elements that went into the formation of the Karaite sect, and that the Qumran element was able, either through sheer spiritual and intellectual weight, or through numbers, or both, to exert a preponderant influence on the medley of heterogeneous groups and individuals that rallied to 'Anan's banner. It is hardly necessary to reiterate that the anti-rabbinic forces did not spring into existence with the apostasy of 'Anan, and that the movement headed by him was far from being a unitary phenomenon. Conceding that some details in Sa'adya's account[1] of the genesis of the Karaite-Rabbanite schism are more fiction than solid historical fact, there is no reason to cast any doubt on his statement that 'Anan's followers were recruited from 'evil and worthless men from among the remnants of the brood of Zadok and Boethus', by which expression he most probably denoted heretics and nonconformists in general.

Daniel al-Qumisi and Jacob al-Qirqisani afford us some glimpses of the bewildering assortment of sectaries that sailed under the flag of Karaism. To cite but two illustrations, it could harbour schismatics that differed from the main sectarian body on such a pivotal question as the fixing of the festivals,[2] which was one of the principal issues dividing Karaites from Rabbanites and the chief cause of enmity and friction between them.[3] It could

[1] Sa'adya's account has been preserved in Elijah b. Abraham's apologetic tract *Ḥilluq ha-Qar'aim we-ha-Rabbanim* (*Liq. Qad.*, App., p. 103). L. Nemoy (*Karaite Anthology*, p. 4) is sceptical about the historicity of the whole account; see, however, S. W. Baron, *op. cit.* V, p. 388 and M. Zucker, *Rav Saadya Gaon's Translation of the Torah*, p. 147f and note 596.

[2] See al-Qumisi's *Epistle*, *JQR*, *ibid.* p. 280: וגם עמדו אחריהם [היינו אחרי רועי גלות הרבנים] הקוראים לנפשם בעלי מקרא ויאמרו לא בשבת חג המצות וסכות, ולא עלינו טומאת מת ומצורע וטומאת גוי... יש גם בבעלי מקרא אומרים משפט ייי על הרוח לבדה ולא על הגוף... וגם כחש בתחיית המתים... וגם בבעלי מקרא שאינם שומרים אביב... מתירים לאכול בשר בקר וצאן היום הזה... וגם שולחים משאות ואגרות בשבת וכאלה הרבה.

As it is obvious from the context, by *ba'alē miqrā'* al-Qumisi denotes a variety of sectarian elements before his time. See also M. Zucker, *op. cit.*, p. 168, note 659, end.

[3] Two revealing illustrations of the focal position of the calendar issue in the Karaite-Rabbanite dissension may be given here. Qirqisani tells us that he asked the Palestinian scholar, Jacob b. Ephraim, why the Rabbanites were on friendly social terms with the followers of *Abū 'Īsā* of Iṣfahān and even intermarried with them, although they acknowledged Jesus and Muhammad as prophets. The reply was: 'Because

accommodate groups like those of Khorāsān and Jibāl that disavowed the belief in the coming of the Messiah and the rebuilding of the Temple[1]—national hopes on the realization of which other partisans bent all their physical and spiritual endeavours.

It appears that 'Anan's activity consisted mainly in canalizing these anti-traditional currents into a major focus of resistance to the hegemony of the rabbinic authorities. His importance for them must have been more of a political and organizational[2] than

they do not differ from us in the observance of the holidays' (see L. Nemoy, *HUCA*, 7 [1930], p. 382). The other illustration is derived from Salmon's commentary on the *Psalms* (p. 50). Commenting on *Ps.* 55, 22 where the psalmist describes the duplicity of the adversaries, Salmon observes: 'It is the same today! How often do you see one of them [the Rabbanites] who, having met you, bids you peace and embraces you fondly, yet forthwith hastens to his synagogue where he thunders anathema against you! When you ask him, 'Why have you condemned me?' he replies, 'Because you desecrate the holy days!' (Engl. tr. by Nemoy, *JQR*, 48 [1957–58], p. 59). On Byzantium see Zvi Ankori, *The Karaites in Byzantium*, Index, *s.v.* 'Calendar'.

[1] See L. Nemoy's translation, *HUCA*, 7, p. 395. The sharp divisions recorded by Qirqisani were not the result of a supposed disintegration of a unified Karaite sect after 'Anan's death; the general course of Karaite evolution was in the direction of greater cohesion and consolidation, rather than the reverse.

[2] Whatever deeper theological implications 'Anan's famous rallying-call (*Search ye thoroughly in the Torah, and do not rely on my opinion*) may enshrine, its immediate impact and significance was that of a political programme. It was calculated, especially in its second part, to reassure his prospective supporters of his tolerant attitude towards the different groups and individuals that were at variance with his religious views but prepared to side with him and recognize him as exilarch. This, of course, does not mean that 'Anan was a liberal and broad-minded person; it merely reveals him as a shrewd politician and opportunist. In order to gain the widest possible support from the various dissident elements all ritualistic and doctrinal differences had to be pushed into the background, as a matter of prudence and practical policy, and the common bond uniting them all had to be emphasized. This bond was first and foremost a negative one: the repudiation of the traditions of the Oral Law. On the positive level they agreed on the written Torah as the sole source of religious legislation; they were agreed on the necessity and duty of intensive searching in the Law, epitomized in the positive part of 'Anan's rallying-call. Its negative part, translated into terms of practical policy, said in effect: 'It is not my intention to impose my own interpretation as *the* interpretation which has to be recognized by those

of a purely religious character. Previously, deviationists had been regarded simply as renegades and outcasts, as belonging to neither of the two great communities of the environment. It was he who secured the right of the deviationists that followed him to a separate, independent and respectable existence side by side with the established Rabbanite community. Heterodox circles which had hitherto led a more or less underground existence,[1] could now raise their heads and join the new organization, headed by a leader of Davidic lineage and bearing the proud and venerable title of exilarch.

Within this melting-pot of schismatics, divided by internal differences in belief and practice but held together by a common interest and naturally longing to integrate themselves somehow or other into a unified fabric, the Qumran section was obviously able to assert itself as a dominant force and thus imprint many of its own characteristics on the single grouping that ultimately crystallized out as the Karaite sect. It is this direct, living contact, rather than merely literary influence, that best accounts for the close links between the two sects.[2] These links, it must be emphasized, partially antedate the discovery of Hebrew manuscripts in the neighbourhood of the Dead Sea at the beginning of the ninth century, reported by Timotheus I, Patriarch of Seleucia.

acknowledging my exilarchic authority; I do not propose to replace the uniformity of the existing regime by a new system, equally uniform, and thus force you to abandon your respective traditions and modes of living.' Cf. also *supra*, pp. 88f.

[1] See al-Qumisi's *Epistle*, *JQR*, 12, p. 285; Sahl b. Maṣliaḥ, *Liq. Qad.*, App., pp. 27, 35; Yefeth b. 'Ali, cited *supra*, p. 151n; Yehudah Hadassi, *Eshkol ha-Kopher*, Alph. 1, letter *gimmel*.

[2] See Salo, W. Baron, *op. cit.*, V, p. 215; Rabin, *Qumran Studies*, p. 129; N. Golb, *Journal of Religion*, 41, pp. 28ff. Cf. also Z. Ankori, *op. cit.*, p. 20.

APPENDIX A

THE CESSATION OF PROPHECY IN KARAITE IDEOLOGY

The most common Karaite description of rabbinic Judaism, frequently occurring in the preceding pages, is מצות אנשים מלמדה, 'commandment of men learned by rote', or more briefly: 'man-made commandments' as opposed to the God-given ones observed by the Karaite sect.[1] If the full significance of this description is to be grasped, its polemical character truly understood and, most especially, if the train of thoughts it evoked in the Karaite mind is to be noticed at all, it is essential to recognize that it is not an isolated formula borrowed from *Isa.* 29, 13, where it figures in a different context, has a different meaning, and a different reference, but that lying behind its usage is a *pesher* exposition of the whole pericope (29, 10–14); that the reference is wider than the actual words quoted; and that it is that *pesher* which imparts to the description its weight and significance, *viz.*, that it is not the Karaite author who is thus stigmatizing the rabbinic brand of Judaism, but rather none other than the prophet Isaiah himself, who first described it in this manner:

(10) *For the Lord has poured out upon you*
a spirit of deep sleep,
And has closed your eyes, the prophets,
and covered your heads, the seers.

(11–12) *And the vision of all this has become to you like the words of a book that is sealed. When men give it to one who can read, saying, 'Read this', he says, 'I cannot, for it is sealed'. And when they give the book to one who cannot read, saying, 'Read this', he says, 'I cannot read'.*

[1] Among Rabbinites the phrase is used in the sense of 'mechanical, unthinking fulfilment of the commandments', the word 'learned-by-rote' being taken as the key-word of the phrase.

(13) *And the Lord said: 'Because this people*
draw near with their mouth,
And honour Me with their lips,
but have removed their heart from Me,
And their fear of Me is a commandment
of men learned by rote;

(14) *Therefore, behold, I will again do marvellous*
things with this people . . .
And the wisdom of their wise men
shall perish,
And the discernment of their discerning men
shall be hid.'[1]

The above pericope in its entirety constitutes a key *testimonium* in the ideological edifice of Karaism. It answers, namely, a searching question which deeply perturbed the Karaite mind: How to explain the tragic fact of far-reaching consequences that the overwhelming majority of the nation could fall into the error of grossly misinterpreting the Torah and supplanting the God-given precepts by allegedly man-made ones? *Pesher* expositors found the answer in the *Isaiah* pericope: It is the effect of the cessation of prophecy[2] which, in its turn, resulted in the spiritual blindness[3]

[1] This verse is used by al-Qumisi in the *Epistle* (*JQR*, *ibid*, p. 279) and in *Pithron*, p. 5 (on *Hos.* 4, 1); p. 26 (on *Joel*, 1, 11).

[2] Cf. al-Qumisi (*JQR*, *ibid*. p. 279): כי אפסו הנביאים מיש׳ ועל כן היו ישראל כעורים ככ׳ ויעצם את עיניהם . . . (ישעי׳ כ״ט, 10) ועל כן אבדה דעת מישראל . . . ועל כן לא היתה דעת לחכמים אשר אחרי הנביאים והם רבנין אשר בבית השני אחרי הנביאים . . . ולא מן התורה למדו לישראל כי בדו מלבם מצות ככ׳ (שם, שם, 13) מצות אנשים מלמדה The *Isaiah* verses are a constant theme for several prominent exponents of Karaism, such as Sahl b. Maṣliaḥ (*Liq. Qad.*, App., p. 35); David al-Fasi (*Kitāb Jāmi' al-Alfāẓ*, II, p. 423); Elijah b. Abraham (*Liq. Qad.*, App., p. 100); Hadassi, 92, *lamed*.

[3] Also *Isa*. 59, 10 (*We grope for the wall like the blind*, *yea*, *as they that have no eyes do we grope*, etc.) is adduced as proof-text of the spiritual blindness of the people; see al-Fasi, *op. cit.*, II, p. 539; Sahl, *Liq. Qad.*, App., p. 35; Elijah b. Abraham, *ibid.*, p. 100. Cf. *Diqduqē ha-Ṭe 'amim*, p. 53.

A prominent place is occupied by the pericope of *Isa*. 56, 10–12, beginning with the words *His watchmen are blind*. The three verses, which were interpreted as a damning characterization of rabbinic

of the nation and led to religious anarchy[1] and the emergence of rabbinic Judaism.

But this is not the entire import of the pericope. At the same time it served as one of the principal weapons in the Karaite armoury employed to undermine the very basis of the rabbinic position: to contest the claim of the historic continuity of tradition, of the unbroken chain of transmission from Moses through the prophets to the sages of the Mishnah. This continuity, Karaite spokesmen insisted, was interrupted by the termination of prophecy, when God turned away His face from His people and withdrew the authentic mediators and interpreters of His will. That is the greatest calamity that has befallen the nation, equal to, if not greater than, the tragedy of the physical exile.[2] In fact, for Daniel al-Qumisi the Hebrew term *Galuth* is not merely a geographical term denoting the countries of the Dispersion; nor does it solely refer to the period commencing with the destruction of the Second Temple; for him, as for other Karaite leaders, *Galuth* has a spiritual connotation and signifies the epoch of the nation's blindness which included practically the whole period of the Second Commonwealth,[3] beginning with the cessation of

leadership, figure as one of the Karaite *testimonia* and are widely cited. Al-Qumisi: *Pithron*, p. 8; *Epistle*, p. 280; Salmon b. Yeruḥim, *The Book of the Wars of the Lord*, p. 82; Yefeth b. 'Ali, commentary on *Isaiah*, MS. British Museum, Or. 2502, fol. 150a; his description of the 'Perfect in the Way', see 'The Qumran Sectaries', p. 290; Hadassi, p. 10, col. a; Alph. 122, end; 123, beginning. See also *supra*, pp. 203, 139n. On *ṣādē majuscula* at the beginning of the pericope see above p. 72n.

[1] In a debate with the Palestinian scholar, Jacob b. Ephraim, Qirqisani went to the length of arguing that the disparity in the massoretic traditions and the pronunciation of Hebrew between the Palestinians and Babylonians was the result of the cessation of prophecy (*Kitāb al-Anwār*, ed. Nemoy, pp. 135ff.; B. Klar, *Meḥqarim we-'Iyyunim*, p. 326).

[2] Al-Qumisi (*ibid.* p. 281) expostulates with his partisans in the Dispersion for not mourning over the cessation of prophecy: ולא מתאבלים על אשר שבתה הנבואה. Likewise Salmon in his commentary on *Lamentations* (MS. B.M., Or. 2515 [Cat. No. 253], fol. 191b) exclaims: כיף לא נבכי עלי עדם אלנבוה̈ ואלנביאים.

[3] See my study 'The Dead Sea Scrolls', etc., p. 78, note 9. Instructive also is the following passage from al-Qumisi's *Epistle* (p. 285; L. Nemoy, *Karaite Anthology*, p. 38): 'Since the beginning of the *Galuth*, in the days of the kingdom of the Greeks, the Romans, and the Magians, the

prophecy, and embraces both Palestine and the Diaspora. Thus, paradoxically, the Holy Land itself, even during Temple times, is Galuth, because dominated by rabbinic Judaism.

These two vital arguments, the termination of prophecy and the spiritual blindness of the nation,[1] form, as it were, the

Rabbanites held the office of princes and judges'; see the Hebrew text *supra*, p. 68, n. 2.

The date must be computed on the basis of the ancient chronology, both rabbinic and karaitic, which telescoped the entire period of the Persian domination to a few decades. According to *Seder 'Olam Rabbah* (ch. 30; ed. Ratner, p. 141) it lasted no longer than 34, or, according to a different reading, 52 years (*ibid.* p. 137, n. 15). Hadassi allocates 50 or 'almost 60' years for the Persian era (125, *'ayin*; 124, *lamed*), while an anonymous Karaite commentator reckons for the interval between Cyrus and Alexander but 56 years (J. Mann, *Texts & Studies*, II, p. 102).

Al-Qumisi's view about the beginning of Rabbanism coincides with Sa'adya's chronological system according to which the termination of prophecy occurred forty years after the restoration of the Second Temple, and, further, that 'our ancestors began to compile the Mishnah forty years after [the rebuilding] of the Second Temple, and continued until 130 years after its destruction, 510 years in all' (*Sepher ha-Galuy*, in S. Schechter's *Saadyana*, p. 5; cf. *Kuzari*, iii, 39, 65; A. Harkavy, *Studien und Mitteilungen*, V, p. 194). For the correct text of the passage see S. Poznanski, *The Karaite Literary Opponents of Saadiah Gaon*, London 1908, p. 41, note 1. Baron's translation (*op. cit.*, VI, p. 203) must be corrected accordingly; 'since the *destruction*' is an obvious *lapsus calami*; read 'rebuilding'.

[1] Karaite *pesher* exegesis interpreted also a number of other scriptural passages as foretelling the same disastrous phase in the history of the people. A few examples will be given. Al-Qumisi (*Pithron*, p. 4) interprets *Hos.* 2, 11, *Therefore will I take back My corn . . . and My wine*, as announcing the termination of prophecy; 'corn' and 'wine' being taken by him as metaphors for 'prophecy' (cf. *ibid.* p. 29, on *Joel* 2, 19, and *supra*, p. 85, n. 3). According to Salmon (*The Arabic Commentary . . . on the Book of Psalms*, p. 78), the psalmist's words *My soul thirsteth for Thee, my flesh longeth for Thee, in a dry and weary land, where no water is* (63, 2) refer to the spiritual dryness brought about by the absence of prophetic instruction. This tragic state of affairs is reflected, according to Yefeth (*The Arabic Commentary . . . on the Book of Hosea*, ed. Birnbaum, p. 32), in *Hos.* 2, 5: *And make her as a wilderness, and set her like a dry land, and slay her with thirst: Mic.* 7, 1–2 was taken by David al-Fasi (*op. cit.*, I, p. 99) as alluding to the intellectual poverty which resulted from the discontinuation of the prophetic gift and the subsequent rise of rabbinic leadership, who *hunt every man his brother with excommunication* (*ḥerem*).

environment of the aforementioned descriptive formula; reference to the formula is a pointer to and a reminder of those arguments by which the Karaite outlaws sought, on the one hand, to shake their opponents' confidence in a monolithic tradition and, on the other, to strengthen their own morale and fortify the barricades against a hostile milieu.

Pre-Sa'adyan Rabbanite polemicists, in their defence of the Oral Law, had to take cognizance of this line of argumentation; and they were driven to develop the rather astonishing theory that the authentic, uninterrupted chain of tradition had been preserved in Babylonian Jewry, whose beginnings dated back to the time prior to the destruction of the First Temple and the discontinuance of prophecy, to the period of Jehoiachin, king of Judah, who was carried into Babylonian captivity in 597, together with the religious leadership, the prophets and the sages. These, by establishing a religious centre in Babylonia, assured the historical continuity of the oral tradition and thus saved the Torah from being forgotten in the subsequent political and religious upheavals. The early deportation of the religious leaders to Babylonia, even before the fall of Jerusalem, was in fact part of the divine design to provide a haven for the preservation of the Oral Law in that land. It was in there that the chain of tradition suffered no hiatus in the course of its history, and it was thus the two Babylonian academies that were the true heirs of the prophetic tradition.[1]

Several authors also invoke *Isa.* 5, 6 (*I will command the clouds that they rain no rain upon it*), expounding the verse as predicting the withdrawal of the prophets; Salmon's MS. commentary on *Lam.* (see above, 261n), fols. 95a, 191b; Yefeth on *Hos.* 10, 12 (*op. cit.*, p. 165); Hadassi, 128, *ṣādē*. This allegorical interpretation, it may be noted, the Karaite exegetes share with the Targum of Jonathan, Aquila (?; according to *Eccl. Rabbah*, xi, 3 and *Yalquṭ ha-Makhiri* on *Isa.*, *ad loc.*; see S. Lieberman, *Greek in Jewish Palestine*, p. 20, n. 32; Gedalyah Allon, *Meḥqarim be-Toldoth Yisra'el*, II, p. 251, footnote); the Church Fathers Eusebius, Jerome and Aphraates (see L. Ginzberg in *Abhandlungen zur Erinnerung an Hirsch Perez Chajes*, Vienna 1933, p. 43; *Jewish Studies in Memory of George A. Kohut*, New York 1935, pp. 283f.).

[1] See *Tanḥuma*, Noaḥ 3; Pirqoy b. Baboy in *'Oṣar ha-Ge'onim*, *Giṭṭin*, pp. 136f.; Ṣemaḥ Ga'on's *responsum* in *Kithbhē Abraham Epstein*, ed. A. M. Habermann, Jerusalem 1950, i, p. 40.

APPENDIX B

AL-QUMISI'S AUTHORSHIP OF *PITHRŌN SHENĒM 'ĀSĀR*

Among the Karaite literary sources utilized in these studies the commentary on the Minor Prophets, published from a unique manuscript in the Firkowicz collection at Leningrad, under the above title,[1] takes a prominent place: both on account of the pre-eminence of its author, who ranks third in the Karaite hierarchy, after 'Anan and Benjamin al-Nahāwendī, and by reason of its being the earliest extant biblical commentary from the pen of a Karaite leader. That this commentary stemmed from the author mentioned had long been taken for granted by all students of Karaism; but most recently, an attempt has been made to impugn al-Qumisi's authorship and declare *Pithron* to be but an epitome of an Arabic commentary of the eleventh century by an unknown author.[2] A re-examination of the problem of authorship has, therefore, become imperative; and in view of the extensive use made of *Pithron* in this volume, the present Appendix will be devoted to this task. None of the arguments adduced in support of the above claim possess, in my view, any cogency; I limit myself to the following observations which are, however, quite sufficient to dispose of any doubt as to al-Qumisi's authorship.

The ascription of *Pithron* to the named Karaite spokesman does not rest solely[3] on the colophon at the end of the Hosea commentary (p. 25); even without it we would have been in a position to identify its author on the basis of the ideas reflected in it and, most especially, on the ground of certain linguistic features characteristic of al-Qumisi's style. *Pithron* belongs, namely, to a group of writings exhibiting identical stylistic forms that earmark them as originating from the same literary pen. Among these there are several whose author is beyond doubt Daniel al-Qumisi:

[1] See Z. Ankori's critical review, *Tarbiz*, 29 [1960], pp. 195–202.

[2] L. Marwick in *Studies in Bibliography and Booklore*, V, pp. 42–61.

[3] Cf. *ibid.*, p. 58.

1. Fragments from his lost *Book of Precepts*, cited in medieval Karaite works and collected by A. Harkavy.[1]

2. A Genizah fragment from his commentary on *Leviticus*, published by S. Schechter, where Daniel is explicitly named as author.[2]

3. A fragment from the same commentary, published by L. Ginzberg,[3] in which the author is clearly indicated by the phrase: . . . אני דניאל אדבר, דע.

4. Portions from his commentary on the *Psalms*.[4] Here, too, the author is similarly indicated by the phrase:[5] אני דניאל אשיבך, דע . . .

All these texts are distinguished by recurrent typical expressions which constitute unmistakable criteria of Daniel's style. The chief criteria are: מדעתי, בדעתי; בזאת תדע; דע כי; טרם (בטרם); על כן (כתוב, אמר, ציוה); למען כי. The first three are the most frequent and most conspicuous ones, and their presence alone would be sufficient evidence of Daniel's authorship.

These same criteria are likewise present—and in profusion—in *Pithron*, and thus stamp it as a literary production by al-Qumisi. It is chiefly by means of these criteria that students of Karaism were enabled to identify a number of other texts[6] as belonging to Daniel. The most notable among these is undoubtedly the *Epistle*.[7] Composed in Hebrew, it bears the imprint of Daniel's style, displaying as it does the peculiarities we are accustomed to

[1] See *Studien und Mitteilungen*, VIII, pp. 187–92.

[2] *Saadyana*, pp. 144–6.

[3] *Ginzē Schechter*, II, pp. 471–4; partly republished *supra*, pp. 60f.

[4] See above, p. 200, n. 2.

[5] *Ha-Ṣopheh*, 9 [1925], p. 136.

[6] They are listed in Mann's *Texts & Studies*, II, pp. 10–15; see also the new fragment identified and published by M. Zucker, *Rav Saadya Gaon's Translation of the Torah*, pp. 184–96. Apart from a solitary reference to al-Qumisi's commentary on *Leviticus* (Mann, *JQR*, 12, p. 474) none of these texts have been mentioned by Marwick.

[7] *JQR*, *ibid*., pp. 273–91.

from the aforementioned works bearing his name.[1] This being the case, it is significant to note that three interpretations in *Pithron* (*Hos.* 12, 8–9; *Hab.* 1, 2–4, 14) are also to be found in that important historical document.[2] A comparison of the two sources discloses not merely an identity of thought but several verbal coincidences as well. Moreover, *Pithron* records an alternative interpretation to *Hos.* 12, 9 (וגם פתרו) the same interpretation which we have in the *Epistle* also (281: וגם יפתרו רבים). The community of ideas is equally revealing; only the most outstanding ones will be mentioned. Both sources stigmatize rabbinic Judaism as idolatry,[3] condemn the practice of offering incense and the use of candles in the synagogue,[4] oppose the giving of priestly dues after the destruction of the Temple,[5] and severely denounce the study of extraneous disciplines as 'an abomination of the Lord'.[6]

Marwick dwells on the Arabicisms in *Pithron*. If these are to be taken as proof that the work was originally written in Arabic and translated into Hebrew by an ignorant epitomizer-translator, it would be just as reasonable to conclude that Maimonides' *Mishneh Torah*, where so genuine an Arabicism as יש שם figures among the first ten words, or Abraham Ibn Ezra's commentary on the Pentateuch, which regularly uses the un-Hebrew expression —but perfect Arabicism—קרוב מן (instead of ל), were originally composed in Arabic and rendered into Hebrew by an ignoramus writing a 'clumsy Hebrew'. The Arabicisms are, indeed, translations, but *mental* translations on the part of the Arabic-speaking *authors* who thought in Arabic but wrote in Hebrew. The recurrent Arabicisms מדעתי, בדעתי are, as indicated, a constant

[1] For instance, the characteristic expression *'al kēn* occurs in it more than forty times; cf. the passage quoted p. 260, n. 2.

[2] It was known to Sa'adya, see M. Zucker, *op. cit.*, p. 175, n. 679.

[3] *JQR*, pp. 277, 278; *Pithron*, p. 22. For further references see *ibid.*, p. 13, n. 26; cf. *supra*, pp. 151ff.

[4] *JQR*, p. 277; *Pithron*, p. 7. Cf. M. Zucker, *op. cit.*, p. 170, n. 666.

[5] *JQR*, pp. 277, 286f.; *Pithron*, p. 9; see also the commentary on *Leviticus*, *Ginzē Schechter*, II, p. 481.

[6] *JQR*, pp. 273, 274; *Pithron*, p. 4, and the references in n. 23.

feature of Daniel's style.[1] In the *Book of Precepts*, unquestionably written in Hebrew, we meet the expression לא מותר לנו which is a 'slavish rendition' of the Arabic לא יגוז. The term יכשר which is a translation[2] of the Arabic יגוז is used in the *Epistle*, pp. 238, 287. Likewise the word *segullah* appears there several times.[3] The unusual phrase במדת דעתי has its parallel in the *Epistle*, p. 277, line 15.

An interesting Arabicism (not mentioned by Marwick) is the use of the term דין in its Arabic sense of 'religion'. It occurs twice in *Pithron* (pp. 19, 67), but its occurrence there is not due to the ignorance of the supposed translator who was unable to find a Hebrew equivalent, and therefore left the Arabic word of the original untranslated. As a matter of fact, the term also occurs in the *Epistle*, p. 284, as well as in the commentaries on the *Psalms*[4] and *Daniel*.[5] The term, appearing as it does in four different works, constitutes an additional link connecting *Pithron* with other writings of al-Qumisi.

This brings us to the Arabic words and phrases occurring in *Pithron*. According to Marwick, these are to be accounted for either by the inability of the supposed translator to render them into Hebrew, or by his 'abandonment of any effort at translation into Hebrew' (p. 46). The fact, however, is that other texts definitely written by al-Qumisi and definitely composed in Hebrew exhibit the same phenomenon.[6] This is indeed a characteristic common to all Daniel's writings at our disposal, as was noted by A. Harkavy[7] long before the discovery of *Pithron*.

[1] Cf., for instance, *Saadyana*, pp. 145, 146; *ha-Ṣopheh*, 9, p. 38 (three times); Zucker, *op. cit.*, pp. 186, 187, 192, 193, 196 (three times).

[2] Cf. Marwick, *art. cit.*, p. 49.

[3] *JQR*, pp. 288, lines 8–9; 290, lines 17–18.

[4] *Ha-Ṣopheh*, 8, p. 333.

[5] *JQR*, p. 517.

[6] Cf., e.g., *Book of Precepts*, pp. 187–9, 190; *Saadyana*, p. 145 (six times); *Epistle*, p. 274 (three times), 276, 284, 289.

[7] *Op. cit.*, p. 178, n. 2.

The greatest difficulty in attributing the commentary to Daniel appears to reside in the fact that on p. 69 it speaks of a memorial prayer offered for ʻAnan throughout the year and especially on the festival of *Sukkoth*. Marwick contrasts this with ʻQirqisani's reference to Daniel's disparagement of ʻAnan as "one of the *Maskilim* who stumbled" and his reference to him as *head of the fools* in lieu of the honour bestowed upon him by the sectaries as *head of the Maskilim*' (pp. 57f.).

First, it should be noted that the disparagement of ʻAnan as ʻone of the *Maskilim* who stumbled' is not found in Qirqisani's work, but in al-Qumisi's commentary on the *Book of Daniel*.[1] Secondly, and this is important in the present context, the epithet ʻ*head of the Maskilim*' was not bestowed upon ʻAnan by the sectaries, but it was al-Qumisi himself who conferred this honorific title upon him. One is therefore bound to ask, Is this not a contradiction? Is not Daniel at variance with himself?

However, if we consult Qirqisani's *Kitāb al-Anwār* we discover the solution of the ʻcontradiction'. The two conflicting passages in *Pithron* and in the commentary on *Daniel*, like the two antithetical epithets, stem from two different periods in al-Qumisi's intellectual evolution and are expressive of his diametrically opposed attitudes towards the founder of the sect. ʻAt[2] the beginning of his career', says Qirqisani, ʻhe [al-Qumisi] used to esteem ʻAnan very highly, mentioned him frequently in his works and called him "head of the *Maskilim*"; subsequently, however, he began calling him "head of the fools".'

In fine, al-Qumisi's authorship of *Pithrōn Shenēm ʻĀsār* remains unshaken.

[1] *JQR*, p. 519.

[2] L. Nemoy, *HUCA*, 7 [1930], p. 321.

ADDENDA

P. 4, line 3. For the translation of *lmdbr* '*in* the wilderness' see J. N. Epstein, *Mābhō' le-Nūsaḥ ha-Mishnah*, pp. 1110ff. A new fragment of the *Rule of the Community* (S^d^) actually reads *bmdbr*, see J. T. Milik, *RB*, 67 [1960], p. 414.

P. 33, n. 2. Cf. also *Midrash Mishlē* on 6, 11 (ed. S. Buber, p. 55): 'This refers to the messianic king who will march at the head of Israel, as it is said (*Mic.* 2, 13): *And their king will pass on before them.*'

P. 46, n. 2. Cf. further Jean Daniélou, *The Bible and the Liturgy*, p. 93: 'The pillar of cloud prefigured Christ, according to Johannine typology.'

P. 46, n. 3. On the idea of the second coming of Moses see now Howard M. Teeple, *The Mosaic Eschatological Prophet*, *JBL*, Monograph Series, vol. X, 1957.

P. 54, n. 2. Cf. further J. M. Baumgarten, *JBL*, 77, pp. 355ff.; A. A. Akavia, *Sinai*, 47, p. 40; David Leibel, *Tarbiz*, 29, p. 296. Talmon replied to his critics, *ibid.*, pp. 394f.

P. 65, n. 3. S. Lieberman also shares the view that the *Mishnah of Rabbi Eliezer* includes anti-Karaite polemics, see his *Tosefta Ki-Fshuṭah*, p. 31, n. 7. Cf. *supra*, pp. 130n and 212, note 3.

P. 69, note. About the obscure passages in the Torah, cf. also M. Zucker, *Rav Saadya Gaon's Translation of the Torah*, p. 109, n. 461.

P. 71, n. 4. To *Ps.* 119, 72 see the quotation from Yefeth's commentary on the *Song of Songs* in 'The Qumran Sectaries', pp. 100f.

P. 74, n. 1. Cf. also N. Allony in *Sepher Tur-Sinai*, Jerusalem 1960, pp. 286f.

P. 85. To the significance of Benjamin al-Nahāwendī's saying, 'I am neither a prophet nor the son of a prophet', see Z. Ankori's different interpretation, *Karaites in Byzantium*, p. 214.

P. 88, n. 1. It is illustrative of the decline of the knowledge of Aramaic (or at any rate of its Babylonian dialect) in Palestine in the eleventh century even among Rabbanites that the Palestinian scholar, Abraham b. Shabbethai, in 1089–90, found it necessary to translate portions of the Babylonian Talmud into Hebrew. See J. Mann, *Texts & Studies*, I, p. 446, n. 2; S. W. Baron, *op. cit.*, VI, p. 256.

P. 90. Cf. further the *widduy* formula published from the Genizah by Israel Abrahams (*HUCA*, i, p. 383): והרגנו נביאי האמונה, which is to be rendered 'and we killed the *true* prophets', and not 'the prophets of faithfulness' (as rendered by Abrahams, *ibid.*, p. 381). Another example see Sahl b. Maṣliaḥ, *Liq. Qad.*, App., p. 35, line 15.

P. 110. Concerning the Karaite *pesher* on *Dan.* 11, 33, see al-Qumisi's explicit statement that 'this verse is written in reference to the kingdom of Yishma' 'el' (*JQR*, 12, p. 286).

P. 111. In his latest work on the Dead Sea Scrolls (*Les écrits esséniens découverts près de la Mer Morte*, Paris 1959) Dupont-Sommer still renders *maskil* by 'wise man' (*homme entendu, intelligent*). Correcting his translation in the *Zadokite Documents*, Rabin in *Qumran Studies*, p. 49, decided definitely in favour of the rendering 'teacher' for *maskil.*

P. 143, n. 3. The employment of the expression *dibbēr sārāh* to describe the falsification of the Torah is likewise found in al-Qumisi's *Book of Precepts* (A. Harkavy, *Studien u. Mitteilungen*, VIII, p. 187).

P. 163, n. 1. A. M. Habermann also takes the phrase *mō'ēd ha-ta'anīth* as signifying the Day of Atonement; see his *Megilloth Midbar Yehudah: The Scrolls From the Judean Desert*, p. 211. So also does Cecil Roth, *The Historical Background of the Dead Sea Scrolls*, p. 59.

P. 166, n. 1. Cf. J. N. Epstein, *HUCA*, 23/2 [1950–51], p. 8 (Hebr. pt.).

P. 185. On the Maḥzor commentary ascribed to 'Eli'ezer b. Nathan of Mayence see now I. H. Levine's study in *Tarbiz* 29 [1960], pp. 162–75.

P. 192. On the custom of visiting the cemeteries of fast-days among the Jews of Kurdistan, see Erich Bauer in *Magnes Anniversary Book* (ed. F. I. Baer and others), Jerusalem 1938, pp. 50–61.

P. 208, n. 3. See now M. Zucker, *op. cit.*, pp. 116ff.

P. 212, n. 2. To the massoretic passage cf. also D. S. Loewinger, *Textus*, I [Annual of the Hebrew University], p. 92.

P. 213, n. 3. To the Karaite rejection of the festival of Hanukkah, see also the passage from *Sepher ha-'Osher* (MS. Leiden) quoted by Z. Ankori, *op. cit.*, p. 282, n. 87.

P. 215, n. 6. In *Megilloth Midbar Yehudah*, p. 34, A. M. Habermann still adheres to his view on the meaning of *Sepher Hagu*, but the name of the book now appears in two forms: 'Book of *Hāgō*' (pp. 84, 86, 87) and 'Book of *Hăgāy*' (p. 59).

P. 242, n. 2. To the abbreviations of the names of God see also G. R. Driver, *Textus*, I, p. 120.

P. 243, n. 3. See now Giorgio Castellino's edition of the Mercati fragments of the Hexapla, *Psalterii Hexapli Reliquiae . . .* Bybliotheca Vaticana, MCMLVIII; cf. further Norman Walker, *VT*, 3, pp. 103f.

P. 253. Notwithstanding P. Wernberg-Møller's vigorous plea for a 'psychological' interpretation of 1QS, III, 13–IV, 26 (*Revue de Qumran*, 3 [1961], pp. 314ff.; see also Marco Treves, *ibid.*, pp. 449ff.), it seems to me that the whole tenor of the passage strongly favours a metaphysical rather than a psychological interpretation.

LIST OF MANUSCRIPTS

INDEXES

I. MODERN AUTHORS

II. TEXTS

III. GENERAL INDEX

(*DoA* =*Day of Atonement; K.* =*Karaite(s); Q.* =*Qumran(ites); R.* =*Rabbanite(s); r.* =*rabbinic*)